ANCIENT CHRISTIAN TEXTS

HOMILIES ON NUMBERS

Origen

TRANSLATED BY

THOMAS P. SCHECK

EDITED BY

CHRISTOPHER A. HALL

SERIES EDITORS

THOMAS C. ODEN AND GERALD L. BRAY

IVP Academic

An imprint of InterVarsity Press
Downers Grove, Illinois

InterVarsity Press
P.O. Box 1400, Downers Grove, IL 60515-1426
World Wide Web: www.ivpress.com
E-mail: email@ivpress.com

InterVarsity Press® is the book-publishing division of InterVarsity Christian Fellowship/USA®, a movement of students and faculty active on campus at hundreds of universities, colleges and schools of nursing in the United States of America, and a member movement of the International Fellowship of Evangelical Students. For information about local and regional activities, write Public Relations Dept., InterVarsity Christian Fellowship/USA, 6400 Schroeder Rd., P.O. Box 7895, Madison, WI 53707-7895, or visit the IVCF website at <www.intervarsity.org>.

Design: Cindy Kiple
Images: Saints Peter and Paul by Carlo Crivelli at Accademia, Venice/Art Resource, NY

ISBN 978-0-8308-2905-7

Printed in the United States of America ∞

InterVarsity Press is committed to protecting the environment and to the responsible use of natural resources. As a member of Green Press Initiative we use recycled paper whenever possible. To learn more about the Green Press Initiative, visit <www.greenpressinitiative.org>.

Library of Congress Cataloging-in-Publication Data
Origen.
   [Homilies on Numbers. English]
   Homilies on Numbers/Origen; translated by Thomas P. Scheck;
   edited by Christopher A. Hall.
      p. cm.—(Ancient Christian texts)
   Includes bibliographical references and index.
   ISBN 978-0-8308-2905-7 (cloth: alk. paper)
   1. Bible. O.T. Numbers—Sermons. 2. Sermons, Latin—Translations
   into English. I. Scheck, Thomas P., 1964- II. Hall, Christopher A.
   (Christopher Alan), 1950- III. Title.
   BR65.O59S34 2009
   222'.1407—dc22

                                                               2009031641

P	24	23	22	21	20	19	18	17	16	15	14	13	12	11	10	9	8	7	6	5	4	3	2	1
Y	30	29	28	27	26	25	24	23	22	21	20	19	18	17	16	15	14	13	12	11	10	09		

This translation is dedicated to the sacred memory
of Erasmus of Rotterdam (1466–1536),
in whose mighty company I shall not now be ashamed

CONTENTS

GENERAL INTRODUCTION / PAGE IX

ABBREVIATIONS / PAGE XVII

TRANSLATOR'S INTRODUCTION / PAGE XIX

ORIGEN'S HOMILIES ON NUMBERS / PAGE 1

Rufinus's Preface / PAGE 1
Homily 1: Numbers 1:1-54 / PAGE 2
Homily 2: Numbers 2:1-34 / PAGE 6
Homily 3: Numbers 3:5-39 / PAGE 9
Homily 4: Numbers 3:39–4:49 / PAGE 13
Homily 5: Numbers 4:1-49 / PAGE 16
Homily 6: Numbers 11:16-25; 12:1-15 / PAGE 20
Homily 7: Numbers 12:1-15; 13:18-34; 14:1-8 / PAGE 24
Homily 8: Numbers 13:18-34; 14:1-38 / PAGE 32
Homily 9: Numbers 17:1-28 (LXX, Heb) = 16:36–17:13 (RSV) / PAGE 35
Homily 10: Numbers 18:1-7 / PAGE 44
Homily 11: Numbers 18:8-32 / PAGE 49
Homily 12: Numbers 21:16-23 / PAGE 62
Homily 13: Numbers 21:24-35; 22:1-14 / PAGE 71
Homily 14: Numbers 22:15-28 / PAGE 79
Homily 15: Numbers 22:31-41; 23:1-10 / PAGE 85

Homily 16: Numbers 23:11-24 / PAGE 91

Homily 17: Numbers 23:25-30; 24:1-9 / PAGE 101

Homily 18: Numbers 24:10-19 / PAGE 110

Homily 19: Numbers 24:20-24 / PAGE 116

Homily 20: Numbers 25:1-10 / PAGE 122

Homily 21: Numbers 26 / PAGE 131

Homily 22: Numbers 27:1-23 / PAGE 134

Homily 23: Numbers 28:1–29:39 / PAGE 139

Homily 24: Numbers 28–30 / PAGE 147

Homily 25: Numbers 31:1-54 / PAGE 153

Homily 26: Numbers 31–32 / PAGE 160

Homily 27: Numbers 33:1-49 / PAGE 168

Homily 28: Numbers 34–35 / PAGE 183

SUBJECT INDEX / PAGE 189

SCRIPTURE INDEX / PAGE 193

GENERAL INTRODUCTION

The Ancient Christian Texts series (hereafter ACT) presents the full text of ancient Christian commentaries on Scripture that have remained so unnoticed that they have not yet been translated into English.

The patristic period (A.D. 95-750) is the time of the fathers of the church, when the exegesis of Scripture texts was in its primitive formation. This period spans from Clement of Rome to John of Damascus, embracing seven centuries of biblical interpretation, from the end of the New Testament to the mid-eighth century, including the Venerable Bede.

This series extends but does not reduplicate texts of the Ancient Christian Commentary on Scripture (ACCS). It presents full-length translations of texts that appear only as brief extracts in the ACCS. The ACCS began years ago authorizing full-length translations of key patristic texts on Scripture in order to provide fresh sources of valuable commentary that previously was not available in English. It is from these translations that the ACT Series has emerged.

A multiyear project such as this requires a well-defined objective. The task is straightforward: *to introduce full-length translations of key texts of early Christian teaching homilies and commentaries on a particular book of Scripture.* These are seminal documents that have decisively shaped the entire subsequent history of biblical exegesis, but in our time have been largely ignored.

To carry out this mission the Ancient Christian Texts series has four aspirations:

1. To show the approach of one of the early Christian writers in dealing with the problems of understanding, reading and conveying the meaning of a particular book of Scripture.

2. To make more fully available the whole argument of the ancient Christian interpreter of Scripture to all who wish to think with the early church about a particular canonical text.

3. To broaden the base of biblical studies, Christian teaching and preaching to include classical Christian exegesis.

4. To stimulate Christian historical, biblical, theological, and pastoral scholarship to-

ward deeper inquiry into early classic practitioners of scriptural interpretation.

For Whom Is This Series Designed?

We have selected and translated these texts primarily for general and nonprofessional use by an audience of persons who study the Bible regularly.

In varied cultural settings around the world, contemporary readers are asking how they might grasp the meaning of sacred texts under the instruction of the great minds of the ancient church. They often study books of the Bible, verse by verse, book by book, in groups and workshops, sometimes with a modern commentary in hand. But many who study the Bible intensively hunger to have available to them as well the thoughts of some reliable classic Christian commentator on this same text. This series will give the modern commentators a classical text for comparison and amplification. Readers will judge for themselves as to how valuable or complementary are their insights and guidance.

The classic texts we are translating were originally written for anyone (lay or clergy, believers and seekers) who would wish to reflect and meditate with the great minds of the early church. They sought to illuminate the plain sense, theological wisdom, and moral and spiritual meaning of an individual book of Scripture. They were not written for an academic audience, but for a community of faith shaped by the sacred text.

Yet in serving this general audience, the editors remain determined not to neglect the rigorous requirements and needs of academic readers who until recently have had few full translations available to them in the history of exegesis. So this series is designed also to serve public libraries, universities, academic classes, homiletic preparation and historical interests worldwide in Christian scholarship and interpretation.

Hence our expected audience is not limited to the highly technical and specialized scholarly field of patristic studies, with its strong bent toward detailed word studies and explorations of cultural contexts. Though all of our editors and translators are patristic and linguistic scholars, they also are scholars who search for the meanings and implications of the texts. The audience is not primarily the university scholar concentrating on the study of the history of the transmission of the text or those with highly focused interests in textual morphology or historical critical issues. If we succeed in serving our wider readers practically and well, we hope to serve as well college and seminary courses in Bible, church history, historical theology, hermeneutics and homiletics. These texts have not until now been available to these classes.

Readiness for Classic Spiritual Formation

Today global Christians are being steadily drawn toward these biblical and patristic sources for daily meditation and spiritual formation. They are on the outlook for primary classic sources of spiritual formation and biblical interpretation, presented in accessible form and grounded in reliable scholarship.

These crucial texts have had an extended epoch of sustained influence on Scripture interpretation, but virtually no influence in the modern period. They also deserve a hearing among modern readers and scholars. There is a growing awareness of the speculative excesses and spiritual and homiletic limitations of much post-Enlightenment criticism. Meanwhile the motifs, methods and approaches of ancient exegetes have remained unfamiliar not only to historians but to otherwise highly literate biblical scholars, trained exhaustively in the methods of historical and scientific criticism.

It is ironic that our times, which claim to be so fully furnished with historical insight and research methods, have neglected these texts more than scholars in previous centuries who could read them in their original languages.

This series provides indisputable evidence of the modern neglect of classic Christian exegesis: it remains a fact that extensive and once authoritative classic commentaries on Scripture still remain untranslated into any modern language. Even in China such a high level of neglect has not befallen classic Buddhist, Taoist and Confucian commentaries.

Ecumenical Scholarship

This series, like its two companion series, the ACCS and Ancient Christian Doctrine (ACD), are expressions of unceasing ecumenical efforts that have enjoyed the wide cooperation of distinguished scholars of many differing academic communities. Under this classic textual umbrella, it has brought together in common spirit Christians who have long distanced themselves from each other by competing church memories. But all of these traditions have an equal right to appeal to the early history of Christian exegesis. All of these traditions can, without a sacrifice of principle or intellect, come together to study texts common to them all. This is its ecumenical significance.

This series of translations is respectful of a distinctively theological reading of Scripture that cannot be reduced to historical, philosophical, scientific or sociological insights or methods alone. It takes seriously the venerable tradition of ecumenical reflection concerning the premises of revelation, providence, apostolicity, canon and consensuality. A high respect is here granted, despite modern assumptions, to uniquely Christian theological forms of reasoning, such as classical consensual christological and triune reasoning, as distinguishing premises of classic Christian textual interpretation. These cannot be acquired by empirical methods alone. This approach does not pit theology against critical theory; instead, it incorporates critical historical methods and brings them into coordinate accountability within its larger purpose of listening to Scripture.

The internationally diverse character of our editors and translators corresponds with the global range of our audience, which bridges many major communions of Christianity.

We have sought to bring together a distinguished international network of Protestant, Catholic and Orthodox scholars, editors, translators of the highest quality and reputation to accomplish this design.

But why just now at this historical moment is this need for patristic wisdom felt particularly by so many readers of Scripture? Part of the reason is that these readers have been long deprived of significant contact with many of these vital sources of classic Christian exegesis.

The Ancient Commentary Tradition

This series focuses on texts that comment on Scripture and teach its meaning. We define a commentary in its plain sense definition as a series of illustrative or explanatory notes on any work of enduring significance. The word "commentary" is an Anglicized form of the Latin *commentarius* (or "annotation" or "memoranda" on a subject or text or series of events). In its theological meaning it is a work that explains, analyzes or expounds a biblical book or portion of Scripture. Tertullian, Origen, John Chrysostom, Jerome, Augustine and Clement of Alexandria all revealed their familiarity with both the secular and religious commentators available to them as they unpacked the meanings of the sacred text at hand.

The commentary in ancient times typically began with a general introduction covering such questions as authorship, date, purpose and audience. It commented as needed on grammatical or lexical problems in the text and provided explanations of difficulties in the text. It typically moved verse by verse through a Scripture text, seeking to make its meaning clear and its import understood.

The general western literary genre of commentary has been definitively shaped by the history of early Christian commentaries on Scripture. It is from Origen, Hilary, the *Opus imperfectum in Matthaeum*, John Chrysostom and Cyril of Alexandria that we learn what a commentary is—far more so than in the case of classic medical or philosophical or poetic commentaries. It leaves too much unsaid simply to assume that the Christian biblical commentary took a previously extant literary genre and reshaped it for Christian texts. Rather it is more accurate to say that *the Western literary genre of the commentary (and especially the biblical commentary) has patristic commentaries as its decisive pattern and prototype.*

It is only in the last two centuries, since the development of modern historicist methods of criticism, that modern writers have sought more strictly to delimit the definition of a commentary so as to include only certain limited interests focusing largely on historical critical method, philological and grammatical observations, literary analysis, and sociopolitical or economic circumstances impinging on the text. While respecting all these approaches, the ACT editors do not hesitate to use the classic word *commentary* to define more broadly the genre of this series. These are commentaries in their classic sense.

The ACT editors freely take the assumption that the Christian canon is to be respected as the church's sacred text. The reading and preaching of Scripture are vital to religious life. The central hope of this endeavor is that it might contribute in some small way to the revitalization of religious faith and community through a renewed discovery of the earliest readings of the church's Scriptures.

An Appeal to Allow the Text to Speak for Itself

This prompts two appeals:

1. For those who begin by assuming as normative for a commentary only the norms considered typical for modern expressions of what a commentary is, we ask: Please allow the ancient commentators to define *commentarius* according to their own lights. Those who assume the preemptive authority and truthfulness of modern critical methods alone will always tend to view the classic Christian exegetes as dated, quaint, premodern, hence inadequate, and in some instances comic or even mean-spirited, prejudiced, unjust and oppressive. So in the interest of hermeneutical fairness, it is recommended that the modern reader not impose on ancient Christian exegetes modern assumptions about valid readings of Scripture. The ancient Christian writers constantly challenge these unspoken, hidden and indeed often camouflaged assumptions that have become commonplace in our time.

We leave it to others to discuss the merits of ancient versus modern methods of exegesis. But even this cannot be done honestly without a serious examination of the texts of ancient exegesis. Ancient commentaries may disqualify as commentaries by modern standards. But they remain commentaries by the standards of those who anteceded and formed the basis of the modern commentary.

The attempt to read a Scripture text while ruling out all theological and moral assumptions—as well as ecclesial, sacramental and dogmatic assumptions that have prevailed generally in the community of faith out of which it emerged—is a very thin enterprise indeed. Those who tendentiously may read a single page of patristic exegesis, gasp and toss it away because it does not conform adequately to the canons of modern exegesis and historicist commentary, are surely not exhibiting a valid model for critical inquiry today.

2. In ancient Christian exegesis, chains of biblical references were often very important in thinking about the text in relation to the whole testimony of sacred Scripture, by the analogy of faith, comparing text with text, on the premise that *scripturam ex scriptura explicandam esse*. When ancient exegesis weaves many Scriptures together, it does not limit its focus to a single text as much modern exegesis prefers, but constantly relates it to other texts, by analogy, intensively using typological reasoning, as did the rabbinic tradition.

Since the principle prevails in ancient Christian exegesis that each text is illumined by other texts and by the whole narrative of the history of revelation, we find in patristic comments on a given text many other subtexts interwoven in order to illumine that text. In these ways the models of exegesis often do not correspond with modern commentary assumptions, which tend to resist or rule out chains of scriptural reference. We implore the reader not to force the assumptions of twentieth-century hermeneutics on the ancient Christian writers, who themselves knew nothing of what we now call hermeneutics.

The Complementarity of Research Methods in this Series

The Ancient Christian Texts series will employ several interrelated methods of research, which the editors and translators seek to bring together in a working integration. Principal among these methods are the following:

1. The editors, translators and annotators will bring to bear the best resources of *textual criticism* in preparation for their volumes. This series is not intended to produce a new critical edition of the original language text. The best Urtext in the original language will be used. Significant variants in the earliest manuscript sources of the text may be commented on as needed in the annotations. But it will be assumed that the editors and translators will be familiar with the textual ambiguities of a particular text, and be able to state their conclusions about significant differences among scholars. Since we are working with ancient texts that have, in some cases, problematic or ambiguous passages, we are obliged to employ all methods of historical, philological and textual inquiry appropriate to the study of ancient texts. To that end, we will appeal to the most reliable text-critical scholarship of both biblical and patristic studies. We will assume that our editors and translators have reviewed the international literature of textual critics regarding their text so as to provide the reader with a translation of the most authoritative and reliable form of the ancient text. We will leave it to the volume editors and translators, under the supervision of the general editors, to make these assessments. This will include the challenge of considering which variants within the biblical text itself might impinge on the patristic text itself, and which forms or stemma of the biblical text the patristic writer was employing. The annotator will supply explanatory footnotes where these textual challenges may raise potential confusions for the reader.

2. Our editors and translators will seek to understand the *historical context* (including social-economic, political and psychological aspects as needed) of the text. These understandings are often vital to right discernment of the writer's intention. Yet we do not see our primary mission as that of discussing in detail these contexts. They are to be factored into the translation and commented on as needed in the annotations, but are not to become the primary focus of this series. Our central interest is less in the social location of the text or the philological history of particular words than in authorial intent and accurate translation. Assuming a proper social-historical contextualization of the text, the main focus of this series will be on a dispassionate and fair translation and analysis

of the text itself.

3. The main task is to set forth the meaning of the biblical text itself as understood by the patristic writer. The intention of our volume editors and translators is to help the reader see clearly into the meanings which patristic commentators have discovered in the biblical text. *Exegesis* in its classic sense implies an effort to explain, interpret and comment on a text, its meaning, its sources and its connections with other texts. It implies a close reading of the text, utilizing whatever linguistic, historical, literary or theological resources are available to explain the text. It is contrasted with *eisegesis* which implies that interpreters have imposed their own personal opinions or assumptions on the text. The patristic writers actively practiced intratextual exegesis, which seeks to define and identify the exact wording of the text, its grammatical structure and the interconnectedness of its parts. They also practiced extratextual exegesis, seeking to discern the geographical, historical or cultural context in which the text was written. Our editors and annotators will also be attentive as needed to the ways in which the ancient Christian writer described his own interpreting process or hermeneutic assumptions.

4. The underlying philosophy of translation that we employ in this series, like that of the Ancient Christian Commentary on Scripture, is termed *dynamic equivalency*. We wish to avoid the pitfalls of either too loose a paraphrase or too rigid a literal translation. We seek language that is literary but not purely literal. Whenever possible we have opted for the metaphors and terms that are normally in use in everyday English-speaking culture. Our purpose is to allow the ancient Christian writers to speak for themselves to ordinary readers in the present generation. We want to make it easier for the Bible reader to gain ready access to the deepest reflection of the ancient Christian community of faith on a particular book of Scripture. We seek a thought-for-thought translation rather than a formal equivalence or word-for-word style. This requires the words to be first translated accurately and then rendered in understandable idiom. We seek to present the same thoughts, feelings, connotations and effects of the original text in everyday English language. We have used vocabulary and language structures commonly used by the average person. We do not leave the quality of translation only to the primary translator, but pass it through several levels of editorial review before confirming it.

The Function of the ACT Introductions, Annotations and Translations

In writing the introduction for a particular volume of the ACT series, the translator or volume editor will discuss, where possible, the opinion of the writer regarding authorship of the text, the importance of the biblical book for other patristic interpreters, the availability or paucity of patristic comment, any salient points of debate between the Fathers, and any special challenges involved in translating and editing the particular volume. The introduction affords the opportunity to frame the entire commentary in a manner that will help the general reader understand the nature and significance of patristic comment on the biblical texts under consideration and to help readers find their critical bearings so as to read and use the commentary in an informed way.

The footnotes will assist the reader with obscurities and potential confusions. In the annotations the volume editors have identified Scripture allusions and historical references embedded within the texts. Their purpose is to help the reader move easily from passage to passage without losing a sense of the whole.

The ACT general editors seek to be circumspect and meticulous in commissioning volume editors and translators. We strive for a high level of consistency and literary quality throughout the course of this series. We have sought out as volume editors and translators those patristic and biblical scholars who are thoroughly familiar with their original language sources, who are informed historically, and who are sympathetic to the needs of ordinary nonprofessional readers who may not have professional language skills.

Thomas C. Oden and Gerald L. Bray, Series Editors

Abbreviations

ACW   Ancient Christian Writers: The Works of the Fathers in Translation. Mahwah, N.J.: Paulist Press, 1946–.

ANF   A. Roberts and J. Donaldson, eds. Ante-Nicene Fathers. 10 vols. Buffalo, N.Y.: Christian Literature, 1885–1896. Reprint, Grand Rapids, Mich.: Eerdmans, 1951–1956; Reprint, Peabody, Mass.: Hendrickson, 1994.

BETL   Bibliotheca ephemeridum theologicarum Lovaniensium. Louvain, Belgium: Peeters, 1947–.

DCB   W. Smith and H. Wace, eds. *Dictionary of Christian Biography, Literature, Sects and Doctrines.* 4 vols. London, 1887. Reprint, New York: AMS Press, 1984.

DEOO   *Desiderii Erasmi Roterodami Opera omnia.* Edited by Jean Leclerc. 10 vols. Leiden, 1703–1706. Reprint, Hildesheim, Germany: Georg Olms Verlag, 1961–1962.

FC   Fathers of the Church: A New Translation. Washington, D.C.: Catholic University of America Press, 1947-.

GCS   Die griechischen christlichen Schriftsteller der ersten drei Jahrhunderte. Berlin: de Gruyter, 1897–.

NPNF   P. Schaff et al., eds. A Select Library of the Nicene and Post-Nicene Fathers of the Christian Church. 2 series (14 vols. each). Buffalo, N.Y.: Christian Literature, 1887–1894; Reprint, Grand Rapids, Mich.: Eerdmans, 1952–1956; Reprint, Peabody, Mass.: Hendrickson, 1994.

PG   J.-P. Migne, ed. Patrologia Graeca. 166 vols. Paris: Migne, 1857–1886.

SC   H. de Lubac, J. Daniélou et al., eds. Sources Chrétiennes. Paris: Editions du Cerf, 1941–.

TRANSLATOR'S INTRODUCTION

Origen of Alexandria (185–254) was probably the most important and influential Christian theologian of the pre-Nicene church.[1] Born the eldest of seven children to Christian parents in Alexandria, Egypt, he became a humble Christian scholar of deep learning in the Scriptures and of heroic sanctity of life. Origen received a thorough education in Scripture and Greek literature from his father, Leonides, who was imprisoned and later beheaded in 202 during the Emperor Septimus Severus's persecution of the Christians. Longing for martyrdom himself, Origen survived this purge, though his life was often in great danger. Evidently, the anti-Christian legislation only affected converts, not the already-baptized.[2] Origen even wrote a letter to his imprisoned father, exhorting him not to shrink back from offering the supreme witness of the faith. Forty years later, while preaching in Caesarea, Origen reflected back on his spiritual heritage and made the following confession: "Having a father who was a martyr does me no good, if I do not live well myself and adorn the nobility of my descent. That is, I must adorn his testimony and confession by which he was illustrious in Christ."[3] Origen's humility and his zeal for martyrdom, which is reminiscent of St. Ignatius of Antioch, are defining characteristics of his personality. He once preached: "If God would consent to let me be washed in my blood, receiving a second baptism by accepting death for Christ, I would surely go from this world. . . . But blessed are they who merit these things."[4] The thirst for martyrdom, which is viewed as a gift that Christ grants to the worthy, is an idea that is present in these homilies as well.[5]

After Leonides's execution the family's goods were confiscated. In order to support his mother and siblings, Origen became a teacher of Greek grammar and literature. He studied philosophy in depth and gained a reputation for his learning, even in the pagan world. Demetrius the Bishop of Alexandria later put him in charge of instructing catechumens, and for some time Origen maintained dual teaching responsibilities, both secular and ecclesial. He later gave up teaching secular literature, sold his library for a meager sum of money, and dedicated himself completely to Christian catechesis. In Alexandria this activity went on during the persecutions, and many of Origen's pupils and

---

[1] The chief primary source for Origen's life work is Eusebius *Ecclesiastical History* 6.
[2] See *Augustan History*, Severus 17.1.
[3] *Homilies on Ezekiel* 4.8. See my forthcoming translation in ACW (2010).
[4] Cf. *Homilies on Judges* 7.12.
[5] Cf. Homily 10.2.1.

converts were killed, while he accompanied them to the execution site. Later in Caesarea, Origen's giftedness as an exemplary Christian teacher was remembered with nostalgia and great emotion by one of his most famous pupils, St. Gregory Thaumaturgus (the Wonderworker), in the *Panegyric to Origen*. Gregory highlighted the fact that Origen's actions corresponded to his words, and that his sincere and Spirit-filled Christian discipleship is what led many others to imitate him. At the beginning of the fourth century, the future martyr Pamphilus of Caesarea noted that Origen was very humble and had deeply Christian character.[6]

It is well known that Origen lived a life of extreme asceticism and self-denial, in conscious imitation of Christ and the apostles. According to some reports, Origen took Matthew 19:12 literally and castrated himself in order to protect his chastity, since many of his students were female. Crouzel wryly remarked that this is the only bit of information the general public usually knows about Origen. This story is increasingly doubted by modern scholars as secondhand hearsay. Most recently, J. McGuckin rejected the tradition as "a smokescreen of Pamphilus's own invention, canonized by Eusebius."[7] The reason for doubt is that the story seems to contradict several passages in his writings, where Origen himself ridicules such a crassly literal interpretation of Jesus' words.[8] Yet the tradition still seems probable to me, since Eusebius, a fervent admirer of Origen, records it. Eusebius knew men and women who had known Origen personally. Moreover, it does not seem consistent with Pamphilus's upright Christian character to suggest that he would have invented this story as a "smokescreen."

At some point in his career Origen traveled to Rome to visit the very famous and ancient church there. According to St. Jerome, in Rome Origen heard St. Hippolytus preach a sermon, and the future martyr acknowledged the presence of his distinguished guest.[9] Origen later moved to Palestine, where, Eusebius reports, bishop Theoctistus of Caesarea allowed him to preach, even though he was a layman. Then, without permission from his home bishop, Origen was ordained a priest in Palestine by the local bishops. This was a canonically irregular procedure in that it took place without permission from Demetrius (Origen's bishop in Alexandria) and it was carried out in spite of the mutilation he had deliberately undergone. According to Eusebius it was for these reasons, that is, canonical irregularities, that Origen was expelled from the church of Alexandria. However, there also seems to have been doctrinal issues involved in Origen's excommunication. Eusebius may have willed to minimize these out of his partiality for Origen. Yet they are attested by Origen himself in his own *Letter to Friends in Alexandria*, which is cited by both Rufinus and Jerome.[10] The doctrinal issue referred to in that letter was Origen's alleged belief

---

[6]Cf. *Apology for Origen* 3. See my new translation in FC 120.

[7]John Anthony McGuckin, ed., *The Westminster Handbook to Origen* (Louisville: Westminster John Knox, 2004), p. 7.

[8]Cf. *Commentary on the Gospel of Matthew*, ad loc.; *Homilies on Numbers* 25.3.5.

[9]Cf. Jerome *On Illustrious Men* 61.

[10]Cf. Jerome *Apology Against Rufinus* 2.18 (NPNF 2 3:511).

that the devil would ultimately be saved, something Origen vehemently repudiates in the same letter. I will say more on this below.

Origen was consulted in theological discussions, one of which survives, *Dialogue with Heraclides*. Unfortunately, only two letters from his once vast correspondence are extant. He journeyed to Arabia and to Antioch, where he had been summoned by Julia Mammaea, the mother of the emperor Alexander Severus, who wanted to learn more about Christianity from him. Such involvements show Origen's substantial reputation among his contemporaries, both Christian and pagan. In 250, shortly after completing his lengthy *Against Celsus* and his *Commentary on the Epistle to the Romans*, Origen was arrested during Decius's persecution. He was imprisoned and severely tortured on the rack, but Origen, like his father, refused to deny his Lord Jesus Christ in order to be released. Had he died during that term of imprisonment, there does not seem to be any doubt that he would have been canonized. Instead, it was the emperor who died, the anti-Christian measures expired, and Origen was released from prison, but in broken health. Origen is thus technically ranked among the church's "confessors," whereas his father is a martyr. He died at the age of 69, probably in 254. His tomb was still being shown to crusaders in the thirteenth century at Tyre, in the church of the Holy Sepulcher.

Origen's Surviving Works

One of the great tragedies of church history is that the vast majority of Origen's writings do not survive.[11] This owes to the condemnation of later developments of his thought at the Fifth Ecumenical Council in 553. Balthasar strikingly compared the destruction of Origen's writings to the shattering of a perfume vessel into a thousand pieces that filled the whole house (of the church) with its fragrance.[12] Some of the missing titles are known from St. Jerome's *Epistle* 33 to Paula. Of Origen's major extant works, table 1 shows their approximate length.[13] (Origen's massive text-critical project, the *Hexapla*, where he displayed in parallel columns up to eight texts and translations of the Old Testament, does not survive except in fragments).

Against Celsus is Origen's magnum opus. As his longest extant writing and final work, it comprises the most important written defense of Christianity from antiquity. As a work of Christian apologetics, the book retains its relevance and interest even to modern

---

[11]Erasmus of Rotterdam (1466–1536) said in this connection: "I can scarcely refrain from tears as I read the lists of ancient authors and see what wealth we have lost. My grief increases when I compare the quality of our losses with what we now commonly read" (*Epistle* 676:32-35; *The Correspondence of Erasmus: Letters 594 to 841*, Collected Works of Erasmus, trans. R. A. B. Mynors [Toronto: University of Toronto Press, 1979], p. 138).

[12]Hans Urs von Balthasar, ed., *Origen, Spirit and Fire: A Thematic Anthology of His Writings*, trans. Robert J. Daly (Washington, D.C.: Catholic University Press, 1984), p. 2.

[13]Most of these calculations are found in C. P. Hammond, "The Last Ten Years of Rufinus's Life and the Date of His Move South from Aquileia," *Journal of Theological Studies* 28, no. 2 (1977): 428-29, who points out that these are very rough estimates owing to the inconsistent length of the additional material found in the footnotes of Migne. (For example, the figures for *On First Principles* are too generous.) Sometimes my independent estimates have differed significantly from Hammond's.

readers. This work has caused misunderstanding because it contains remarks by Origen where he argues that the allegorization of the biblical narratives is no more unreasonable than the allegorization, or rationalization, of the Greek myths which was fashionable in the erudite Greek world of his day. Some scholars have extrapolated from this that Origen's exegetical principles were derived from Neo-Platonic allegorization of Homer.

Table 1. Extent of Surviving Text of Origen's Works

Title of Work (with ancient Latin translator)	Number of columns in Migne (PG 11-17)
*Against Celsus	493
Commentary on Romans (Rufinus)	455
*Commentary on John	405
*Commentary on the Gospel of Matthew (on Mt 16:13–22:33)	382
On First Principles 1-4 (Rufinus)	296
Homilies on Numbers (Rufinus)	220
Commentary Series on the Gospel of Matthew (on Mt 22:24–27:66) [traditionally called Homilies]	199
Homilies on Leviticus (Rufinus)	169
Commentary on the Song of Songs (Rufinus)	136
Homilies on Joshua (Rufinus)	123
Homilies on Genesis (Rufinus)	117
*Homilies on Jeremiah (Jerome)	107
Homilies on Exodus (Rufinus)	100
Homilies on Luke (Jerome)	99
Homilies on Ezekiel (Jerome)	96
Homilies on Psalms 36–38 (Rufinus)	90
*On Prayer	73
Pamphilus's Apology for Origen (Rufinus)	72
Homilies on Judges (Rufinus)	40
*Exhortation to Martyrdom	36
Homilies on the Song of Songs (Jerome)	21
Homily on 1 Samuel (Rufinus?)	17

* Indicates that the work survives in Greek as well.

However, de Lubac showed long ago that, in spite of the widespread scholarly misunderstanding of Origen's *ad hominem* remarks here, these statements simply do not become principles which are found in Origen's exegesis.[14] The same applies to Origen's theoretical hermeneutical principles found in *On First Principles*, book 4. De Lubac forcefully argued that scholars should observe Origen at work, in his actual exegesis, to determine the principles of his hermeneutics. What makes the modern misapprehension of Origen all the more tragic is that in the very book *Against Celsus*, and in all his other works, Origen

---

[14]Henri de Lubac, *History and Spirit: The Understanding of Scripture According to Origen*, trans. A. Nash (San Francisco: Ignatius, 2007), pp. 33-42.

refuses to treat the Bible, or any part of it, like a Platonic myth. He defends historical Christianity against the attacks of Gnosticism, down to the very details concerning the dimensions of Noah's ark.[15]

Origen's commentaries on Romans, John, Matthew and Song of Songs became classics in the West.[16] They show Origen "at work" in the verse-by-verse exposition of individual books of the Bible. All but the commentary on Romans place their main focus on bringing out the deeper spiritual meaning of the text. The *Commentary on Romans*, on the other hand, approaches being a literal exposition of Paul's words. His treatises *On Prayer* and *Exhortation to Martyrdom* are important thematic treatments that exemplify the way Origen grounded theology in the explanation of Scripture. They too remain stimulating reading to this day. Pamphilus's *Apology for Origen* (309) is listed here because it is a work comprised mainly of excerpts from a diverse selection of Origen's writings, many of which are no longer extant. Composed by the martyr Pamphilus (d. 310), with the collaboration of Eusebius of Caesarea, the author defends Origen's orthodoxy against the attacks of some contemporaries (probably Methodius). Other more recently discovered works of Origen are not listed here and include the previously mentioned *Dialogue with Heraclides* and his treatise *On the Passover* (or *The Pascha*).

Origen's first book, *On First Principles*, is also his most controversial treatise.[17] It was the main source of posthumous accusations against Origen's orthodoxy. In this work Origen became the first Christian theologian to attempt a theological reflection on the essential doctrines of the Christian faith, beginning with the Holy Trinity, using the tools of reason, scripture and apostolic tradition. His stated aim is to defend the church's faith against the heretics. Two centuries after Origen's death, in 543, some of Origen's opinions that are discussed in *On First Principles* were condemned by emperor Justinian. In 553 fifteen anathemas were laid down against Origenian doctrines by the Fathers of the Fifth Ecumenical Council outside the official sessions of the Council. The condemned doctrines included Origen's theories about the preexistence of human souls and of Christ's soul, the spherical shape of resurrection bodies, the animate nature of the stars and heavenly bodies, the suggestion that Christ may have to be crucified in the future age on behalf of demons, the view that the power of God is limited, and the conjecture that the punishment of demons and impious men is only temporary.[18] Many scholars today would deny that Origen ever affirmed some of these points. All agree that Origen spoke tentatively and never intended his discussions of these matters to be taken as defined

---

[15]Cf. *Homilies on Genesis* 2.1.

[16]For a study of the legacy of Origen's *Commentary on Romans*, see Thomas P. Scheck, *Origen and the History of Justification* (Notre Dame: University of Notre Dame Press, 2008).

[17]For a good discussion of some of the textual issues involved in this work and its modern editions, see R. Rombs, "A Note on the Status of Origen's *De Principiis* in English," *Vigiliae Christianae* 61 (2007): 21-29.

[18]This summary is taken from the *Canons Against Origen* (from the book against Origen of the Emperor Justinian, 543), reproduced in Henry Denzinger, *The Sources of Catholic Dogma*, trans. R. Deferrari from the 13th edition of Henry Denzinger's *Enchiridion Symbolorum* (Fitzwilliam, N.H.: Loreto, 1954), pp. 203-11.

doctrine. Moreover, H. Crouzel, a very competent expert on Origen in the twentieth century, states that the action of Emperor Justinian in 543 was really directed against sixth-century "Origenists," and not against the historical Origen. This would mitigate the authority and relevance of the action with respect to Origen. What is an undeniable fact is that in the Western church, Origen's writings were cherished in the form of the Latin translations that were carried out by St. Jerome and Rufinus of Aquileia. Their author was considered to be fundamentally orthodox. The reader is referred to the standard treatments of Origen's life and doctrine by H. Crouzel and J. Daniélou, as well as the theological classic *History and Spirit* by Henri de Lubac, for more detailed discussions of these matters.

Origen's Homilies

A large percentage of Origen's surviving writings are homilies on Scripture, which illustrates how deeply Origen was connected to the church of his day, both as a priest, catechist and pastor of souls. Origen's reflections on the institutional church in his homilies are extremely valuable, as a sort of window into the church of the third century.[19] More generally, Origen's homilies represent the oldest surviving corpus of Christian sermons. As such, they were in their Latin translations a source of endless inspiration to Christians of later generations in the Western church. To give some examples, the very learned priest-scholar Erasmus of Rotterdam (d. 1536) recommended the writings of Origen for the Christian's edification. He expressed admiration of Origen's successful allegorical interpretations found above all in Origen's *Homilies on Numbers* and emulated Origen's approach in his work *Handbook (Enchiridion) of the Militant Christian* (1503).[20] Recently Pope Benedict XVI commended the writings of Origen to his Roman Catholic audience.[21]

Rufinus of Aquileia

Some of Origen's homilies were translated by St. Jerome, but the greater part, including the present *Homilies on Numbers*, were translated by Rufinus of Aquileia (345–411). Rufinus is best known to posterity as a Latin translator.[22] He was, in fact, the most productive translator of Greek patristic texts of antiquity and stands alongside St. Jerome as one of the greatest Latin translators of all time. In addition to the works of Origen, Rufinus also translated into Latin several other important works of the Greek Fathers, including

---

[19]This aspect is one of the main focuses of Jean Daniélou's *Origen*, trans. Walter Mitchell (New York: Sheed & Ward, 1955).

[20]Cf. J. P. Dolan, trans., *The Essential Erasmus* (New York: Signet Classics, 1964), pp. 63, 78. See also A. Godin, "The *Enchiridion Militis Christiani*: The Modes of an Origenian Appropriation," *Erasmus of Rotterdam Society Yearbook* (1982), pp. 47-79.

[21]Weekly General Audience, Wednesday April 25, 2007; May 2, 2007.

[22]The classic and still unsurpassed study is by F. X. Murphy, *Rufinus of Aquileia (345–411): His Life and Works* (Washington, D.C.: The Catholic University of America Press, 1945). Also thought provoking is the approach taken by the feminist scholar E. Clark, *The Origenist Controversy: The Cultural Construction of an Early Christian Debate* (Princeton: Princeton University Press, 1992).

Eusebius's *Ecclesiastical History*, the [pseudo]-*Clementine Recognitions*, the *Dialogue of Adamantius on the Orthodox Faith*, the *Homilies of Gregory of Nazianzus*, the *Homilies of St. Basil*, *History of the Monks in Egypt*, *Rule of St. Basil*, *The Blessings of the Patriarchs* and the *Sentences of Evagrius*. Rufinus also wrote in his own name an important *Apology Against Jerome* and the *Commentary on the Apostles' Creed*.

Rufinus was born in Concordia, educated in Rome, baptized in Aquileia, and ordained in Jerusalem by Bishop John, the successor of Cyril. In his youth Rufinus was on intimate terms with St. Jerome, and he maintained close friendships with the best minds of Christian Italy throughout his life. He spent about seven years in Egypt, where he was a disciple of Didymus the Blind. Rufinus himself became a "confessor" when, after the death of Athanasius in 373, an Arian ruler in Egypt persecuted, imprisoned and exiled him along with several bishops because of their Nicene orthodoxy.[23] Later he traveled with St. Melania to Palestine, where he lived as a monk for many years on the Mount of Olives. The last part of his life, from about 397–411, was spent in Aquileia, Rome, southern Italy and finally Sicily, where he died. This final fortnight of years was devoted principally to the task of translation.

Rufinus always maintained a clear and stable attitude toward Origen, whom he regarded as his teacher. He believed that Origen was the outstanding exegete and theologian of the early church and that a translation of Origen's works would be of considerable profit to the church in the West. After his death in 411, Rufinus's translations and ecclesiastical services were highly praised by Palladius, John Cassian and Cassiodorus. Unfortunately, a conflict with the fatefully eloquent but intemperate St. Jerome damaged Rufinus's reputation in the West until quite recently. Jerome's irresponsible and malevolent defamation of Rufinus's character and orthodoxy was written during the unproductive Origenist controversies of the late-fourth and early-fifth centuries. Fortunately Rufinus did not allow himself to become discouraged by this quarrel, and by his patient and selfless translation effort, carried out at the request of his superiors, he saved from certain destruction some of the most precious writings of Christian antiquity. His translations were "destined to form Latin minds for many years to come."[24]

Rufinus's Translation Method

Rufinus's translation technique, particularly for the work *On First Principles*, has been the subject of reproach since the days of Jerome. By his own free admission, Rufinus suspected that the Greek manuscripts of Origen's writings had been tampered with by heretics.[25] Because of this suspicion, in his Latin translations Rufinus sometimes omitted

---

[23]See Rufinus's *Apology to Anastasius* 2 (NPNF 2 3:430).
[24]De Lubac, *History and Spirit*, pp. 45-46.
[25]Rufinus documents his suspicions in the prefaces to *On First Principles*, in his *Apology Against Jerome*, and in his work *On the Adulteration of the Works of Origen* (NPNF 2 3:421-27).

or altered the wording of the original in order to make the text conform more adequately to Origen's plainly orthodox statements found elsewhere in his writings. For obvious reasons Rufinus was particularly concerned to defend Origen against the charge of "proto-Arianism."[26] Yet Rufinus denies on repeated occasions that he had added anything of his own. He says that he simply restored Origen to himself.

In spite of such claims, Rufinus's translation procedure is blemished in part by an honest but serious text-critical misjudgment. He mistakenly believed that the spurious *Dialogue of Adamantius on the Orthodox Faith* was an authentic work of Origen. Buchheit thought that Rufinus falsified the authorship of this work deliberately.[27] However, Hammond has shown that this is wrong and that Rufinus had good reasons for his mistaken attribution of this work.[28] As late as the nineteenth century, the *Dialogue of Adamantius* was judged to be an authentic work of Origen. Rufinus himself had translated this work into Latin with the intention of exhibiting Origen as a champion in the fight against heresy.[29] The *Dialogue* contains statements such as "I believe that . . . God the Word is consubstantial and eternal,"[30] and "the blessed Trinity is consubstantial and inseparable."[31] Such formulations seem to point to the recent determination of the Council of Nicaea.[32] Yet by a mistaken text-critical judgment, Rufinus thought these were Origen's own expressions. He therefore felt free to borrow such formulations and put them into Origen's mouth in certain thematically related texts, whenever he was convinced that heretics had inserted their own corruptions into Origen's original text. When judged by his own contemporary standards of literary criticism, Rufinus's mistake was honest and excusable. The few passages from the *Homilies on Numbers* that may be affected by Rufinus's practice will be noted below.[33] Apart from such christological and trinitarian passages, Rufinus's Latin translation can be received as generally reliable.[34]

In the preface to the *Homilies on Numbers*, Rufinus reports to his dedicatee Ursacius that conditions have not been favorable for completing the translation, since he has been forced in 410 to flee across the Straits of Messina to Sicily during the invasion of the

---

[26]See: R. Williams, "*Damnosa hereditas*: Pamphilus's *Apology* and the Reputation of Origen," in *Logos: Festschrift für Luise Abramowski zum 8. Juli 1993*, ed. H. C. Brennecke, E. L. Grasmück and C. Markschies (Berlin: W. De Gruyter, 1993), pp. 151-69. For a good discussion of Rufinus's method of translation, see R. Heine's introduction to Origen, *Homilies on Genesis and Exodus*, FC 71 (Washington, D.C.: Catholic University of America Press, 1982), pp. 27-39.

[27]V. Buchheit, "Rufinus von Aquileja als Fälscher des Adamantiosdialogs," *Byzantinische Zeitschrift* 51 (1958): 314-28 (p. 319).

[28]Hammond, "The Last Ten Years of Rufinus's Life," 391.

[29]Cf. PG 11.1713-1884.

[30]Cf. PG 11.1718: *Deum unum, eumque conditorem et effectorem omnium esse credo: Deumque Verbum qui ex eo natus est, qui ejusdem est ac ille essentiae, qui semper est, qui extremis temporibus hominem ex Maria assumpsit.* "I believe that there is one God and that he is the founder and creator of all things; and [I believe] that God the Word, who was born from him, who is himself of the same substance, who is eternal, assumed a human nature from Mary in the last days."

[31]Cf. PG 11.1883: *Ejusdem enim essentiae est, inseparabilisque beata Trinitas.* "For the blessed and inseparable Trinity is of the same substance."

[32]Cf. *DCB* 1:40.

[33]Cf. Homily 12.1.4.

[34]This has been confirmed recently for a different work of Origen by M. Beyer Moser, *Teacher of Holiness: The Holy Spirit in Origen's Commentary on the Epistle to the Romans* (Piscataway, N.J.: Gorgias Press, 2005).

Italian peninsula by Alaric, ruler of the Goths. Thus the present group of homilies was completed in Sicily. It represents Rufinus's last surviving translation.[35] Rufinus remarks in the preface that he has supplied additional material to the homilies from Origen's "Excerpts" or *Scholia*, his more detailed commentary notes. The *Scholia* on Numbers are no longer extant except in what is preserved here. Rufinus says that he did this in order to fill in exegetical gaps that existed in Origen's homilies on the book of Numbers and to make the work more complete and coherent.[36] Therefore the genre of the present work is a mixture of the homily and of Origen's more detailed exegesis of the Old Testament text. When he is judged by ancient standards of translation, Rufinus's procedure of supplying additional Origenian material from other exegetical writings is not reproachable. For his declared aim was to edify his Latin readers, who longed to read more of Origen's exegesis of Numbers than was found in the original homilies. We can be grateful for the added exegesis, since otherwise it would not have survived, even if it means that the present form of the homilies is not the exact form in which Origen originally delivered them.

Origen's Exegetical Method

Origen's spiritual exegesis of the Old Testament is grounded on the historical revelation of the Christian mystery. The presupposition of all ancient Christian exegesis is that the coming of Jesus Christ, the incarnate Word of God and Messiah of Israel, has brought the fulfillment of the long-awaited time of salvation (cf. Mk 1:15), of the Mosaic law (cf. Mt 5:17; Rom 13:10), and of the Old Testament Scriptures (cf. Mt 26:31, 54; Lk 22:37; Jn 13:18; Acts 3:18; 1 Cor 15:3-4). In light of the historical fulfillment, the Old Testament must now be received as a period of preparation for the messianic/ecclesiastical age and as a period of divine pedagogy (cf. Gal 3:23-25). The fulfillment of the Old Testament in the New Testament implies a surpassing or going beyond what was imperfect and incomplete in the Old Testament; indeed it introduces a certain obsolescence of the ceremonial and ritual aspects of the law. The Christian principle admits that Old Testament moral precepts remain in force, and that the Old Testament had a positive role in that it procured religious education for the Jews and led them to Christ. But the law was a temporary and provisional regime from which Christians have now been set free.

Origen's basic hermeneutical principle for interpreting the Old Testament is derived from Christ himself, who taught his followers that the Old Testament prefigures the spiritual realities that constitute the New Testament. Jesus explained the meaning of his life and death using the rites of the Sinai covenant (cf. Lk 22:20). The four Evangelists develop this way of reading the Old Testament, as do Revelation and the Catholic Epistles.[37] Origen endeavors, quite simply, to sit at Jesus' feet as a devoted pupil and learn

---

[35]See Hammond, "The Last Ten Years of Rufinus's Life," 393.
[36]The words added to this effect at the end of 19.4.6 appear to be Rufinus's.
[37]Cf. Mt 2:15; 1 Cor 5:7; 9:9; 10:4; Eph 5:31-32; Heb 9:5; 12:17; 1 Pet 1:19; 2:6-9; Rev 14:8.

from him how to read the Old Testament. He wants to perpetuate and develop in detail the interpretive methods that are used by the authors of the New Testament when treating Old Testament texts. Origen brings this christological and ecclesiological interpretive program to bear on the smallest details of the Old Testament text. Nothing authorizes the reader of Origen, therefore, to see in his method a concern to "Hellenize." Rather, Origen was following his interpretive guides, Jesus, Paul and the other sacred writers. In 7.5.3, Origen tells his hearers to go back to the Gospels and Paul to find examples of "spiritual interpretation."

Programmatic texts for Origen's hermeneutics are the following:

Hebrews 10:1: "For since the law has but a shadow of the good things to come instead of the true form of these realities, . . ."

1 Corinthians 10:11: "Now these things happened to them as a warning, but they were written down for our instruction, upon whom the end of the ages has come."

Romans 15:4: "For whatever was written in former days was written for our instruction, that by steadfastness and by the encouragement of the scriptures we might have hope."

2 Timothy 3:16-17: "All scripture is inspired by God and profitable for teaching, for reproof, for correction, and for training in righteousness, that the man of God may be complete, equipped for every good work."

In light of St. Paul's claims about the Old Testament in these passages, Origen asks in 7.1.1: What foreshadowing, what warning, what instruction, what encouragement, reproof, correction or exhortation, do we find in the narratives recorded in the book of Numbers?

In addition to adhering closely to the New Testament patterns of interpretation of the Old Testament, it is also evident that Origen had an almost excessive admiration of ancient Jewish methods of exegesis. In 13.5.1 he mentions a Jewish convert to Christianity, the son of a Palestinian rabbi, who taught him influential principles of Scripture interpretation. Links to the renowned Philo of Alexandria are not difficult to find in Origen's *Homilies on Numbers*.[38] Indeed, it is to Origen that the West owes the survival of Philo's writings.[39] Origen also subtly praises the type of symbolic interpretation found in the intertestamental Jewish book 1 Enoch, a work that is quoted in the New Testament book of Jude 14.[40] Thus it is clear that many tributaries fed into Origen's exegetical method. Yet Origen did not derive his principles from pagan thought or from intertestamental Jewish exegesis or from the rabbis. Of fundamental importance to him was the pattern of interpretation found in the New Testament itself, which he felt Christian exegetes and homilists ought to imitate.

---

[38]Cf. Homily 26.4.1.
[39]See D. Runia, "Philo of Alexandria," in *The Westminster Handbook to Origen*, ed. J. A. McGuckin (Louisville: Westminster John Knox, 2004), pp. 169-71.
[40]Cf. Homily 28.2.1.

Origen's method of interpretation has been much maligned and misunderstood by modern scholars. Some of these professedly Christian critics are equally offended and embarrassed by the New Testament itself and the way its writers, and even Jesus himself, interpret the Old Testament.[41] This fact not only places Origen in good company, but shows that some of Origen's critics themselves recognize that his hermeneutical principles do not stem from a spirit of rationalism, a Platonist's anti-historicism, or the intention to "demythologize" the Old Testament, but from the New Testament writers.[42] Origen sought to imitate St. Paul; he endeavored to preserve the Old Testament for the church, to edify his congregation, to equip his hearers for spiritual warfare,[43] and to see souls renewed in the image of Christ. Origen had the heart of a pastor. To him, the question for the homilist is not whether the stories in the book of Numbers literally occurred in history. For the most part Origen assumed that they did. As H. Crouzel intelligently reminds us, "In spite of the spontaneous reactions of many modern scholars it must not be concluded from the fact that Origen allegorizes a story that he does not believe in the historicity of the literal account, which is perfectly compatible with the quest for a spiritual meaning."[44] Rather, the question is, Assuming the literal factuality of these narratives, why were they preserved by the Holy Spirit in the church? What spiritual lessons and warnings do these stories offer the Christian? How can our souls be edified by these readings? In Homily 26.3 Origen justifies his interpretive approach by citing Luke 16:29: the Old Testament was written to help us avoid going to the place of torments. Accordingly, by his spiritual interpretation of the text of Numbers, Origen aims to save souls.

Origen concedes that sometimes believers' souls can be edified by the literal application of the Old Testament text. For example, Origen refers to the warning to avoid sexual immorality that is based on the example of the seduction of the men of Israel by the Midianite women.[45] Ancient Israel was often edified by this level of interpretation, and sometimes Christians are too, though the physical sword of Phinehas has been removed by Christ from the hands of his redeemed people.[46] Indeed, the whole world benefits from the literal application of parts of the law of Moses.[47] But even when literal applications

---

[41]For example, the Bultmannian Catholic Old Testament scholar J. L. McKenzie claims that St. Paul's methods of interpreting the Old Testament fall into the same basket with the New Testament view of the three-decker universe. *A Theology of the Old Testament* (Garden City, N.Y.: Doubleday, 1976), pp. 339-40. For a critique of McKenzie, see G. V. Villegas, *The Old Testament as a Christian Book: A Study of Three Catholic Biblical Scholars: Pierre Grelot, John L. McKenzie, and Luis Alonso Schökel* (Manila: Divine Word Publications, 1988).

[42]R. Hanson compares Origen to Rudolf Bultmann. *Allegory and Event* (Richmond, Va.: John Knox Press, 1959), p. 366.

[43]De Lubac, *History and Spirit*: "What he thus describes, that to which he exhorts, particularly in his homilies, under the symbols of the Old Testament, is spiritual combat" (p. 171). "He conceived the Christian life above all as a combat initiated at baptism, and it is to this combat that he did not cease to exhort his listeners" (p. 212).

[44]H. Crouzel, *Origen: The Life and Thought of the First Great Theologian*, trans. A. S. Worrall (Edinburgh: T & T Clark, 1989), p. 63.

[45]Cf. Homily 20.1.5.

[46]Cf. Homily 20.5.1.

[47]Cf. Homily 22.1.2. For other examples, cf. *Against Celsus* 4.47; *Homilies on Judges* 5.2; *Homilies on Genesis* 8. These are discussed in de Lubac, *History and Spirit*, pp. 110-11.

are valid and beneficial, Origen strives to find symbolic meaning in all narratives. For instance, the book of Numbers speaks of censuses to which the sons of Israel were subjected during their exodus wanderings. Origen asks: What improvement do those who read about this obtain from this knowledge?[48]

Doubtless, the fact that the followers of Marcion denied that the Old Testament narratives have any use whatsoever played a role in inspiring Origen to find a practical and spiritually edifying use even for seemingly insignificant details in the text of the Old Testament.[49] Clearly Origen goes too far at times and plays games with allegorical exegesis that lead to forced and farfetched interpretations. Origen sometimes expresses himself provocatively and his reasoning lends itself to misunderstandings. Yet Origen does not claim finality for his spiritual interpretations, and in fact he often offers more than one. Frequently, he challenges his hearers to pursue their own investigations into the mystical meaning. All that matters is that the minds of the hearers be lifted up to heaven, equipped for spiritual combat and better suited to make progress in their spiritual journey toward the Promised Land. This brief summary shows that Origen's homiletical exhortations should be judged chiefly for what they are: material aimed to edify Christian souls by bringing out the potential Christian meaning of the Old Testament, based chiefly on the conscious imitation of Pauline/Hebrews methods of Old Testament interpretation. These homilies are not designed to inform historical scholars of ancient near eastern history.

Lienhard argued the important thesis that Origen's main achievement was to assure the Old Testament a permanent place in the Christian church. Origen did this

> not by an abstract theory but by working his way through the entire Old Testament, book by book, sentence by sentence, and word by word. Origen provided the church with the first Christian commentary on virtually the entire Old Testament. Seldom, if ever again, would there be any doubt that this book had its proper and rightful place in the Christian church.[50]

This is a fitting assessment of Origen's great contribution to Christian thought.

Concluding Remarks

The classic study of Origen's practice of Scripture interpretation is now available to English readers.[51] De Lubac refutes the widespread distortions of Origen's hermeneutical method that continue to be perpetuated by scholars who have read little of Origen's exegesis. In this work de Lubac does not assume the role of apologist for Origen, except indirectly, by correcting the misreading of Origen that has gone on in the past. Nor does

---

[48]Homily 1.2.
[49]Cf. Homily 27.2.1.
[50]J. T. Lienhard, "Origen and the Crisis of the Old Testament in the Early church," *Pro Ecclesia* 9, no. 3 (2000): 362.
[51]De Lubac, *History and Spirit.*

---

he undertake to rehabilitate Origen's interpretative method as if it should be emulated by modern exegetes. On the contrary, de Lubac invites modern exegetes to use other methods of interpretation than those used by the authors of the New Testament.[52] This shows that R. E. Brown misses the point of de Lubac's book when he passes the judgment that de Lubac and Daniélou have failed in their endeavor to give great value to patristic exegesis *as exegesis* and then declares confidently: "I think we must recognize that the exegetical method of the Fathers is irrelevant to the study of the Bible today."[53] Brown fails to understand that de Lubac's task was corrective and explanatory. By his unparalleled and exhaustive knowledge of Origen's writings, he demonstrated convincingly that, contrary to the allegations of Origen's critics, Origen's exegesis does not entail the negation of the literal sense. De Lubac showed that the basic principle of Origen's approach to interpreting Scripture is his Christian response to the mystery of Christ. Origen's Christian faith was situated between the interpretations of Judaism, on the one hand, and of the heretics, on the other.

The all too common reproach of Origen's spiritual exegesis of the Old Testament, popularized by R. P. C. Hanson, is that it proves that Origen was only interested in history as parable. One recent interpreter of Origen, in the footsteps of de Lubac, has handled this criticism in a responsible manner. Peter Martens writes:

> If concern for history in biblical scholarship indeed is to equate to restricting the meaning of a passage to what its human author(s) intended for their audience at that time, to hold that the resources of the exegete are solely aimed at unveiling the milieu from which biblical writings emerged and the milieu to which they were originally addressed, then Origen can be fairly labeled as uninterested in history. But this is hardly a self-evident conclusion. Could one not, for example, turn this argument on its head and argue that history is only taken seriously when the exegete takes the full symbolic potential of an event into consideration?[54]

The lesson here is that Origen's exegesis is often unfairly criticized on the basis of modern academic assumptions about what exegesis should be about. These objections are inapplicable to Origen's ecclesiastical context, since Origen's exegesis was given in the context of the liturgy. It was therefore aimed at a different audience and grounded on different principles than those of modern critical exegesis. Was the liturgy designed to be the forum for history lessons or for the edification of Christian souls?

Text and Scripture Citations

The following translation is based on Baehrens's critical Latin text (GCS 30, 7 [1921]),

---

[52]For a fine survey of de Lubac's basic ideas, see M. D'Ambrosio, "Henri de Lubac and the Critique of Scientific Exegesis," *Communio* 19 (Fall 1992): 1-17.

[53]"The Problems of the Sensus Plenior," *Ephemerides Theologica Lovanienses* 43 (1967): 463. It appears to me that Brown's credentials as a "Catholic" exegete are seriously undermined by this conclusion.

[54]Peter William Martens, "Origen on the Reading of Scripture" (dissertation, University of Notre Dame, 2004), p. 102.

as that text appears in SC 415, 442 and 461. I have been greatly assisted by the updated French translation of M. Borret and L. Doutreleau, who revised the original SC translation of André Méhat (SC 29 [1951]). The footnotes in this new edition have also proven valuable. Also, I consulted the excerpts found in the anthologies by Hans Urs von Balthasar and R. Tollinton. For Homily 27, I took advantage of the existing English translation by R. Greer and based my new translation on it. The great study of Origen's ecclesiology by F. Ledegang, *Mysterium Ecclesiae*, and de Lubac's *History and Spirit*, provided me with many of the references to parallel passages in Origen and in other early Christian literature. For the wording of the Scripture citations, I have tried to follow the RSV text as closely as possible. It is important to recall, however, that both Origen and Rufinus viewed the Greek Septuagint as the divinely inspired text of the Old Testament. Although Origen often mentions variant Hebrew readings as well as Hebrew etymologies, his exegesis turns entirely on the Septuagint (LXX) readings. The reader is well advised to consult an English translation of the LXX for clarification of Origen's exegesis.[55] Scripture references in the footnotes are given according to their location in the RSV so long as the reading corresponds generally with the RSV text. Where the LXX text departs significantly from the RSV, reference is made to the LXX. In the Psalms, readers will find that the LXX numbering often differs by one from the RSV numbering.

---

[55]See Sir Lancelot C. L. Brenton, *The Septuagint with Apocrypha: Greek and English* (Peabody, Mass.: Hendrickson, 1987; first published 1851).

ORIGEN
Homilies on Numbers

Rufinus to Ursacius:[1]

Brother, I will address you in the words of the blessed martyr:[2] "You are right to remind me, dearest Donatus, but I too remember my promise,"[3] to collect all that Adamantius[4] wrote in his old age on the law of Moses and to translate into the Latin language things worth reading. But the time for fulfilling the promise was not "seasonable,"[5] as that one[6] says, but was tempestuous[7] for us and full of confusion. For what opportunity is there for composition when there is fear of the enemy's missiles, when the devastation of cities and fields is before one's eyes, when one has to flee from dangers of the sea, and even in exile there is no freedom from fear? For as you yourself saw, the barbarian was within sight of us.[8] He had set fire to the town of Rhegium, and our only protection against him was the very narrow sea that separates the soils of Italy from Sicily.[9]

Well, to those who find themselves in such a position, what security could there be for writing, and especially for translating, where one's purpose is not to develop one's own thoughts but to adapt those of another? However, when there was a quiet night, and our minds were relieved from the fear of an attack by the enemy, and we had at least some little leisure for thought, as a solace from our troubles and to relieve the burden of our pilgrimage, we have found all that Origen had written on the book of Numbers, whether in the homiletical style or even some of those writings that are called "Excerpts."[10] At your urging, we brought these writings together from diverse sources and arranged them into a single sequence. Then we translated them into the Roman tongue to the best of our ability. You assisted my labor with all your might, Ursacius. Indeed, you were so extremely eager about this that you thought the youth who acted as secretary was too slow in carrying out his service.

But I want you to know, brother, that this reading, to be sure, clears paths for understanding, but it does not deal with each clause separately as you have read in Origen's commentaries. The rationale for this is to prevent the reader from becoming idle himself, but,

---

Rufinus to Ursacius [1]Ursacius was the friend of Rufinus who was with him when he took refuge in Sicily from the invasion of the Italian peninsula by the Goths under Alaric (410). It was at Ursacius's instigation that Rufinus translated the *Homilies on Numbers*. Ursacius also provided Rufinus with secretarial assistance. [2]That is, Cyprian bishop of Carthage who was beheaded in 258. [3]Rufinus cites verbatim from Cyprian's *Epistle* 1 ("To Donatus"), a letter that to some extent can be regarded as an anticipation of Augustine's *Confessions*, since in it Cyprian tells us of the spiritual crisis that led to his conversion. Cf. ANF 5:275; SC 291:35, 75. [4]Eusebius *Ecclesiastical History* 6.14.10 says that Origen was known as Adamantius, i.e., "man of adamant," during his own lifetime and that it referred to his rock-like opposition to the heretics. Jerome, *Epistle* 43, thought it referred to his industry in producing innumerable books. Adamantius was also the name of an author whose *Dialogue on the Orthodox Faith* Rufinus had translated into Latin, under the mistaken impression that it was an authentic work of Origen. [5]Lat *tempestivum*. [6]I.e., Cyprian in the letter cited. [7]Lat *tempestuosum*. [8]The reference is to Alaric and his army of Goths. [9]He means the straits of Messina. [10]Rufinus admits here that he has integrated some of Origen's *Excerpts on Numbers* into his translation of Origen's *Homilies on Numbers*. The "excerpts" (Latin for "selections") are also known as "Scholia." They were advanced commentary notes on the books of Exodus, Leviticus, Numbers, Isaiah, Psalms 1-15, Ecclesiastes and John. None of Origen's *Scholia* survive intact or complete, though chap. 27 of the *Philokalia* contains selections from Origen's *Scholia on Exodus*. Rufinus's admission means that the present translation is a mixed genre of homily and commentary.

as it is written, "let him stir up his own heart" and "let him produce a meaning,"[11] and when he has heard the good word, he should add to it, as one who is wise.[12]

Therefore, as I am able, I am striving to achieve what you have enjoined. Indeed, now of all the writings that I have found on the Law, the brief orations on Deuteronomy alone are lacking. If the Lord offers his help, and if he gives soundness to my eyes, we desire to add these to the remaining body of the work,[13] although our very loving son Pinianus[14] is enjoining yet other tasks from me. Because we have in common a devotion to chastity, I am blessed by his religious companionship in my exile. But pray together with us that the Lord may be present, and give peace to our times, and bestow grace on those who are laboring, and make our work fruitful for the progress of the readers.

Homily 1
Numbers 1:1-54

1.1. Not everyone is worthy of the divine numbering,[1] but those who ought to be comprised within the number of God are designated by certain privileges.

Now this book that is inscribed "of Numbers," contains clear proof of this fact. It reports that by God's command women are not summoned to the numbering.[2] Doubtless this is due to the obstacle of feminine weakness. Nor is any slave summoned, insofar as they are ignoble in life and character. Nor is any Egyp-

tian counted, of those who had been mixed in [with the people], for the obvious reason that they were foreign-born and barbarians. But only Israelites are counted, not all of them, but those "from twenty years old and upwards."[3] And it is not merely the consideration of age that is taken into account, but it is asked if he shows a strength that is adequate for war. For it is indicated through the word of God that "everyone that goes forth in power[4] is numbered."[5] So it is not solely age, but power too that is required of the Israelite. Those who are of a young age are not numbered, nor are they considered suitable for the divine reckoning, unless they happen to be firstborn or descend from priestly or Levitical stock. These alone among the young men are summoned to the numbering. But absolutely no female is summoned.

1.2. And what does this seem [to indicate]? Can these things be void of mysteries? Are we to believe that the Holy Spirit, who dictated these things to be written, composed these things for the sole purpose of informing us who was numbered among the people at that time, and who remained outside of the number? Just what progress will come from this to those who are eager to be instructed by the sacred volumes? For what profit is there in having learned this? Or what is conferred to the soul's salvation, if one knows that a certain part of the people was numbered in the desert, but a part was left uncounted?

1.3. But if we follow the thought of Paul and believe that "the law is spiritual,"[6] and if we

---

[11]Cf. Sir 2:18 (23). The Vulgate has a different versification than the Greek. [12]Cf. Sir 21:15 (18 Vg). The meaning here is that Origen's homiletical style aims at edification, not line-by-line commentary, and thus he leaves many questions unanswered. He often challenges his hearers to investigate matters that he has mentioned but has not treated in detail. Cf. Rufinus's Epilogue to *Origen's Commentary on Romans.* [13]Rufinus died in 411 (cf. Jerome *Commentary on Ezekiel, Prologue*) before being able to complete this proposed work, and no translation of Origen on Deuteronomy survives. However, Cassiodorus possessed one consisting of *sermones iiii in quibus est minuta nimis et suptilis expositio* ["four homilies in which there is an extremely brief and subtle exposition"], which he includes in a list of Origen on the Octateuch without naming the translator (*Institutes* 1.1.9). Cf. C. P. Hammond, "The Last Ten Years of Rufinus's Life and the Date of His Move South from Aquileia," *Journal of Theological Studies* 28, no. 2 (1977): 393. [14]Pinianus was the husband of Melania the Younger (daughter of Rufinus's friend, Melania the Elder), who, after four childless years of marriage, consented with Melania to take a vow of continence, though they continued living together. Palladius (*Lausiac History* 119) reports that Pinianus was the son of Severus, a Prefect. He and Melania inherited the estates of the elder Melania and were generous in showing hospitality. They were acquainted with Augustine. See *DCB* 4:397. **Homily 1** [1]Lit. "numbers," and below. [2]Cf. Num 1:1-4. [3]Num 1:3. [4]LXX *dynamis*. The Latin *virtus* carries the meaning of both power and virtue. [5]Num 1:3. [6]Rom 7:14.

listen spiritually to what it contains, then enormous progress to the soul will appear in these things that are written. For the present reading teaches me that, if I rise above the foolishness of youthful age, if I cease being an infant in thoughts and, "having become a man, I lay aside the things of an infant,"[7] if, I say, I become a young man, and the kind of young man that I "conquer the evil one,"[8] I will seem suitable to be among those of whom it is written: "all who go forth in the power of Israel."[9] Then I will be counted worthy of the divine numbering. But as long as any of us are characterized by a childish and unstable understanding, or an effeminate and dissolute laziness, or if we have Egyptian and barbaric morality, then we do not deserve to be reckoned by God in the holy and consecrated number. For in the writings of Solomon those who perish are said to be "unnumbered"; but all who are saved are "numbered."[10]

1.4. Now do you want me to show you that the number of saints is computed by God? Listen to how David speaks about the stars of heaven: "He who numbers the multitude of stars and calls them all by name."[11] In fact the Savior not only appointed his chosen disciples in accordance with a number, but he even says that the "hairs of their head are numbered." For he says: "Even the hairs of your head are numbered."[12] By these words he was assuredly not saying that those hairs are numbered which are ordinarily cut with scissors and fall to the ground, or which are lost and vanish. Rather, he means that those hairs of the head are numbered by God which were on the Nazarenes, in whom there was present the power of the Holy Spirit for overthrowing the foreign nations.[13] Therefore, by "the hairs of the head" that come as it were from the head of the apostles, he means the virtues[14] of the soul and the abun-

dance of meanings which were produced from the principal part[15] of the mind.

But we have digressed somewhat extensively in these things. Let us now return to the subject.

2.1. It says: "And the Lord spoke to Moses in the desert of Sinai,"[16] namely, all the things that we have summarized above in the brief narration, where he is commanded "to number all who go forth in the power[17] of Israel from twenty years old and upwards."[18] So, if someone "goes forth in power," and not in just any kind of power, that is, in the power of the Egyptians or in that of the Assyrians or Greeks, but if he goes forth in the power of Israel, then he is numbered by God. For there is a power of the soul that Greek philosophers teach; but it is irrelevant to the number of God, for it is not exercised for God but for human glory. There is also a power of the Assyrians, or Chaldeans, which is extolled in the study of astrology; but it is not that Israelite power and therefore it is irrelevant to God. There is also a power of the Egyptians in what they call "the secrets of wisdom," but this does not enter in to the calculation of God. With God only the Israelite power is numbered. This is that power that is taught by God, which is learned through the divine Scriptures, which is handed down through the apostolic and gospel faith. And this is why he says that they alone will be numbered, "who go forth in the power of Israel."

2.2. Moreover, let us consider why it is that the people are not numbered immediately after they came out of Egypt; for they were still being pursued by Pharaoh.[19] But they are not said to be numbered when they cross the Red Sea and come to the desert; for they had not yet been tested; they had not yet been attacked by the enemy. They clash with Amalek and conquer,[20] but not even then are they numbered; for a sin-

---

[7]Cf. 1 Cor 13:11. [8]Cf. 1 Jn 2:13. [9]Num 1:3. [10]Cf. Lk 13:23. [11]Ps 147:4. [12]Mt 10:30. It is noteworthy that Origen cites this Scripture at the conclusion of his last homily (28) on Numbers. [13]Cf. Judg 16:15-17; *On First Principles* 4.3.12; *Dialogue with Heraclides* 22.10-12; Clement *Miscellanies* 4.17.153.2-3. [14]Or "powers." [15]The Greek term *hēgemonikos* according to the Stoics was one of the eight parts of the soul and the one that governed the five senses, the faculty of speech and the generative force. [16]Num 1:1. [17]Lat *virtus*. [18]Num 1:3. [19]Cf. Ex 14:6-28. [20]Cf. Ex 17:8-13.

gle victory is not enough for one who is striving for perfection. They receive manna as food and they drain the cup of water from the "rock that followed them,"[21] but not then are they numbered; for they had not yet matured to the point of being considered suitable for numbering. The "tabernacle of testimony"[22] is constructed, but not even with this has the time arrived for numbering the people. The law is given through Moses,[23] the practice of sacrifices is handed down, the rites of purification are shown, the laws and mysteries of sanctification are established, and then the people are summoned to the numbering by the command of God.

2.3. "Inscribe these things," O hearer, "on your heart" twice and "three times."[24] Consider what great things you must pass through, what great things you must endure, by means of how many progressions, tests and battles you must fight and win, in order to be able to attain to the divine numbering, that you may somehow be taken into account by God, that you may be considered worthy to be numbered among the holy tribes, that you can be visited and registered by God's priests Aaron and Moses in the census records of the numbering.[25] In the first place you must receive God's law, the law of the Holy Spirit;[26] sacrifices must be offered, purifications must be fulfilled; all that the law of the Spirit[27] teaches must be done, so that you can at some time attain to the Israelite numbering.

3.1. I perceive a still deeper mystery in this book "of Numbers." For thanks to the apostle Paul, who sprinkles in for us seeds of the spiritual understanding, the reckoning of the tribes, the distinction of ranks,[28] the grouping of families and the entire arrangement of the camps suggest to me indications of immense mysteries.

3.2. Come then, and let us see what this whole reckoning of numbers holds for the mystical understanding, and what this diversity of ranks contains.

For us the expectation of a resurrection from the dead is a certainty, since at the advent of Christ "those who are alive, those who are left, will not precede those who have fallen asleep."[29] But united and grouped together with them, "they will be caught up in the clouds to meet Christ in the air."[30] That is to say, abandoning the corruption of this earthly location and the habitations of death, either all will remain "in the air"—as Paul declares—or some will go to paradise, or some are to be transferred to some other locations out of the many stages[31] that are with the Father.[32] Now the distinction in destination and glory will doubtless be bestowed based on the merits and deeds of each one. Each will be in that ranking that the merits of his deeds have earned for him, as Paul himself attests when he says of those who rise: "But each in his own ranking."[33]

3.3. From this, then, it will come to pass in the resurrection that each one will be assigned on the basis of spiritual indicators, either to the tribe of Reuben, on account of the fact that one really possessed a likeness and affinity to Reuben in character or deeds or life. But another will be assigned to the tribe of Simeon, possibly on account of obedience. Another is assigned to the tribe of Levi, I think because he presided well over the priesthood, or because he "gained a good standing for himself" by ministering well.[34] Another is assigned to the tribe of Judah, doubtless because he has borne royal aspirations and has ruled the people well, who are within him, namely the people comprised of the insights of his mind and of the thoughts of his heart.[35] Moreover, each one will be grouped with each of the tribes on the basis of these things which he possessed either in his actions or character, which became known to each of these tribes. So there will be certain rankings of this sort in

---

[21]Cf. Ex 17:6; 1 Cor 10:4. [22]Ex 36–40. [23]Cf. Lev 1:1; cf. Jn 1:17. [24]Cf. Prov 22:20. [25]Cf. Num 2:32. [26]Cf. Rom 8:2. [27]Cf. Rom 8:2. [28]Or "orders." [29]1 Thess 4:15. [30]1 Thess 4:17. [31]Lat *mansiones*. This term will become important in Homily 27 where Origen will discourse at length on it. [32]Cf. Jn 14:2. [33]Or "order." Cf. 1 Cor 15:23. [34]Cf. 1 Tim 3:13. [35]Cf. *Homilies on Joshua* 19.3; F. Ledegang, *Mysterium Ecclesiae: Images of the Church and Its Members in Origen*, BETL 156 (Leuven : Leuven University Press, 2001), p. 461.

the resurrection of the dead, just as the apostle indicates.[36] It seems to me that a type and figure of these rankings is prefigured in this book.

3.4. Moreover, the order and position of the marking off of the camps is described by means of a certain association and connection between the tribes. Doubtless this relates to some sort of status at the resurrection of the dead. I do not think any of the following descriptions are pointless: that three tribes are said to be positioned "toward the east," and three "toward the west," and three "toward the sea," and the final three "toward the north [wind]"—which is called the hard wind;[37] moreover, the fact that the tribe of Judah, which is regal, is stationed "toward the east."[38] It is from this [tribe] "our Lord descended."[39] Nor is it pointless that Issachar is joined to this tribe and Zebulun, and that this triune number is ordained in four parts—which [parts], although they have different characteristics of their positions, nevertheless are all contained within the number of the Trinity. Consider also that through all four of these parts the same Trinity is always gathered into one number. Doubtless this is in view of the fact that under the one name of Father, Son and Holy Spirit, all who come from the four parts of the world and call on the name of the Lord are assessed, when they "recline with Abraham, Isaac and Jacob in the kingdom of God."[40]

3.5. We had to point these things out in a general way, because we wanted to summarize briefly the mystical content of this entire sacred volume, so that each [reader] may receive an opportunity for a spiritual interpretation of these things and pursue a similar investigation in the remaining details, or even a superior and more lofty investigation, should God reveal more to

him.[41] For I judge myself to be truly unequal to the task of explaining the mysteries that this book of Numbers contains; and I am even more inadequate for explaining the things that the book of Deuteronomy contains.[42]

3.6. And for that reason we need to hasten to reach Jesus,[43] not that son of Nun, but Jesus Christ. But only by first taking advantage of Moses as our pedagogue,[44] and by "leaving behind the elementary matters of infancy"[45] with him. Let us thus strive for the perfection of Christ. For Moses did not suppress many wars; but Jesus held all wars in check; in fact he gave peace to everyone. Thus it is written that "the land ceased from wars."[46] The Promised Land, the land of inheritance, the "land that flowed with milk and honey,"[47] is divided up by Jesus: "For blessed are meek, for they will inherit the land"[48] through Jesus.[49]

3.7. Moreover, you will find that types and images of that division preceded. For it is not pointless that land beyond the Jordan is distributed to some, but to others is given land inside the Jordan. And to some, it is given as to the first, but to others as to those who are second; and to a few as to the third; and in this way that the inheritance of the land is divided "in order," where "each may rest under his own fig tree and under his own vine, and there is no one more to cause terror."[50] All of these things that have been prefigured in splendid mysteries, the Lord Jesus himself will fulfill for each one in truth, on the day of his coming. This will be no longer "in a mirror and in an enigma," but "face to face,"[51] in accordance with the fact that he knows everyone's merits. He is the "knower of the heart,"[52] "to whom be the glory and power in the ages of ages. Amen."[53]

---

[36]1 Cor 15:23. [37]Cf. Sir 43:20. [38]Cf. Num 2:3. [39]Heb 7:14. [40]Mt 8:11. [41]Notice Origen's humility. He scarcely claims that his spiritual interpretations are final and definitive interpretations of the sacred text. Cf. Henri de Lubac, *History and Spirit: The Understanding of Scripture According to Origen*, trans. A. Nash (San Francisco: Ignatius, 2007), pp. 370-74. [42]Origen's interpretation of Deuteronomy does not survive. [43]Heb *Joshua*. In the Greek language and in Origen's text, the same word, *Jesus*, is used for both names. By retaining the Greek form, I have endeavored to highlight Origen's understanding of Joshua son of Nun as an image and prefiguration of Jesus Christ. [44]Cf. Gal 3:24. [45]Cf. 1 Cor 13:11. [46]Josh 14:15. [47]Ex 33:3. [48]Or "earth." [49]Mt 5:5. [50]Mic 4:4. [51]Cf. 1 Cor 13:12. [52]Cf. Jer 17:10. [53]1 Pet 4:11.

Homily 2
Numbers 2:1-34

1.1. The first reading from "Numbers" showed that the army of God that came forth from the land of Egypt and made a journey through the desert was "inspected," that is, numbered by Moses and Aaron. And having been separated into individual tribes, it was assessed by a determinate number.[1] We have explained the meaning of this, together with the entire content of this little book, when we said that a form had been written down in advance of how the people of God, coming forth from the Egypt of this world to the Promised Land, that is, either to the place of virtues or to the glory of the kingdom of heaven.[2] They hasten to the inheritance and are brought by certain rankings and degrees of merits. And through this we showed that the magnificence of the "good things to come"[3] is foreshadowed in the images of the law.

1.2. But now, the initial part of this reading that has been recited today teaches us how the ordering of the camps is arranged by those who have been transferred over to God and who do not "entangle themselves in secular affairs."[4] And it says: "And the Lord spoke to Moses and Aaron, saying: Let the sons of Israel set up camps, a man according to his own rank and according to his signs, according to the houses of his families; let the sons of Israel encamp opposite one another in a circuit around the tabernacle of witness."[5] Moses says: "Let a man advance into the camps according to his rank [ordo] and according to his signs and according to the houses of his families."[6] And Paul says: "Let all things be done decently and according to order [ordo]."[7] Now does it not seem right to you that it is the same Spirit of God who speaks both in Moses and in Paul? Moses commands them to advance into the camps "in order." Paul commands all things to be done

in the church "in order." And Moses, who was a minister of the law, commands that order be kept in the camps. Paul, however, as a minister of the gospel, wants there to be Christian orderliness not only in actions, but also in dress. For he says as much: "Women likewise in orderly dress."[8] This leads me to think that they not only want order maintained in the discharge of duties and in dress, but that they intend it also to be understood that there is a certain order in the soul as well, concerning which it is said that "each one ought to advance according to his own order."

1.3. This order is revealed principally by the fruit of works; but no less by the greatness of one's thoughts. For it often happens that one who bears base and banal thoughts and who thinks earthly things occupies an elevated rank in the priesthood, or sits in the seat of the teacher. But sometimes one who is spiritual and is so free from an earthly manner of life that he can "examine all things and is himself judged by no one,"[9] holds a rank [ordo] of lesser ministry, or is even relegated to the common crowd. But this is to show contempt for the statutes of both the law and the gospel, and to do nothing "according to order."

Moreover, if any of us is anxiously concerned about food and drink[10] and devotes all his concern to secular affairs, but who assigns to God one hour or two out of the whole day, and comes to the church for prayer, or who listens to the word of God in passing, but who devotes his chief interest to anxious concern for the world and for his own belly[11]—such a man does not fulfill the command that says that a man should "advance according to his own order," or that says: "let all things be done according to order."[12] For the "order" [ordo] appointed by Christ is "to seek first the kingdom of God and his justice,"[13] and to believe that God adds these things to us in the second place.[14] As a

---

Homily 2 [1]Cf. Num 2:32. [2]Cf. Homily 1.1.3-4. [3]Cf. Heb 10:1. [4]Cf. 2 Tim 2:4. [5]Num 2:1-2. [6]Num 2:1-2. [7]1 Cor 14:40. [8]1 Tim 2:9; cf. Tit 2:3. [9]1 Cor 2:15. [10]Cf. Mt 6:31. [11]Cf. Phil 3:19. [12]1 Cor 14:40. [13]Mt 6:33. [14]Cf. Mt 6:34.

consequence, let a "man advance according to his order."

1.4. Do you think that they who fill the priestly office and boast of their priestly rank [ordo] "advance according to their order" and do all that is worthy of this order? Do you think likewise that the deacons "advance according to the order" of their ministry? Why, then, do we often hear people blaspheme and say: Behold, what a fine bishop! Or, what a fine priest![15] Or, what a fine deacon! Are not such things said when either a priest[16] or a minister of God has been seen going contrary to his order in some matter, or acting in some way that is contrary to the priestly or Levitical order? But what shall I say of virgins or the continent or of all those who are seen in the religious profession? If something they do is immodest or aggressive or insolent, will not Moses immediately accuse them and say: "Let a man advance according in his order."[17] Therefore, let each one know his order and understand what is worthy of that order he has received. And let him weigh his actions and speech very carefully, let him be moderate in his entrance and in his attire, so that it agrees with the profession of his order. Otherwise, he may hear God say to him: "Because of you my name is blasphemed among the Gentiles."[18]

2.1. Now let us see what the meaning of what he says is: "And according to their signs."[19] I think that signs are those things by which the unique characteristics of each person are designated; for instance, all human beings are alike, to be sure, but there is a certain unique distinction in each one, either in our face or height or posture or dress. It is by means of these, for instance, that Paul is shown to be Paul, and Peter is shown to be Peter, and not Paul. Now sometimes the distinction of each one's "sign" is given even to those who do not see it, so that by the voice and speech one recog-

nizes that this or that one is speaking. And each one is recognized according to the sign of his unique qualities, even without his being physically in view. In this way, I think, there are also diverse signs in souls. One man is emotionally quite mild in spirit, meek, calm, tranquil, even-keeled; another fellow is vehement, arrogant, harsh, easily incited, rather brash. Another is circumspect, cautious, full of foresight, attentive, diligent; another is lazy, remiss, negligent and incautious; and in these qualities one has more, another less. Now I shall dare to say that perhaps to the extent that there is diversity inherent in men's facial appearance, so there are differences to be found also in souls. For I recall that the very wise Solomon says in a certain passage: "Just as faces differ from faces, so also the hearts of men are different."[20] But let each one, as Moses says, "advance according to his own signs,"[21] that is, let not the one whose signs are base and contemptible[22] advance more arrogantly and loftily than the signs of his soul demand.

2.2. Let us also add the following as well in order to further clarify the meaning of the diversity of signs.

Everyone who knows how to read and write has learned the letters of the alphabet.[23] It is certain that there are twenty-four in the Greek alphabet, and twenty-three in the Latin. And with them, they write all that needs to be written. And yet the sign A, for example, which Paul writes is different from what Peter writes; and thus you will find in every person who knows how to read and write different ways of writing the signs of each individual letter. Thus the handwriting of each individual is recognized by certain characteristic signs and indications. And even though the alphabet is the same, there are still in the very similarity of the letters a great dissimilarity in the signs. If, then, the example of the thing proposed has

---

[15] Lat *presbyter*. [16] Lat *sacerdos*. [17] Num 2:2-4. [18] Rom 2:24; cf. Ezek 36:21. [19] Num 2:2. [20] Prov 27:19. [21] Num 2:2. [22] Lat *humilis et despectus*. Above in Homily 2.1.3 he uses *humiles et abiectus*. [23] Cf. Homily 4.1.2.

become quite clear to you, come now to the movement of the mind and of souls. By these movements they are stirred into action. Notice the "handwriting" and see how, for instance, the soul of Paul purposed to be chaste, and the soul of Peter does this as well; yet there is a certain chastity that is uniquely Peter's and another that is Paul's, even though it may seem one and the same. After all, the chastity of one of them is such that it requires him "to buffet his body and subject it to slavery," and which still says: "lest perhaps."[24] But the chastity of the other is not afraid of this "lest perhaps."[25] Likewise justice also has its unique character in Paul, and it has this in Peter as well. The same applies to wisdom and the other virtues.

2.3. Now if even in these names we have mentioned as examples it is possible for there to be some differences in the particular way they possess the virtues, even though they are one through the Spirit of God, how much more will all the rest of humanity bear certain unique signs in the movements of their minds and in the virtues of their soul! Perceiving this in its mystical account, Moses writes in the law: "let each one advance into the camps according to his own signs."[26]

2.4. Now it can happen that we may go from inferior signs to better and more magnificent ones by having zeal for good works. For if we have correctly understood that all things that are written down in the law[27] are the "forms of future things"[28] and of that age that we hope for based on the resurrection, then it is certain, assuredly, that, if in the present life we have zeal for better things, and if, according to the example of the apostle, "forgetting what is behind, we strive toward the things that are ahead"[29] in the resurrection of the dead, where "just as star differs from star in glory, so also the merits of each one will shine,"[30] then we shall assuredly

be able to be transferred from inferior signs to better and more resplendent ones and to be put on a level with the more brilliant stars. And in this life human nature is capable of advancing so far that in the resurrection of the dead it can be put on the same level, not merely of the glory of the stars, but even of the splendor of the sun, according to what is written: "the just will shine like the sun in the kingdom of God."[31] It is on this basis, then, that in what comes later he says: "according to their signs by the houses of their families."[32]

2.5. As for what he says: "by the houses of their families," the same Greek word is recorded that the apostle uses when he says: "for this reason I bow my knees to the Father of our Lord Jesus Christ from whom all fatherhood in heaven and on earth is named."[33] What the Latin translator has recorded in the passage in Numbers as "families," Paul speaks of here as "fatherhood," but in Greek it is one and the same word.

So these are the fatherhoods, or families, that Paul now points to in heaven; but Moses, still under the figures of the law, describes them on earth. He warns us to advance according to them, that we may be able to be grouped with the heavenly fatherhoods. For just as Paul has declared above, there are perhaps some, whether these are to be called families or fatherhoods in heaven, and there is that one whom the same Paul names in another passage "the church of the firstborn ones inscribed in heaven."[34] We will be grouped with the latter if we "advance according to order,"[35] and if "we do all things according to order."[36] If nothing disordered is found in us, no disturbance, nothing dishonorable, then we too "will shine like the firmament,"[37] and "gleam like the stars" or even the sun itself[38] in the kingdom of God, through Christ our Lord, "to whom is the glory and power in the ages of ages. Amen."[39]

---

[24]1 Cor 9:27. [25]Cf. 1 Pet 4:1-5. [26]Num 2:2. [27]Cf. Rom 15:4. [28]Cf. Heb 10:1. [29]Phil 3:13. [30]1 Cor 15:41. [31]Mt 13:43. [32]Num 2:2. [33]Eph 3:14-15. The referent is *patria*. [34]Heb 12:23. [35]Num 2:2. [36]1 Cor 14:40. [37]Dan 12:3. [38]Sir 50:7. [39]1 Pet 4:11.

Homily 3
Numbers 3:5-39

Concerning what is written: "I have taken Levites from the midst of the sons of Israel for every firstborn who has opened the womb,"[1] and so forth.

1.1. It is written about the manna of that time that if one receives it in the way God had commanded, he would be nourished by it; but if one wanted to receive it contrary to God's command and contrary to the divinely established manner, he would not enjoy it as life-giving food, but "worms would spring forth" from it.[2] And thus it came to pass that one and the same kind of manna generated for some worms and putrefaction, but for others it gave food that was health-giving and necessary for life. Now then, our manna is the Word of God, and with us the word of God is effective for salvation for some, but for others it yields punishment. And for this reason, I think, the Lord and Savior himself, who is "the living word of God,"[3] said: "For judgment I came into this world, that those who do not see may see, and those who see may become blind."[4] How much better would it have been for some people not to have heard the word of God at all, than to hear it with malice, and to hear it with hypocrisy! Now we speak of "better" in comparison with evil things; for it is truly better and truly more right and more perfect that the one who hears the word of God hears it with a good and simple heart, that he hears it with an upright and ready heart, so that he might bear fruit and grow as in the good earth, as it were.[5]

1.2. We have said these things as a preface on account of some of those who gather to hear with a mind that is neither simple nor faithful. I am talking about certain catechumens with whom perhaps some even of those who have already received baptism may be grouped. "For not all who are from Israel are Israelites,"[6] nor are all who have been washed in the water immediately also washed by the Holy Spirit; just as, on the contrary, not all who are numbered among the catechumens are estranged from and devoid of the Holy Spirit. For in the holy Scriptures I find that some catechumens were worthy to be indwelt by the Holy Spirit, and others who had received baptism were unworthy of the grace of the Holy Spirit. Cornelius was a catechumen, and before he came to the waters, he merited to receive the Holy Spirit.[7] Simon had received baptism, but because he approached this grace with hypocrisy, he is rejected from the gift of the Holy Spirit.[8] I do not want you to doubt that even now there are some Corneliuses among the crowd of catechumens, to whom it could be said that "your acts of mercy and your prayers have ascended to God."[9] On the other hand, there are also some Simons in the crowd of believers, to whom it ought to be boldly said: "O you who are filled with all deceit and deception, son of the devil, enemy of all justice."[10] I am saying these things as a rebuke to my own self, not merely to the hearers. For I too am one of those listening to the word of God.[11]

2.1. But let us hear what the divine word says to Moses. It says: "And the Lord spoke to Moses, saying: Behold, I have received the Levites from the midst of the sons of Israel, for every firstborn that opens the womb from the sons of Israel; they shall be their ransoms, and the Levites shall be mine. For every firstborn is mine. From the day on which I struck every firstborn in the land of Egypt, I sanctified to myself every firstborn of Israel; both of man and of beast, it will be mine; I am the Lord."[12] The Levites are received for the firstborn, since they assuredly are not firstborn. Indeed Levi is the third born

Homily 3 [1]Num 3:12. [2]Cf. Ex 16:19-20. [3]Cf. 1 Pet 1:23; Heb 4:12. [4]Jn 9:39. [5]Lk 8:15. [6]Rom 9:6. [7]Cf. Acts 10:47. [8]Cf. Acts 8:13, 18-19. [9]Acts 10:4. [10]Acts 13:10. [11]Erasmus of Rotterdam, in his *Edition of Origen*, 1536 (*DEOO* 8:438), praised the way Origen in his homilies frequently included himself among those whom he was rebuking. [12]Num 3:11-13.

from Leah. For the first was Reuben, the second Simeon, the third Levi.[13] Now those who are not firstborn by nature are received as firstborn.

2.2. Are we to believe that these things were written in God's law pointlessly? Or does this not teach us that with God they are not considered to be firstborn who come first in terms of physical birth, but rather it is those whom God himself, who has examined the purpose of their mind, indicates are to be received into the order of the firstborn? For thus Jacob, who was born later, was adjudged by God to be the firstborn, and he received the blessings of the birthright that the divine superintendence procured owing to his father's blindness.[14] For on the basis of the purpose of his heart, which was exposed to God, even "before they were born in this world or did anything good or evil,"[15] the Lord declares of them: "Jacob I have loved, but Esau I have hated."[16] Therefore Levi's sons are not firstborn according to the flesh, but they are received for the firstborn. Thus it is something more to be received for the firstborn than to be born the firstborn.

2.3. "Behold," it says, "I have received the Levites from the midst of the sons of Israel."[17] Simply say: I have received the Levites from the sons of Israel. Why is it that you add "from the midst" of the sons of Israel? From which "midst," then? As we said above, Levi is the third of Israel's sons. I should like to know, then, from what "midst" the Levites are taken. In the Scriptures I find that that blessed Shunamite, who once took care of the prophet, answered with confidence to the king of Israel, who wanted to confer a favor on her. She said, "I dwell in the *midst* of my people."[18] And even more marvelously I see it written in the Gospels about our Lord and Savior, when John says, "In your *midst* stands one whom you do not know."[19] I think, then, that one who has never

"turned aside to the right or to the left"[20] can be said to "stand in the *midst*," he who "committed no sin nor was deceit found in his mouth."[21] And therefore, since he always stands, he is said to "stand in the *midst*"; but if one imitates him, like all the saints do and like that blessed woman of whom we made mention above, one is not said "to stand"—for it cannot happen that one never turns aside to the right or to the left, "for no one is clean from defilement not even if his life should last one day"[22]—but he is said "to dwell in the *midst* of the people."[23] And the Levites, therefore, "are taken from the *midst* of the sons of Israel."[24]

2.4. For the Levites are those who did not know their right hand and their left, but by following Moses, that is, by following the law of God, they did not spare father and mother.[25] And you, therefore, if when temptation comes, if when the wrath of sin comes, "you do not turn aside to the right hand or to the left,"[26] if you do not transgress God's law, but stand firm and stable "in the midst" and "do not turn aside" and do not "bow your knees"[27] to sin, and do not follow the head of the beast,[28] that is, the image of foolishness, you will be "received from the midst of the sons of Israel" and you will be placed in the number of the firstborn. These things have been said in view of what is written: "And I will receive the Levites from the midst of the sons of Israel."[29]

3.1. But if it seems good, let us turn back again to the order of the historical narrative that is reported in Numbers. From that order, let us contemplate the mystery of the firstborn, where or how it ought to be investigated. Therefore let us reconsider more attentively how the twelve tribes are arranged in four parts by threes and how they encamp in a fixed place in each of the zones of the sky.[30] Indeed we find that Judah is stationed in the east with Issachar

---

[13]Cf. Gen 29:34. [14]Cf. Gen 27:1-29. [15]Rom 9:11. [16]Mal 1:2-3. [17]Num 3:12. [18]2 Kings 4:8, 13. [19]Jn 1:26. [20]Cf. Num 20:17. [21]1 Pet 2:22. [22]Job 14:4-5. This is an important text for Origen's understanding of the human condition, according to which all human beings enter bodily life in a fallen condition. [23]2 Kings 4:13. [24]Num 3:12. [25]Cf. Ex 32:27-29; Mt 10:37. [26]Num 20:17. [27]Cf. Rom 11:4. [28]Cf. Ex 32:4-5. [29]Num 3:12. [30]Cf. Num 2:1-2.

and Zebulun,[31] but Reuben is stationed in the west with Simeon and Gad.[32] In the south is Ephraim with Benjamin and Manasseh,[33] but in the north is Dan with Naphtali and Asher.[34] Of all of these tribes that are located in a circuit, as it were, according to the four poles of the earth, the Levites are appointed in their midst, as nearest to God, around the very tabernacle of God. Moses and Aaron are in the camps of Judah that are in the east; but Gershom is in the camps of Reuben. Yet Kohath is in the camps of Benjamin. But the text locates Merari where Dan set his camps. And thus the sons of Levi seem to be in the midst of the sons of Israel on every side and in a circuit. They are inserted and interwoven as it were among the others.

3.2. These are the things the letter of the law sets forth for us, so that, by gathering seeds of mysteries from these details, we might ascend by degrees, as it were, from low to higher matters and from earthly to heavenly things. So ascend now, O hearer, if you can, and rise up from earthly thoughts by the contemplation of your mind and by the clear perception of your heart. Forget earthly things for a little while; move beyond the clouds and beyond heaven itself by going there with your mind. Seek there the tabernacle of God where "Jesus our forerunner entered for us,"[35] and "is now present before the face of God interceding for us."[36] There, I say, seek these four orders and positions of the camps; there perceive the columns of the Israelites and the watches of the saints, and there examine these mysteries of the firstborn ones which we are now seeking.

3.3. But I do not dare to ascend there alone, nor do I dare to immerse myself in such secret recesses of mysteries without the authority of some great teacher. I cannot ascend there unless Paul goes before me and shows me the way of this new and arduous journey. He himself, then,

the greatest of the apostles,[37] who knew that there were many churches not only on earth but also in the heavens, of which John enumerates a certain seven,[38] nevertheless Paul himself, wanting to show that there is in addition a certain church of the firstborn ones, says when writing to the Hebrews: "For you have not come to a burning and tangible fire, but you have come to Mount Zion and to the city of the living God, the heavenly Jerusalem, and to multitudes of praising angels, and to the church of the firstborn ones, which is written in heaven."[39] This is why Moses describes the people of God as divided on earth by four encampments, and why the apostle describes four orders of saints in heaven. He calls each of us to come to each of them. For not everyone comes to each of these places, but some come to "Mount Zion"; but those who are a little better than these come to the "city of the living God, the heavenly Jerusalem"; and those who are more eminent even than these come to the "multitude of praising angels"; and those who are beyond all these come to the "church of the firstborn ones, which is written in heaven."

3.4. So if you have understood from these things what is the order of the firstborn ones and what is the mystery of that term, prepare yourself and strive as hard as you can to make progress in actions, life, character, faithfulness and principles, in the hope that perhaps you may be able to come to the "church of the firstborn ones, which is written in heaven."[40] But if you are not that strong, but are a little weaker, then come to the "multitude of praising angels."[41] But if you cannot reach that order, strive at least to hasten to the "city of the living God, the heavenly Jerusalem."[42] But if you are not suitable for that, at least strive for "Mount Zion,"[43] that "you may be saved on the mountain."[44] All that matters is that you

---

[31]Cf. Num 2:3-9. [32]Num 2:10-14. [33]Cf. Num 2:18-24. [34]Num 2:25-31. [35]Heb 6:20. [36]Heb 7:25. [37]As the context shows, the referent is to the author of Hebrews, which Origen took to be Paul. [38]Cf. Rev 1:4, 11. [39]Heb 12:18, 22-23. [40]Heb 12:23. [41]Heb 12:22. [42]Heb 12:22. [43]Heb 12:22. [44]Gen 19:17; cf. Acts 2:40.

not reside on earth, that you not remain in the valleys, that you not continue in the submerged lower places. It seems to me that this is how one should understand the reception of the firstborn sons of Levi who minister to God and serve at his altar and tabernacle, and who concelebrate divine ministries by means of perpetual watches.

4.1. Moreover, it does not appear to me that the words: "for every firstborn who opens the womb,"[45] can easily be explained or discussed. For not everyone who "opens the womb [vulvam]" should immediately be considered worthy of the sanctification of the firstborn, since even in the Psalms we read: "Sinners are estranged from the womb [vulva], they have gone astray from the belly [ventre], they have spoken false things."[46] This assuredly cannot in any way hold good according to the letter. For how could one go astray from God's way immediately when he has come forth from his mother's womb? Or how could a newborn child speak false things, or even utter any words at all? Therefore, since it is impossible both for one to go astray from the belly and to speak false things, it will be necessary to examine the kind of belly and womb to which this statement can apply, namely: "Sinners are estranged from the womb and they have gone astray from the belly, they have spoken false things."[47] Well, there exists that womb which every firstborn opens who is sanctified to God. Once "God opened Leah's womb,"[48] which had been closed, and she gave birth to the patriarchs. The same thing happened to Rachel, so that she likewise gave birth,[49] she whose "face was clear and her appearance beautiful."[50] Moreover, in many other passages of Scripture, you will find that wombs are opened. If you look into each of these in the respective passages, you will discover how "sinners go astray from the womb,"[51] and others who "open the womb" are sanctified

in the order of the firstborn ones.

4.2. It says: "And the Levites will be mine; for every firstborn is mine; from the day on which I struck every firstborn in the land of Egypt, I have sanctified every firstborn to myself."[52] What the historical narrative contains about these matters is well known: when the people of Israel were led out of Egypt, the firstborn of the Egyptians were struck down.[53] So this is what is being indicated in this passage: the firstborn of Israel were not sanctified before the firstborn of the Egyptians had been struck down. And it records that the death and destruction of those Egyptians is the cause, as it were, of Israel's sanctification. Based on this, one should understand here that there are certain firstborn even among the Egyptians, that is, among the contrary powers, chosen, as it were, for their wickedness and "first" among the demons. Until they are struck down and annihilated, the firstborn of the Israelites cannot receive sanctification at all. Who is it, then, who struck down the firstborn of the Egyptians, that is, the "principalities and powers"[54] of the demons? Is it not my Lord Jesus Christ, who is "the firstborn of all creation,"[55] who "exposed the principalities and hostile powers, triumphing over them in the cross."[56] Surely unless he had struck them down and triumphed over them, in no way could the sanctification of the firstborn have come to us. But in order to give us the blessings of the firstborn, he himself first becomes "firstborn from the dead, that he might be the one who holds the primacy in everything."[57] And on behalf of the firstborn ones, he received us who believe in his resurrection and placed us into the order of the firstborn. But this only applies if we hold firmly to the grace of the blessings until the end, aided by the mercy of our Lord Jesus Christ, "to whom is the glory and power in the ages of ages. Amen."[58]

---

[45]Num 3:12. [46]Ps 58:3. [47]Ps 58:3. [48]Gen 29:31. [49]Cf. Gen 30:22. [50]Gen 29:17. [51]Ps 58:3. [52]Num 3:12-13. [53]Cf. Ex 12:29. [54]Col 2:15. [55]Col 1:15. [56]Col 2:15. [57]Col 1:18. [58]1 Pet 4:11.

Homily 4
Numbers 3:39–4:49

Concerning what is written: "The number of the Levites was found to be twenty-two thousand, and the number of the firstborn of the sons of Israel was twenty-two thousand two hundred and seventy-three."[1]

1.1. In the book of Numbers that is being read to us, there are many differences in the numbers that are recorded for the sons of Israel. But after the sons of Israel, the Levites are also numbered separately. For they had not been assessed with the sons of Israel, and their number is considered set apart, as it were, and exceptional beyond the others, according to which all together they are reported to be found to be "twenty-two thousand,"[2] so that neither more nor less than this number is found. After this the Lord commanded as well the firstborn of the sons of Israel to be numbered by the same ordering by which the Levites had been numbered, that is, "from one month and above," and the firstborn of the sons of Israel are found to be "twenty-two thousand two hundred and seventy-three."[3] Do you think that Moses wanted to teach us through this the mere record of census numbers and encased no mystery in this, as is his usual manner in the differences between these numbers? Will it seem to be meaningless that the firstborn of Israel are said precisely to be in excess of "two hundred and seventy-three," and that the Levites are described as not exceeding or falling short at all from the number "twenty-two thousand"?

1.2. Now if one observes the divine Scriptures, one will frequently find that the number

"twenty-two" has been recorded for important reasons. For the Hebrews hand down the tradition that there are twenty-two letters in the alphabet.[4] Once again, twenty-two fathers are enumerated from the first-formed [father], Adam, to Jacob, from whose seed the twelve tribes receive their commencement.[5] They also hand down the tradition that the species of all the creatures of God are restricted to within twenty-two. Moreover, if one investigates quite carefully, one will find many other things in the Scriptures that have been consecrated by this number. So it is for this reason that the Levites, that is, those who serve God devotedly, and the firstborn of the sons of Israel, are identified by this admirable and sacred number.

1.3. Nor does what is added in respect to the sons of Israel, "two hundred seventy-three," appear pointless to me, though I do not perceive an easy road for finding the solution, unless the Lord deems it good to open up and "remove the veil" placed over these letters by Moses.[6]

Well then, those who are skilled in such matters claim with regard to the human race in the flesh that the embryo[7] stays in the womb for nine months; but it is reported that it is not brought to birth before it passes three days of the tenth month.[8] In this way one finds that that number, that is, "two hundred seventy-three" would indicate these days that are calculated from nine months and three days of the tenth, and together they come to these "two hundred seventy-three days" by which the entrance into this world is granted to the human race.[9] And so, in the numbers twenty and two, the sum of all creatures is tallied by mystical reasons; but in these numbers which are found from what abounds among the firstborn

---

Homily 4 [1]Cf. Num 3:39, 43. [2]Num 3:39. [3]Num 3:43. [4]Cf. Homily 2.2.2; *Selecta on Psalms* 1; Hilary, *Commentary on Psalms* 1. [5]Cf. Wis 10:1. [6]Cf. 2 Cor 3:16. [7]Lat *generatio*. [8]I am not certain about Origen's source for this. My colleague Joel Kalvesmaki informs me of a reference in the Hippocratic text, *De octimestri partu* 13.18, to a 280-day birth. Another medical text, anonymous and probably not datable, discusses a 275-day birth: *De generatione et semine* 25 (Ideler, *Physici et medici Graeci minores* 294-96). There is also an uncanny parallel in St. Augustine, *On the Trinity* 4.5 (9), where Augustine extrapolates from Jn 2:20 (this temple was built in 46 years) 46 x 6, which equals 276, representative of the new womb of his perfect body, and the number of days between the annunciation on March 25 and his birth on December 25. [9]The calculation apparently assumes 30 days per month ([9 x 30 = 270] + 3 = 273).

of Israel, the mystery of human generation is likewise being set forth.

1.4. After this, when the sons of Levi were divided into three orders, and each of the orders was assessed by the name of the three rulers, in this too certain distinctions are described that do not lack mysteries. For in the first place the order of the sons of Kohath[10] is described, and deservedly so, for from it Moses and Aaron descend to whom the essence[11] of the priesthood is entrusted. "For from him is born Amram; and from Amram Moses and Aaron."[12] The second order is that of Gershom[13] who is indeed considered first in birth, but second in order; for this is what the Scripture says: "Now the sons of Levi are Gershom, Kohath and Merari."[14] But from the sons of Kohath once again two orders are deployed: and indeed those who descend from Aaron are entrusted with the priesthood.[15] But the remaining portion are those who are ordained to serve the priests.[16] And the reason the duties are divided out to the four portions of the Levites is so that Aaron and his sons may carry out the priesthood.[17] Consequently, those who are left over from the people of Kohath carry the "Holy of Holies" on their shoulders.[18] The sons of Gershom, on the other hand, take care of the things that pertain to the tabernacle of testimony, to its court and skins, or even veils, and to whatever things are less rigid and lighter in weight.[19] As for the sons of Merari, they carry the columns of the tabernacle and its bases and the bars.[20] This is why even in those who have to be counted, Scripture expressly records that the force[21] of Merari is counted;[22] for virtue is needed to carry moveable gear of this sort.

2.1. But it is time for us to go back to the apostle Paul, who while beholding all these things with a now free and unveiled eye of his mind, and while casting aside the veil of the Old Testament[23] says that the first people, in constructions of this sort, "were serving the copy and shadow of heavenly things."[24] And while you hear this, consider whether perhaps these four orders of camps are a copy and shadow of those four orders, which Paul, while writing to the Hebrews, enumerated in the heavens.[25] And again, to the four Israelite orders, add the four groups of the Levites. Let it be sufficient that we have indicated and fleetingly glanced at these things. We have not so much explained and opened them up, as merely touched on them, and we have done so with a view toward purer thoughts—supposing that there are some of us who have brought to these things thoughts that are pure and free from worldly thinking.

2.2. It says: "Take the number of the sons of Kohath."[26] Behold again another order of numbers is introduced. The sons of Levi were already numbered "from one month and above."[27] Now the sons of Levi are numbered "from twenty-five years old,"[28] but it does not say, as it does for the others: "and above," but "up to the fiftieth year."[29] And that number becomes an important and chosen one. For it is added to these: "All," it says, "who advanced to minister at the works of the tabernacle of testimony."[30] These are ones who are numbered by a better and more important number. For as it was said with respect to the sons of Israel: "All who advanced for battle among the sons of Israel,"[31] so also here it is said: "All who advanced to minister, in order to do works in the tabernacle of testimony."[32]

2.3. After this it is told what are the "works of the sons of Kohath in the midst of the sons of Levi according to their clans in the taberna-

---

[10]Lat *Caath*. Cf. Num 4:2. [11]Lat *summa*. [12]Cf. Num 26:59. [13]Lat *Gerson*. [14]Num 3:17. [15]Cf. Num 3:4. [16]Cf. Num 3:6-9. [17]Cf. Num 3:3. [18]Cf. Num 4:4, 7, 9. [19]Cf. Num 4:24-28. [20]Cf. Num 4:29-33. [21]Lat *virtus*, which also means "virtue." [22]Cf. Num 3:33-34. [23]Cf. 2 Cor 3:16. [24]Cf. Heb 8:5. [25]Cf. Heb 12:22. See above at Homily 3.3.3. [26]Num 4:2. [27]Num 3:15. [28]Num 8:24. [29]Num 4:3. [30]Num 4:3. [31]Num 1:3-45. [32]Num 4:30.

cle of testimony."[33] It says: "Aaron and his sons will go in when the camps have been raised, and will take down the veil by which the holy things are covered and with that veil they will cover the ark of testimony."[34]

And after this seven kinds of objects are enumerated which they are commanded to cover. In the first place, as something more precious than everything else, the ark of the testimony is covered "with the veil by which it was first covered";[35] moreover, it is covered "from above with a hyacinth skin."[36] Another "hyacinth veil from above" is added as well.[37] In the second place, the "table" is covered,[38] in the third place the "candlestick,"[39] fourth, the "golden altar,"[40] then the "vessels of service,"[41] sixth, a covering of the altar is placed with certain veils,[42] in the seventh place, the basin is also covered[43] and nothing of all these things is left bare or revealed.[44] Finally, a precept of the following sort is added as well: "Do not," it says, "destroy the clan of Kohath from their tribe,"[45] that is to say, they should know that they will be destroyed if they set their hands to move these things without each object having first been covered by the priests.

3.1. So now let us return to that tabernacle of "the church of the living God,"[46] and see how these details are to be observed in the church of God by Christ's priests. If someone is truly a priest, to whom the sacred vessels, that is, the secrets of the mysteries of wisdom, have been entrusted, let him learn from these things and take heed to guard these things inside the veil of his conscience. He should not be too ready to show them in public. But if circumstances demand that he show these things to the inferior, that is, to transmit them to the ignorant, he should not show them uncovered. Let him not display them in an open and completely exposed way; otherwise, he commits murder

and "destroys the clan."[47] For everyone is cut off who touches the secret things and the ineffable sacraments. He has not yet been transferred into the order and rank of priesthood by his merits and knowledge. For it is only to the sons of Aaron, that is, to priests, that it has been granted to see in a bare and revealed fashion the very ark of testimony and the table and the candlestick and anything else of those things we have summarized above. But others should look at these things covered up, or rather, they should carry them on their shoulders as these things that have been veiled over.[48]

3.2. And the sons of Kohath, although they are not priests, nevertheless, since they are near the priests, they are able to carry these things "on their shoulders." But others put their bundles and ministrations not on their shoulders but on their wagons.[49] Let us now anticipate the reading and say a few things also about these things, since the passage has given a warning. When wagons are presented by each of the tribes, the sons of Merari received four of them, the sons of Gershom two,[50] but those who are better than these do not receive wagons.

3.3. So consider the manner in which the distribution of the duties of divine service is made, and how these holy things are not placed on speechless animals to be carried, but rational men should be the ones to carry "on their shoulders" the equipment by which the Holy of Holies is served. On the other hand, the things that are harder and heavier are not put on rational animals so much as on speechless ones to be carried. Moreover, there are some differences among these. For those who watch over the harder and heavier ministrations have more animals; for "four wagons" are given to the sons of Merari; but for the sons of Gershom, since they were near the sons of Kohath, merely "two

---

[33]Cf. Num 4:4. [34]Num 4:5. [35]Cf. Num 4:5. [36]Num 4:6. [37]Cf. Num 4:7. [38]Cf. Num 4:7. [39]Cf. Num 4:9. [40]Cf. Num 4:11. [41]Cf. Num 4:12. [42]Cf. Num 4:13. [43]Cf. Num 4:14. [44]Cf. Num 4:15. [45]Cf. Num 4:18. [46]Heb 12:22. [47]Cf. Num 4:18. [48]Cf. Num 7:9. [49]Cf. Num 7:3. [50]Cf. Num 7:7-8.

wagons suffice."[51] From this it is shown that
for harder works, and so to speak, fatter ones,
there are more who serve as animals; but for the
things that are procured by rational beings, few
approach from those who seem less instructed
or learned. For to those things that are mystical and hidden away in secrets and are exposed
only to priests, not only does no "animal man"[52]
approach, but not even those who seem to have
some learning and training, yet have not yet
ascended to the grace of the priesthood by their
merits and life. For not only do they see these
things "through a mirror" and "in a riddle,"[53]
but also they receive them covered and veiled,
and they carry them "on their shoulders,"
namely so that they may recognize these things
more by the action of works than by the revelation of knowledge.

3.4. Since therefore such is the dispensation
of the mysteries of God[54] and of the service that
concerns the holy things, we should present
ourselves to be of such quality that we become
worthy of the order of priesthood. Otherwise,
heavy burdens will be placed on us, as on irrational beasts, as it were. But let us be regarded
as holy and rational with respect to the priestly
duties.

For we are "a royal priesthood and a people
for his possession,"[55] but on the condition that
we are equal in the merits of our life to the
received grace and are considered worthy of the
holy ministry, so that, when we depart from
this life, we may merit to be received, as we said
above, among the priests of God and among
those who serve the ark of the covenant, that
is to say, the secret and concealed mysteries.
Thus "with our face unveiled may we look on
the Lord's glory"[56] and enter the holy land, the
inheritance of which will be given to us by our
Lord Jesus Christ, "to whom is the glory and
power in the ages of ages. Amen."[57]

Homily 5
Numbers 4:1-49

*Concerning what is written: "Do not destroy
the clan of Kohath[1] from its tribe."[2]*

1.1. While giving a response to Moses and
Aaron, the Lord speaks and says: "Do not
destroy the clan of Kohath from its tribe out
of the midst of the sons of Levi; but do this to
them and they will live and they will not die,
when they approach the Holy of Holies," and
so on.[3] First, let us understand the things that
are reported according to the letter, and then,
with the Lord assisting, let us ascend from the
understanding of the letter to the understanding of the Spirit.

Well then, first understand the position of
the "tabernacle of testimony";[4] understand also
the "Holy of Holies," which is separated from
the holy things by a veil placed between,[5] which
no one is permitted to look at except the priests
alone. After this, understand how, when it
was moved, when the sons of Israel move their
encampments, the tabernacle is taken down,
and Aaron and his sons, the priests, cover up
everything within the Holy of Holies with their
coverings and veils; and leaving these things
covered in the very same place where they had
been, they bring in the sons of Kohath, who
were appointed to this duty, and they make
them lift these things on their shoulders, everything that the hand of the priest had covered.
And for this reason it is said by the Lord: "You
shall not destroy the clan of Kohath from its
tribe,"[6] as if they would have to be destroyed if
they had touched the Holy of Holies bare and
exposed, which was not only unlawful to touch,
but even to look at, when it was not veiled.

1.2. If you have understood what the order
of history contains, ascend now to the splen-

---

[51]Cf. Num 7:7-9. [52]Cf. 1 Cor 2:14. Origen's jarring phrase will be preserved in the translation. [53]Cf. 1 Cor 13:12. [54]Cf. 1 Cor 4:1. [55]Cf. 1 Pet 2:9. [56]Cf. 2 Cor 3:18. [57]Cf. 1 Pet 4:11. **Homily 5** [1,3,3]Lat *Caath*. [2]Num 4:18. [3]Num 4:18-19. [4]Cf. Ex 26:33-34; Num 4:20. [5]Cf. Num 4:5-6. [6]Num 4:18.

dor of the mystery and contemplate the light of the spiritual law,[7] if the eye of your mind is pure.[8] If one of those who minister to God is worthy to take in the divine things and to look at the mysteries that the rest are less capable of contemplating, he is understood to be an Aaron or one of Aaron's sons. He can enter into things which it is not lawful for others to approach. So if someone is like this, to him alone is the ark of the covenant exposed.[9] It is he who sees the urn that contains the manna, who considers and understands the propitiatory. He gazes at both cherubim and the holy table and the candlestick of light and the altar of incense.[10] That person considers these things and understands them spiritually, that is, the one who exerts himself in the word of God and in the mysteries of wisdom and who occupies himself only with God in the sanctuary. Of course this person to whom these things are revealed and to whom these things are believed to be examined spiritually should know that it is not safe for him to disclose these things and to make them accessible to those to whom it is not allowed to be given access. Instead, he should cover up each of these things and hand over each of these things covered up, to be carried on the shoulders and placed on the necks[11] of others who are less capable. For when all the teachers who have been perfected and instructed from the mystical words impose works on the people,[12] and the people[13] do these things and fulfill what is commanded, and yet do not understand the reason for the things that are being carried out, what else is being done but that the Holy of Holies, covered up and veiled, is being carried on their shoulders?

1.3. And in order that you may consider still more clearly what is being said, we will inform you from the examples that are exhibited in the divine books. Doubtless Moses understood what the true circumcision was.[14] He under-

stood what the true Passover was.[15] He knew what the true new moons were and the true sabbaths.[16] And although he had understood all these things in the Spirit, he nevertheless kept them veiled by means of words through the forms and foreshadowing of physical[17] realities. And though he knew that "Christ our true Passover had to be sacrificed,"[18] he commanded a physical sheep to be sacrificed at the Passover.[19] And though he knew that the "feast day ought to be celebrated with the unleavened bread of sincerity and truth,"[20] nevertheless he gave instructions about the unleavened bread of flour.[21] So this and things like this were the "Holy of Holies," which, although Moses handed down that it was to be carried by others, that is, it was to be fulfilled in reality and in works, yet he handed these things down covered up and veiled by means of a common communication of words. Now we have often shown in many passages of Scripture that "shoulders" may indicate works.

1.4. Moreover, in the ecclesiastical observances there are some things of this sort, which everyone is obliged to do, and yet not everyone understands the reason for them. For the fact that we kneel to pray, for instance, and that of all the quarters of the heavens, the east is the only direction we turn to when we pour out prayer, the reasons for this, I think, are not easily discovered by anyone. Moreover, who would readily explain the reasons for the way we receive the Eucharist, or for the rite of explanation by which it is celebrated, or for the things that are done in baptism, the words, actions, sequences, questions and answers? And yet, we carry all these things on our shoulders, though they are covered and veiled, when we fulfill them and follow them in such a way that we have received them as handed down and commended by the great high priest and his

---

[7]Cf. Rom 7:14. [8]Cf. Mt 6:22; Eph 1:18. [9]Cf. Ex 25:10-30; cf. Heb 9:4-5. [10]Cf. Heb 9:4-5. [11]Cf. Num 7:9. [12]Lat *populi*. [13]Lat *plebs*, translated "clan" above. [14]Cf. Rom 2:26-27. [15]Cf. 1 Cor 5:7. [16]Cf. Col 2:16-17. [17]Lit. "bodily." [18]Cf. 1 Cor 5:7. [19]Cf. Ex 12:3. [20]Cf. 1 Cor 5:8. [21]Cf. Ex 12:8.

sons. So when we carry out all these things and things similar to these, and yet do not follow the reason for them, we raise to our shoulders and carry divine mysteries that are concealed and covered, unless there be some Aaron among us, or Aaron's sons, to whom it is granted to gaze on these things bare and revealed. Yet it is conceded in such a way that they know in themselves that these things are to be veiled and covered, when reason demands these things to be given to others and to be set forth as a work.

2.1. After this it is said of the Levites that they are to work, from twenty-five years old and above to the fiftieth year.[22] "Everyone," it says, "who goes forth to the work of works and to the works that are carried in the tabernacle of testimony."[23] In these things, observe the distinction of the words of the divine Scripture. Where it speaks of the works of the sons of Israel, it does not say "works of works," but only "works"; but when it speaks about the duties of the Levites, it did not say only "works," but "works of works." For just as there are certain "holy [objects]" [sancta], but there is another "Holy of Holies" [sancta sanctorum], so there are certain "works" and other "works of works." This is why it seems to me that Moses, when he sensed that there are certain works that are visible, but there is another inner mystical and secret meaning of them, these he called not merely "works" but "works of works." But the works that he understood to be common and only for the present time, he named these only "works." So there are certain "works of works," which I think are all these things of which either in the present reading or in Exodus and in other passages are commanded under secret mysteries and are to be fulfilled partially in the present time, partially in the future. But the things that are called "works of works," as we have said, are commanded as things that must

be handed down not to just anyone but to the Levites alone.

2.2. And among the Levites themselves, no one is called to these works unless he is precisely "in the twenty-fifth year of his life up to his fiftieth."[24] But not even these numbers of years, twenty-five and fifty, are without a mystery. For in the number twenty-five, the perfection of the five senses is made known, so that five times five are calculated. Assuredly this indicates that one who is found to be perfect in every aspect in the senses that have been multiplied and purified is called to "works of works" that are to be done in mystery. But we have often and abundantly shown in many passages of the Scriptures that the number fifty contains the mystery of forgiveness and pardon.[25] For there is both the fiftieth year which is called Jubilee by the Hebrews, in which there is remission both of property and slavery and debt,[26] and there is the tradition in the law that the fiftieth day after Passover is a feast day.[27] Moreover, in the Gospel, when the Lord was teaching the parable of forgiveness and pardon, he introduces some debtors, "one who owed fifty denarii and the other five hundred."[28] Now the numbers fifty and five hundred are related; for ten times fifty makes five hundred. Moreover, in another respect that number is made sacred; for if the perfection of the number one is added to the seventh seven, it makes fifty days. Likewise if the consummation of one decade is added to the seventh seventy, it makes five hundred.

2.3. But if it is pleasing to gather still more abundant mysteries of the numbers fifty and five hundred, we also have in this very book of Numbers that is in hand the passage where certain ones offer as gifts to God the fiftieth portion from the spoils of the enemies, those who have not gone out to war, but certain ones

---

[22]Cf. Num 4:47; 8:24-25. [23]Num 4:47. [24]Cf. Num 4:47. [25]Cf. *Homilies on Numbers* 22.1; 25.4; *Homilies on Genesis* 2.5; 16.6; *Homilies on Leviticus* 13.4; *Homilies on Exodus* 9.3; Philo *On the Change of Names* 228; *On the Life of Moses* 2.80; *On the Special Laws* 2.176-177; Clement *Miscellanies* 6.87.2. [26]Cf. Lev 25:10. [27]Cf. Lev 23:15. [28]Cf. Lk 7:41.

offer a five-hundredth;[29] and surely this number too, fifty and five hundred, are not given without a reason. Moreover, in Genesis when God was discussing pardoning the Sodomites, if they should obtain a pardon, the patriarch Abraham, aware of mysteries of this sort, begins to plead to the Lord for pardon to the Sodomites based on the number fifty. He says: "If fifty be found in the city, will you not save the city on account of the fifty?"[30]

3.1. But let us return to our theme. So it is necessary that the Levites "up to fifty years" work among the holy things;[31] those who are inferior do "works," those who are better do "works of works,"[32] but those who are superior to these must serve spiritual duties and enter into the Holy of Holies. There they must cover the things that have to be covered and hand over to the sons of Kohath the things that have to be carried on the shoulders and conveyed with the hands.[33] Moreover, the rest are set in order, each one in accordance with the things that have been explained higher up on repeated occasions. But lest this excessive caution regarding the coverings and veils provoke despair as it were and grief among the hearers, we shall attempt to explain a few things, which it may be both safe for us and right for you to look at—since indeed as we have said earlier, we are called "a royal race and priesthood, a holy nation and a people for his possession."[34]

3.2. So let us interpret the tabernacle of testimony [testamentum] to refer to all the saints who are assessed under God's covenant [testamentum]. In this tabernacle are some who are more exalted in their merits and superior in grace, and some of these are called the "candlestick,"[35] perhaps the apostles themselves, who illuminate those who draw near to God. Moreover, if there are any others in this tabernacle of God who show the light of knowledge

and teaching to all who enter, they may all be named the mystical "candlestick."[36] Others are the "holy table,"[37] whosoever has the loaves of God and refreshes and feeds souls that "hunger for justice."[38] Others are the "altar of incense," whosoever "by means of prayers and fasting day and night does not leave the temple"[39] of God, who pray not only for themselves, but also for the entire people. Designated as the "ark of the testament"[40] of God are those to whom God entrusted the secret mysteries and committed the secrets of the hidden judgments of his providence. And still more are those ones to be named the "propitiatory,"[41] who with all confidence propitiate God to men by means of the sacrifices of prayers and the victims of supplications, and those who intercede for the transgressions of the people. But those who have merited an abundance of knowledge and who abound in the wealth of the knowledge of God can be understood as the "cherubim."[42] For cherubim is translated "abundance of knowledge" in our language.

3.3. But it is necessary that all these be carried, who are described through each of these details that have been listed above. Moreover, they must be carried "on the shoulders." In my judgment it may be for this reason that angels, who "have been ordained for the sake of those who are inheriting salvation,"[43] are the ones who carry each of these whom we have mentioned above. For when this tabernacle is taken down and we begin to enter into those holy places and go to the place of promise, doubtless those who are truly holy and are considered to be in the Holy of Holies advance, being conveyed by angels. Up to the point where the tabernacle of God rests, "they are carried on the shoulders and they are lifted up in their hands." This is what the prophet foresaw in the spirit[44] when he said: "Since he commanded his angels

---

[29]Cf. Num 31:28-30. [30]Gen 18:24. [31]Or "in the sanctuary." [32]Num 4:47. [33]Cf. Num 4:5-15. [34]1 Pet 2:9. [35]Cf. Num 4:9. [36]Cf. Num 4:9; Heb 9:2. [37]Cf. Num 4:7; Heb 9:2. [38]Cf. Mt 5:6. [39]Cf. Lk 2:37. [40]Cf. Num 4:5; Heb 9:4. [41]Cf. Ex 25:17; Heb 9:5. [42]Cf. Ex 25:18, 22; Heb 9:5. [43]Heb 1:14. [44]Or "by the Spirit."

concerning you that they should lift you up in their hands, lest you strike your foot against a stone."[45]

3.4. To be sure, the devil thought this statement was to be understood about the Savior, but he had been blinded by malice and did not understand the mystical utterances. For my Savior did not need angels to prevent him from "striking his foot against a stone." The devil misrepresented the divine Scripture when he produced these statements in connection with the Savior. For this is said not about him, but about all the saints, that God, on behalf of his people, commanded his angels that they should not "strike their foot against a stone." Moreover, everything that is written in this Psalm corresponds to just persons more than to the Savior. For it is not the Savior that the Lord delivers "from destruction and from the mid-day demon"[46]—far be it from us to think such a thing! Rather, this is said of every just person. For the just are those who need the help of angels of God, to keep them from being overwhelmed by demons, so that their hearts not be pierced by "an arrow flying in the darkness."[47]

By these same angels Paul, under the same mystery, affirms that certain ones will be carried in the clouds, when he says: "But even we who live, who are left, will be caught up together with them in the clouds to meet Christ in the air."[48] So those who have been completely cleansed from transgressions and have become light are *caught up* by angels; but those who are still weighed down by certain lingering faults are *carried*.

3.5. So both the "posts of the tabernacle" and the other objects of the court that are mentioned by the Scripture are carried by certain people.[49] But they are not carried by Israelites but by Levites in accordance with this meaning that we seem to have briefly touched on in pass-

ing. We leave this to the interpretation of the hearers, so that if anyone burns with a greater desire for these things, he may kindle the light of knowledge for himself and may infer greater things than these with his more penetrating eye.[50] But may the Lord grant to us that we be carried and lifted up by workmen such as these, that we be delivered and defended from "the arrow flying in the darkness" and from "the destruction and the mid-day demon." Otherwise we may "strike our foot against the stone."[51] May we come finally to the place of promise of the saints, through Christ Jesus our Lord, "to whom is the honor and the power in the ages of ages. Amen."[52]

Homily 6
Numbers 11:16-25; 12:1-15

Concerning what is written: "Moses went out to the people,"[1] and concerning the seventy elders[2] and concerning the Ethiopian woman whom Moses took for a wife.[3]

1.1. Many things have been read aloud for us simultaneously, and neither our time restraints nor the greatness of the mysteries permit us to speak about all these things. It is permitted, however, to pick a few little flowers from the vast fields and to pluck, not as much as the field grows in abundance, but as much as suffices to catch the fragrance. It is just as when someone comes to a spring. He does not need to draw all that the deep reservoir pours forth, but as much as soothes the mouths of those parched with thirst. Otherwise, when more than a due measure of health-giving water is consumed, it may become harmful to the one drinking.

1.2. It says: "And Moses went out to the people and spoke the words of the Lord."[4] As long as Moses is hearing "the words of God," and is

---

[45]Ps 91:11-12. [46]Ps 91:6. [47]Cf. Ps 91:5. [48]1 Thess 4:15-17. [49]Cf. Num 4:31-32. [50]Origen often leaves to the hearer the responsibility of investigating details he has mentioned but left unexplained. [51]Cf. Ps 91:5, 6, 12. [52]1 Pet 4:11. **Homily 6** [1]Num 11:24. [2]Cf. Num 11:16-17. [3]Cf. Num 12:1. [4]Num 11:24.

being taught by him, he is inside and stays in inner things and is held in secret things; but when he speaks "to the crowds"[5] and ministers to the people with whom he is not able to stand when inside, he is said "to go outside." So what reality do such words contain? That every doctor and teacher of the church, if he stirs up something from the deeper mysteries, if he brings forth "among the perfect"[6] some hidden and concealed thing from the wisdom of God, as long as he is involved in deep interpretations, one should say that he is inside and abides in inner matters. But when "he speaks to the crowds" and brings forth things that advance to those who are outside and which the common people can listen to, he is said to have gone "outside and to speak the words of the Lord to the people."[7]

1.3. I see that Paul did this too. He was inside when he said: "But we speak wisdom among the perfect, but wisdom not of this world, nor of the rulers of this world, who will be destroyed. But we speak God's wisdom in a mystery, hidden, which none of the rulers of this world recognized."[8] You see how Paul, when he says these things, is on the inside and penetrates into the internal and hidden matters of divine wisdom. But listen to what he says when he "goes forth to the people":[9] "Let no evil speech go forth from your mouth,"[10] and "Let him who is stealing, steal no longer,"[11] and "Let each man have his own wife," and "Let each woman have her own husband."[12] Paul says these things, and other things that are like this, by going outside to the people in accordance with the example[13] of Moses.

2.1. But let us look at another section as well where it is reported that "Moses chose seventy men from the elders of the people and kept them before the tabernacle of testimony";[14] and "God, taking from the Spirit of Moses, gave to the seventy elders," and "when the Spirit rested on them," it says, "they all prophesied."[15] You should not understand the words: "Taking from the Spirit of Moses, he gave the Spirit to the seventy elders," as though God is removing some material and physical substance from Moses and dividing it into seventy portions, and as though he were giving a scanty particle to each of the elders. It is impious to understand the nature of the Holy Spirit in this way. But attend to the figure of these mysterious words in the following manner. It is as if Moses, and the Spirit who was in Moses, were the lamp of some very brilliant light from which God kindled seventy other lamps. The principal splendor of that light came to the others in such a manner that the very origin of the light suffered no loss from the sharing of its source.[16] In this manner a pious interpretation is offered for what is written, that "God took from the Spirit of Moses and gave to the seventy elders."[17]

3.1. But let us see what it is that he is saying in what follows: "And the Spirit rested," it says, "on them and they all prophesied."[18] We do not read that the Spirit "rests" on just any men, but on the saints and the blessed. For the Spirit of God rests on those "who are pure in heart,"[19] and on those who purify their souls from sin. But on the other hand he does not dwell in a body subject to sins, even if he may have once dwelled therein. For the Holy Spirit cannot suffer the company and fellowship of an evil spirit. For it is certain that an evil spirit is present in each one's heart at the moment of sin, and it plays its part. Assuredly when room is given to an evil spirit, and we receive it through evil thoughts and wicked lusts, the Holy Spirit, feeling grieved and having been, so to speak, crowded out, flees from us.[20] This is why the apostle, knowing that these things happen in this way, gave a warning when he said: "Do not grieve the Holy Spirit with whom you were

[5]Cf. Mt 12:46; 13:36. [6]Cf. 1 Cor 2:6-7. [7]Num 11:24. Cf. Num 21:2; *Homilies on Leviticus* 4.6. [8]Cf. 1 Cor 2:6-7. [9]Cf. Num 11:24. [10]Eph 4:29. [11]Eph 4:28. [12]1 Cor 7:2. [13]Lat *forma*. [14]Num 11:24. [15]Cf. Num 11:25. [16]Cf. Philo *On Giants* 25. [17]Cf. Num 11:25. [18]Num 11:25. [19]Mt 5:8. [20]Cf. *Commentary on Romans* 1.18.8-10.

sealed for the day of redemption."[21] Therefore, by sinning we "grieve the Holy Spirit," but by behaving justly and holily we prepare a resting place for him within us. This is also why in what he now says about the seventy elders, that "the Spirit rested on them," he has set forth the praiseworthy quality of their life as well as their virtues. After all, since the Holy Spirit "rested" in view of the purity of their heart, the sincerity of their mind and the capacity of their understanding, he becomes immediately active in them and he wastes no time, wherever material that is worthy of his action is available. For the Scripture says, "And the Spirit rested on them and they prophesied."[22]

3.2. So on all who have prophesied, the Holy Spirit has rested, yet on none of these has he rested as he did on the Savior. This is why it is written of him that: "A shoot shall arise from the root of Jesse, and a flower shall grow from his root. The Spirit of God will rest on him, the Spirit of wisdom and understanding, the Spirit of counsel and fortitude, the Spirit of knowledge and of piety; and the Spirit of the fear of God will fill him."[23] But perhaps someone says: You have shown nothing more written about Christ than is written about the rest of men; for just as it is said about the others, that "the Spirit rested on them," so also it is said about the Savior: "The Spirit of God will rest on him." But notice that on no other is the Spirit of God described as having rested with this sevenfold virtue. Doubtless this is because the prophecy concerns the very substance of the divine Spirit, which "rests on the shoot that was proceeding from the stock of Jesse."[24] Because that substance could not be explained under one term, it is set forth under diverse designations.

3.3. I have another testimony whereby I can show that the Holy Spirit rested on my Lord and Savior in an excessive degree and in a completely different way than is reported in respect to others. For John the Baptist says of him: "He who sent me to baptize in water said to me: The one on whom you see the Spirit descending and remaining in him, he is the one."[25] If he had said: "the Spirit descending," and would not have added: "and remaining in him," the Savior would seem to possess nothing remarkable over the others. But now he has added: "and remaining in him." So this was a sign of the Savior that could be shown in no other; for of no one is it written that the Holy Spirit "remained in him."

3.4. And lest anyone think that I am detracting from the prophets by saying this, the prophets themselves know that I am not detracting from them when I prefer my Lord Jesus Christ. For they recall each of their own statements and find that of no other is it said: "He did not commit sin, nor was deceit found in his mouth."[26] For since he is the only one "who did not commit sin," therefore in him alone did the Holy Spirit "remain" and continue to remain.[27] For if he is the one of whom something unique and remarkable is said, namely what we said above, that he "did not commit sin," then it is established that all the rest were "under sin."[28] If all of them were, then the prophets too were under it, necessarily. So how is it right for us to say that the Holy Spirit had "remained" in them at the moment of sin?

3.5. Or, if it seems incredible to you that the prophets, after they received the Holy Spirit, were able to sin, let us turn back to this same Moses, whom we have in hand, who was assuredly the greatest and most remarkable of the prophets.[29] He writes of himself and gives testimony about himself, that he sinned in what he said: "Hear me, O unbelieving ones; must we produce water for you from this rock?"[30]

---

[21]Eph 4:30. [22]Num 11:25. [23]Is 11:1-3. [24]Is 11:1-2. [25]Jn 1:33. [26]Is 53:9; 1 Pet 2:22. [27]For the distinction between "remain" and "continue to remain," see Philo On Giants 28. [28]Cf. Rom 3:9. [29]Cf. Homily 22.3. Henri de Lubac, History and Spirit: The Understanding of Scripture According to Origen, trans. A. Nash (San Francisco: Ignatius, 2007), p. 299, refers to this passage and says: "Like Philo, like Josephus, and like all the Jews, he [Origen] is dazzled by the greatness of Moses." [30]Num 20:10.

For in these statements, he did not sanctify the Lord "at the water of contradiction,"[31] that is, he did not trust in the power of God; and he said that "God is able to bring forth water for you from this rock," but, from weakness and a kind of hesitation, as it were, he answered and said: "Can we bring forth water for you from this rock?"[32] Since therefore the Lord reckons these words to him as a sin, it is certain that when he was saying these things, he did not speak from the Holy Spirit, but from a spirit of sin. But if such a great prophet as Moses is shown by the testimony of Scripture to have had the Spirit of God in him at one time, but at another time not to have had it, namely at the moment of sin, then it is certain that a similar idea[33] should be maintained respecting the rest of the prophets.

3.6. Now what should I say about David? He prays for the Holy Spirit not to be taken from him, as though it is possible to take the Spirit from him, and he says: "Cast me not away from your presence, and take not your Holy Spirit from me."[34] But in what follows, he demands back the gift that had been taken from him as it were by his own fault and says: "Return to me the gladness of your salvation and strengthen me with your governing Spirit."[35]

But what should I call to mind about Solomon as well? Surely no one will say that it was without the Holy Spirit that he either carried out his judgments,[36] or built the temple to the Lord,[37] or, on the other hand, that it was in the Holy Spirit that he made temples to demons[38] or turned his heart toward impious wives.[39]

Even that prophet who was sent "into Bethel" by the Lord in the third book of Kingdoms surely spoke the words of God in the Holy Spirit;[40] yet one should not believe that he transgressed the Lord's command in the Spirit of God, since he had been commanded "not to eat bread" in Bethel. On that account he was

killed by a lion.[41] But it would take too long to go into the details.

3.7. Now I think, though I would not declare this absolutely, that among the common actions of men, there may be some in which, though they may be free from sin, nevertheless do not seem worthy for us to think that the Holy Spirit is present in them. I would say, for instance, that lawful marriage is free from sin,[42] nevertheless at that time when conjugal acts are being done, the presence of the Holy Spirit will not be granted, even if the one who is complying with his responsibility to reproduce seems to be a prophet. Moreover, there are many other things in which human power alone suffices for itself, and the thing does not require, nor is it befitting, that the presence of the Holy Spirit be there.

But here we are falling into a digression, as it were, while wanting to show that the Spirit of God ever "remained" only on my Lord and Savior Jesus, but on all the other saints, just as also on the seventy elders, who served as a point of departure for these words, the Spirit of God merely "rested." He operated in them at that time when it was expedient for them through whom he was working and it was useful to those to whom he was ministering.

4.1. Moreover in what follows, the reading that was read aloud contains the statements: "Moses married an Ethiopian wife, and Miriam[43] and Aaron spoke disparagingly of Moses because he married an Ethiopian wife, and they said: Has God spoken to Moses alone? And the Lord heard it," it says.[44] And after this he commands them "to go out to the tabernacle of testimony" and there, when a certain trial was conducted, Miriam becomes leprous until a certain time and then she is called back to the camp.[45]

To explain this quite briefly, we can say that Miriam contained a form of the first people.

---

[31]Num 20:13. [32]Num 20:10. [33]Lat *forma*. [34]Ps 51:11. [35]Ps 51:12. [36]Cf. 1 Kings 3:16-28. [37]Cf. 1 Kings 6:15. [38]Cf. 1 Kings 11:7. [39]Cf. 1 Kings 11:1. [40]Cf. 1 Kings 13:1-6. [41]Cf. 1 Kings 13:17-24. [42]Cf. 1 Cor 7:28. [43]Lat *Maria*. [44]Num 12:1-2. [45]Cf. Num 12:4-15.

Moses represents the law of the Lord. He entered into a marriage with this Ethiopian woman, who was gathered from the Gentiles. Therefore Moses, that is, the spiritual law, took this wife; and for this deed Miriam, who now is the synagogue, is indignant and speaks disparagingly, together with Aaron, that is to say, with the priests and Pharisees.[46] To the present day, then, that people speak disparagingly, since Moses is with us, and it seems disgraceful to them that among us he does not teach "the circumcision of the flesh"[47] or the observance of the sabbath or of new moons[48] or the blood-sacrifices. Instead he instructs on the circumcision of the heart,[49] on rest from sinning, and on feast days "in the unleavened bread of sincerity and truth"[50] and on "sacrifices of praise,"[51] and on victims, no longer of slaughtered cattle, but of slaughtered vices.

4.2. So God passes judgment concerning these things and he confirms the marriage with the Ethiopian woman and he freely allows Moses to live and rest with her, but he expels Miriam "outside the camp"[52] and puts her far from the tabernacle of testimony. Aaron is likewise expelled with her. But in addition, Miriam even becomes leprous.[53]

Now look at that people and see the extent of the foulness of their observance, the extent of the baseness of their mental view. Nevertheless, this leprosy does not abide forever, but when the week of the world[54] has begun to be fulfilled, they will be called back to the camp. For at the end of the world, "when the fullness of the Gentiles has entered in, then even all Israel will be saved."[55] At that time the leprosy will cease from the countenance of Miriam; for she will receive the beauty of the faith and she will accept the splendor of the knowledge of Christ,[56] and her face will be restored, when "both will

become one flock and one shepherd."[57] One must truly say to this: "O the depth of the riches both of the wisdom and knowledge of God,"[58] who "has enclosed all under sin, so that he may be merciful to all,"[59] in Christ Jesus our Lord, "to whom is the glory in the ages of ages. Amen."[60]

Homily 7
Numbers 12:1-15; 13:18-33; 14:1-8

Once again the things that had remained concerning the Ethiopian woman and concerning the leprosy of Miriam [Maria].

1.1. As the apostle says: "All these things happened to them in a figure, but they were written as a warning to us."[1] My question is: What warning do we receive from what has been read to us, that "Aaron and Miriam[2] spoke disparagingly of Moses,"[3] and on that account were chastised? In fact, Miriam even becomes "leprous."[4] Now the concern about this chastisement was so great that while Miriam was spending a week's time with leprosy, the people of God were not making their journey to the Promised Land, nor was the tabernacle of testimony moved.

In the meantime I am warned, first of all, from this action, and I am warned in a useful and necessary way, not to "speak disparagingly of a brother."[5] I should not speak evil of my neighbor; I should not open my mouth to speak disparagingly, not only of holy people, but of any of my neighbors, when I see the extent of God's indignation that arose from this, the extent of the vengeance that proceeded from this. After all, even in the Psalms we see that God was roused into action against this sin by a similar indignation where he says: "You sit and

---

[46]Cf. Procopius *Commentary on Numbers* 12.1; Irenaeus *Against Heresies* 4.20.12. [47]Eph 2:11. [48]Cf. Col 2:16. [49]Cf. Rom 2:29. [50]1 Cor 5:8. [51]Ps 50:14. [52]Cf. Num 12:14. [53]Cf. Num 12:10. [54]Apparently the phrase refers to the church age up to the second coming of Christ. [55]Cf. Rom 11:25. [56]Cf. 2 Cor 4:6. See Homily 7.4; *Commentary on Song of Songs* 2.1; *Homilies on Song of Songs* 1.6. [57]Cf. Jn 10:16. [58]Rom 11:33. [59]Cf. Rom 11:32. [60]Cf. 1 Pet 4:11. **Homily 7** [1]1 Cor 10:11. [2]Lat *Maria*. [3]Cf. Num 12:1. [4]Cf. Num 12:10. [5]Ps 50:20.

speak disparagingly of your brother and you put a stumbling block against your mother's son."[6] Likewise in another Psalm, under the persona of a just man who knows how particularly displeasing this is to God, it is said: "I pursued the one who secretly disparaged his neighbor."[7] So then, based on all these words of the divine Scripture, which are as it were "sharp double-edged swords,"[8] let us cut off the vice of denigrating holy people and of disparaging brothers. For leprosy comes to those who denigrate and speak evil.

1.2. But after this let us pass from moral subject matter to the mystical understanding. Although a few things have already been said in the previous discussion, nevertheless let us add what seems to have been lacking. Let us see, then, who it is who "speaks disparagingly of Moses," who speaks evil of him.

Not merely the Jew, but also the heretics, who do not receive the law and the prophets, they, too, speak disparagingly of Moses. After all, they are accustomed to fasten even a criminal charge against him when they say that Moses was a murderer, for he killed an "Egyptian."[9] And with their blasphemous speech they concoct many other things either against him or the prophets. Therefore, since they "speak disparagingly of Moses,"[10] they have leprosy in their soul and they are leprous in the inner man, and therefore they are considered to be "outside the camp"[11] of the church of God. So whether it is the heretics who "speak disparagingly of Moses" or those of the church who speak disparagingly of their brothers and who speak evil of their neighbors, there is no doubt that everyone who practices this vice is leprous in his soul.

1.3. And Miriam [Maria] indeed, thanks to the intervention of Aaron the high priest, is cured on the seventh day;[12] but if we contract

leprosy in our soul by the vice of detraction, we will remain leprous in our soul and unclean until the end of the week of the world,[13] that is, until the time of resurrection; but if not, while there is time for repentance, let us receive correction and having been converted to the Lord Jesus and appeasing him through repentance, let us be cleansed from the uncleanness of our leprosy. But I think that it is not merely that first people nor the heretics alone, whom we have mentioned above, who "speak disparagingly of Moses." For all who understand the writings of Moses badly and those who receive the spiritual law in a carnal fashion also speak disparagingly of Moses, because from words that proceed from the Spirit, they teach people in a fleshly way.

You have heard for yourself what judgment and condemnation befalls detractors and evil speakers. Now listen to what a great benefit they confer on those whom they detract. We have never found that God spoke such great praises about Moses his servant as we now observe are spoken when these people had spoken disparagingly of him.

2.1. Listen, then, to what it relates in what follows and what praises the Holy Spirit pours forth on Moses. It says: "And the Lord descended in a pillar of cloud, and he stood at the door of the tabernacle of testimony; and Aaron and Miriam were called, and they both stood there. And he said to them: Hear my words: If one of you is a prophet of the Lord, I will both be made known in visions and I will speak to him in dreams. With my servant Moses it is not so. He is faithful in all my house. I will speak to him mouth to mouth, in outward reality, and not in an enigma, and he has seen the glory of the Lord. And why were you not afraid to speak disparagingly of my servant Moses? And the anger of the Lord's fury came on them and

---

[6]Ps 50:20. [7]Ps 101:5. [8]Cf. Rev 1:16; Heb 4:12. [9]Cf. Ex 2:12. The heretics in view here seem to be Marcion and the Gnostics. Cf. Irenaeus *Against Heresies* 1.27.2. [10]Cf. Num 12:1. [11]Cf. Num 12:14. [12]Cf. Num 12:15. [13]Cf. *Homilies on Leviticus* 8.4; *Commentary on Romans* 2.13.21; *Barnabas* 15.9.

they departed. And the cloud withdrew from the tabernacle, and behold Miriam became leprous as snow."[14] You see what punishment the detractors brought down on themselves, but also what praise they obtained for the one against whom they had spoken in detraction. For themselves, they obtained disgrace, for him splendor; for themselves they procured leprosy, for him glory; for themselves opprobrium, for him magnificence.

2.2. Moreover, before Moses took the Ethiopian woman, it was not written that God spoke to him "in outward reality and not in enigmatic speech." But when he took the Ethiopian woman, then God says of him: "I shall speak with him mouth to mouth, in outward reality and not in enigmatic speech."[15] For it is only recently, when Moses came to us and was joined to this Ethiopian woman of ours, that the law of God is no longer known in figures and in images as before, but is known in the very outward reality of truth. And the things that were formerly signified in an enigma now are fulfilled in reality and in truth. And so the one who was explaining the forms of the figures and enigmas says: "But we know that our fathers were all under the cloud and all were baptized in Moses in the cloud and in the sea, and all ate the same spiritual food, and all drank the same spiritual drink. For they drank from the spiritual rock that followed them; but the rock was Christ."[16] You see the manner in which Paul solves the enigma of the law and teaches the forms of the enigmas and says that "the rock" was an enigma to Moses, before it was joined to this Ethiopian woman of ours. Now, in outward reality, "the rock is Christ," for now God "speaks mouth to mouth" through the law. Previously, baptism was "in an enigma, in the cloud and in the sea," but now, in reality, it is a "regeneration in water and in the Holy Spirit."[17] At that time the manna was food "in an enigma," but now, "in

reality," the flesh of the Word of God is "true food," just as he himself says: "My flesh is truly food and my blood is truly drink."[18] So then, even now Moses takes his place among us and unites with this Ethiopian woman. Either he himself speaks to us, or God speaks to him, "not in an enigma, but in reality."

2.3. Now to these things is added: "And he saw the glory of the Lord."[19] When did Moses see the glory of the Lord? I would say at that time when the Lord "was transfigured on the mountain" and "Moses was present with him, together with Elijah, and they were conversing with him."[20] And therefore, it is rightly added in what follows: "And why were you not afraid to detract from my servant Moses?"[21] Indeed, clearly this statement is directed against those who, to be sure, appear to receive the Gospels, but they speak disparagingly of Moses, and they are deservedly reproached, since, although they learn through the Gospel that Moses, together with Elijah, saw the glory of the Lord, they have dared to speak disparagingly of the law and the prophets.[22] And therefore, let us not detract from Moses. Let us not speak disparagingly of the law, but let us be not only "hearers of the law, but also doers,"[23] so that we may deserve "to be glorified together"[24] with Moses himself.

2.4. But I think that they also supply material for denigrating Moses, who, for instance, when the book of Leviticus is read, or a reading from Numbers, do not show how these things which have been written "in an enigma,"[25] ought to be understood "in outward reality,"[26] that is, they do not explain spiritually the things that are read in the law. For inevitably those who hear the rites of sacrifice, or the observation of sabbaths, or of other similar things being read aloud in the church are offended and say: "What need is there for this to be read in the church? What good are Judaic precepts to us

---

[14]Num 12:5-10. [15]Num 12:8. [16]1 Cor 10:1-4. [17]Cf. Tit 3:5; Jn 3:5. [18]Jn 6:55. [19]Num 12:8. [20]Cf. Mt 17:1-3. [21]Num 12:8. [22]The referent is probably to the Gnostic sects, including the Marcionites. [23]Jas 1:23. [24]Cf. Rom 8:17. [25]1 Cor 13:12. [26]Num 12:8.

and the observances of a rejected people? These things belong to the Jews; let the Jews look after them!" Therefore, lest minor stumbling blocks of this kind occur to the hearers, an effort must be made to attain to the knowledge of the law. And what is read must be understood and explained in accordance with the fact that "the law is spiritual."[27] Otherwise, thanks to the learned, or rather, thanks to laziness and negligence, Moses may be denigrated by the unlearned and by those who lack expertise. But "let us be converted to the Lord" so that he may "remove the veil" of the letter for us.[28] Then the face of Moses will not seem ugly to us, but glorious and lovely. Then we will not merely refrain from disparaging him, but we will even confer on him praise and glory for the greatness of his meanings.

2.5. "And the anger of the Lord's fury came on them, and they departed. And the cloud withdrew from the tabernacle, and behold Miriam [Maria] became leprous like snow."[29] The anger of the Lord's fury comes on those who speak evil and detract. Nevertheless, with respect to the words "the cloud withdrew from the tabernacle and behold Miriam became leprous like snow," one must consider very carefully the fact that first the cloud withdraws, and then she is filled with leprosy.[30] This shows that even if the grace of the Holy Spirit is in someone and that person disparages and detracts, it withdraws from that person after the detraction, and then the soul is filled with leprosy. For even that first people had the grace of God within it, but after they stretched forth their blasphemous tongues against the true Moses, our Lord Jesus Christ, the cloud departed from them and passed to us "on a very high mountain," where our Savior "was transfigured and a gleaming cloud overshadowed" his disciples and "a voice came from the cloud saying: This is my beloved Son, in whom I am well pleased."[31]

After this, then, "Miriam became leprous like snow." While the cloud was present, Miriam was not leprous, but when it departed.[32] For while the presence of God was among that people, they were not leprous; but when it departed, the shame of its face covered them. Moreover, let us fear lest we cause this cloud to flee from us by means of evil speaking, evil doing and evil thinking. And then the leprosy of sin will appear in us, when the grace of God has abandoned us.

3.1. "And Aaron looked at Miriam and behold she was leprous. And Aaron said to Moses: I beseech you, Lord, do not impute the sin against us, for we did not know that we sinned. Let her not be like death, and as a miscarriage expelled from her mother's womb, and it devours half of her flesh."[33] Here he wants to show that that people was indeed formed in the womb of the mother of its synagogue. Yet it could not attain to a perfect and complete birth. For just as a miscarriage is an incomplete and disordered birth, so also that people was at one time within the womb of the mother, that is, it was placed under the instruction of the synagogue; but it was not able to be made alive and to be completely formed because of the sins that intervened. And for that reason they were expelled like a miscarriage, incomplete and premature, namely with sin devouring half of her flesh, as it says.

And yet, sometimes there can even be a good miscarriage. Now a miscarriage is called good when it is compared with other things, as even Ecclesiastes says: "And I said: A miscarriage is good rather than that one."[34] Who is "that one"? It says: "He who enters into vanity and walks in darkness."[35] So he is not calling a miscarriage good in the absolute sense, but good in comparison with a life that is led in vanity and in the darkness of ignorance. And in Ecclesiastes a certain comparison is made between the two.

---

[27]Rom 7:14. [28]Cf. 2 Cor 3:16. [29]Num 12:10. [30]Cf. Num 12:9. [31]Cf. Mt 17:5. [32]Cf. Num 12:10. [33]Num 12:10-12. [34]Eccles 6:3. [35]Eccles 6:4.

3.2. For Ecclesiastes also says elsewhere: "The dead are good in comparison with the living."[36] Once again if you compare a miscarriage with those things, you will say that it is good in comparison with both. So if you consider those who are alive and those who are dead, a miscarriage is better than these, because it has not even tasted of the advantages of life in this world. By making the comparison, you will discover the differences. So consider that he does not call others "living" except those of whom it is said in the Psalms: "Nevertheless every living man is vanity."[37] So then, [a miscarriage is better] than every man who lives in vanity; for not every life is in vanity, but that life which is "according to the flesh"[38] and according to the errors and pleasures of the world, that is a life of vanity. And beyond this life are all who are dead to this life and who say: "Now to me the world has been crucified and I to the world,"[39] and of whom it is said: "Therefore you are dead with Christ."[40] These ones, then, are better than those living ones. But a miscarriage is said to be beyond these because, although it may seem to have come into the flesh, nevertheless it did not receive any commencement of the vanity of this life. Nevertheless, Ecclesiastes introduces someone else as well, as it seems, who is better even than the former, of whom he says: "And best beyond these is the one who has not yet been born,"[41] that is, who does not even come to the conclusion of the fleshly womb and to the injury of a physical birth.

3.3. Moreover, consider what Ecclesiastes also says: "I praised all the dead more than the living, those who live until now."[42] Does he not show plainly that he has called those ones better who are dead to the world, and he would declare those ones inferior who are living for the world? For if you want to understand this according to the letter, how is it that the dead deserve to be praised more than the living? For normally one is praised because he acts with a good will and intention. But that common death comes to no one from his will or intention. How then will one seem worthy of praise for what he endures contrary to his intention? Otherwise even Pharaoh the king of Egypt, who was drowned in the sea, will be praised beyond Moses, who escaped from the sea alive. And the Egyptians who died in the waters will be praised more than the people of God who "passed through on dry ground in the midst of the sea."[43] Therefore do not understand it this way, but know that you will have to be praised as one who is dead, when you are able to say: "I have been crucified with Christ. But I no longer live, but Christ lives in me."[44] If you have renounced the world, if you have rejected vices, if you are no longer provoked to sin, but you are dead to sin, then you are better than the one who lives to sin; and that praiseworthy death will be in you. For no one is praised for this common death, which comes to everyone by the law of nature.

3.4. Although this was a digression, it still had to be discussed in connection with the passage where the word of God says that Miriam became a miscarriage for her fault of detraction and as a wound of chastisement.[45] We needed to show that there is both a reproachable and a praiseworthy kind of miscarriage. After all, even the apostle was aware that among these orders of which we have spoken above there is a praiseworthy order of miscarriage. He says even concerning himself: "But last of all, as to a miscarriage, he appeared also to me."[46] He numbers himself ahead of those who are alive and ahead of the dead, yet behind those who are not yet born. Therefore, Miriam becomes "like a miscarriage"; for that people was not able to be formed "unto perfection" in the law, as Paul too declares when he says: ""For the law brought no one to perfection."[47] Finally, the same apostle

---

[36]Eccles 7:1. [37]Ps 39:5. [38]Cf. Rom 8:4-5. [39]Gal 6:14. [40]Col 3:3. [41]Eccles 4:3. [42]Eccles 4:2. [43]Ex 14:29. [44]Gal 2:20. [45]Cf. Num 12:12. [46]1 Cor 15:8. [47]Heb 7:19.

says the following about certain ones who had fallen away from the faith and had converted themselves, so to speak, into miscarriages, in his effort to renew them again to the principles of a perfect birth: "My little children, for whom I again suffer birth pains until Christ is formed in you."[48]

4.1. "And Moses cried to the Lord saying: God, I beg you, heal her."[49] And who if not Moses should pray to the Lord for the healing of that people? Moses prays for them. And perhaps this was what he discussed in his conversation with the Lord Jesus Christ, when he was transfigured on the mountain.[50] Perhaps he asked him that all Israel be saved, once "the fullness of the Gentiles has entered."[51]

4.2. "And the Lord said to Moses: If her father had spit in her face, would she not be ashamed for seven days? Let her be separated for seven days outside the camp, and after this she will enter."[52] What does this mean: "If her father had spit in her face, she would be ashamed for seven days"? We have put Miriam in the place of the synagogue. The synagogue's own father spit in its face. To spit in the face is a sign of repudiation. After all, in the passage in the law where it is commanded that the nearest neighbor should marry the woman who has been left desolate, it is written that if the neighbor wants to repudiate the marriage, the man whose sandal was loosed should be spit on in the face.[53] And this was given as a sign of repudiation. So then, Miriam [Maria], that is, that people, when it is repudiated by God, is said to be spit on in the face.

4.3. In another passage as well we have a significance of spittle, when Isaiah says: "All the nations are reputed as a drop in the bucket and as spittle."[54] So there it is shown that even that people was rejected like the other nations, which "are reputed as spittle." And in fact if you consider that former honor, when

the high-priestly order flourished among them, when there were the insignia of the priests, the Levitical services, the majesty of the temple, the prophetic splendor, and when they had the advantage of heavenly associations on earth—what honor that was, what glory! And again if you look at them now, with what terrible shame do they shrink back! They are without their temple, without an altar, without sacrifice, without a prophet, without the priesthood, without any visitation from heaven. They are scattered over the whole earth and live as refugees! Could anyone fail to recognize that "her father has spit in her face" and drenched their face with shame?

4.4. So she is "separated for seven days outside the camp."[55] We have already said above that these seven days indicate the week of this world;[56] for in seven days the substances of the entire visible creation seem to have been produced.[57] For at that time things that did not exist came into being. In fact, in the week of the whole world the secrets will also be explained by a certain dispensation known to God alone, which were produced at that time. Meanwhile, in this week in which Miriam was sequestered, the camps of the sons of Israel are not moved, but they stay closed in one location and there is no progression at all for them, "until Miriam is cleansed"[58] of her leprosy.

5.1. It says: "And after this the people moved forward from Aseroth and encamped in the desert of Pharan."[59] Aseroth translates as "perfect houses." So after Miriam has been purged, the people progress from their perfect houses, and come to Pharan, which translates as "visible mouth." A visible mouth seems to me possibly to be understood to refer to the fact that "the Word became flesh"[60] and "the invisible became visible." And this can signify that after the end and perfection comes of all that had to be done to that people, then they cross over[61] and come

---

[48]Gal 4:19. [49]Num 12:13. [50]Cf. Mt 17:3. [51]Rom 11:25-26. [52]Num 12:14. [53]Cf. Deut 25:5-10. [54]Is 40:15. [55]Num 12:14. [56]Cf. Homily 7.1. [57]Cf. Gen 1:1–2:3. [58]Num 12:15. [59]Num 12:16. RSV Hazeroth, Paran. [60]Jn 1:14. [61]Cf. Heb 11:29.

to the one in whom they had not previously believed, namely the "Word made flesh."

5.2. "And the Lord spoke to Moses saying: Send out men and let them survey the land of the Canaanites, which I am giving to the sons of Israel for a possession,"[62] and the remaining things in which are narrated the story of the spies who were sent and report that the land is good and admirable, but that the sons of the giants dwell there in whose sight the people of God seemed like locusts.[63] And the majority despair of being able to be saved from the sons of the giants, but Jesus[64] does not despair, but strengthens the faith of the people, along with "Caleb, who is from the tribe of Judah," and they say: "If God loves[65] us, let him bring us into this land."[66]

5.3. So which land does this refer to according to the spiritual understanding? Which land indeed is a holy and good land, but is inhabited by the ungodly? And who are these enemies who inhabit the land of the saints? And how should they be expelled, so that once expelled the saints may succeed in their place? Let us go back to the Gospels, let us go back to the apostle. The Gospels promise the saints the kingdom of heaven. The apostle says: "But our commonwealth[67] is in heaven."[68] So then, the place of inheritance that is promised to the saints is in heaven. And what makes us think that in these places that are promised to you, there is now no inhabitant whom you must drive out of there by means of battle? Why then would the Lord say: "In the days of John the Baptist the kingdom of heaven suffers violence, and those who do violence plunder it"?[69] For if there were not those whom one must treat with violence, if there were not those who must be expelled and driven out of there, he would never have said: "the kingdom of heaven must be plundered by means of violence."[70] And unless

there were those with whom we are engaged in a struggle and combat, the apostle would never have said: "Our struggle is not against flesh and blood, but against principalities and powers, against the rulers of this darkness of this world, against the spiritual forces of wickedness in the heavens."[71] It appears that the following statement of God through the prophet should be understood about this as well, where he says: "And my sword has been made drunk in heaven."[72] So it is necessary that you overcome those who are said to be the "spiritual forces of wickedness in the heavens," who are the true Canaanites. You must drive them out of the heavenly places, so that you may dwell there instead of them.

5.4. Yet please recognize that they are giants. Everything that puts up resistance against God is called a "giant." Thus whoever opposes God and is against truth, which is their principal activity, is deservedly called a giant. It is granted to you, then, to expel the giants and to enter into their kingdom. Or was it not written about one of them: "Who will take spoils from a giant?"[73] Likewise the Lord said of him in the Gospel: "No one can enter into the house of the strong man and plunder his possessions unless he first ties up the strong man."[74]

At the present time, then, when one makes a comparison between the human and demonic nature, we are "locusts" and they are "giants." And this is especially the case if our faith is wavering. For they will truly be giants and we will truly be locusts if unbelief terrifies us. But if we follow Jesus[75] and believe his words and are filled with his fidelity, in our sight they will be as nothing. For listen to how he encourages us and says: "If God loves[76] us, let him bring us to this land,"[77] since it is good and its fruit is marvelous.[78]

5.5. Therefore, the type and figure that preceded in the fathers is completed in us. They

---

[62]Num 13:2-3. [63]Num 14:7; 13:28, 33. [64]Heb *Joshua.* [65]Lat *diligit.* The Greek has *hairetizō.* [66]Num 14:8. [67]Lat *conversatio.* [68]Phil 3:20. [69]Mt 11:12. [70]Cf. Mt 11:12. [71]Eph 6:12. [72]Is 34:5. [73]Is 49:24. [74]Mt 12:29. [75]Heb *Joshua;* cf. Num 14:6-9. [76]Lat *amat.* [77]Num 14:8. [78]Cf. Num 14:7.

expelled nations and attained their inheritance; for they acquired the whole land of Judea and the city of Jerusalem and Mount Zion. These things were fulfilled among them, but what is being said to you? It does not say: "you have come to things that are visible" but "to things that are invisible."[79] For it says: "You have come to the mountain of the living God and to the heavenly city of Jerusalem and to a multitude of angels."[80] Moreover, elsewhere the same apostle says: "The Jerusalem that is above is free, which is the mother of us all."[81] If one does not adapt the faith to the words of the apostle when he says: "Jerusalem is heavenly," then one can reject these words of ours as well. But if the faith must be applied to Paul's words, just as it surely is to be applied, and if we believe that Jerusalem is heavenly as a type of this earthly one, by means of the spiritual understanding, then we should also more correctly relate what appears to be written about this earthly one to that heavenly one. Therefore, just as Paul says, "we have come to the heavenly Jerusalem," doubtless we also come to the heavenly Judea; and just as they expelled the Canaanites from the earthly Judea, and Perizzites and the Hivites and the other nations,[82] so also we who "have come to the mountain of God" and to the heavenly kingdoms, must necessarily expel from there the opposing powers and the "spiritual forces of wickedness from the heavenly places."[83] And just as they expelled the Jebusite from Jerusalem[84] and the place that had formerly been called Jebus was afterward named Jerusalem,[85] so also we should first expel the Jebusite from Jerusalem and thus attain to the inheritance of it. But they did these things with visible weapons, whereas we use invisible ones. They conquered by means of physical battles, but we overcome by means of spiritual combat.

6.1. Would you like to hear how Paul fought first? He is not only the "teacher of the Gentiles,"[86] but he is also the teacher of this army.[87] Listen to what he writes about himself, as we also mentioned above. He says, "Our struggle is not against flesh and blood, but against the principalities and powers, against the rulers of the darkness of this world, against the spiritual forces of wickedness in the heavenlies."[88] This is why he musters spiritual weapons and invisible arrows for the combatants of this spiritual and invisible combat and says: "Put on the breastplate of love and the helmet of salvation, and take up the shield of faith by which you can extinguish all the flaming arrows of the evil one."[89] Moreover, he says: "Take up the sword of the Spirit, which is the word of God."[90]

6.2. So then, when you arm yourself with weapons like these, and follow the general Jesus, you will not fear these giants. For you will see how Jesus will subject them to himself. And just as the fathers trampled on the necks of the nations,[91] so also you will trample on the necks of demons. For he himself says to those who follow him faithfully: "Behold I have given to you power to trample on serpents and scorpions and on every power of the enemy."[92] For Jesus always wants to do miraculous things, he wants to conquer giants by means of locusts, and to overcome heavenly wickedness by things that are on the earth. And perhaps this was what he was saying in the Gospels, that "he who believes in him" will not only do the things that he himself did, but "he will do," he says, "even greater things than these."[93] For it truly seems to me to be something greater when a human being, here in the flesh, weak and inclined to fall, armed solely with faith in Christ and with his word, overcomes giants and legions[94] of demons. Although he is the one who conquers in us, nevertheless he calls it something "greater," that he is conquering through us, than for him

---

[79]Cf. Col 1:16; Heb 12:22. [80]Heb 12:22. [81]Gal 4:26. [82]Cf. Josh 9:1-2. [83]Cf. Eph 6:12. [84]Cf. 2 Sam 5:6-7. [85]Cf. Josh 18:28. [86]Cf. 2 Tim 1:11; Rom 15:16. [87]Cf. *Homilies on 1 Corinthians* 15.2-3; *Homilies on Joshua* 15.1. [88]Eph 6:12. [89]Cf. Eph 6:14, 16, 17. [90]Eph 6:17. [91]Cf. Josh 10:23-24. [92]Lk 10:19. [93]Cf. Jn 14:12. [94]Cf. Mk 5:9.

to conquer through his own self.

6.3. All that remains for us is to be constantly armed with these weapons and that "our commonwealth be always in heaven."[95] Let every movement of ours, every act, every thought, every word be heavenly. For the more fervently we ascend there, the more precipitously will they come down from there; and the more we increase, the more they will become inferior. If our life is holy, if it is in accordance with God, he will inflict death on them; if our life is lazy and characterized by luxury, he will make them strong and gigantic against us. Therefore, to the extent that we grow in strength, they become correspondingly inferior and weak, just as, on the contrary, if we grow weak and seek earthly things,[96] they become stronger. And to the extent that we are spread out into the lands, to that extent we give up larger spaces to them in the heavenlies. This is why we must instead act in such a way that they be diminished, while we increase, that they be driven out, while we enter in, that they fall, while we ascend; just as that one fell of whom the Lord says in the Gospel: "Behold I saw Satan falling like lightning from heaven."[97] Therefore, let them be cast down from there, that the Lord Jesus may bring us in and allow us to receive his heavenly kingdom. "To him be the glory in the eternal ages of ages. Amen."[98]

Homily 8
Numbers 13:18-33; 14:1-38

Concerning the things that are reported back by the scouts, and concerning the Lord's anger and the supplication of Moses and Aaron.

1.1. Twelve spies were sent from the sons of Israel "to survey the land,"[1] which had been promised to them. When they return after forty days, they report back diverse things.[2]

For ten of them cast the people into despair, to the point that they wanted to reject Moses and select another leader and return to Egypt.[3] But two others report good things[4] and encourage the people to persevere in faith. They say: "If the Lord loves us, let him bring us into this land."[5] But the people are plunged headfirst into the desperation of infidelity and jump up to stone those who are reporting the good things.[6] But the Lord's majesty covers them in clouds. "And the Lord says to Moses: I will strike them with death and destroy them, and I will make you and the house of your father into a great and numerous nation, more than this one is."[7]

1.2. So then, such a great threat from the Lord comes, not to expose the divine nature as capable of suffering and subject to the vice of anger, but in order through this to make known to Moses the love he had for the people, and to make known the goodness of God, which surpasses all thought. For it is written that God becomes angry and threatens the destruction of the people in order that man may be taught that he has so much opportunity with God, and there is so much ground for confidence, that even if there is some anger in God, it may be mitigated by human prayers, and that man is able to procure so much from him that he may even change God's own decrees. For the goodness that follows wrath shows both the confidence of Moses before God and that the divine nature is estranged from the vice of anger.

1.3. At the same time the words here contain a mystery that will be fulfilled in the future ages whereby God promises to raise up another people after this one is rejected. For he says: "I will strike them with death and I will destroy them and make you and the house of your father into a great nation, much more than this one is."[8] So this threat is not an expression of wrath, but a prophecy. For another nation had to be received, that is, that people of the nations, but not

---

[95]Cf. Phil 3:20; *Commentary on Song of Songs* 3.14, 28. [96]Cf. Col 3:1-2. [97]Lk 10:18; cf. Is 14:12. [98]Cf. 1 Pet 5:11. **Homily 8** [1]Cf. Num 13:3-4. [2]Cf. Num 13:26. [3]Cf. Num 14:1-4. [4]Cf. Num 14:6-7. [5]Num 14:8. [6]Cf. Num 14:10. [7]Num 14:11-12. [8]Num 14:12.

through Moses. For indeed Moses excused himself. For he knew that that great nation which is promised was not to be summoned through Moses, but through Jesus Christ, and it was to be called not a Mosaic, but a Christian people.[9] On that account, therefore, Moses pleads many times for that people. But the Lord dispenses the means of chastisement with balanced moderation[10] and says that "the men who came forth from Egypt and have tempted me."[11] Those who have persisted in their unbelief "will fall in the desert."[12] He also says: "they will not see the land which I swore to their fathers,[13] but the sons of those who are with me here,[14] whoever does not know good or evil."[15]

There may possibly be an even more hidden mystery in the words of the Lord who says: "The sons of those who are with me here." Where is the "here"? In what sense are they "with me"? "He who has ears to hear, let him hear!"[16]

1.4. For the moment we say that our fathers were that first people, but we are "the sons of those." So, because they sinned, they were rejected and fell; but we, their sons, have arisen in their place and have been raised up, "we who did not know good or evil." For we are "from the nations,"[17] we who have not known either the good things that come from God, or the evils that are produced by sin. But if we succeed in the place of those who were rejected, let us fear the precedent of such a great fall, listening to the warning of Paul which says: "But see the severity and goodness of God, for those who have fallen, severity, but for you the goodness of God, but only if you persevere in goodness, otherwise you too will be cut off. And they, if they do not continue in unbelief, will be grafted in."[18]

1.5. Now after this the Lord goes on to say:

"But your sons will be inhabitants of the desert for forty years."[19] And he clarifies the mystery that that number contains when he says: "In accordance with the number of days," he says, "during which you surveyed the land, forty days, a day for a year, you will receive for your sins for forty years."[20] I fear to discuss the secrets of this mystery; for I see that the reckoning of sins and punishments is comprehended here. For if as a punishment for the sin of one day a year is prescribed to each sinner, and if an equal number of years will have to be completed in the penalties, in accordance with the reckoning of days in which the sin is committed, I fear that perhaps for those of us who sin daily and who perhaps do not spend a day of our life without sin, that perhaps the very ages, or even the ages of ages may not be able to suffice for the punishments that will have to be paid. For in the fact that that people are tormented in the desert for forty years for a transgression of forty days, and they are not permitted to enter the holy land, a certain likeness of the future judgment seems to be shown, when the reckoning of sins needs to be made up. Yet it might be possible that there will be a sort of compensation for good works, or even a compensation for "the evils that each one has received in this life," as Abraham showed concerning Lazarus.[21] But to have complete knowledge of these things belongs to no one except to him to whom "the Father has committed all judgment."[22] Now the idea of a day of sin being reckoned as a year of punishment is shown not only in this book, in which there is absolutely nothing that can be doubted, but similar things are also indicated in the little book *The Shepherd*, if indeed that writing seems deserving to be received by anyone.[23]

1.6. But perhaps someone denies that it is compatible with the goodness of God that he

---

[9]Cf. *Commentary Series on Matthew* 101. [10]Num 14:13-14. [11]Cf. Num 14:22. [12]Cf. Num 14:29; 1 Cor 10:5. [13]Cf. Num 14:23. [14]Cf. Num 14:31-33. [15]Cf. Deut 1:39. [16]Mt 11:15. [17]Cf. Rom 9:24. [18]Rom 11:22-23. [19]Num 14:33. [20]Num 14:34. [21]Cf. Lk 16:25. [22]Cf. Jn 5:22. [23]Cf. Hermas *Shepherd, Similitude* 6.4.4. Origen did not consider *The Shepherd* of Hermas to be canonical, but he did view it as extremely useful and even divinely inspired. Cf. *On First Principles* 1.3.5; 2.1.5; 3.2.4; *Selecta on Psalms, Homily* 1 on Ps 37; *Commentary on Matthew* 14.21; *Commentary Series on Matthew* 53; *Homilies on Luke* 35.3; *Homilies on Ezekiel* 1.5.2; *Commentary on Romans* 10.31.

pays back a year of punishments for the sin of one day; or rather, perhaps someone says: even if he renders a day for a day, granting that he is just, yet he does not seem to be merciful or kind. Consider then whether we can possibly explain the difficulty of this matter by very clear examples. Suppose a wound is inflicted on the body or a bone is broken or a nerve center ruptured. Wounds of this sort usually happen to bodies in the space of one hour, and then are barely healed with great pain and suffering over a long period of time. For how much swelling and what great pain arises from the wounded spot? But now, suppose someone is repeatedly wounded in the same spot, or suppose the same bone is broken more than once. By what tremendous pain and agony can this be healed and cured? And by what length of time is this brought to healing, if indeed it is even possible at all? And scarcely ever will one be cured in such a way that he avoids a physical infirmity or a nasty scar.

1.7. Pass now from the example of the body to the wounds of the soul. As often as the souls sins, just so often it is wounded. And lest you be in doubt that it is wounded by sins, as if by arrows and swords, listen to the apostle when he admonishes us to take up "the shield of faith by which," he says, "you can extinguish all the flaming arrows of the evil one."[24] So you see that sins are the "arrows of the evil one," which are aimed at the soul. But not only does the soul suffer the wounds of arrows, but it also experiences fractures of its feet, when "snares are prepared for its feet,"[25] and when its "steps are made to trip."[26] Well, how long do you think it will take for these wounds and others like them to be cured? Indeed, if we could only see how with each sin our inner man is wounded, how bad words inflict a wound! Have you not read the words: "swords inflict wounds, but not as

much as the tongue."[27] The soul is wounded, then, even by the tongue. It is also wounded by evil thoughts and desires, but it is fractured and shattered by the works of sin. If we could see all this and feel the scars of a soul that has been wounded, we would certainly resist sin unto death.[28] But now, just as those who are filled with a demon or the mentally insane do not perceive it when they are wounded, because they lack natural senses, so is it with us. Since we have become crazed by the desires of the world,[29] or intoxicated with vices, we cannot feel the extent of the wounds or the extent of the grief we are bringing on our soul by sinning. And therefore it is perfectly consistent that the reckoning of the punishment, that is, of the medical treatment and cure, be extended over time, and that for each wound the length of healing be prolonged as well, according to the nature of the wound.[30]

1.8. So then, the justice and kindness of God will also become evident in those very penalties of the soul. Let the one who hears this who has committed sin come to his senses and sin no more.[31] For conversion in the present life and a penance that is carried out fruitfully will bring swift medicine to wounds of this sort. For penance not only heals a past wound, but it does not allow the soul to be wounded further by sin. Or rather, I should add this: If, for instance, I am a sinner, will the same punishment be mine if I have sinned once in a matter in which I also sin a second and third time and even more frequently? It will not be like that, but rather, the measure of the punishment must also be determined by the manner, number and measure of the sin. For God will give to us "the bread of tears" and he will offer drink to us "in tears," but this will be "according to measure."[32] Now the measure will be what each one has acquired for himself in his own life, either less or more,

---

[24]Eph 6:16. [25]Ps 57:6. [26]Ps 37:31. [27]Sir 28:18. [28]Cf. Heb 12:4. [29]Cf. 1 Jn 2:16. [30]Origen's purgatorial understanding of divine punishment is revealed here. Cf. *Commentary on Romans* 2.2.2; 7.5.10; 8.12.8; *On First Principles* 2.5.3; 2.10.6; *Homilies on Ezekiel* 1.2. [31]Cf. Jn 8:11. [32]Ps 80:5.

by means of sinning. Moreover, it is said: "the cup in the hand of the Lord is full of undiluted wine, well-mixed."[33] So doubtless it is mixed by each person, and it will become his judgment, not only based on the evils that he has done, but also for the good things. And yet, when the two are mixed, "his dregs," which I think refers to the part of the evil things, "will not be drained completely."[34]

1.9. But as we have said, these things are "in the hand of God." Our task is to hasten to correction quickly, to be converted to repentance without pretense, to bewail our past, to be on guard for the future, to invoke God's help; for immediately when you convert and groan, you will be saved.[35] For you will find "an advocate, who intercedes for you to the Father, the Lord Jesus,"[36] who is much more preeminent than Moses was,[37] who nevertheless "prayed for that people,"[38] and he was heard. And perhaps the reason it is written that Moses interceded for the sins of the first people and procured pardon was so that we might have much more confidence, since "Jesus our advocate" will undoubtedly procure a pardon from the Father. But this only applies if we are converted to him and if "our heart does not draw back,"[39] just as John too says in his epistle: "Now I say these things, little children, so that you will not sin. But if one of you sins, we have an advocate with the Father, Jesus the just, who intercedes for our sins."[40] "To him be the glory in eternal ages of ages. Amen."[41]

Homily 9
Numbers 17:1-28 (Heb, lxx) = 16:36–17:13 (rsv)[1]

Concerning the censers[2] of Korah[3] and the sedition of the people against Moses, and concern-ing the rods among which the rod of Aaron sprouted.

1.1. With God, as it is granted that he is to be understood, there is nothing that is not beneficial, there is nothing pointless, but even the things that seem alienating to people and worthy of rejection are found to play some necessary role. Now the present reading suggests this understanding to us, which speaks of the censers of Korah and of the rest who sinned with him. For God does not command even these censers to be rejected, but to make them into "beaten plates" and "to surround the altar with them."[4] So Scripture relates that by the command of God, "Eleazar the son of Aaron the priest took the bronze censers," it says, "which those who had been burned had offered, and they made disks of these, and they placed them on the altar as a commemoration to the sons of Israel, so that no foreigner who is not of Aaron's seed would approach to put incense before the Lord, lest he become as Korah and his conspiracy, just as the Lord said by the hand of Moses."[5]

1.2. Through the prophet the Lord says manifestly in a certain passage: "My counsels are not like your counsels, nor are my thoughts like your thoughts."[6] If this case were judged to-day among men and if an examination were held among the rulers of the churches concerning those who have endured the penalty of divine vengeance, because, for instance, they teach things that are different from the churches, would it not be judged that, whatever they have said, whatever they have taught, whatever they have left behind in writing, all of it should utterly perish equally with their own ashes? But God's judgments are not like our judgments. For listen to how he commands the censers of

---

[33]Ps 75:8. [34]Ps 75:8. [35]Cf. Is 45:22. [36]Cf. 1 Jn 2:1; Rom 8:34. [37]Cf. Heb 3:3. [38]Cf. Num 21:7. [39]Ps 44:18. [40]Cf. 1 Jn 2:1-2. [41]Cf. 1 Pet 5:11.　**Homily 9**　[1]The Hebrew and lxx versions have a different versification than English versions of the passages discussed in this homily. The lxx and Hebrew Num 16:36 = Num 17:1 in English versions. The lxx and Hebrew Num 17:1 = 17:16 in English versions.　[2]A censer, or fire-pan, is a vessel used for holding incense.　[3]Lat *Chore*.　[4]Cf. Num 16:38 (17:3 Heb).　[5]Num 16:39-40 (17:4-5 Heb).　[6]Is 55:8-9.

those who have risen up against God's prophet to be made into beaten plates and to be affixed around the altar.[7] Korah contains a figure of those who rise up against ecclesiastical faith and the teaching of the truth. Thus it is written of Korah and his company that they offered the incense of "strange fire" in bronze censers.[8] God commands the strange fire to be dispersed and poured out, "but the censers," it says, "since they have been sanctified, make them into beaten plates, and surround the altar with them, since they were offered before the Lord and have been sanctified."[9] Well, to me what seems to be shown through this figure is that these censers, which the Scripture calls "bronze," contain a figure of the divine Scripture. On this Scripture, the heretics place a "strange fire" by introducing a meaning and an interpretation that is estranged from God and contrary to the truth. They do not offer a sweet incense to the Lord, but a detestable kind. And therefore this example [forma] is given to the priests of the churches, that if at some time some such thing should arise, those things that are indeed alien from the truth should be immediately expelled from the church of God. But if some things from the meanings of the divine Scripture are found inserted into the words even of heretics, let these things not be rejected equally with those things that are contrary to the truth and to the faith. For the things that are brought forth from the divine Scripture have been sanctified and offered to the Lord.[10]

1.3. Yet the command to join and associate with the altar things that come from the censers of sinners can be understood in still another way. First of all, the fact that they are called "bronze" does not seem to be superfluous. For when the faith is true and the proclamation of the word of God is whole, they are called either silver or gold. Thus the gleam of the gold declares the purity of the faith, and the "silver tested by fire" signifies "utterances that have been examined."[11] But those that are called "bronze" consist in the mere sound of the voice, not in the power of the Spirit, and they are, as the apostle says, like "a sounding bronze or a clashing cymbal."[12] So if we bring these "bronze censers," that is, the words of the heretics, to the altar of God, where there is divine fire, where the true proclamation is, the truth itself will gleam more brightly in comparison with what is false. Let me give an example. Suppose I take the statements of Marcion[13] or Basilides[14] or any other heretic and refute them using words of the truth and testimonies from the divine Scriptures, as if I were using the fire of the divine altar. Will not their impiety appear more clearly by the very comparison? For if the teaching of the church were simple and not surrounded from without by assertions from the teachings of the heretics, our faith would not be able to seem as clear and as examined. But the reason why catholic teaching undergoes attacks from those who contradict it is so that our faith will not grow sluggish from inactivity, but will be refined by such exercises.

1.4. This, after all, is the reason that the apostle said: "Now there must be heresies among you, in order that those who are proven may be manifested among you."[15] This means it is necessary to surround the altar with the censers of the heretics,[16] so that the distinction between believers and unbelievers may become certain and manifest to all. For when ecclesiastical faith begins to shine like gold and her proclamation gleams before those who behold it like silver that has been tested by fire, then the words of the heretics, obscured with baseness and disgrace, will appear dim because of the

---

[7]Cf. Num 16:38 (17:3 Heb). [8]Cf. Num 26:61. [9]Cf. Num 16:36-40 (17:1-3 Heb). [10]Cf. *Homilies on Exodus* 9.6; Clement *Miscellanies* 6.66.5. [11]Cf. Ps 12:6. [12]1 Cor 13:1. [13]Marcion was one of the principal heresiarchs of the second century. He believed that the Creator God was just but cruel, while the Father of Jesus was loving but not just. He rejected the Old Testament entirely, and purged the New Testament of everything that related it to the Old Testament. [14]Basilides was a Gnostic teacher of the second century who lived in Alexandria. Cf. Irenaeus *Against Heresies* 1.24.3. [15]1 Cor 11:19. [16]Cf. Num 16:38 (17:3 Heb).

vileness of the bronze.

1.5. Now do you want to know that good things are better known to be good in comparison with what is worse? Who would know that light is good if we did not perceive the darkness of night? Who would know the sweetness of honey unless he had taken a taste of what is bitter? In fact, ultimately, if you take away the devil himself and the contrary powers who fight against us, the virtues of the soul cannot shine without the struggle. So then, the glory of faithful priests cannot shine, unless it is commended by the rejection and punishment of the unfaithful.

1.6. Moreover, from these things we have read, each of the just seem to be considered brighter before God by comparison with the rest. After all, of Noah it is written that he was "just and perfect in his generation."[17] There it is shown not that he was completely perfect, but he was "perfect in his own generation," and he was pronounced just in comparison with others. I believe that one should think of Lot in a similar way. For to the extent that the Sodomites became worse day by day, to that degree Lot appeared more just.[18] Moreover, in this very book that we have in our hands, when those who had surveyed the land returned and ten of them struck the people with despair by their terrifying words,[19] but the remaining two, namely Caleb and Jesus,[20] gave a good report and encouraged the people to persevere in their intention, it was not so much for their confession as because of the terror of their comrades that the Lord conferred immortal merit on them. For the virtue of their minds would not have shone so splendidly in them had not the base fear and laziness of the other ten been exposed.

1.7. Now we have said these things concerning the censers of those who were condemned, which are commanded to be affixed to the altar.

For it is by comparison with what is inferior that the just appear brighter. At the same time an example has been given to posterity to prevent anyone from presuming an arrogant spirit and seizing to himself the priestly duty that is given by God. Instead, let him yield to him who has acquired the office neither by human ambition nor by corrupted favor. Moreover, let offices not be usurped by means of reprehensible donations. Instead, let them be assumed by the consciousness of merits and by the will of God.[21]

2.1. After this it is reported and said: "And the sons of Israel murmured against Moses and Aaron, saying: You have killed the people of the Lord. And it came to pass when the congregation rushed on Moses and Aaron, in a rush they fled to the tabernacle of testimony. But the cloud covered it, and the majesty of the Lord appeared. And Moses and Aaron went in to the presence of the tabernacle of testimony."[22]

2.2. We have not previously read that a cloud covered the tabernacle and the majesty of the Lord appeared and received Moses and Aaron into the cloud, but only now, when the people rose up against them and wanted to stone them.[23] Let us learn from this how great is the benefit that comes during the persecutions of Christians, how much grace is bestowed, how God becomes their champion, how the Spirit is abundantly poured out. For it is especially at that time that the Lord's grace is present, when human cruelty is aroused. At that time we have peace with God,[24] when we endure wars from men for the sake of justice.[25] "For where sin abounded, grace superabounded."[26]

2.3. So then, the cloud of the tabernacle "covered them" and the "congregation rushed on Moses and Aaron and the glory of the Lord appeared."[27] However great in meritorious living were Moses and Aaron, however strong they

---

[17]Gen 6:9. [18]Cf. Gen 13:13. [19]Cf. Num 13:31-33. [20]Cf. Num 14:6-9. [21]For another allusion to intriguing for episcopal offices, see Homily 22.4. [22]Num 16:41-43 (17:6-8 Heb). [23]Cf. Num 14:10. [24]Cf. Rom 5:1. [25]Cf. Mt 5:9-10. [26]Rom 5:20. [27]Num 16:42 (17:7 Heb).

were in the virtues of the soul, nevertheless the glory of God could not appear to them except when they were placed in the midst of persecutions, tribulations, dangers, and were brought practically to the point of death. Therefore neither should you think that the glory of the Lord can appear to you when you are asleep or at leisure. Or did not even Paul the apostle merit to attain God's glory by this means? Does he not list himself beyond all the others to have been "in tribulations, in difficulties, in prisons"? Does he not say that he was "three times beaten with rods," was "once stoned," that he suffered "shipwreck three times," that he had "dangers at sea, dangers from rivers, dangers from robbers, dangers from false brothers"?[28] To the extent that such circumstances abound, so much the more do they confer the glory of God on those who bear them patiently.

3.1. "And the Lord spoke to Moses and Aaron saying: Depart out of the midst of this congregation, and I will consume them at once. And they fell on their faces."[29] Once, in Sodom, a minimum of ten were sought by means of whom those who lived in the five cities of the Sodomites were scarcely able to be saved;[30] but now two are able to suffice to save the whole nation of the Israelites, but only if they are found to be men of the quality that Moses and Aaron were. So what more shall we say is in these two men? What virtue is so great, what merit, whereby more than six hundred thousand were delivered from the destruction of the devastator? I think that in Moses the law is signified, which teaches people the knowledge and love of God; in Aaron there is an example of supplicating God and of praying to him. So if it comes to pass at some time that God is indignant with us or with the whole people of God, and if a verdict of revenge is already proceeding from the Lord, but the law of God returns to our heart, admonishing us and teaching us to repent, to

make satisfaction for our transgressions, to make supplication for our faults, the anger will at once cease, the indignation will grow quiet, the Lord will be propitiated, as if Moses and Aaron were interceding for us and were making supplication for the whole people.

3.2. Now if at some time God's indignation arises and a severe chastisement comes for our sins, but our hearts are hardened, so that we are not "converted to the Lord"[31] or "humbled in his sight,"[32] so that we soothe his disposition and anger by the confession of supplications; if instead, we say: "God doesn't care about the life of mortals, nor do these things pertain to God. A long time ago he abandoned us, and these things do not reach his awareness." If we think such things in our hearts, and if these things proceed from our mouth, it is certain that there is no Moses and Aaron among us, that is, knowledge of the law and the fruit of repentance, through which we could be able to escape the destruction of imminent death.[33] I think that this happened even to that people who preceded us, when they "all turned aside, together they became useless, and there was no one who has done good, there was not even one."[34] For if these things had been present, surely God would never have abandoned them. But let us too fear lest something similar be found in us; for I fear that sentence in which our Lord and Savior, who foreknows all things, says as if he is in doubt: "Do you think that the Son of Man, when he comes, will find faith on the earth?"[35]

3.3. So Moses and Aaron are commanded "to go out from the midst of the congregation, so that the congregation may be destroyed at once."[36] But let us see what these men do. They are holy, they are perfect, and what is more, they are disciples more of the gospel than of the law; and so "they love their enemies" as well and they "pray for their persecutors."[37] For while they are coming to kill them, these men "fall on

---

[28]Cf. 2 Cor 11:23-26. [29]Num 16:44-45 (17:9-10 Heb). [30]Cf. Gen 18:32. [31]Cf. 2 Cor 3:16. [32]Cf. Jas 4:10. [33]Cf. Mt 3:1-7. [34]Ps 14:3; cf. Rom 3:12. [35]Cf. Lk 18:8. [36]Num 16:44-45 (17:9-10 Heb). [37]Cf. Mt 5:44.

their faces on the ground."[38]

4.1. "And Moses said to Aaron: Take a censer, and put on it fire from the altar, and put incense in it, and carry it away quickly into the camp, and intercede for them. For wrath has gone forth from the presence of the Lord, and it has already begun to destroy the people."[39] But since we have reached these passages, I want to admonish the disciples of Christ about the goodness of God, lest any of you perhaps be troubled by heretics, if ever a conflict should occur while they tell you that the God of the law is not good, but just, and that the law of Moses does not contain goodness, but justice.[40] Let those who incriminate both God and the law notice how Moses himself and Aaron have previously done what the Gospel subsequently taught. Behold, Moses "loves his enemies and prays for his persecutors."[41] This is precisely what Christ teaches us to do in the Gospels. For listen to how they "fall on their face on the ground" and pray for those who had risen up in an insurrection to kill them. So then, the power of the gospel is found in the law, and the Gospels are understood as being supported by the foundation of the law; nor do I even give the name "Old Testament" to the law, if I understand it spiritually.

4.2. The law becomes an "Old Testament" only for those who want to understand it in a fleshly way; and for them it has necessarily become old and aged, because it cannot maintain its strength. But for us, who understand and explain it spiritually and according to the gospel-meaning, it is always new. Indeed, both are "New Testaments" for us, not by the age of time but by the newness of understanding. Or does not the apostle John perceive this very thing in his epistle when he says: "Little children, I give you a new commandment, that you love one another"?[42] For he surely knew that

the commandment of love was long ago given in the law.[43] But because "love never fails,"[44] and the commandment of love never grows old, he pronounces what never grows old to be ever new; for the commandment of love continually renews in the Spirit those who observe and keep it. But for the sinner and for the one who does not preserve the covenant of love, even the Gospels grow old. Nor can it be a "New Testament" for the one who does not "lay aside the old man and put on the new man and the one created according to God."[45]

4.3. So Moses encourages the high priest to offer "incense in the camp and to intercede for the people." For "already," it says, "the people began to be destroyed."[46] Moses saw in spirit what was being done. He saw that power had gone forth into the camp and was devastating and destroying sinners; and on that account he encourages the high priest "to take a censer, to put fire from the altar in it, to throw incense on top and to go out" and "stand between the living and the dead," lest the "destruction" proceed any further, or assuredly "shattering," as the more correct reading of Scripture contains.[47]

5.1. But first, if it seems appropriate, let us describe the image of the historical narrative itself. Only then, when the outward form of the accomplished event becomes clear, should we ask if there is anything mystical in the passage as well. So understand that people of Israel arranged in camps by the orders of tribes and families.[48] But consider how a power was sent by God to ravage the people with death, not sporadically, but it began with a certain first portion, and it proceeds in order to wreak the havoc of death. After this, observe how the high priest wearing the priestly garments goes forth carrying the "censer and fire with incense" and heads for the place to which the death borne by the destroying angel had reached.[49] He stands

---

[38]Num 16:45 (17:10 Heb). [39]Num 16:46 (17:11 Heb). [40]These are Marcionite themes. [41]Cf. Mt 5:44. [42]Cf. 1 Jn 2:8; 3:23. [43]Cf. Lev 19:18. [44]1 Cor 13:8. [45]Cf. Eph 4:22, 24. [46]Num 16:46 (17:11 Heb). [47]Text critical comments may be original to Origen, or they may be Rufinian glosses. [48]Cf. Num 2:2. [49]Cf. Ex 12:23.

in that place in which death had given an end to the first [victims], and he was near the ones who would follow. Behold the priest standing there and separating the living from the dead by a sort of intervention of his own self. But the power of his propitiation and the mystery of incense shamed the destroying angel,[50] and here the death came to an end, but life was restored.

5.2. If you have understood the order of the historical narrative and have been able to perceive with your eyes, so to speak, the high priest standing between the living and the dead, ascend now to the loftier heights of these words. Behold how the true high priest Jesus Christ has taken on the censer of human flesh and placed on it the fire of the altar. Doubtless this refers to that splendid soul of his with which he was born in the flesh. He has added incense to his soul as well, namely the immaculate Spirit. He has stood between the living and the dead and has caused death to stop advancing. But as the apostle says, "he destroyed him who had the power of death, that is, the devil,"[51] so that "he who believes in him" may no longer die, but "live forever."[52]

5.3. So this was the mystery which came later but even then had terrified the devastator of the people. For he recognized the figure of the censer, of the fire and of the incense. And the one who was appointed to be in the midst of the living and the dead foresaw what sort of sacrifice had to be offered to God. And at that time the prefigured image saved them, but the very truth of salvation came to us. For that devastating angel did not blush at the purple and wool garments of the high priest woven from linen, but he understood these coverings of the high priest that were coming, and assuredly he yielded to these things before which the whole creation was inferior.

5.4. But I think that this form was fulfilled not only at the first coming of our Lord and Savior, but possibly the same form will be preserved also at the second coming. For the Son of man will come again, and doubtless when he comes, he will find some to be dead and some living. Now we can understand this also in the following way, that some may be found still in this condition of life in which we now are, when many dead ones have already preceded. But it can be understood in another way, that we understand the "dead" as bodies, but "the living" are souls. Yet I remember that some of those who have interpreted this passage before us[53] said that the dead are those who are understood to be dead in their sins because of the excessiveness of the wicked deeds, whereas the living are those who have continued in the works of life. Nevertheless, by both means of interpretation, this great high priest and Savior of ours will even in the future stand in the midst of the living and the dead. Moreover, at that time perhaps one must say that he is in the midst of the living and the dead, when "he will put the sheep on his right and the goats on his left," and he will say to those who are on his right: "Come, you who are blessed by my Father, receive the kingdom which has been prepared for you from the foundation of the world,"[54] and so forth. But to those who are on his left, he will say: "Go into the eternal fire, workers of iniquity,[55] which my Father prepared for the devil and his angels; for I never knew you."[56] And assuredly they are dead who are sent into eternal fire; but they are living who are sent into the kingdom.[57]

6.1. It says: "And the devastation ceased," or, as we said is read in other copies: "shattering,"[58] which will agree more with the interpretation of truth; for "shattering" is what happens as it were to clay vessels. Therefore, sinners become clay vessels, as Jeremiah the prophet indicates in the Lamentations when he says: "The sons of Zion, who were honorable and puffed up with gold, how have they been reckoned as clay ves-

---

[50]Cf. Ex 12:23. [51]Heb 2:14. [52]Jn 3:15. [53]Cf. Philo *Who Is the Heir?* 201. [54]Mt 25:33-34. [55]Cf. Mt 7:23; Lk 13:27. [56]Cf. Mt 25:41; Mt 7:23. [57]Cf. Mt 25:41; Lk 13:27. [58]Num 16:50 (17:15 Heb).

sels, the works of the hands of a potter?"[59] And the apostle says: "In a large house there are not only gold and silver vessels, but also wood and clay ones, and some are for honor[able use], but others are for dishonor[able use]."[60] So there are clay vessels for honor, which are capable of being shattered.

6.2. But let us consider more carefully what the apostle says about these clay vessels in what follows. He says: "If someone cleanses himself from these things, he will be a vessel for honor, sanctified and useful to the Lord, prepared for every good work."[61] Here he seems to show that one and the same man is what the vessel itself is, what it becomes and of what it is made. Therefore, we should understand that human intention is operative here, but that the remaining part of man is that vessel that is made either for honor or for dishonor. Thus when our mind chooses what is good and draws us to a good way of life, it makes us into a useful vessel. But when it becomes negligent and our resolution falls away from the good, we become a "vessel for dishonor." So if our understanding is caked with mud and is always thinking about mud[62] and earthly things, we become a "clay vessel" and the "work of the hands of a potter."[63] And possibly this is why the apostle rebukes the man who is like this, as one who, although he has a mind of mud and earth, yet he is raising questions about great matters, which he is incapable of comprehending. Such a man says: "So why does he still find fault? For who resists his will?"[64] The apostle responds to him as if to a piece of clay: "Who are you, O man, who answers back to God? Does the clay say to the one who formed it: Why did you make me this way?"[65]

6.3. It is further said that our body is both a "clay vessel" and also the "letter of the law," when the apostle says: "But we have this trea-

sure in clay vessels."[66] For both meanings can be accepted in this passage in that, while we are placed in the body, the Lord gives to us a treasure of grace through the Holy Spirit, and that in the words of the law, which are considered base and contemptible in the sense that they do not seem polished by any rhetorical craft, "the treasure of wisdom and knowledge of God is stored," so that it could be said fittingly that in these things "the treasures of wisdom and knowledge of God are hidden."[67]

6.4. Let these things be said concerning the "shattering" which is reported to have "ceased."[68] But now let us discuss a few things about the subsequent historical narrative as well, in which a mention of rods is introduced.

7.1. "And the Lord spoke to Moses saying: Speak to the sons of Israel, and take a rod from them according to the houses of their families from all their rulers, twelve rods; and write each one's name on his rod. And write the name of Aaron on the rod of Levi; for it is one rod; they shall give them to you according to the tribe, by the houses of their families. And you shall put them in the tabernacle of testimony opposite the ark, by means of which I will be made known to you from there. And it will be that the rod of whichever man I shall choose shall sprout; and I will remove from you the murmuring of the sons of Israel, which they are murmuring about you."[69]

7.2. Every ruler of a tribe and people has a rod; for it is impossible for anyone to rule a people unless he has a rod. This is why the apostle Paul, since he was a ruler of a people, said: "What do you want? Shall I come to you with a rod, or with love and a spirit of gentleness?"[70] So it is necessary that all rulers of tribes have their rods, but there is one alone, as the Scripture relates, the high priest Aaron, whose rod "sprouted." But since, as we have

---

[59]Lam 4:2. [60]2 Tim 2:20. [61]2 Tim 2:21. [62]Or "clay." [63]Cf. Lam 4:2. [64]Rom 9:19. [65]Rom 9:20. The interpretation given here is consistent with what Origen offers in his *Commentary on Romans* 7.16.1-4. Origen understands Rom 9:19 as the words of Paul's imaginary opponent, whom Paul rebukes in his own persona in 9:20. [66]2 Cor 4:7. Cf. *Homilies on Exodus* 7.1. [67]Cf. Col 2:3. [68]Num 16:50 (17:15 Heb). [69]Num 17:1-5 (17:16-20 Heb). [70]1 Cor 4:21.

repeatedly shown, Christ is the true high priest, he alone is the one the rod of whose cross not only sprouted, but bloomed and bore all this fruit in the form of the believing peoples.

7.3. But what is that fruit that it bore? "Almonds,"[71] it says, which is, in the first place, a fruit that is bitter in its outer covering. It is protected and covered by its next layer, but with its third layer it feeds and nourishes the one who eats it. In the school of Christ, then, the teaching of the law and the prophets is like this: at first glance the letter is very bitter. It prescribes the circumcision of the flesh, it commands sacrifices and the other things that are designated as "the letter that kills."[72] Throw all this away, as you would the bitter rind of a nut. In the second place you will reach the protective covering of the shell in which moral teaching or the definition of self-control is described. These are, of course, necessary to protect what is contained inside, but doubtless they too are to be cracked and removed. For instance, we would say that abstinence from food and chastisement of the body is undoubtedly necessary, as long as we are in this body, corruptible as it is and susceptible to passions. But when it is broken and dissolved and, at the time of its resurrection, has been rendered from corruption into incorruption, and from animal into spiritual, then it will no longer be dominated by the labor of affliction or the punishment of abstinence, but rather by its own proper nature, and not by any physical corruption. So this is why there now seems to be a necessary rationale for abstinence, but afterwards this will not have to be sought. But in the third place you will find hidden and concealed in the [law and the prophets] the meaning of the mysteries "of the wisdom and knowledge of God"[73] by which the souls of the saints are nourished and fed, not only in the present life but also in the future. For this is that priestly fruit about which the promise is given to those "who hunger and thirst for justice," that "they shall be satisfied."[74]

7.4. So it is in this way that the reckoning of this threefold mystery runs through all the Scriptures. And so it is that wisdom admonishes us that in our response to those who "propose a word of truth" to us,[75] we should describe these things in *three* ways to ourselves in our hearts. So it is that Isaac the patriarch dug *three* wells, of which the third alone is called by him "width" or "breadth."[76] Now since the rod of almond is a priestly mystery, for this reason I think that Jeremiah as well, who was one of the priests of Anathoth, saw an almond rod and prophesied of it the things that are written, either about the almond rod or about the cauldron or the boiling pot. It is as if through these objects he saw that life was in the almond rod and death was in the boiling cauldron.[77] For life and death are set before our face,[78] and Christ, in the mystery of the almond, is indeed life, but the devil, in the figure of the boiling cauldron, is death. Therefore, if you sin, you will place your portion with the boiling cauldron; but if you act justly, your portion will become in the rod of almond with the great high priest. Moreover, in the Song of Songs the bride is said to have gone down into the "garden of almond,"[79] where it is recorded that she found equally as well an abundance of priestly pomegranates, so to speak,[80] along with the nuts.[81]

7.5. However, since we began to speak about rods, God promised *one* fruit to come on the rod, but he gave several. Now pay very careful attention to see whether we can show how the generosity of God outstrips even the very promises. Perhaps even from these things, we can fathom and track down that unspeakable goodness of God, which is always read in the letter of Scripture. For we see that he is more generous in bestowing than in promising.

8.1. So then, the words of Scripture of which

---

[71]Num 17:8 (17:23 Heb). [72]2 Cor 3:6. [73]Col 2:3. [74]Mt 5:6. [75]Cf. Prov 22:20-21. [76]Cf. Gen 26:15, 18, 22. [77]Cf. Jer 1:1, 11, 13. [78]Cf. Deut 30:15. [79]Song 6:11. [80]Cf. Philo *On the Life of Moses* 2.186. [81]Cf. Song 6:11.

we are now speaking contain this: It says: "And it will be that the rod of whichever man I choose will sprout."[82] God promised only one thing, that "the rod of the one whom he has chosen will sprout." But when we arrive at the outcome, when what was promised is shown to have been fulfilled, it is not the one thing that had been promised that is said to have been brought into effect, but see how many things are added. For it says: "And behold, the rod of Aaron in the house of Levi sprouted."[83] Doubtless this is the one thing that had been promised, but other things are added as well, and it is said: "And it produced buds and put forth blossoms and sprouted almonds."[84] So then, though only a sprout had been promised, notice how much God gives: not only did it produce a "sprout" but also "buds," and not only "buds," but also "blossoms," and not only "blossoms," but also "fruit." What then should we conclude and contemplate from these things? First of all, the mystery of the resurrection from the dead; for a dry rod sprouted, when a dead body began to come to life again. But what are these four things which will be given to the body when it rises again? That "what is sown in corruption will rise in incorruption, and what is sown in weakness will rise in power, and what is sown in dishonor will rise in glory, and what is sown an animal body will rise a spiritual body."[85] These are the four things which the rod of our dried out body will sprout in the resurrection.

8.2. Moreover, in the second place we will say that just as here God gave quadruple for his promise, and bestowed many more very precious things than he promised, how much more is it the case that in all passages of Scripture, when some promise of God is contained, in the future it will be prepared in multiple form, but only if one merits to attain to that promise. And thus what the apostle says will truly be ful-

filled: "Eye has not seen nor ear heard nor has it ascended into the heart of man what God has prepared for those who love him."[86] See, then, how great and of what nature are the things which not only no one can see or hear, but which cannot even "ascend into the heart," that is, into human thinking. Therefore, whether you speak of the earth or the sky, or this sun and the brightness of this visible light, all these things the eye has seen and the ear has heard; so they cannot be those things which "eye has not seen, nor ear heard, nor ascended into the heart of man." So move beyond all these things and transcend everything that you see, that you hear, even that you can think of, and know that what is laid up for "those who love God" is what could not even ascend into the thinking of your heart. I think that this is why, in promises of this kind, no physical[87] thing should be thought of. For the rational definition of physical matter has not wholly escaped the comprehension of human thought. But these are things that cannot "ascend into the heart" of anyone, into the mind of anyone, things which are contained only in the wisdom of God.[88]

8.3. But by this reckoning whereby the goods of the promises are given in greater measure than had been promised, the same applies to the punishments that are threatened to sinners. They must be inflicted with the torments that have been multiplied, just as we explained higher up where a year is appointed in vengeance for a day.[89] On the other hand, it is possible that someone should think that a third eventuality could come to pass. He may derive some comfort from what is contained in that threat that came to David, when a period of three days is declared for the devastating death that is coming; yet the time of punishment seems to have been shortened to six hours.[90] But these things are able to advance there where a

---

[82]Num 17:5 (17:20 Heb). [83]Num 17:8 (17:23 Heb). [84]Num 17:8 (17:23 Heb). [85]1 Cor 15:42-44. [86]1 Cor 2:9. [87]Lat *corporeal*. [88]Notice Origen's keen awareness of God's incomprehensibility and of his mysterious nature. [89]Cf. Num 14:34. See Homily 8.1.5. [90]2 Sam 24:13-16.

time of repentance and an opportunity for satisfaction is granted. Nevertheless, it is recorded that God, with respect to evils, "repays unto the third and fourth generation,"[91] but with respect to good things, he shows mercy not only "unto the third and fourth generation," but, as the Scripture says, "unto a thousand generations."[92]

9.1. But let us return to the things that we began to say about rods. We can still understand the differences of those things that sprouted in the rod in the following manner as well. All who believe in Christ first die, and after this are reborn; and the fact that the dry rod subsequently sprouts is likewise a figure of this. Thus, a person's first confession of Christ is the first sprouting. Secondly, he buds, when he has been reborn and receives the gift of grace by the sanctification of the Spirit of God. Then he bears blossoms, when he has begun to advance and be arrayed with a charming attractiveness of character that exudes the fragrance of mercy and kindness. Finally, he also bears the fruit of justice, by which he not only lives, but also bestows life on others. For when he comes to perfection, and brings forth the word of faith from himself, the word of the knowledge of God, and wins others,[93] this is to have produced fruit for others by means of which they may be nourished.

9.2. So then, everyone who believes is sprouted from the rod of Aaron, who is Christ. In the four different kinds of sprouts are indicated, in other Scriptures, the four periods of life which the apostle John in his epistle has comprehended with a mysterious distinction; for he says: "I have written to you, children," and "I have written to you, young men," and "I have written to you, youths," and "I have written to you, fathers."[94] Surely it is not physical ages that he is recording, but differences in the levels of progress of the soul, as we have observed

is designated as well in this sprouting of the priest's rod. So all these things are considered not so much as applying to the rod of Aaron as to that rod which "came forth from the root of Jesse and the blossom that came up from his root, on which the Spirit of God rested."[95] Here it does not seem superfluous that the rod is said to "come forth" and the blossom "comes up." For although Christ is one in substance, he becomes diverse to each one, in accord with the need of each one in whom he works. Thus the one who is more sluggish and who becomes quite negligent in discipline, for him Christ becomes a "rod," and with respect to a rod, one does not speak of "going up" but of "coming forth." For it is necessary for one who is inactive and sluggish to "come forth" from the state in which he is wrongly staying, and he must pass to another condition, as one who has been compelled by means of a rod, that is, who has been warned by the severity of more strict teaching. But Christ is said to "come up" in one who is just, since "the just will blossom like a palm."[96] So then, the rod "comes forth" to the one who requires a beating; but it "comes up and blossoms" in the one who is making progress toward justice. But it "comes up" to the point that he bears the fruit of the Spirit, which is "love, joy, peace, patience"[97] and the other virtues in Christ Jesus our Lord, "to whom is the glory and power in the ages of ages. Amen."[98]

Homily 10
Numbers 18:1-7

Concerning what is written: "And the Lord said to Aaron: You and your sons and the house of your father with you, you will take on the sins of the saints."[1]

1.1. Those who are better always take on the

---

[91]Cf. Ex 20:5. [92]Cf. Ex 20:6; Deut 7:9. [93]Cf. 1 Cor 9:22. [94]1 Jn 2:12-14. Cf. F. Ledegang, *Mysterium Ecclesiae: Images of the Church and Its Members in Origen*, BETL 156 (Leuven : Leuven University Press, 2001), p. 234. [95]Is 11:1-2. [96]Ps 92:12. [97]Gal 5:22. [98]1 Pet 4:11. **Homily 10** [1]Num 18:1.

faults and sins of those who are inferior. For thus also the apostle says: "You who are stronger, sustain the infirmities of the weak."[2] If an Israelite sins, that is, a layman, he cannot get rid of his own sin, but he requires a Levite, he needs a priest, or rather, he seeks something still more eminent than these: there is need of the high priest in order to be able to receive the remission of sins. But if the priest or high priest transgresses, he can cleanse his own sin, but only if he does not sin against God; for concerning sins of this nature, we see in the letters of the law that a remission is not easily achieved.[3]

1.2. We have said these things on behalf of what was read aloud for us: "And the Lord spoke to Aaron," it says, "saying: You and your sons and the house of your father with you, you will take on the sins of the saints."[4] This passage can be explained in the following way: that by means of the things that the high priest offers for the sin of each one and purifies the one for whom he has made the offering, it is written: "You and your sons with you will take on the sins of the saints."[5] Nevertheless, it does not seem superfluous to me that it makes mention of the sins of the *saints*; for indeed in many passages of Scripture, this word is repeated. This is why one must ask how it is that some are called "saints," and yet their sins are recorded.

1.3. For it is not the case, as some think, that as soon as one has begun to be a saint, he can no longer sin and immediately is reckoned to be without sin. For if a saint did not sin, it would assuredly not be written: "You will take on the sins of the saints." If a saint were without sin, the Lord would not say through Ezekiel the prophet to the angels whom he sent to punish sinners: "And you will begin with my saints."[6] For if saints are without sin, how is it that they themselves are the first to succumb to the penalties for sins? If the saints were without sin, Scripture would never have said: "Let

the just man, at the beginning of his words, become his own accuser."[7] If the saints were without sin, the apostle Paul, while writing to the Romans, would never have said: "Do not destroy the work of God for the sake of food,"[8] to people to whom at the beginning of the letter he had written: "To all who are in Rome, to those beloved of God, to those called *saints*."[9] And again, the same apostle, when writing to the Corinthians, says: "Paul, a called apostle of Jesus Christ,"[10] and after a few things: "To the church of God which is in Corinth, to those sanctified in Christ Jesus, to those called *saints*."[11]

1.4. Well, listen to what great sins he reproaches in those whom he calls "sanctified" and "saints." For he says in what follows: "For since there is jealousy and contention among you, are you not fleshly, and are you not walking according to man?"[12] And again: "Already you have become rich, without us you are reigning, and would that you were reigning!"[13] And again: "But some are puffed up as if I were not coming to you";[14] and a little later: "Fornication is actually reported among you, and the kind of fornication which is not found among the nations!"[15] Indeed, in what comes next he says: "And you are puffed up and do not instead have sorrow!"[16] Surely here he has left no one unscathed, while he attributes to some the charge of fornication, to others of being puffed up and arrogant. He brands them also in what follows, even with respect to lawsuits, and he says: "Even the fact that you have lawsuits among you at all is already a fault with you."[17]

1.5. He convicts those whom he had called "saints," and in view of the fact that they are eating things sacrificed to idols,[18] he pronounces this verdict, as it were, among them and says: "But while sinning against brothers in this way and wounding their weak consciences, you are sinning against Christ."[19] Moreover, he

---

[2]Rom 15:1. [3]Cf. 1 Sam 2:25. [4]Num 18:1. [5]Num 18:1. [6]Ezek 9:6. [7]Prov 18:17. [8]Rom 14:20. [9]Rom 1:7. [10]1 Cor 1:1. [11]1 Cor 1:2. [12]1 Cor 3:3. [13]1 Cor 4:8. [14]1 Cor 4:18. [15]1 Cor 5:1. [16]1 Cor 5:2. [17]1 Cor 6:7. [18]Cf. 1 Cor 8:7. [19]1 Cor 8:12.

reproaches them not only for no less a matter than sacrifices, but also for presuming to take the "cup of demons." And he says: "You cannot drink from the cup of the Lord and the cup of demons, you cannot share in the Lord's table and the table of demons."[20] To these people he also says the following: "When you come together in the church, I hear there are divisions."[21] And again: "For each one presumes to eat his own meal, and one person goes hungry, and another gets drunk."[22] And on account of these transgressions, he says: "Therefore many among you are weak and sick, and many sleep. But if we judged ourselves, we would surely not be judged."[23]

1.6. But after this he heaps up against them no longer moral delinquencies but sins against the faith. For he says: "How is it that some among you say that there is no resurrection of the dead?"[24] And again: "But if Christ has not risen, your faith is in vain, and you are still in your sins."[25] But it would take too long and it would not befit the present moment to produce further evidence of these matters by which it is proven that those who are called "saints" should not necessarily also be understood to be without sin. But those who hold to this opinion are people who do not look carefully and diligently into the divine Scriptures, in which there are shown to be many differences between the saints, as we have talked about in greater detail in other treatments of this matter. But now as well, we will say as much as the passage requires.

1.7. The same people are called saints and sinners, namely, those who have devoted themselves to God and have separated their life from the common crowd's manner of living, in order to serve the Lord. Thus a man like this is called a saint in accordance with the fact that he has cut off other behaviors and has sold himself out

to the Lord. Now it can happen that in his service to the Lord he does not carry out all that is fitting to carry out. Instead he transgresses in some matters and commits sin. For just as the one who withdraws himself and separates himself from all other activities in order to master the discipline of medicine or philosophy, for instance, will assuredly not, immediately on his handing himself over to the learning of these things, be so perfect that he is not found to fall short in anything. Rather, he will commit many errors and will scarcely ever reach perfection. And yet, as soon as he hands himself over to such schools, it is certain that he is registered among the doctors or philosophers. One should understand something similar to this concerning the saints. As soon as one has made this his intention, he is called a saint. But in accordance with the fact that he necessarily transgresses in many things, he will likewise be called a sinner, until, by means of practice and instruction and diligence, the habit of sinning is cut off from him.

1.8. But I will add something further, namely, that if one does not have a holy intention and if one is not zealous for sanctity, when he sins, he does not know how to do penance for his sin; he does not know how to seek a remedy. Those who are not saints die in their sins; those who are saints do penance for their sins, they feel their wounds, they understand their failures, they seek out a priest, they ask for healing, they seek purification through the high priest.[26] For this reason, then, the words of the law carefully and expressly indicate that high priests and priests not only "take on sins" of just anyone, but of "saints."[27] For one who cures his sin through the high priest is a saint.

2.1. But let us return to our high priest, "the great high priest who has passed through the heavens, Jesus,"[28] our Lord, and let us see how

---

[20]1 Cor 10:21. [21]1 Cor 11:18. [22]1 Cor 11:21. [23]1 Cor 11:30-31. [24]1 Cor 15:12. [25]1 Cor 15:17. [26]Jean Daniélou's *Origen*, trans. Walter Mitchell (New York, Sheed & Ward, 1955), p. 71, comments on this passage: "It would be impossible to state more clearly than this that sins of weightier moment were remitted by absolution from a priest." [27]Num 18:1. [28]Heb 4:14.

he himself, together with his sons, namely, the apostles and martyrs, take on the sins of the saints.[29] Indeed, no one who believes in Christ is unaware of the fact that our Lord Jesus Christ came "to take away the sin of the world,"[30] and that he blotted out our sins by his death. But, if we are equal to the task, we will attempt to prove from the divine Scriptures how his sons too, that is, the apostles and martyrs, take away the sins of the saints. First, listen to what Paul says: "For I will freely spend," he says, "and be spent for your souls";[31] and in another place: "For I am already on the point of being sacrificed," he says, "and the time of my departure"—or "dissolution"—"has come."[32] Thus the apostle speaks of his being "spent" and "offered up as a sacrifice" for those to whom he was writing. But when a sacrifice is offered, it is offered for the purpose of purging the sins of those for whom the victim is killed. Now the apostle John writes in the Apocalypse about the martyrs, that "the souls of those who had been slain because of the name of the Lord Jesus stand near the altar."[33] But whoever stands near the altar is shown to be doing the duty of a priest; but the duty of a priest is to intercede for the sins of the people.[34] This is why I am apprehensive that perhaps because martyrs are not being made, and the sacrifices of saints are not being offered for our sins, there may come no remission of our sins.[35] And consequently I am apprehensive, that while our sins continue to remain in us, it may come to pass to us what the Jews say concerning themselves, that since they have no altar nor temple nor priesthood, and on that account do not have those who offer sacrifices, "our sins," they say, "remain in us," and therefore "no pardon is obtained." We, on the contrary, ought to say, "The victims of the martyrs are not being offered for us, and this is why our sins remain in us"; for we do not deserve to experience persecution for the sake of Christ, nor to die for the name of the Son of God.[36]

2.2. And this is why even the devil does not want to incite public persecutions against us from the pagans, because he knows that remission of sins comes through the suffering of martyrdom. For he knows that if "we are brought before kings and governors on account of the name of Christ" in testimony to Jews and Gentiles,[37] there will be joy and exultation with us, because "great will be our reward in heaven."[38] The enemy does not cause this, either because he is jealous of our glory, or possibly because the One who foresees and foreknows all things knows that we are not capable of enduring martyrdom. Yet "the Lord knows who are his,"[39] and he has his treasures in those in whom this is not expected: "for God does not see as man sees."[40] But I do not doubt that even in this assembly there are some who are known to

---

[29]Cf. Num 18:1. [30]Jn 1:29. [31]2 Cor 12:15. [32]2 Tim 4:6. [33]Rev 6:9. On the death of martyrs as sacrifice for sins, see Homily 24.1.3-9. [34]Cf. Heb 5:1-2. [35]Origen's reflections here are grounded on the idea of the mystical body of Christ. According to Col 1:24, there is no lack in the sufferings of Christ as *head*; but many sufferings of Christ are still lacking, or are still to come, in his *body* the church and his *members* the faithful. As the head of the body, the church, Christ suffered to procure the forgiveness of sins. His sacrifice is the fount of all other forms of forgiveness. The sufferings of the members of his body can assist in procuring forgiveness for other members. In *Homilies on Leviticus* 2.4 Origen discusses seven means of obtaining forgiveness of sins in the gospel: baptism, martyrdom, alms, Christian brotherly forgiveness, leading others to repentance, love and tearful confession to a priest. In the present passage, Origen seems to be combining St. Paul's thoughts with 2 Macc 7:37-38, which speaks of the bloody deaths of Jewish martyrs having a vicarious atoning value before God that can be transferred to the good of others, an idea that is developed in 4 Macc. Also, 2 Macc 12:43-44 affirms that some who have "fallen asleep in godliness" will need prayer and sacrifices "that they may be loosed from sins." Clearly the Jews of the second century B.C. built on their antecedent tradition and developed a profound conviction of the vicarious atoning value of martyrdom and of the need for an intermediate state of purification after death. Relevant discussions can be found in R. Daly, "Sacrificial Soteriology in Origen's Homilies on Leviticus," in *Studia Patristica* 17, no. 2 (1982): 872-78; Gary A. Anderson, "Redeem Your Sins by the Giving of Alms: Sin, Debt, and the 'Treasury of Merit' in Early Jewish and Christian Tradition," *Letter & Spirit* 3 (2007): 39-69. [36]This remarkable passage indicates that Origen views martyrdom as a reward meted out to the worthy. Cf. Homily 9.2.2; Lk 20:35. [37]Cf. Lk 21:12; Mt 10:17. [38]Mt 5:12. [39]2 Tim 2:19. [40]1 Sam 16:7.

him alone, who in his sight are already martyrs, prepared for the testimony of conscience, to pour out their blood for the name of our Lord Jesus Christ, if anyone should demand it. I do not doubt that there are some who "have taken up their cross and follow him."[41] Although these things have been said as a sort of digression, yet they seem necessary for us to understand how it is through the high priest and through the sons of the high priest that remission of sins comes to the saints.

3.1. After this follows the words: "And you and your sons will receive the sins of your priesthood. And take to yourself your brothers, the tribe of Levi, the family of your father, and let them be joined to you and let them minister to you, and you and your sons with you shall observe your watches in the sight of the tabernacle of testimony and the watches of the tabernacle."[42] It is particularly fitting for those who glory in belonging to the order of the priesthood very carefully to observe and pay attention to these things that are written, so that they may know what the divine law commands them to observe. It says: "You and your sons with you, in the sight of the tabernacle of testimony, observe your watches both of the altar and of the tabernacle."[43] Now the commands are definite and clear, that we ought to observe the "watches of the tabernacle and of the altar and of the priesthood." Now, of course, who the one is who observes and does the things that are commanded to the priests, and who it is who takes advantage of the order and office of priesthood, but fails to observe the works and ministry of the priesthood, that One alone can know who "searches the minds and hearts."[44] Now it is not only things that are external that are commanded to be observed, but above all priests must tend to those things, it says, "which are inside the veil."[45] It is as if he were saying: Let it be a concern to the priests both to fulfill

the clear and manifest commands of the divine law, and to contemplate its hidden and veiled mysteries with all keenness of mind.

3.2. But if you want to refer the tabernacle of testimony to the human being, since indeed Paul calls the human body a tabernacle, when he says: "For we who are in this tabernacle are weighed down with groaning, because we do not want to be stripped, but to be clothed"[46]—if therefore we refer the tabernacle to the human being, we will call the interior of the veil, where inaccessible things are covered, the governing part of the heart, which is the only part that can receive the mysteries of truth and is capable of receiving God's secrets.

3.3. Now I think the significance of there being two altars, that is, an interior and an exterior one, is that an altar is a symbol of prayer.[47] For this is what the apostle says: "I will pray with the spirit, I will also pray with the mind."[48] For when I pray "in my heart," I enter into the inner altar. I think this is also what the Lord says in the Gospels: "But you, when you pray, go into your room and shut your door, and pray to your Father in secret."[49] Thus the one who prays like this, as I said, approaches the altar of incense which is within.[50] But when one pours forth prayer to God with a clear voice and with words that have been brought forth vocally, as one who would edify those who hear, this is the one who "prays with the spirit"[51] and who seems to offer a sacrifice on the altar, the altar which is set up outside for the people's burnt offerings.[52] So it is necessary for priests in particular to attend to these things and to guard the things that are covered inside within the veil, lest anything there be defiled, lest anything be found unclean. That is to say, they must attend to the inner man and to the secrets of the heart, so that immaculate things may continue to abide there.

3.4. By "cherubim and propitiatory,"[53] one

---

[41]Mt 16:24. [42]Num 18:1-3. [43]Num 18:2-3. [44]Ps 7:9. [45]Num 18:8. [46]2 Cor 5:4. [47]Cf. *Homilies on Leviticus* 9.1. [48]1 Cor 14:15. [49]Mt 6:6. [50]Cf. Ex 27:1; Heb 9:3-4. See *On Prayer* 20.2. [51]1 Cor 14:15. [52]Cf. Ex 20:24. [53]Heb 9:5; cf. Ex 25:17-18; Rom 3:25.

should understand the knowledge of the Trinity; for the translation of "cherubim" points to a "multitude," that is, a perfection "of knowledge."[54] And what else is the "perfection of knowledge" if not to know the Father and the Son and the Holy Spirit? So this must be attended to by priests, that it be preserved undefiled and unharmed.

3.5. Moreover, "the jar holding the heavenly food of manna"[55] is undoubtedly the treasure of the divine word. In my judgment the "golden ark" in which are the "tablets of the covenant"[56] indicates nothing else than our mind in which we ought to have the law of God inscribed. Now this mind should be of gold, that is, pure and precious. We should always have the law of God inscribed on it, as the apostle says: "Written not with ink, but with the Spirit of the living God, not on tablets of stone, but on the tablets of the fleshly heart."[57] For this is what is also said about certain ones: "Who show the work of God written in their hearts."[58] But who if not God has written it on their hearts "with his finger"?[59] Assuredly the natural law that God gave to the human race, he has also written into the minds of all.[60] From this source we take a commencement and receive certain seeds for thoroughly searching for truth. If we cultivate these seeds well, they will bring forth the fruit of life in us in Christ Jesus our Lord, "to whom is the glory in the ages of ages. Amen."[61]

Homily 11
Numbers 18:8-32

On the offering of the first fruits.[1]

1.1. The law commands that the first fruits of the whole harvest and of all animals be offered to the priests.[2] And so, everyone who possesses a field, a vineyard, an olive tree, or even a garden, and anything that is cultivated in the ground, and anyone who raises cattle of any kind, must offer to God from these things all that is first, that is to say, he must bring it to the priests. For it says that what is given to the priests is offered to God. And this is what we are taught from the law, since no one licitly or lawfully may enjoy the harvest that the earth has produced, or the animals that the offspring of cattle have brought forth, unless the first fruits from each of these things are offered to God, that is, to the priests.

1.2. Now I think that it is necessary for this law to be observed even according to the letter. This is also the case for some of the other laws. For now and then there are commands of the law that even the disciples of the New Testament keep as necessary observances. And if it seems fitting, let our discourse first engage those things which are written in the law, to be sure, but they are written as things that have to be observed under the Gospels. After we bring these things into the open, let us then also investigate what also should be understood spiritually in these things. For there are some who say the following, that if there is anything at all that must be observed according to the letter, why then should not everything be observed? But if the things that the law contains are to be referred to the spiritual understanding, then nothing at all should be discerned according to the letter, but instead everything ought to be understood spiritually. But we will attempt to

---

[54]Cf. *Commentary on Romans* 3.8; *Homilies on Ezekiel* 1.15; *Commentary on Song of Songs* 2; Philo *On the Life of Moses* 2; *Questions and Answers on Exodus* 2.62; Clement *Miscellanies* 5.6.35.6. [55]Heb 9:4. [56]Ex 25:21. [57]2 Cor 3:3. [58]Rom 2:15. [59]Cf. Ex 31:18. [60]In Origen, *Homélies sur les Nombres*, ed. Louis Doutreleau, SC 415: 289, Doutreleau observes that one can see here the first seeds of a "natural theology." Cf. Augustine *Against Faustus the Manichaean* 22.27; *On Free Will* 5.6; Thomas Aquinas *Summa theologica* Ia, Iiae, Q.94, art. 4. The same author asserts that the idea of a natural law is of Stoic origin. Cf. Cicero *De republica* 3.22. On the other hand, B. Dunkle, "A Development in Origen's View of the Natural Law," *Pro Ecclesia* 13, no. 3 (2004): 337-51, argues that Origen develops his theory of a moral natural law not by direct reference to any particular philosophical position, but rather by reflection on Scripture. [61]Gal 1:5. **Homily 11** [1]The length of this homily suggests that it is one in which Rufinus has inserted material from Origen's *Scholia* (*Excerpta*), as he says he did in the Preface. [2]Cf. Num 18:8-19.

qualify the excessiveness of both claims and set forth, on the basis of the authority of the divine Scriptures, what kind of rules should be followed in the words of this sort of law.

1.3. It is written in the eighteenth Psalm: "The law of the Lord is above reproach, converting souls, the testimony of the Lord is faithful, offering wisdom to little children; the precept of the Lord is clear, illuminating the eyes. The fear of the Lord is pure, continuing for ever and ever;[3] the justices of the Lord are right, causing hearts to rejoice; the judgments of the Lord are true, justified in themselves, to be desired beyond gold and very precious stone and sweeter than honey and the honeycomb."[4] Now then, if these terms did not differ from each other in meaning, surely the divine Scripture would never have indicated unique distinctions for each one. Thus it says one thing about the law of the Lord, something else about the command, something else about justifications, something else about judgments. So then, as we have just shown, the law is one thing, the precept is something else, a testimony is something else, a justification is something else, and a judgment is something else. Moreover, within the law itself, there is a very plain distinction between these things. This is indicated when it is said: "This is the law and the commandments and the justifications and the precepts and the testimonies and the judgments, which the Lord commanded Moses."[5]

1.4. So, since these things are proven to be so by means of testimonies from the law itself, and they differ from one another by these distinctions, we should more carefully consider in these things that are read aloud from the law that, just as it is written, for instance, this is a "command," the command must not immediately be received as *law*; or, when it is written that these are "justifications," the justifications

must not be thought of as either *law* or *command*. Likewise, when "testimony" or "judgments" are recorded, the one is not to be understood in a way that would confuse it with the rest, but each one is different from the others.

1.5. So, if we read that it is written, "the *law* contains the shadow of good things to come,"[6] we are not immediately compelled to believe that the command as well, or the justices, or the judgments, concerning which this statement does not apply, are the "shadows of the good things to come." Finally, to give one example from the many that could be given, it is not written: this is the *command* of the Passover, but "this is the *law* of the Passover."[7] And since "the law is the shadow of the good things to come," doubtless the law of the Passover is the shadow of the good things to come.

1.6. So then, when I come to the passage that describes the Passover, I should understand in that physical[8] sheep a "shadow of the good thing to come."[9] I should perceive that "Christ our Passover has been sacrificed."[10] In a similar way, you will find it written also concerning "unleavened bread"[11] and the other observances of feast days. Since all these things are written in the law under the designation of "law," since the law necessarily points to the good things to come by means of the shadow that is present, I should ask what is the unleavened bread "of the good things to come." If I do, I will find that the apostle tells me: "Let us celebrate the feast day, not with the old leaven nor with the leaven of malice and wickedness, but with the unleavened bread of sincerity and truth."[12]

1.7. Moreover, it is written of circumcision: "This is the *law* of circumcision."[13] Since, then, circumcision too is assessed under the designation of *law*, but the law is a shadow, I ask what "shadow of good things to come" does circumcision contain. Otherwise, Paul could possibly

---

[3]Lit. "in the age of age." [4]Ps 19:7-10. [5]Num 36:13. [6]Heb 10:1. [7]Ex 12:43. [8]Lit. "bodily." Cf. Ex 12:5. [9]Cf. Heb 10:1. Good is now singular, whereas above he cited it in the plural. [10]1 Cor 5:7. [11]Ex 12:8. [12]1 Cor 5:8. [13]Origen's memory may have slipped, since this is not a direct quotation from the Old Testament. In any case, circumcision is given as a law in Gen 17:9-14; Paul speaks of it as the law in Rom 2:17-28, as does Jesus in Jn 7:23.

say to me, as one who is standing in the shadow of circumcision: "If you are circumcised, Christ will not benefit you";[14] and "For that circumcision is not the circumcision that is manifest in the flesh; nor is he a Jew who is manifest in the flesh, but he who is a Jew in secret, and circumcision is of the heart in the Spirit, not the letter, whose praise is not from men but from God."[15] You will find nearly all of these particular things designated under the designation of *law* in the writings of Moses, yet the apostle says that they are absolutely not to be observed according to the letter.

1.8. Now in fact in the passage where it says: "You shall not kill, you shall not commit adultery, you shall not steal,"[16] and the other things of this sort, we do not find that the term *law* is said first in respect to these things. Rather, these things seem to be *commandments*; and for that reason this Scripture is not done away with for disciples of the gospel, but is fulfilled.[17] For, as I have said, it is not the *commandment* but the *law* that is said to contain "a shadow of the good things to come."[18] And therefore, we must observe these things according to the letter. It speaks this way in other passages as well: "Justly follow after what is just."[19] What need is there in this to look for an allegory, when even the letter edifies?

1.9. So we have shown that there are some things which are absolutely not to be observed according to the letter of the law, and there are some things which allegory ought not to completely transform, but they should be observed in every way just as the Scriptures state concerning these things. My next question is whether there are certain things which, even according to the letter, cannot, in fact, stand, yet of necessity an allegory should be sought in these things as well. And see if we are able to fortify this with apostolic and Gospel authority.

1.10. It is written in the law: "For this reason a man will leave his father and mother and will cleave to his wife and the two will be one flesh."[20] Because these words contain mystical allegories, Paul, when he cited this example in his epistle, declares and says: "This is a great mystery, but I am speaking of Christ and the church."[21] Now the Lord and Savor himself teaches that it is necessary for this to be kept also according to the letter when he says: "It is written: for this reason a man will leave his father and mother and will cleave to his wife, and the two will be one flesh. Therefore what God has joined together, let not man separate."[22] And he certainly shows that these things are to be observed even according to the letter when he adds: "What God has joined together, let not man separate." Moreover, in other passages, where the apostle says that "Abraham had two sons, one from the slave woman and one from the free,"[23] who doubts that these things ought to stand according to the letter? For it is certain that both Isaac by Sarah and Ishmael by Hagar were sons of Abraham.[24] Yet the apostle adds to this and says: "Now these things are allegorical."[25] He converts them into "two testaments," and in fact he speaks of the children of the New Testament as the offspring of Sarah, who gives birth to them in freedom, but he has identified the offspring of Hagar, "who gives birth unto slavery," as the sons of the earthly Jerusalem.

1.11. We have shown, I think, by the authority of the divine Scripture, from these things that are written in the law, that some things are to be absolutely fled from and avoided, so that they are not to be observed according to the letter by the disciples of the gospel. Yet certain things are to be retained in every way, just as they were written. Other things, however, have a truth of their own according to the letter, but they also contain an allegorical meaning that is beneficial and necessary.

2.1. Now it will be [the task] of a wise scribe,

---

[14]Gal 5:2. [15]Cf. Rom 2:28-29. [16]Rom 13:9. [17]Cf. Mt 5:17. [18]Cf. Heb 10:1. [19]1 Tim 6:11. [20]Gen 2:24. [21]Eph 5:32. [22]Cf. Mt 19:5-6. [23]Gal 4:22. [24]Cf. Gen 21:3; 16:15. [25]Gal 4:24.

and of one who is "instructed about the kingdom of God, who knows how to bring forth new and old things from these treasures,"[26] to know how in each passage of Scripture either to reject completely the "letter that kills" and to seek "the spirit that gives life,"[27] or to confirm it in every way and prove the teaching of the letter to be useful and necessary, or to fittingly and properly introduce a mystical meaning, even while the historical sense remains.

2.2. I think this is applicable as well to the words that we have in hand; for it is befitting and useful for first fruits to be offered to the priests of the gospel as well. For "thus also the Lord has arranged that those who announce the gospel should live from the gospel, and those who serve at the altar should partake of the altar."[28] And just as this is worthy and befitting, so on the contrary it is unbecoming and unworthy, or rather, impious, that he who worships God and enters the church of God, who knows that the priests and ministers assist at the altar and minister either in the Word of God or in the ministry of the church, that he should not offer the first fruits to the priests from the harvest of the lands, a harvest that God granted by producing his sun and by serving by his rains.[29] A soul of this sort does not seem to me to have remembered God, nor does it seem to think or believe that God has given the harvest that he has taken in, which he stows away as if it had nothing to do with God. For if he believed that it were given to him by God, he would surely know how to honor God by rewarding the priests from his gifts and presents.[30]

2.3. And in order to show still more fully by means of the words of the Lord himself that these things must be observed even according to the letter, let us add the following. The Lord says in the Gospels: "Woe to you, scribes and Pharisees, hypocrites, you who tithe"—that is, you give a tenth—"of mint and cumin and dill, and you neglect what are the greater matters of the law; hypocrites, these things ought to be done and the others not omitted."[31] So consider very carefully how the Lord's words mean that the greater matters of the law are by all means to be done, yet these things that are according to the letter are designated as things that are not to be neglected. But if you reply that he said these things to the Pharisees, not to the disciples, listen again to this same One, who says to the disciples: "Unless your justice abounds more than that of the scribes and Pharisees, you will not enter into the kingdom of heaven."[32] So then, what he wills to be done by the Pharisees, in much greater measure and with more abundance does he will to be fulfilled by the disciples; but what he does not will to be done by the disciples, he does not command to be done by the Pharisees. Now the manner in which he wants it to be done in greater measure by the disciples than the Pharisees are doing, he makes clear in the passage where he says: "It was said to the ancients: you shall not kill";[33] and the Pharisees observe this. But to his disciples he says: "But I say to you that if anyone becomes angry with his brother, he will be liable to the judgment."[34] He speaks in a similar fashion in respect to what is written: "You shall not commit adultery," in that for his disciples he wills that their justice abound more, so that they do not even "look on a woman to lust for her."[35]

2.4. Therefore, from these few things which we have brought forth, if any are diligent in the study of the divine Scriptures, they can very easily assemble distinctions from other passages as well. "For if a wise man hears," it says, "not only will he praise the word, but he will add to it."[36] What will he add? He will go on to

---

[26]Mt 13:52. [27]2 Cor 3:5. [28]Cf. 1 Cor 9:14, 13. [29]Cf. Mt 5:45. [30]Origen's spirited appeal for the adequate remuneration of messengers of the gospel follows the teaching of Paul (cf. 1 Cor 9:5-14; 1 Tim 5:17-18) and Jesus (cf. Lk 9:3-6), and reflects the established custom of the third-century church. His literal defense of tithing follows in the next section. [31]Mt 23:23. [32]Mt 5:20. [33]Mt 5:21. [34]Mt 5:22. [35]Cf. Mt 5:28. [36]Sir 21:15.

investigate and penetrate into each chapter of the law, in order to determine when the letter of the law is to be fled from, when it is to be embraced, and also when the narration of history is in agreement with the mystical explanation. For "Christ redeemed us from the curse of the law";[37] he did not redeem us from the curse of the *commandment*, nor from the curse of the *testimony*, nor from the curse of the *judgments*, but "from the curse of the *law*," that is, that we should not be subject "to the circumcision of the flesh,"[38] nor to the observation of sabbaths, and other things similar to these,[39] which must be said to be contained not in the *commandments* but in the *law*.

2.5. How then is our justice abounding "more than that of the scribes and Pharisees"[40] if they do not dare to taste of the harvest of their land before offering to the priests the first fruits and separating off a tenth for the Levites, while I do none of these things, but use[41] the harvest of the land in such a way that the priest does not know about it, the Levite is unaware of it, the divine altar does not perceive it?

2.6. Now the following must be said as a warning, that the law is spoken of in a twofold way; for all these things generally, that is, the commandment, justifications, precepts, testimonies and judgments, are called law; but a certain part of these which are written in the law are said to be law in a unique sense, such as those things we discussed above. Law in a general sense is signified, for instance, when it is said of the Savior that he "came not to destroy the law, but to fulfill it."[42] And likewise in another passage is says: "Therefore the fullness of the law is love."[43] In that passage obviously he has designated as law everything together that is written in the law. We say these things in order to clarify that the command concerning first fruits of the crops or of the livestock ought

to stand even according to the letter.

3.1. But now let us see how it bears an allegorical, that is, spiritual sense. So let us investigate whether in Scriptures other than these on which we have spoken above, we find first fruits named; for he has said here: "All the first fruits of oil and wine and grain, the first fruits of all these things which had been offered to God, I have given them to you."[44] So now my question is, where are first fruits named in addition to this passage? For if all the first fruits pertain to the high priest, a high priest must necessarily be sought for us too, to whom even these first fruits should pertain, which we have found introduced in other passages of Scripture.

3.2. Now first of all, we read that it is written of Christ the Lord himself that he is the "first fruits of the dead."[45] Thus he is himself the "first fruits" in some fashion. And again we find that the apostle speaks of certain ones as the "first fruits of Asia,"[46] and others are the "first fruits of Achaia."[47] Based on this, it is consistent that some believers in every church be designated as the first fruits, but only those whom the apostolic spirit would approve. I think that Cornelius is also one of these, who is deservedly called "first fruits" of the church of Caesarea, along with those with whom he merited to receive the Holy Spirit.[48] And Cornelius should be called first fruits not only of this church, but possibly of all the Gentiles[49] as well; for he was the first to "believe from the Gentiles,"[50] and the first to be "filled with the Holy Spirit,"[51] and therefore he will be rightly called the first fruits of the Gentiles.

3.3. But you may possibly ask who offers these first fruits to God, or who is the high priest to whose accounts these things fall due. I think that in accordance with the word of the Lord, "this world" is said to be "the field,"[52] but the field not of the earth only, but human

---

[37]Gal 3:13. [38]Cf. Rom 2:28. [39]Cf. Col 2:16. [40]Cf. Mt 5:20. [41]Lat *abutor*, which means both "use" and "abuse." [42]Mt 5:17. [43]Rom 13:10. [44]Num 18:12. [45]Cf. Col 1:18; 1 Cor 15:20. [46]Rom 16:5. [47]1 Cor 16:15. [48]Cf. Acts 10:1-48. [49]Or "nations." [50]Cf. Acts 21:25. [51]Cf. Acts 10:44; Lk 1:67. [52]Cf. Mt 13:38.

hearts are understood. This is the field that the angels of God have received for cultivation. Thus they indeed possess the harvest of their own cultivation, and they hold it, namely, those who "live under governors and managers"[53] and have not yet come to the height of perfection. Indeed if their hearts are carefully cultivated and are led to perfection, they offer them as first fruits to the great high priest, as those who are chosen and the best of the rest. After all, we have found that Cornelius himself, before he received instruction in the word of God or the grace of baptism from Peter, had heard from the angel that his "prayers and alms had ascended to God."[54] And for this reason it seems that through that very angel Cornelius was offered to God as the first fruits.

3.4. We can also say about Peter and Paul that they themselves offer the first fruits of those who believe through themselves, just as the apostle says, that he had "completed the gospel of Christ from Jerusalem in a circuit up to Illyricum," and he had preached the gospel in this manner, "not where Christ had been named, lest he should build on someone else's foundation."[55] So then, consider Paul to be offering as his own harvest all those whom he taught, all those to whom he preached, who made progress in the faith because of him. Consider how he daily seeks new fields to cultivate and new ground in which to sow seed, and how he speaks about this to certain people: "For I desire to come to you, in order to have a harvest even among you as also among the other Gentiles."[56] Consider this, I say, how he indicates that some are chosen from this whole harvest, and he says of some, as we have said above, that they are the "first fruits of Asia,"[57] and others are "first fruits of Achaia,"[58] and how he chooses first fruits from each of the churches and offers them to God. Now possibly he even

esteems some as "firstborn ones." I believe, however, that he would regard those who are inferior to these, whom he could offer neither as the "first fruits" nor as the "firstborn ones," as the "tithes."

3.5. Moreover, I think that every teacher would seem to cultivate the field of that church in which he teaches, that is, the hearts of the believers, in view of the fact that he teaches, preaches and instructs hearers. Thus he too has fruit from this cultivation and doubtless among this harvest he finds someone chosen and outstanding, whom he offers as first fruits. He also finds those whom he offers as firstborn ones and others as tithes. But if it does not seem reckless to be bold in such matters, possibly those men can be called the firstborn ones of whom it is written: "they have not defiled themselves with women, for they have remained virgins,"[59] or this can even seem to be said about martyrs. And the church's virgins can no less be understood as first fruits; and as the tithes can be understood those who have lived chastely and continently after a marriage.[60]

4.1. Our discussion began with the first fruits of angels, which we had said they offer from their cultivation of the human race. We were then diverted to a discussion of the apostles by the passage that follows, and from there to every teacher. Let us now return to the source of the things that we had begun to discuss. Each of the angels, then, will be present in the judgment at the consummation of the age, bringing with itself those over whom it was in charge, those whom it had aided and instructed, those for whom it "always looked on the face of the Father in heaven."[61] Now I think that even there an inquiry will take place [to determine] whether the angel fell short in the cultivation of his people, or whether human negligence should answer for having utterly failed to re-

---

[53]Cf. Gal 4:2. [54]Acts 10:4. [55]Rom 15:19-20. [56]Rom 1:13. [57]Rom 16:5. [58]1 Cor 16:15. [59]Rev 14:4. [60]Virginity and celibate widowhood appear to have been recognized states of life in Origen's day, not yet officially organized or patronized by the church, but voluntary, and, as this passage indicates, ranking high on the scale of merit. [61]Mt 18:10.

spond worthily of the angelic cultivation. And so, God's judgment will determine whether there was some sort of negligence on the part of the ministering spirits, "who have been sent for ministry and aid on behalf of those who are receiving the inheritance of salvation,"[62] or whether there was laziness in those who are helped by them, so many are the falls that come to a human life.[63]

4.2. But if this is so, there will therefore be a judgment of God also between angels and men, and perhaps some who come from the multitude of believers will be judged with Paul and will be compared with his labors and fruits; and perhaps he will be found to be superior even to some angels in his labors, and doubtless it was for that reason that he said: "Or do you not know that we will judge angels?"[64] It is not that Paul himself will judge angels, but that Paul's work which he did in the gospel and in respect to the souls of believers will judge some; not indeed all, but some of the angels. And for this reason perhaps even Peter, considering these matters, said: "Into which things even angels long to look."[65] I grant that the apostles themselves make use of the angels they have as helpers in order to fulfill the mission of their preaching and to complete the work of the gospel. For this is what was said in the Acts of the Apostles, that it was Peter's angel who knocked on the gate.[66] Similarly then there is understood to be both an angel of Paul, just as there is of Peter, and another of another apostle, and of each one by ranking or for their merits, which assuredly consist in their labors and teaching, either of the apostles or of the rest of the teachers after them. It is necessary that the angels have the first portions even of the souls which they have led after them, and that they

bring this harvest to the Lord's threshing floor, together with those men through whom they have effected this. Thus there will be in the gathering of the harvest, that is, in the choosing of believers, this one, for instance, who was outstanding in that church and the best of the first fruits; and that one who was superior even to the former, a firstborn of that church, who was offered, for instance, by that angel.

4.3. And so everything that is foreshadowed in the law, since "the law holds the shadow of the good things to come,"[67] will in some such manner be fulfilled in the truth of the good things to come through the services of angels. Thus the things that are prefigured in that Israel which is said to be "according to the flesh,"[68] are fulfilled in the true and heavenly Israelites. For the name Israel has reached to the angelic orders, except that they will be called Israel much more truly, to the extent that they are more truly "a mind seeing God"; for this is what Israel means when translated.[69] For I think that just as we see certain names recorded in the Scriptures, both of nations and of rulers, which without any hesitation should be referred to evil angels and to hostile powers, as, for instance, Pharaoh king of Egypt and Nebuchadnezzar[70] the Babylonian or Assyrian,[71] so also things that are written about holy men and about a religious nation, we ought to refer to the holy angels and to the good powers.[72] Now to prove that Scripture refers to the king of an impious nation as a malignant power, listen to how Isaiah speaks about Nebuchadnezzar: He says: "And I will bring a sword over a great nation,[73] over the ruler of the Assyrians. For he says: I will act with my power,[74] and by the wisdom of my mind I will destroy the boundaries of the nations, and I will plunder their power."[75] And

---

[62]Heb 1:14. [63]Cf. *Homilies on Luke* 35 in Jean Daniélou, *Origen*, trans. Walter Mitchell (New York, Sheed & Ward, 1955), p. 243. [64]1 Cor 6:3. [65]1 Pet 1:12. [66]Cf. Acts 12:13, 15. [67]Heb 10:1. [68]1 Cor 10:18. [69]The etymology is founded on Gen 32:30; 35:10: *anēr horōn theon*. Cf. Homilies 15.2; 16.7; 17.4; *Commentary on John* 1.35(40).260; 2.31(25).189; *On First Principles* 4.3.8; *Homilies on Genesis* 15.3; 16.6; *Homilies on Exodus* 1.5; *Commentary on Romans* 7.14.2; 8.12.6. [70]Lat *Nabuchodonosor*. [71]Cf. Dan 1:1; Jdt 1:1. [72]Or "virtues." Lat *virtus*. [73]The LXX (Origen's text) of Is 10:12 has "great *noun*," "mind," not "nation." Rufinus may have misread the Old Latin's *mentem* (mind) as *gentem* (nation); or possibly his amanuensis misheard the dictation. [74]Lat *virtus*. [75]Lat *virtus*; Is 10:12-13.

again elsewhere, speaking as if about the ruler of some nation, he says: "How has Lucifer, who rose in the morning, fallen from heaven?"[76] So, if the reckoning of the truth compels all these things to be referred to certain angels of malignant power, is not the consequence of the same that what is also written down about the good rulers or nations is to be referred to the angels and ministers of the good powers, as we have said above?

4.4. Moreover, consider the Scripture we read in Genesis, when God, doubtless speaking to the angels, says: "Come, let us confound their tongues."[77] What else should one think but that it was the angels who worked out the different languages and dialects that people speak? For instance, there must have been one who inspired a man with the Babylonian language, and one who gave to another the Egyptian language, and another who inspired the Greek language. And thus, possibly these were the very princes of the various nations who were apparently the authors of the different languages and dialects. But the language that had been given at the beginning through Adam—in our opinion it was Hebrew—remained in that part of humanity that never became the portion of any angel or ruler, but which continued to remain God's portion.[78]

4.5. Meanwhile, as we began to say, the angels offer the first fruits, each, I believe, of its own nation, and again each of its own church. These are the angels John seems to be writing to in the Apocalypse, for instance, "to the angel of the church of the Ephesians,"[79] or "of the Smyrnaeans,"[80] or "of the Laodiceans,"[81] and of the others that are recorded. So each of the angels offers the first fruits of its own church or nation, which it has been entrusted to manage. Or perhaps there may even be other angels in addition who gather each of the faithful from all nations. And let us consider whether

perhaps, just as in some city where, for instance, there are no Christians as yet, if someone goes there and begins to teach, labor, give instruction and lead them to the faith, and he himself later becomes the ruler and bishop for those whom he has taught, so likewise, in the future the holy angels may themselves even become the rulers of the people whom they have gathered in from the various nations, the people whose progress they have secured by their labor and ministry. Thus Christ would be called not so much a king, as a "King of kings," and not so much a Lord, as a "Lord of lords."[82] For if they become kings of those whom they rule and cause to make progress, then they themselves offer some to the high priest, some indeed to the sons of the high priest,[83] that is, to the higher powers and archangels, some also to the Levites,[84] that is, to those a little inferior. But this only applies if it seems reasonable that the angelic orders are distinguished in outward form in some way that is similar to the way the Israelites are distinguished, seeing that the Israelites are said "to serve the shadow and copy of the heavenly things."[85]

4.6. Therefore, we can say that perhaps in the future, when the whole harvest will be gathered at the threshing floor, there will be a certain portion of the high priest, but of that true high priest, Christ. There will also be another portion of the Levites, as we already said above, set apart either for the angels or for the other heavenly powers. But I think that there will even be a portion of men, at any rate of those who were wise and faithful stewards of the true God in this life. For the Lord indicates this in the Gospels, I think, when he says to him to whom five minas had been entrusted and he had made of them ten: "Have authority over ten cities";[86] but to the one to whom he had entrusted one, and he made of it five, [he says]: "Have authority over five cities."[87] For what authority

---

[76]Is 14:12. [77]Gen 11:7. [78]Cf. Deut 32:9; See Daniélou, *Origen*, p. 236. [79]Cf. Rev 2:1. [80]Cf. Rev 2:8. [81]Cf. Rev 3:14. [82]Cf. Rev 19:16. [83]Cf. Num 18:10. [84]Cf. Num 18:24. [85]Cf. Heb 8:5. [86]Lk 19:17. [87]Lk 19:19.

over cities should be understood here, if not the management of souls? Whence also it seems to me that it was not without reason also among these angels that some bear authority and lordship over others, but others are subject and obey authority. Just as in the case of the one to whom the authority of ten cities is given, or of him to whom five cities is given, because he multiplied the money entrusted to himself, it is not even without merit that he attains to the authority of this sort. For with God everything happens according to reason and judgment, not gratuitously, but for merit's sake one is appointed to be the ruler of many, another is appointed to be subjected to another's lordship.

4.7. We may perhaps seem to have wandered into a rather extensive digression, but it was necessary to discuss these things as well while explaining the first fruits, seeing that the divine Scriptures contain this term that is of such great honor that even Christ himself is termed "first fruits"[88] and the "first fruits of those who sleep."[89] And just as Christ is "King of kings" and "Lord of lords"[90] and "shepherd of shepherds"[91] and "high priest of high priests,"[92] so he will consistently be said to be "first fruits of first fruits." These first fruits are offered no longer to the high priest, but to God, in accordance with the fact that "he offered himself as a sacrifice to God,"[93] and by rising from the dead "he sat down at the right hand of God."[94] And he is called the "first fruits" and "firstborn of all creation."[95] The present moment is not the time to pursue whether this ought to be understood in the same way in which all creatures should be understood, or in some loftier and more divine understanding.

5.1. So let us return to the account of the first fruits which we said are offered through angels, which are gathered from the fields of this world. Now the fields of angels are our

hearts. Thus each of them offers to God the first fruits from the field that it cultivates. And if today I should be deserving to bring forth some great interpretation that is worthy of the supreme high priest, so that from all these things that we speak and teach, there would be something outstanding that would necessarily please the highest priest, it could possibly happen that the angel who presides over a church would choose something from all these statements and would offer it to the Lord in the place of the first fruits from the little field of my heart. But I know that I am not deserving of that, nor am I aware in myself that such an interpretation would be found in me, which the angel who cultivates us would judge worthy to offer to the Lord as the first fruits, or as the firstborn things. But would that what we speak and teach would be of such quality that we should not deserve to be condemned for our words.[96] This grace would be sufficient for us.[97]

5.2. So then, the angels offer the first fruits of us and each one cultivates those whom it converts to God from errors by its own zeal and diligence; and each person is the portion of, or under the care of, this or that angel. It is as it was at the beginning of this world, "when God dispersed the sons of Adam, he appointed boundaries for the nations according to the number of angels of God."[98] And each nation came to be under this or that angel, but there was one chosen nation, Israel, which was "the Lord's portion" and "the line of his inheritance."[99] Thus I believe also that at the end of this world and the beginning of another [world] of the future ages, once again the Most High may "divide the sons of Adam." Those who are unable to be so "pure in heart" that "they see God"[100] and be the Lord's portion may at least see the holy angels. And may they be both "his people Jacob" and "the line of his inheritance

---

[88]1 Cor 15:23. [89]1 Cor 15:20. [90]1 Tim 6:15; Rev 19:16. [91]Cf. 1 Pet 5:4. [92]Cf. Heb 4:15. [93]Cf. Eph 5:2. [94]Col 3:1. [95]Col 1:15. [96]Cf. Mt 12:36-37. [97]For a similar expression of humility, cf. Homily 3.1.2 above. [98]Deut 32:8. [99]Deut 32:9. [100]Recall the interpretation of Israel as "mind seeing God" above at Homily 11.4.3.

Israel" according to the number of the angels of God.

5.3. Thus it is desirable, as we have said, to make such progress that each one deserves to be chosen among the first fruits or the firstborn things, and to be offered to God, and to be "the Lord's part." But if not this, it is desirable at least to deserve to be a portion of the holy angels. Only let no one be found among those of whom it is written: "They will enter into the lower parts of the earth, they will be handed over to the hand of the sword, they will be the portions of foxes."[101] So you see that at the time of resurrection, when "the Most High" begins "to divide the nations," and "to disperse the sons of Adam"[102] according to their merits, there will be some who "enter into the lower parts of the earth" and become "the portions of foxes," that is, the portions of demons. For those are the "foxes that ruin the vineyards."[103] Herod was one of these, of whom it is said: "Go tell that fox."[104]

5.4. Therefore, let us flee from earthly deeds and an earthly understanding. Otherwise, weighed down by earthly thoughts, we may be said to "enter into the lower parts of the earth and become the portions of foxes." For they enter into the lower parts of the earth who receive God's law and the goods of the promises with an interpretation that comes from an earthly way of thinking and who do not spur on the souls of the hearers to the expectation of heavenly things and to reflection on the things above. For the apostle plainly says: "If you have been raised together with Christ, seek the things that are above, where Christ is at the right hand of God, not the things on the earth."[105] Doubtless the apostle was speaking to those who, with an earthly observance, were saying: "Do not take, do not taste, do not touch,"[106] to whom he adds: "all which things are for corruption by the very use according to

the commandments and teachings of men."[107]

6.1. After this he adds: "And the Lord spoke to Aaron saying: Behold I have granted to you to guard the first fruits."[108] Although in some of the copies of the Latins it is written as "to observe," yet it is more true to read "to guard." But one must ask how first fruits will be guarded according to the law. For the priests receive the first fruits not to keep them but to consume them. Why then does he say: "Behold I have given the first fruits to you to guard"? From this it is established that this cannot be applied to the law of the letter, but to the law of the Spirit.[109] For the first fruits that we have explained above spiritually *can* be guarded. Moreover, if according to the apostle Christ is the first fruits,[110] then it is true indeed that these first fruits have been given to us "to guard." For what is so blessed as a soul that always guards Christ, whom it has received, and always having him abiding within itself? Such a soul truly receives the first fruits to guard it. For those first fruits that were offered in the law were consumed as food, and "having entered into the belly were digested and passed into the pit,"[111] as the Gospel says. But the one who eats these first fruits and tastes "the bread that came down from heaven"[112] will not die, but remains unto eternal life. For that is the bread that, though it is always being consumed, it always abides, or rather, it is always increased. So there is, as the apostle says, a "spiritual food,"[113] which, the more it is consumed, the more it grows. For the more you take in the word of God, the more you devour that food assiduously, the more richly it will abound in you. Let these things be said on behalf of what is written: "to guard the first fruits."

7.1. And here is what follows: "of all the things that are sanctified to me from the sons of Israel."[114] Not without a mystery is this said; for God does not will to receive first fruits from

---

[101]Ps 63:9-10. [102]Deut 32:8. [103]Song 2:15. [104]Lk 13:32. [105]Col 3:1-2. [106]Col 2:21. [107]Col 2:22. [108]Num 18:8. [109]Cf. Rom 8:2. [110]Cf. 1 Cor 15:20. [111]Cf. Mt 15:17. [112]Cf. Jn 6:51, 58. [113]Cf. 1 Cor 10:3. [114]Num 18:8.

anywhere else but from the things that have been sanctified of Israel. For it can happen that even among the Gentiles some works worthy of God are found. For even among them, certain virtues of the soul have been cultivated and to some small extent philosophy is not lacking in some of them. But God is not willing that these things be offered as first fruits. God wills to accept good deeds from those whose "mind sees God,"[115] and who are sanctified to God by faith. But the pagan, even if he seems to be morally upright in character, this kind of uprightness is not sanctified, because he does not attribute his soul's virtue to God, but he vaunts it as his own. And for this reason it is not received among the first fruits.[116] Now in terms of defining the letter of the law, it appears to exclude even the proselytes from offering a gift of this sort; for he wants only those sanctified from the sons of Israel to offer first fruits.

7.2. Now I think that one can be called an Israelite by virtue of the fact that it is permitted to him to enter the church[117] of God. For it is written: "You shall not abhor the Idumean, since he is your brother, nor the Egyptian, since you were a foreigner in the land of Egypt. If sons are born to them, in the third generation they shall enter into the church of God."[118] So as long as the Egyptian or Idumean does not bear fruit and has not produced sons in the first, second and third generations, he cannot "enter into the church of the Lord," but it is the generation of sons that causes them "to enter into the church of the Lord."

7.3. Let the one who reads divine literature pay very careful attention and not pass over the words of Scripture as he pleases, but let him look at each word. Notice that it did not say: "if sons or daughters are born to them," but: "if sons are born to them, in the third generation

they will enter into the church of the Lord."[119] And consider, if you are able, in accordance with the mystical meaning, why it is sons alone, and not daughters as well, who cause the fathers "to enter the church of the Lord." After all, you will find that even saints to whom God gives outstanding witness bore daughters with difficulty but they did bear sons. Abraham did not father daughters, nor did Isaac. Only Jacob fathered one, and she was a burden to her brothers and parents;[120] for when she was defiled by Hamor the son of Shechem,[121] she stirred up ill-will against her family and the fury of vengeance in her brothers. Moreover, "every *male* is commanded to appear before the Lord three times per year";[122] the female is not summoned to appear before the Lord. So then, if one looks carefully into the divine Scriptures, he will find that it is not idly that one passage names daughters as well along with the sons, but another passage makes no mention of daughters. Here then, the first fruits which are offered are commanded to be offered by those who are sanctified as sons of Israel, not by the daughters as well. According to the spiritual understanding, however, this is to be related not to the distinction of sex, but to that of souls.

7.4. It says: "To you I have given these things as an honor and to your sons after you, as an eternal legal formality."[123] "To you," it says. To whom? Doubtless you will answer: Aaron. But the words that follow suggest instead that one should understand Christ the true high priest, and his sons the apostles, and the teachers of the churches. For it says: "eternal legal formality." Well, how can what is visible be eternal, when the apostle says: "The things that are seen are temporal; but what are not seen are eternal"?[124] So if the first fruits which are offered to Aaron are visible, things that are visible can-

---

[115]This is the meaning of Israel. Cf. Homily 11.4.3. [116]Origen is quite positive about the natural capacity of man to know about God and the spiritual world, but he is rather negative about the way in which the philosophers made use of this capacity. He certainly does not view philosophy as any sort of passport into heaven. [117]Lat *ecclesia*. [118]Deut 23:7-8. [119]Deut 23:8. [120]Cf. *Homilies on Luke* 4.2. [121]Cf. Gen 34. [122]Cf. Ex 23:17. [123]Num 18:8. [124]2 Cor 4:18.

not be said to be eternal. In a similar way, the circumcision that is visible and the unleavened bread that is visible and the Passover that is visible are of necessity not eternal but temporal. For "the things that are seen are temporal." And again, if "the things that are not seen are eternal," then also the invisible circumcision, "which is in secret,"[125] is eternal, and the "unleavened bread of sincerity and truth,"[126] it too is eternal, since it is from those things "which are not seen." In a similar manner, then, these "eternal legal formalities" are not said to him "who is a Jew outwardly," but to him "who is a Jew in secret," and who keeps the law "in the spirit, not the letter,"[127] and "according to the inner man."[128]

"And let this be to you from these holy things that are sanctified."[129]

8.1. While looking over this very same thing concerning sacrifices, several times I have asked myself just what are these "holy sanctified things." It seems to me that he has said "holy sanctified things" here as if to distinguish them from those that are not holy sanctified things. Now I think that the Holy Spirit is so holy that he has not been sanctified; for to him no sanctification has come in addition and from elsewhere, which was not there previously. On the contrary, he was always holy. His sanctity did not have a beginning. In a similar manner one should understand concerning the Father and the Son; for the substance of the Trinity is unique in that it did not receive its sanctification from the outside, but its own nature is holy.[130] But every creature will be called "holy sanctified things" either by the privilege of the Holy Spirit or by reason of its merits. So then we also read that it is written: "Be holy, for I am holy, says the Lord God."[131] One should not immediately posit a likeness of sanctity in

God and in human beings; for it is said of God, that he *is* holy, but people are commanded to *become* holy, as if they were not always so. After all, these words in Greek, where we have "be holy," express rather this: "become holy." But our translators have indifferently recorded "be" for "become."[132] Each of us, then, becomes holy from the time when he comes near to the fear of God and receives the divine teaching within himself, from the time when he has sold himself out to God, but only if he has sold himself out from the heart. A person can be called a sanctified holy one; but God alone is truly and always holy.

8.2. Now do you want me also to reveal to you a distinction of this sort from the divine Scriptures? Listen to how Paul speaks when he writes to the Hebrews: "For are not he who sanctifies and those who are sanctified all from one?"[133] Who then is the one who sanctifies? Doubtless Christ. And who are those who are sanctified? Those who believe in Christ. Therefore it is clear that he who sanctifies is holy, since he is always holy; but those who are sanctified must be called not simply holy but the holy sanctified ones.

Do not think that what we read as written about Christ contradicts this interpretation: "He whom the Father has sanctified and sent into this world."[134] For there he who is sanctified is Christ according to the flesh, not according to the spirit.[135] For Christ says equally according to the spirit and according to the flesh: "I sanctify myself for them."[136] Thus he who sanctifies is understood according to the spirit, and he who is sanctified for the sake of his disciples is understood according to the flesh. Yet it is one and the same Christ, who at one time sanctifies in the spirit, at another time is sanctified in the flesh.

[125]Cf. Rom 2:29. [126]1 Cor 5:8. [127]Cf. Rom 2:28-29. [128]Cf. Rom 7:22. [129]Num 18:9. [130]Cf. *On First Principles* 1.8.3. [131]Lev 20:7. [132]According to Doutreleau, SC 442:60 n. 1, this philological remark comes from Origen, who is referring to a variant reading of the *Hexapla*. When he speaks of "our translators," he means those whose translations he has preserved in the columns of the *Hexapla*. A variant of the lxx reading of Lev 20:7, *hagioi esesthe*, as *hagiasthēsesthe*. [133]Heb 2:11. [134]Jn 10:36. [135]Cf. Rom 1:3-4. [136]Jn 17:19.

8.3. So, the "holy sanctified" first fruits are to be offered from the whole harvest,[137] but to the spiritual high priest. From what harvest, then, shall we offer spiritual first fruits? Listen to the number of fruits the apostles lists: He says: "The fruit of the Spirit is love, joy, peace, patience,"[138] and so forth. Well then, what first fruits from the fruit of love, which is the first fruit of the Spirit, should I indeed offer to the high priest? I think that the first fruits of love are that I shall "love the Lord my God with my whole heart, with my whole soul, and with my whole mind."[139] These are the first fruits. But from that fruit of love, what should I have in the second place? That "I should love my neighbor as myself."[140] Therefore, these first fruits of love are offered to God through the high priest, but those that come in the second position are left to my uses. Still, I think that there is something from this fruit that should be considered in the third place: that "I should love even my enemies."[141]

8.4. Now if you are able, in a similar fashion look to find similar first fruits of the other fruits of the Spirit as well. "Joy" is recorded in the second place as a fruit of the Spirit. So if I rejoice in the Lord[142] and rejoice in hope,[143] and if I rejoice when I have suffered mistreatment for the name of the Lord,[144] in all these things, and in other things similar to these, I have offered to God the first fruits of joy through the true high priest. Moreover, if I endure "the plundering of my goods with joy,"[145] and if I put up with tribulations, poverty and every kind of insult, while rejoicing, that too is for me the fruit of joy, which takes the second place among the fruits of the Spirit. For if I rejoice over secular affairs, honors or wealth, those are false joys springing from the "vanities of vanities."[146] But if I rejoice in evils and exult over the ruin of others, those are not only vain but even diabolical joys, or rather, they do not even deserve to

be called joys. For "there is no rejoicing among the impious, says the Lord."[147] I still want to investigate another fruit of joy, or rather, other first fruits of joys. If I rejoice in the word of God, if I rejoice in the knowledge of the mysteries of God, if I rejoice that I am deemed worthy to recognize the secret and hidden things of God's wisdom, if I rejoice that I have abandoned all things that are in this world, not only the useless things, but also the useful ones, not only vain things, but also necessary ones, and that I have handed myself over to the word of God alone and to his wisdom: in all these things that I have received, sufficient first fruits of joy will be offered to God. Moreover, at each one's leisure (lest we drag on our homily longer than is right), it will be permissible to adapt what is suitable concerning the rest of the fruits of the Spirit.

9.1. It says: "And from all their gifts."[148] As for the one who has offered a gift to God, the first fruits must once again be offered to the high priest. I think this can be established in the following way by an allegorical explanation. If one distributes to his own or to those in need, or if one does some good work, he has offered a gift to God for the sake of the commandment. But he will offer the first fruits of this gift if he gives away not only food or money, for instance, but also if he has the affection of one showing mercy and exercising compassion. For this is what God requires of a person, that the very mind be filled with and formed by pious and merciful feelings.

9.2. "And from all their offerings."[149] That spiritual offering is what we read: "Offer a sacrifice of praise to God and pay your vows to the Most High."[150] Thus to praise God and to offer the vows of prayer is to make an offering to God. But the first fruits of this offering will be offered through the high priest in the following way, if we pray not only with words and voice,

---

[137]Lit. "fruits." [138]Gal 5:22. [139]Mt 22:37. [140]Mt 19:19. [141]Mt 5:44. [142]Cf. Phil 4:4. [143]Cf. Rom 15:13. [144]Cf. Mt 5:12. [145]Cf. Heb 10:34. [146]Cf. Eccles 1:2. [147]Is 57:21. [148]Num 18:9. [149]Num 18:9. [150]Ps 50:14.

but also with the mind and heart, in accordance with what the apostle counsels: "I shall pray with the spirit, I shall pray also with the mind; I shall sing a psalm with the spirit, I will sing a psalm also with the mind."[151]

9.3. For the angels of God, as the tillers and cultivators of our hearts, assist now and search to see if there is in any of us a mind of this sort, so solicitous, so attentive, which has received the word of God as divine seed, with all eagerness. They search to see if it shows fruit at once, when we rise for prayer, that is, if we collect and gather our thoughts in order to pray to God, if the mind does not wander and its thoughts fly about. Otherwise, our mind would indeed be bent over with the body in prayer, but it would be running in different directions in its thoughts. If anyone, I say, senses that his entreaty is directed and focused, if he understands who it is who is assisting him in these visions of God, and if, there in this ineffable light, he pours out his "prayers and supplications and requests and thanksgivings,"[152] troubled by no external images, this one knows by means of the angel who is assisting him that the first fruits of his offering have been brought to the great and true high priest, Christ Jesus our Lord, "to whom be the glory in the ages of ages. Amen."[153]

Homily 12
Numbers 21:16-23

Concerning the well and its song.

12.1. There has been read to us from the book of Numbers the reading about the well and the song that Israel sang at the well. We see that this reading abounds in mysteries, as is usual, or even beyond what is usual. For it says: "And from there, a well; this is the well of which the Lord spoke to Moses: Gather the people together and I will give them water to drink."[1]

Yet in these statements it does not seem to me that the literal historical sense has much claim. For what is the sense of the Lord giving special orders to Moses to gather the people in order to give them water to drink from a well? As if the people, even of their own accord, would not assemble at the well to drink! Why then is the prophet so specially bidden by his own insistence and effort to gather the people to draw water from the well?

1.2. Thus, the low value of the letter sends us back to the treasure of the spiritual interpretation. And on this account, I think it is appropriate to collect mysteries about wells from other passages of Scripture, so that by a comparison of several passages any obscure point in the words now before us may become clear. And so, the Spirit of God says by Solomon in the Proverbs: "Drink waters from your own cisterns, and from the spring of your own wells. And let not your waters be dispersed abroad beyond your spring"—although in other copies we have read: "And let your waters be dispersed abroad beyond your spring." "Your waters are to be for you alone and no stranger is to share in them."[2] So, according to this description, each one of us has a well within himself. Or rather, we will say something more: each one of us has not one well but many wells, not one cistern of water but many cisterns. For it did not say: "Drink waters from your own *cistern*," but "from your own cisterns." And it did not say: "and from the spring" of your well, but, "from the spring of your own wells." We read too that the patriarchs had wells; Abraham had one,[3] and Isaac had one.[4] I think that Jacob had one too.[5] Making a start with these wells, run through all Scripture, searching for wells, and come right through to the Gospels and there you will find the well on which our Savior "sat" and rested "after the toil of his journey," on the occasion when the woman of Samaria came and

---

[151]1 Cor 14:15. [152]Cf. 1 Tim 2:1. [153]Gal 1:5; cf. 1 Pet 4:11. **Homily 12** [1]Num 21:16. [2]Prov 5:15-16. [3]Cf. Gen 16:13-14; cf. Gen 21:25. [4]Cf. Gen 24:13-15, 42-46; 26:17-22. [5]Cf. Jn 4:6.

wished to draw waters from the well.[6] There the virtue of the well, or of the wells, in the Scripture is explained, and a comparison is made of the waters, where also the secrets of the divine mystery are revealed.

1.3. For it is said that "if anyone drinks of these waters," which that earthly well contained, "he will thirst again; but he who drinks of those [waters] that Jesus gives, in him there will be a fountain of water springing up unto eternal life."[7] Now in another passage in the Gospel there is mention no longer of a fountain or of a well, but of something more. It says: "He that believes in him, as the Scriptures says, out of his belly shall come forth rivers of living water."[8] So you see that he that believes in him has within himself not only a well, but even wells, and not only springs but even rivers; but springs and rivers which would not only refresh this mortal life but even give a life that is eternal.

Therefore, in accordance with the things written in Proverbs which we have set forth, wherever wells and a spring are mentioned together, we must believe that the Word of God is intended, a well, to be sure, if it covers some deep mystery, but a spring if it flows forth and abounds for the people.

1.4. Now it would not be pointless to ask how we can explain the plural number of the wells and the singular number used of the spring. For Wisdom says in the Proverbs: "Drink waters from the spring of your own wells."[9] So let us see what are the wells which he speaks of as having one spring. I think the knowledge of the unbegotten Father can be understood as one well, and the recognition of the only begotten Son should be understood as a second well. For the Son is different from the Father, and he that is the Father is not also the Son, as he says himself in the Gospels: "There is another who speaks testimony about me, the Father."[10] And again I think a third well can be seen in the knowledge of the Holy Spirit. For he too is different from the Father and from the Son, as it is said of him no less in the Gospels: "The Father shall send you another Paraclete, the Spirit of truth."[11] So there is this distinction of three persons in the Father and the Son and the Holy Spirit, which is recalled in the plural number of the wells. Yet of these wells there is one spring. For the substance and nature of the Trinity is one.[12] And in this way the distinction in holy Scripture which says, "From the spring of your wells," will be found not without meaning. But he has carefully expressed the mystical language, so that what was said in the plural of the persons would be in keeping with the substance in the singular.

1.5. But even those wells can apparently be considered concerning whose knowledge that man who was filled with the wisdom of God said: "For he granted to me from those things that are true knowledge, to know the substance of the world and the power of the elements; the beginning and end and middle of seasons; the alternation, variations and changes of seasons; the circuits of the year and the positions of the stars; the nature of living creatures and the tempers of wild beasts; the violence of winds and the thoughts of men; the diversities of plants and the virtues of roots."[13] Do you see how many wells there are in the knowledge of things? The knowledge of plants, for instance, is a well, and possibly the nature of each plant has a well of its own. There is a well too in the knowledge of living creatures, and possibly each

---

[6]Cf. Jn 4:6-26. [7]Cf. Jn 4:13-14. [8]Jn 7:38. [9]Prov 5:15. [10]Jn 8:18. [11]Jn 14:16-17. [12]This passage, with its apparently post-Nicene language of consubstantiality, may have been added by Rufinus. This exact language is found in the spurious *Dialogue of Adamantius on the Orthodox Faith*, a work translated into Latin by Rufinus, who believed that Origen was its true author. Cf. PG 11:1718, 1883. However, an original Origenian discussion of the three persons of the Trinity fits the context of the present passage, and the basic "trinitarian" orientation of Origen's theology, grounded in Mt 28:19, has been demonstrated by C. Kannengieser, "Divine Trinity and the Structure of *Peri Archon*," in *Origen of Alexandria: His World and His Legacy*, ed. C. Kannengiesser and W. L. Petersen (Notre Dame, Ind.: University of Notre Dame Press, 1988), pp. 231-49. [13]Wis 7:17-20.

species of living creature has its own well. Again there is a well in the reckoning of the seasons, in their alternation and change. Since every one of these contains knowledge, deep and profound, they are rightly called wells figuratively. And as long as the mystery of Christ was "hidden from the ages and the generations,"[14] the knowledge of these things was rightly called wells. But when, as Paul says, "God revealed" them to believers "through his Spirit,"[15] all these things become springs and rivers, so that the knowledge of them is not so much now contained in secret, but it is brought forth to many and it provides water to believers and satisfies them.

I believe that this is why the Savior said to his disciples that "he who believes in him" and drinks the water of his teaching, in him shall be no more a well or a spring, but "rivers of living water."[16] For just as the one well, which is the Word[17] of God, becomes wells and springs and countless rivers, so too the human soul, which is in the image of God,[18] can possess in itself and produce from itself wells and springs and rivers.

1.6. Still it is true that the wells that are in our soul require someone to dig them out. For they must be cleansed, and all that is earthly must be cleared away from them, so that those channels of rational thought, which God has implanted in the soul, may produce streams that are pure and undefiled. For as long as earth covers up the channels of the waters and clogs the outflow of the stream, the wave of pure water[19] cannot flow forth. This, after all, explains what is written, that "the servants of Abraham dug wells, and the Philistines filled them and covered them with earth."[20] Moreover, Isaac, who had received his father's inheritance, "dug the wells again" and removed the "Philistines' earth," which they "through jealousy"[21] had thrown into the waters. Moreover, we have observed the following in Genesis, from which

book it seems that this historical narrative is taken, that while Abraham was alive, the Philistines did not dare to fill up the wells or throw earth into them. But when he had departed from this life, then the Philistines grew strong and plotted against his wells. But a little later the wells are repaired by Isaac and return to their proper condition.

1.7. Besides this, when Isaac sets out to betroth or marry a wife, the servant of Abraham finds Rebecca, which translates as "patience,"[22] "at the wells."[23] She does not become the wife of Isaac anywhere else except "at the wells." In the same way when Jacob, in his turn, came to Mesopotamia, having received an order from his father not to take a wife of another race or of foreign blood, he finds Rachel also "at the wells."[24] And Moses finds Zipporah "at the wells."[25] So, if you have understood the significance and character of the wives of the saints, then you too, if you wish to win patience as your bride, or wisdom, or the other virtues of the soul, should say what is said about wisdom: "Her did I seek to make my wife."[26] Come often to those wells, be persistent, and there you will find a wife of this sort. For it is certain that by the "living waters,"[27] that is, by the streams of the living Word, all the virtues of the soul dwell.

1.8. So there are many wells which we have spoken of as within the soul. And there are many others, which are understood in particular passages and meanings of Scripture. Yet that well is more eminent and exceptional beyond others about which in the present passage the Scripture says that it was not just ordinary men who dug it, but the "rulers" and the others even more exalted, whom it termed "kings."[28] For this reason a hymn is sung to God "at this very well."[29] And for that reason it is written: "Go," he says, "to the well." This is the well of which

---

[14]Col 1:26. [15]1 Cor 2:10. [16]Jn 7:38. [17]Lat *sermo*. [18]Cf. Gen 9:6. [19]Lat *latex*. [20]Gen 26:15. [21]Cf. Gen 26:15. [22]This etymology is found in Philo *On the Preliminary Studies* 37 et passim. [23]Gen 24:10-16. [24]Cf. Gen 29:3-12. [25]Ex 2:15-21. [26]Wis 8:2. [27]Cf. Jn 4:10. [28]Cf. Num 21:18. [29]Cf. Num 21:17.

the Lord said to Moses: "Gather the people and I will give them water from the well, [says the Lord]."[30] Moses is commanded to gather the people, that they may assemble at the well and drink water. Now we have often shown that Moses should be understood as the law. So it is the law of God which summons you to come to the well. To what well, but that of which we have spoken above, Jesus Christ, the Son of God, existing in his very substance, yet with the Father and the Holy Spirit named as the one spring of Deity? To this well, then, that is, to the faith of Christ, the law summons us. For he says himself that "Moses wrote about me."[31] To what purpose does he summon us? That "we may drink waters and sing to him a song," that is, "that we may believe with the heart for justice, and confess with the mouth for salvation."[32]

2.1. It says: "Begin with it, [to sing of] the well."[33] Here is the meaning: Put the well, he says, as the beginning of all things, as the apostle also says, that he is "the beginning and firstborn of every creature and in him all things were created."[34] So, "Begin with it, the well," that is, confess that the well is the beginning of all things. Now it can also be understood in this manner, that the words seem to be addressed by the persona of Moses to the people, who is exhorting them and saying: "Make a start in your heart to begin to understand who the well is from whom spiritual waters are to be drawn and the faithful people are to be refreshed. So, "begin with it," that is, with Israel, this well, so that if there is anyone who sees God with his heart,[35] he can draw out the mystical meaning from the depths.

Therefore, the fact that it is Moses, that is, the law, who gathers us to that well does not seem to have been said pointlessly. For it can happen that someone seems to come to that well, but unless he is gathered by Moses, he is not received by God. Marcion seems to have come to that well by himself, also Basilides and Valentinus,[36] but because they did not come through Moses and they have not received the law and the prophets, they cannot praise the Lord God for the springs of Israel. So those who are like this do not come to the well which "rulers dug and kings hammered out."[37]

2.2. But do you want me to show you from the Scriptures to which wells they come? There is a certain "salt valley," in which valley there are wells of bitumen.[38] Thus every heresy and every sin is in the valley and in the salt valley. For sin and iniquity do not ascend upwards, but always descend to the lowest places below. So it is in the valley that every salty and bitter heretical interpretation and every sinful act has been placed—for what sweetness and pleasantness can sin have? Moreover the passage contains something more. For if you come to a heretical opinion, if you come to the bitterness of sin, you have come to the wells of bitumen. Bitumen is the fuel and nourishment of fire. So if you have tasted water from those wells, if you have consumed a heretical interpretation, if you have taken in the bitterness of sin, you will be preparing remedies of fire in yourself, even the fires of Gehenna. And for that reason it is said to those who are unwilling to drink water from this well, "which the rulers and kings dig,"[39] but who [prefer to drink] from those that are in the valley of sin and that feed the material of fire: "Advance in the light of your fire and of the flame that you have kindled for yourself."[40]

2.3. So what is sung at this well? It says: "Begin with him, the well, the rulers have dug it, the kings have hewn it." On the one hand, rulers and kings can seem to be identical; but if it is necessary to distinguish them, we should understand rulers as the prophets. For they

---

[30]Num 21:16. [31]Jn 5:46. [32]Rom 10:10. [33]Num 21:17. The LXX has *exarchete autō phrear.* The whole passage is difficult to translate literally. [34]Col 1:15-16. [35]Cf. Homily 11.4.3. [36]Valentinus was a Gnostic heretic of the second century who taught in Rome and denied that the free choice of the will plays any role in salvation. His doctrine was refuted by St. Irenaeus in *Against Heresies.* [37]Num 21:18. [38]Gen 14:10. [39]Num 21:18. [40]Is 50:11.

have established the prophetic meaning about Christ that was buried and submerged in the depths of the letter. And this is why one of them said: "Unless you hear in secret, your soul will weep."[41] And likewise another prophet says to the Lord: "How great is the abundance of your sweetness, O Lord, which you have hidden for those who fear you."[42] So these are the rulers who "dug" this well, but the kings are the ones who have "hewn it." Now this word "hewn" was taken from *excudo* [to dig out of rock], not from *excido* [to dig].[43] For something that is either cut or formed in stone is said to be hewn. Therefore, "rulers," as those who are a little inferior, are said to *dig* a well, that is, to dig down into the soft earth, as it were, to some depth. But those whom he calls "kings," since they are stronger and more eminent, not only penetrate into the depths of the earth, but into the hardness of rock. Thus they are able to reach the deeper waters and, if it can be said, they scrutinize the very veins of the abyss in it, knowing that "the judgments of God are a great abyss."[44]

2.4. Thus we shall fittingly identify these kings with the apostles, who are able to scrutinize such profound and hidden matters of the well. One of them said: "But God revealed it to us through his Holy Spirit. For the Spirit searches all things, even the deep things of God."[45] Therefore, since they too can scrutinize through the Spirit the deep things of God and can penetrate the deep and profound mysteries of the well, for this reason they are said to be kings, who have hewn that well even in rock and who have penetrated the hard and difficult secrets of knowledge. Now I think that the fact that apostles too can be called kings can be easily verified from what is said about all believers: "But you are a royal race, a great priesthood, a holy nation."[46] So if they call kings those who

have believed through their word, how much more should they themselves be deemed kings who create kings! Moreover, it is easily inferred from this: for if kings are named from ruling, assuredly everyone who rules the churches of God will fittingly be called kings, and much more correctly will those ones be called kings by whom the churches are ruled, since they rule them by their statements and writings. And, on this account, the Lord is deservedly called "King of kings";[47] for unless those and the others who imitate them also become kings, he will not seem to be "King of kings." Moreover the apostle Paul himself, when writing to the Corinthians and rebuking them by means of a bit of irony, says to them: "You are reigning without us, and would that you were reigning, so that we too might reign with you."[48] In that passage he declares, on the one hand, that the Corinthians assuredly ought to be kings, and that he himself wishes to reign with them; but he accuses them of being puffed up over an office that they have not yet deservedly received.

2.5. Therefore, all these "rulers dig that well and the kings of the nations hew it."[49] For the apostles are the "kings of the nations" par excellence, who have gathered the nations to the obedience of faith,[50] and have made known to all the knowledge of Christ, "in whom are hidden the treasures of wisdom and knowledge of God."[51] In accordance with the Lord's instruction, they went around the world fulfilling what was commanded, that they should "teach all nations, baptizing them in the name of the Father and of the Son and of the Holy Spirit."[52] And by this means they hewed, that is, they made known the knowledge of the well, and they made all the nations familiar with it.

Moreover, these matters that we now have in hand, which have been read aloud for us, are a well, together with all the Scripture of the law

---

[41]Jer 13:17. [42]Ps 31:19. [43]The LXX uses two verbs, *oryssō* for the rulers and *eklatomeō* for the kings, the first in the sense of digging and the second in the sense of digging in rock. [44]Ps 36:6. [45]1 Cor 2:10. [46]1 Pet 2:9. [47]Rev 19:16. [48]1 Cor 4:8. [49]Num 21:18. [50]Cf. Rom 1:5. [51]Col 2:3. [52]Mt 28:19-20.

and prophets. The Gospels too together with the apostolic writings are one well, which people are not able to dig into or hew into unless they are found to be kings and rulers. For they deserve to be considered true kings and true rulers who can remove the earth from this well and take away the surface of the letter and produce spiritual meanings like living water[53] from the inner "rock, where Christ is."[54] So it is befitting for those alone to do this who are either kings or rulers; they are called kings because they have driven out the rule of sin from their bodies[55] and have prepared a kingdom[56] for justice in their members.[57] For it is befitting that those who teach others be ones who have first done these things that they are teaching. For thus it is written: "He who has done and taught thus to men, he will be called great in the kingdom of heaven."[58] But to be "great in the kingdom" is to be a king.

It says: "Kings of the nations have hewn it in their kingdom, while they held dominion over them."[59] For in truth they cannot dig that well or open up the hidden deposits of living water unless they have first held dominion over the barbarian nations. For if they have overcome everything whatsoever that was iron within them in their actions, whatever was barbaric in their habits, and subjected it to the royal sense and have taken dominion over these things, so that henceforth they act not in pagan fashion but in accordance with law, they are truly kings who fathom the depths of the well and who scrutinize the secrets and mysteries of the Word of God.

3.1. After this it says: "And from the well they set out for Mattanah,[60] and from Mattanah to Nahaliel and from Nahaliel to Bamoth and from Bamoth to the grove which is in the field of Moab by the top of the mountain that is cut, which looks down on the face of the desert."[61] These names, which seem to be the designations of places, in the significations that they contain in their original language, seem to be pointing more to inferences concerning mysterious matters than to designations of names. For it says: "Having set out they come to Mattanah." For Mattanah translates as "their gifts." So you see that if someone drinks from this well, "which kings and rulers dug," immediately he sets out to this place, so that he may have gifts to offer to God. But what is it that a human being offers to God? It is namely what is written in the law: "My gifts, my presents."[62] Therefore, it is from these things that God has granted that human beings no less make offering to God. What has God given to humanity? The knowledge of himself.[63] What does the human being offer God? His faith and love.[64] This is what God seeks from a person. After all, it is written as follows: "And now, Israel, what does the Lord your God demand of you, but that you fear the Lord your God, and walk in his ways, and love him, and keep all his commandments, and serve the Lord your God with your whole heart and with your whole soul."[65] These are the gifts, these are the presents, which ought to be given to the Lord. But we give these gifts of our heart to the Lord after we have come to know him and have drunk from the depth of his well in the knowledge of his goodness.

3.2. Observe however how the prophet has said: "And now Israel, what does the Lord your God demand of you?"[66] These words are an embarrassment to those who deny that human free will plays a part in salvation.[67] For how could God make demands from humanity, unless man had something in his power that ought

---

[53]Cf. Jn 4:10-11. [54]1 Cor 10:4. [55]Cf. Rom 6:12. [56]Cf. Mt 25:34. [57]Cf. Rom 6:13, 16, 19. [58]Mt 5:19. [59]Num 21:18-20. [60]Rufinus: Mathanaim. [61]Num 21:18-20. [62]Num 28:2. [63]Cf. Wis 13:1-5; Rom 1:20-21. [64]Lat *affectus*. [65]Deut 10:12. [66]Deut 10:12. [67]Lit.: "deny that there is choice in man that he be saved." Certainly the Valentinians denied the free choice of the will in salvation. Many Fathers drew this inference for Marcion as well, since the Marcionites blamed the Creator God for subsequent human sin. See Tertullian *Against Marcion* 2.5-8; 4.41. See my discussion in Thomas P. Scheck, *Origen and the History of Justification* (Notre Dame: University of Notre Dame Press, 2008), pp. 23-29.

to be offered to God, who is demanding it? So then, there are things that are given by God, and there are things that are offered by man. For instance, there was in man that "one mina produced ten minas,"[68] or "one mina produced five minas";[69] but it depended on God that the man had the mina from which he could produce ten minas. But when he offered the ten minas that came from himself, he again received from God no longer money, but power and rule over ten cities.[70] Again, God asks Abraham to offer his own son Isaac to him "on whichever mountain he showed him."[71] Abraham, untroubled, "offered his only begotten,[72] placed him on the altar, and drew the knife to slay him."[73] He is immediately hindered and a ram is given to him as a victim in place of his son. So you see that what we offer to God remains with us, but in these things he makes demands of us in order that our love[74] for God may be tested and our faith may be proved. We have said these things in response to the passage: "The sons of Israel set out from the well and came to Mattanah,"[75] which translates "their gifts."

3.3. But "from Mattanah," we came to "Nahaliel,"[76] which translates as "from God." What is "from God"? After we ourselves have offered what is from us, we come to the point that we attain those things that are "from God." For when we have offered our faith and love[77] to him, then he himself bestows on us the various gifts of the Holy Spirit, of which the apostle says: "But all things are from God."[78]

And "from Nahaliel" we come to "Bamoth," which translates as: "coming of death." Which "coming of death" are we to understand here, if not that death by which we "die together" with Christ "so that we may also live together with him,"[79] and by which we ought "to mortify our members which are on the earth";[80] and again:

"for we have been buried with him by baptism into death"[81]? Thus if someone observes the sequence of this way of salvation, he should make a journey through each of these things we have mentioned, and after many things come to this place which we said means "coming of death." But as we are taught from the Scriptures, there is a death that is inimical to Christ, and another which is amicable to him. Thus he is not speaking [here] about that death that is hostile to Christ, of which it is said: "The last enemy will be destroyed, death, "[82] who[83] is the devil, but of that death by which "we die together with him so that we might also live together with him,"[84] in accordance with which death God says: "I will kill and I will make alive."[85] For he kills in order that we may die together with Christ, and he makes alive in order that we might deserve to be made alive with Christ.

3.4. "And from Bamoth," it says, "into the grove that is in the field of Moab, from the top of the mountain that is cut, which faces the desert."[86] If we undertake this journey, which a rational explanation has asserted consists not so much in the names of places, as in the soul's stages of progress, after all these things we come to a grove, or as it reads in other copies, "in Janen,"[87] which is translated "ascent" or "top of the mountain." So it is through these things that one reaches that very famous grove of the divine paradise and the pleasant delights of the ancient habitation, or, at least, the peak of perfection and the summit of blessedness,[88] so that you too can say: "He has raised us with him and has made us sit in heaven in Christ."[89] Do you see how far one has come from the well? Do you see by means of what stages,[90] or rather, by means of what progressions, the soul's journey is prepared for heaven? If you carefully look into these things, examining within yourself your

---

[68]Lk 19:16. [69]Lk 19:18. [70]Cf. Lk 19:16-18. [71]Gen 22:2. [72]Cf. Heb 11:17. [73]Gen 22:9-10. [74]Lat *affectus*. [75]Num 21:19. [76]Num 21:19. [77]Lat *affectus*. [78]1 Cor 8:6. [79]Cf. 2 Tim 2:11; 1 Thess 5:10. [80]Cf. Col 3:5. [81]Rom 6:4. [82]1 Cor 15:26. [83]Lat *qui* is masculine and refers to the devil *(diabolus)*, not to death *(mors)*, which is feminine and would require *quae*. Cf. *Commentary on Romans* 5.7.8 (1037). [84]Cf. 2 Tim 2:11; 1 Thess 5:10. [85]Deut 32:39. [86]Num 21:20. [87]Lat *Ianam*. [88]Cf. *Commentary on Song of Songs* 1.4; *Homilies on Genesis* 1.7. [89]Eph 2:6. [90]Lat *mansiones*. Cf. Jn 14:2.

own daily progress, you will know where you are and how near to the kingdom of heaven you are considered to be, just as the Lord himself said of someone: "You are not far from the kingdom of God."[91]

4.1. After this another narrative follows. For it says: "And Moses sent"—or as it reads in some copies "and Israel sent"—"ambassadors to Sihon[92] king of the Amorites with peaceable words saying: 'We will pass through your land, we will pass through the road, we will not turn aside to the field or to the vineyard. We will not drink water out of your cistern, we will go by the royal road, until we pass your boundaries. And Sihon did not allow Israel to pass through his borders; and Sihon gathered all his people, and he went out to wage war against Israel in the desert; and he went into Jahaz,[93] and he came together with Israel. And Israel struck him with the slaughter of the sword, and they became lords of his land."[94]

4.2. The history is clear, but let us ask the Lord to enable us to discern something worthy in the story's interior meanings. Sihon[95] translates in two ways, either as "unfruitful tree" or as "puffed up." Therefore, "Israel sends ambassadors to Sihon," he sends to the unfruitful tree, he sends to the puffed up and arrogant one. Now this Sihon is king of the Amorites. Their name translates as "leading to bitterness," or "speaking."[96] So then, "Moses sends to Sihon king of the Amorites with peaceable words, saying: 'We will pass through your land.'" If, according to the spiritual understanding, we say that Sihon the king contains a figure of the devil, since he was puffed up and unfruitful, I think that you should not be amazed that I call him a king, when you hear even our Lord and Savior himself speaking of him this way in the Gospels: "Behold now the ruler of this world is coming, and he will not find anything in me";[97] and again: "Behold now the ruler of this world

will be cast outside."[98] So, if he is said in the Gospels to be the "ruler of this world," it should not seem absurd if he is compared with Sihon king of the Amorites, or even with any other kings of nations.

4.3. Now he is called ruler of the world, not because he created the world, but because there are many sinners in this world. But because he himself is the ruler of sin, for that reason he is likewise called ruler of the world, namely, in those who have not yet abandoned the world by converting to the Father. For the following is likewise spoken in accordance with this, that "the whole world lies under the evil one."[99] For what good does it do us to say that Christ is our ruler, if we are convicted by the facts and by our deeds, that the devil holds lordship over us? Or is it not plain under what ruler the immodest, unchaste, and unjust person is living? Can a person of that sort say, "I am doing these things under Christ," even if he may seem to be registered under the name of Christ? In the person in whom Christ exercises lordship, no impurity and iniquity is committed, nor can unjust desire have any room. And so, in this manner Christ will rightly be called the ruler of the virtues, and the devil will be called the ruler of evil and of all iniquity.

4.4. Therefore, "Israel sends ambassadors to the king of the Amorites,"[100] to the king of those who provoke bitterness, the unfruitful king, the arrogant king. How will the devil be shown to be arrogant and puffed up? It is he who said: "I shall act by my power, and by the wisdom of my intellect will I remove the boundaries of the nations, and I will spoil their strength; and I will shake the cities which they inhabit, and I will seize with my hand the whole world like a nest."[101] And again, here the proud and arrogant one says: "I will ascend to heaven, I will put my throne above the stars of heaven, I will sit on the high mountain above

---

[91]Mk 12:34. [92]Lat *Seon*. [93]Lat *Assaar*. [94]Num 21:21-24. [95]Lat *Seon*. [96]Cf. Philo *Allegorical Interpretation* 3.232. [97]Jn 14:30. [98]Jn 12:31. [99]1 Jn 5:19. [100]Lat *Amorrhaei*; Num 21:21. [101]Is 10:13-14.

the tall mountains which are to the north, I will ascend beyond the clouds, and I will be like the Most High."[102] Are you still asking if he is puffed up and arrogant? Yes, and in fact there is this one who is arrogant and puffed up, and there is that one who is his only-begotten, as it were,[103] of whom it is written that "He will be lifted up beyond everything that is called God or that is worshiped, so that he sits in the temple of God showing himself as though he were God."[104] So everyone who is puffed up and arrogant is either a son of this puffed up one or his disciple and imitator. And for that reason the apostle says of someone: "Lest perchance, having become puffed up, he fall into the judgment of the devil."[105] Through this he shows that everyone who is puffed up will be condemned with a judgment similar to the devil's.

4.5. Thus, we are those who want to pass through this world so that we can come to the holy land which is promised to the saints. And we "send to Sihon with peaceable words," promising that we will not "dwell in his land" or "tarry with him," but we will only "pass through" and will "travel on the royal way and will never turn aside either to a field or vineyard, but we will not drink water from his cistern."[106] Well then, let us see when we made these promises, when we declared these words to the devil. Let every believer recall the time when he first came to the waters of baptism, when he received the first seals of the faith, and approached the font of salvation. What words did he use at that time and in that place? What did he declare to the devil? That he would not make use of his pomp or indulge in his works or submit in any way to any of his services and pleasures.[107] And this is what is

foreshadowed in these words of the law, that "Israel will not turn aside either to his field or to his vineyard,"[108] but he promises that he will not "drink from his cistern."[109] For the faithful will no longer take a drink from the devil's doctrine, from astrology, magic or from any teaching whatsoever that instructs anything contrary to piety toward God. For the believer has his own springs and he drinks from the springs of Israel, he drinks from the springs of salvation; he does not drink water from Sihon's cistern, nor does he "abandon the spring of living water"[110] and gather broken cisterns for himself. Moreover, he promises "to go on the royal way [via]."[111] What is the royal way? Doubtless it is the one that says: "I am the way [via] and the truth and the life."[112] And it is deservedly "royal"; for he is the one of whom the prophet says: "God, give your judgment to the king."[113] Therefore one must go along the royal way and never turn aside either to his field or to his vineyard. This means that the mind of the faithful must no longer turn aside to diabolical works or thoughts.

4.6. Now how is it that we want to pass through the borders of the Amorites[114] with peace? The Amorites can be understood as the party of unbelievers who are in this world; but as we said above, they translate as either "those leading to bitterness" or "those speaking." Now, on the one hand, the sense in which unfaithful and unbelieving people bring God to bitterness does not require an explanation; but his words, "those speaking" can be applied to that party, because infidels and those who live under the ruler of the devil know merely how to speak, but what they say is nonsense. For instance, their poets, astrologers and even many of their philosophers speak nonsensi-

---

[102]Is 14:13-14. [103]I.e., the antichrist. [104]2 Thess 2:4. [105]1 Tim 3:6. [106]Num 21:22. [107]This is an important text witnessing to the rites employed in ancient baptismal services (mid-third century). F. Ledegang, *Mysterium Ecclesiae: Images of the Church and Its Members in Origen*, BETL 156 (Leuven : Leuven University Press, 2001), p. 430 comments: "Origen probably keeps here close to the official formula, which was used at the *renuntiatio*. . . . In Rome it took place at the time with the words: *Renuntio tibi, Satana, et omni servitio tuo et omnibus operibus tuis* ['I renounce you, Satan, and all your service and all your works']"; cf. Hippolytus *The Apostolic Tradition* 21. [108]Num 21:22. [109]Num 21:22. [110]Jer 2:13. [111]Num 21:22. [112]Jn 14:6. [113]Ps 72:1. [114]Lat *Amorrhaei*.

cal and worthless things. But for the faithful, "the kingdom of God is not in words but in power."[115]

Therefore we want to pass through the world peaceably, but this very fact incites the ruler of the world[116] all the more, that we claim that we do not want to stay with him, nor linger, nor do we want to touch anything of his. For that reason he is frustrated all the more, for that reason he is lifted up and enraged and incites persecutions against us; he stirs up dangers, he is intent on torture. And this is why it says: "Sihon gathered all his people, and he went out to clash against Israel."[117] Who are "all the people" of Sihon whom he incites against Israel? The rulers and judges of the world and all the servants of wickedness who always fight against and persecute God's people.

4.7. But what does Israel do? It says: "She came to Issaar."[118] Issaar translates as "fulfillment of the command." So, if we come to that place, that is, to the accomplishment of the commandments, even if Sihon himself, that puffed up and arrogant devil, comes against us with his whole army and clashes against us, if he incites all his demons against us, we overcome him if we fulfill God's commands. For to fulfill the commandments, this is to overcome the devil and his whole army. And then the apostle's prayer will be fulfilled in us which says: "Our God will crush Satan under your feet swiftly";[119] and what the Lord says: "Behold I give to you power to trample on serpents and scorpions, and on all the power of the enemy, and nothing will harm you."[120] For none of those things will be able to harm us, if "we come to Issaar," that is, if we keep the commands and precepts of our Lord Jesus Christ, "to whom is the glory and power in the ages of ages. Amen."[121]

Homily 13
Numbers 21:24-35; 22:1-14

Concerning the things that were left over from the previous discussion, and concerning Balaam and his donkey.

1.1. Yesterday we spoke about how Sihon[1] king of the Amorites, who is a puffed up and unfruitful tree, engaged Israel and was defeated. Scripture says expressly of him that he fell "by the slaughter of the sword," or, as we read elsewhere, "by the mouth of the sword."[2] But if you want to know more precisely by what sword that unfruitful and puffed up one fell "like a cedar of Lebanon,"[3] let us learn it from the apostle Paul who says: "For the word[4] of God is living and efficacious and sharper than any sword."[5] And again in another place he says: "And the sword of the Spirit, which is the word[6] of God."[7] Thus the spiritual Sihon, who is the devil, fell "by the slaughter of this sword."

1.2. After this it is added: "And the sons of Israel," it says, "became lords over all his land." This entire earthly region is called the land of Sihon, but Christ and his church are lords over the whole land of Sihon. "And they became lords from the Arnon to the Jabbok."[8] Arnon and Jabbok were cities of the kingdom of Sihon. The beginning of his kingdom was Arnon and the end was Jabbok, and this is why it is said that "they became lords from Arnon to Jabbok." Now Arnon translates as: "their curses." Thus, curses mark the beginning of the kingdom of this puffed up and unfruitful Sihon. But the end is Jabbok, which translates as "struggle." For it is necessary that everyone who wants to come out of the kingdom of the devil and escape from his borders will encounter a struggle, and the devil's ministers and satellites will incite combats against him. But if one struggles and

---

[115]1 Cor 4:20. [116]Cf. Jn 14:30. [117]Num 21:23. [118]Num 21:23. RSV *Jahaz.* [119]Rom 16:20; cf. Gen 3:15. [120]Lk 10:19. [121]1 Pet 4:11.
Homily 13 [1]Lat *Seon.* [2]Num 21:24. The former reading is found in the LXX and Old Latin version; the latter is Jerome's reading. [3]Ps 37:35. [4]Lat *sermo.* [5]Heb 4:12. [6]Lat *verbum.* [7]Eph 6:17. [8]Num 21:24.

conquers, it will no longer be a Jabbok, the city of Sihon, but it will be a city of Israel. This, of course, is what we read about the patriarch Jacob as well, that when he had come to a certain place, a struggle was prepared for him and, having struggled there through the entire night, when he had held fast and grown stronger for God, his name was repeatedly called Israel.[9]

1.3. It says: "And Israel took all those cities; and Israel dwelled in all the cities of the Amorites."[10] This Israel, which is the Israel in Christ, and not the Israel in the flesh, nor the "Jew in appearance,"[11] itself dwells in all the cities of the Amorites. For the churches of Christ are spread throughout the whole world. Moreover, each of us was first a city of king Sihon, of the puffed up king; for folly was reigning in us, arrogance, impiety and everything that is on the devil's side. But when the strong man was attacked and defeated, and when his goods were "plundered,"[12] we became cities of Israel and an inheritance of saints, but only if that power, which was previously exercising dominion over us, is utterly cut off in us, and the unfruitful tree is cut down, and the puffed up king is cast down, and we are under that king who says: "Learn from me, for I am meek and humble in heart."[13]

1.4. After this it enumerates one by one the cities of the arrogant and unfruitful king and says: "In Heshbon[14] and in all its borders."[15] What is this that it has named as the chief city of the kingdom of Sihon: "Heshbon"? Heshbon translates as "thoughts." Deservedly then the greatest part of the devil's kingdom and most of his power reigns in the thoughts. For the Lord too has said this: "From the heart proceed evil thoughts, murders, adulteries, thefts, false testimonies, blasphemies; and these are what defile a man."[16] And this is the reason that city is necessarily burned and set on fire.[17] With which fire?

With that one, of course, of which the Savior speaks: "I have come to set fire to the earth, and how I wish that it were kindled."[18]

2.1. Now after a few things something is reported about that city. It says: "On this account the enigmatists[19] will say: Come to Heshbon, so that the city of Sihon may be built up and constructed; for a fire has gone forth from Heshbon, and a flame from the city of Sihon, and it has devoured up to Moab."[20] Sihon, as we have said, was a king whose city was Heshbon. So then, one must understand the order of the words, since these enigmatists say: "Come, so that Heshbon," which was Sihon's city, "may be built up and constructed."

But let us now ask who are these "enigmatists." Figurative speech is called an enigma; therefore, enigmatists refer to those who speak figuratively. And who else is there who have spoken in figures but "the law and the prophets"?[21] For listen to how David speaks: "I will open my mouth in parables, I will speak propositions[22] from the beginning."[23] Moreover, Isaiah, since the things he wrote are enigmas, declares in this fashion: "And the words of this book," he says, "will be like the words of a sealed book, which, if they put into the hands of an illiterate man and say to him: 'Read,' he will say: 'I cannot read.' But if they give it to one who can read, he will say: 'I am not able to read it, for it is sealed.'"[24] Now the book is said to be sealed because it is entangled with figures and wrapped in enigmas.

2.2. "Therefore these enigmatists say: Come to Heshbon so that it may be built up."[25] That first Heshbon has fallen, or rather, it has been overturned and burned; another must be rebuilt. But let us show how this happens by giving an example. If you see a pagan living a disgraceful life in religious error, you should not hesitate to say of him that here is the city

---

[9]Cf. Gen 32:24, 28. [10]Num 21:25. [11]Rom 2:28. [12]Mt 12:29. [13]Mt 11:29. [14]Lat *Esebon*. [15]Num 21:25. [16]Mk 7:21-23. [17]Cf. Num 21:28. [18]Lk 12:49. [19]RSV "ballad singers." Origen will explain the meaning of the LXX term below. [20]Num 21:27-28. [21]Cf. Mt 7:12. [22]The LXX has *problēmata*, "problems," which Rufinus has rendered with *propositiones*. [23]Ps 78:2; cf. Mt 13:35. [24]Is 29:11-12. [25]Num 21:27.

of Heshbon in the kingdom of king Sihon; for an unfruitful and puffed up king reigns in his thoughts. If Israel, that is, a son of the church, approaches this pagan, and utilizes the javelins of the word of God and draws the sword of the Spirit[26] against him, if he destroys in him all the fortifications of pagan dogmas and burns the pretensions of his arguments with the fire of truth,[27] in this one, I say again, that city of Heshbon that belongs to Sihon has been overthrown. But he is not necessarily abandoned and left destitute, this man in whom the dogmas of the pagans have been overturned. For it is not the practice for the sons of Israel to leave in ruin the cities they have destroyed. But when they have undermined and overthrown evil thoughts and impious sentiments in a man, they rebuild again in the heart of the one they have destroyed. They will implant good thoughts, pious feelings and the teaching of the truth. They will hand down the rites of religion, they will teach the manner[28] of living, they will admonish upright morals and the established observances.

2.3. And then those enigmatists will truly say to themselves: Come and let us build up Heshbon, which was the city of Sihon. For these, that is, the sons of the church, since they understand the figures and enigmas of the law spiritually, are called enigmatists.[29] This is what Jeremiah also indicates in speech that is no less figurative, when the Lord says to him: "Behold I have put my words into your mouth; behold I have appointed you today over nations and kingdoms to uproot and overturn and rebuild and replant."[30] What does he uproot and what does he overturn? The city of Heshbon, which was Sihon's city. What does he uproot in it and what does he overturn? Impious and impure thoughts. What does he rebuild in it and what does he replant? Pious and chaste thoughts, that it might become a city of Heshbon, not of

the Amorites, but of the sons of Israel.[31]

3.1. But if we want to pursue the details, we will be prevented from discussing those things that have been read aloud to us concerning Balaam. The reading that concerns him is so difficult that we can hardly arrive at a coherent explanation of the historical account. So how great will the difficulty be for us, if the very first glance at the letter is entangled in such great difficulties? But although we are seized with a desire to discuss things that are more obscure, nevertheless the things that are likewise reported in the middle should not be completely omitted.

For after the sons of Israel had gained possession of the cities of the Amorites, they also "ascended the road that leads to Bashan,"[32] where "Og king of Bashan" was.[33] But they do not deem it fitting to send ambassadors to him or to request of him passage through his land,[34] but they immediately clash with him and they conquer both "him and his people."[35]

3.2. Let us see, then, what "Bashan" refers to. Bashan translates as "moral turpitude." Deservingly, then, they do not send ambassadors to this nation or demand passage through his land.[36] For there should be no passage, no access, for us into moral turpitude, but from the start we must immediately fight against it and beware of it in every way. Now Og, who is said to be the king of Bashan, means "obstacle." He can represent a figure of all fleshly and material things, by the love and desire for which the soul that is detained in these things is excluded and separated from God. Thus a command is given to wage such a war against these things that it says "you should leave nothing in it alive."[37] For it is necessary that the sons of Israel leave nothing alive in the kingdom of moral turpitude and disgrace. But it befits Israelite power[38] to cut down and cut off morally base things and to re-

---

[26]Cf. Eph 6:16-17. [27]Cf. 2 Cor 10:5. [28]Lat ordo. [29]Cf. Homilies on Leviticus 7.5. [30]Jer 1:10. [31]Cf. Homilies on Jeremiah 1.15-16. [32]Lat Basan. [33]Cf. Num 21:33. [34]Cf. Num 21:21-22. [35]Num 21:35. [36]Cf. Num 21:21-22. [37]Num 21:35. [38]Or "virtue." Lat virtus. The word can also refer to (armed) forces.

build in the soul everything pious and to plant in it religious and morally upright things.

3.3. Of neither the kingdom of Sihon nor of the kingdom of Moab is it written that no one is to be left alive; for perhaps we have some need of them and we require some of them for the struggles and training of this life; "otherwise we would have to leave this world."[39] Yet from Bashan, that is, from moral turpitude, we require absolutely nothing, and we should leave nothing [alive] in it; everything must be cut down, all the works of moral turpitude must be overthrown. For what is morally base cannot be an honorable thing in anyone.

4.1. "And having set out from there, the sons of Israel camped to the west of Moab by the Jordan opposite Jericho. And when Balak son of Zippor[40] looked,"[41] and the rest. Already the entire historical narrative that is written about Balaam and his donkey is full of difficulties; but the interior meaning is much more difficult, and I do not know if it will be easy to explain even the bare historical statements. Yet, as God grants, let us touch briefly on what we are capable of understanding.

4.2. War is threatening you, O king Balak, son of Zippor; "six hundred thousand" armed troops are invading your borders.[42] You had to prepare arms, muster the army, give thought to battle formation, so that "while the enemy is still a long way off,"[43] you may meet him equipped with weapons. But you "send to Balaam,"[44] a divine, and you send many gifts and promise even greater ones, and you say: "Come, curse for me the people who have come forth from Egypt."[45] But Balaam, as the Scripture teaches, referred these things to God, by whom he is hindered from going. But the king sends ambassadors again and, disregarding his arms, sets all his hope in Balaam, that he might come and bring down words and hurl curses instead

of javelins at the people, in the hope that the people, whom the king's army was unable to overcome, could be conquered by the words of Balaam.[46]

What logical coherence does this historical narrative have? What sort of plan is he showing? Where or when has it been heard that a king, who is threatened by war, forgets about his arms, disregards his army, and takes flight in the words of some divine or soothsayer? This is why, again and again, we need to implore the grace of God, so that we may be able to explain these things, not by means of "fables and Judaic stories"[47] but by reasonable interpretations that are worthy of the divine law.

4.3. First of all, then, one should confess that in certain cases words have more power and efficaciousness than persons,[48] since what an army of many nations seeks to bring about, what it was unable to obtain by sword and arms, is brought into effect by words; and I do not say by holy words or by the words of God, but by certain words, which are formulated among people; words that somehow I do not know how to name. Yet they are composed by a futile art, for this art has the freedom to name things the way it wants to. So there is, as I have said, a human effect that comes about by means of words. Yet it is the kind of effect that cannot be fulfilled except by means of the great strength of a person.[49]

4.4. For instance, there were enchanters and magicians[50] in Egypt. Who among men can transform a branch into a serpent by physical strength,[51] which is what it is reported that they did? Or who can change water into blood by physical strength? Yet the enchanters and magicians of the Egyptians did this.[52] For Moses had done these things first.[53] But because the king of Egypt knew that these things could be done by a certain craft of words, which is formulated

---

[39]Cf. 1 Cor 5:10. [40]Lat *Balach, filius Sephor.* [41]Num 22:1-2. [42]Cf. Num 26:51. [43]Cf. Lk 14:32. [44]Cf. Num 22:5. [45]Num 22:6. [46]Cf. Num 22:8, 12, 15. [47]Cf. Tit 1:14. [48]Lit. "bodies." [49]Lit. "body." [50]Lat *magi.* [51]Lit. "strength of body." [52]Ex 7:11, 22. [53]Cf. Ex 7:10, 20.

among men, he thought that even Moses had done these things not by the power of God, but by magic art, and, since the king had done it by a human craft, he could feign the thing that had been done by the power of God. Immediately [Pharaoh] "summons the enchanters and magicians of the Egyptians."[54] He causes there to be a contest between the one who worked by the power of God and those who invoked demons. Yet "in a similar way" the contrary power makes the branch into a serpent, just as the power of God had done; but the serpent that was made through the power of God "swallowed" and devoured all those serpents that had been turned into serpents from branches by magic art.[55] For the demonic power was not able to restore back to the good the evil that it had made from the good. It was able to make a serpent from a branch, but it was not able to render a branch from a serpent; and for that reason they are all consumed by that branch that had been turned into a serpent by the power of God. But later through divine power [the branch] is restored to its own nature, that it might acknowledge the Lord of nature.

4.5. "The enchanters of the Egyptians caused" water to be turned into blood, but they were not able to turn the blood back into water.[56] But God's power turns not water but the whole river into blood,[57] and again, when Moses prayed, he rendered it back into its clear and natural flow. And once again the magicians of the Egyptians produced gnats, but they were not able to repel them;[58] but Moses both produced gnats and restored things; for our God causes grief and restores again; but the hostile power can indeed cause something bad, but he cannot restore it again whole.

4.6. We have said all these things as a preface, so that we can turn attention to the works of Balaam, or his words. For there are some differences among magicians. For some

have more strength, and some have less. This Balaam was very famous in the magic art, and was very powerful in effecting harmful incantations. For he did not have the power or craft of words for the purpose of blessing, but he had it for cursing; for demons are invited to curse, not to bless. And for that reason, he was, so to speak, an expert in such things in the opinion of all who were in the East. For unless a good number of his attempts had preceded, which had repeatedly turned aside an armed enemy by means of curses, assuredly this king would not have presumed that what was scarcely capable of being accomplished by sword and battle line could be fulfilled by words. So Balak, certain of this and having experienced it on multiple occasions, leaves aside all the instruments and helps of war, and sends ambassadors to him saying: "Behold a people[59] has come forth from Egypt and covers the face of the land; and it has settled near me."[60]

4.7. Moreover, I think there is something else that incited the king; for he seems to have heard that the sons of Israel are accustomed to defeat their enemies by prayer, not by arms, not so much by the sword as by prayers. For Israel raised no arms against Pharaoh, but it was said to Israel: "The Lord will fight for you, and you will be silent."[61] But not even against the Amalekites was it so much the force of arms as the prayer of Moses that prevailed. For "when Moses raised his hands" to God, Amalek was conquered; but when his arms relaxed and lowered, this caused Israel to be conquered.[62] Balak king of Moab had actually heard about these things. For it is written: "The nations heard and were enraged; pains seized hold of those dwelling among the Philistines. Then the leaders of Edom and the rulers of the Moabites were anxious;[63] trembling took hold of them."[64] You see that what Moses had predicted in the Canticle[65] when they crossed the Red Sea had

---

[54]Ex 7:11. [55]Cf. Ex 7:12. [56]Cf. Ex 7:22. [57]Cf. Ex 7:21. [58]Cf. Ex 8:18. [59]The SC text reads *populis*. Presumably this is a misprint of *populus*. [60]Num 22:5. [61]Ex 14:14. [62]Cf. Ex 17:11. [63]Lit. "hastened." [64]Ex 15:14-15. [65]He means the song of Ex 15.

come on them. So the king of Moab had heard that this people conquers by means of prayers, and fights against its enemies with its mouth, not its sword. And doubtless it was for this reason that he thought to himself and said: "Since indeed no arms can match the prayers and supplications of this people, for this reason I must seek such supplications and such weapons that consist in words and such prayers, which would be able to overcome their prayers."

5.1. But that you might know that the king had been thinking in this way, understand from the words of Scripture that have been set forth, which I learned from a certain teacher who had become a believer from the Hebrews.[66] Thus it is written: "And Moab said to the elders of Midian.[67] Now this assembly[68] will lick up all that are round about us, as a calf will lick up the grass of the field."[69] Well, that Jewish convert[70] used to say: Why has he made use of such an example, saying, "as a calf will lick up the grass of the field"? Doubtless for this reason: with its mouth a calf tears up grass from the field, and with its tongue as a sickle, as it were, it cuts whatever it finds. In the same way this people fights with its mouth and lips like the calf, and has weapons in its words and prayers. So the king, aware of this, sends to Balaam, that he himself might bring down words against their words and prayers against their prayers.

5.2. You should not be astonished if such a thing exists in the magical art; for even Scripture makes clear that this craft exists, but it forbids its use.[71] Indeed Scripture also makes clear that demons exist, but it opposes their being worshiped and prayed to.[72] Rightly, then, it forbids the use of magic too, since the ministers of magic are renegade angels and evil spirits and unclean demons; for none of the holy spirits obey a magician. A magician cannot invoke

Michael, Raphael or Gabriel;[73] how much more can a magician not invoke the Almighty God, or his Son Jesus Christ our Lord or his Holy Spirit.[74] We alone have received authority for invoking his Only Begotten Jesus Christ. But I insist on the following: he who has now received authority to invoke Christ, cannot again invoke demons, and he who has become a sharer of the Holy Spirit[75] should no longer summon the unclean spirits. For if he invokes unclean spirits, the Holy Spirit flees from him.

5.3. There are magicians who invoke Beelzebul. After all, that people knew this, and for that reason, they were lying against my Lord Jesus and were saying false things when they said: "This man expels demons by Beelzebul the ruler of demons."[76] But the Savior, knowing that it is indeed true that there is a certain ruler of the demons, Beelzebul, does not accuse them of lying in this, but he answers them: "If I expel demons by Beelzebul, by whom do your sons expel them?"[77] Thus it is established that some demons are evil. When they are invoked by magicians, they are present to them for evil, not for good; for they are prepared to do evil, but they do not know how to do good. And so it is those demons who had yielded to Balaam in a pact of friendship, so to speak, by a certain craft and by the composition of words. Relying on their friendship, he appeared to be great among men.

So it is on this account that the king sends to him and says: "Come now and curse this people for me, for they are stronger than we are; perhaps we can strike some of them and expel them from the land."[78] It seems to me that this king does not have complete confidence in the divine Balaam. He has been terrified, I believe, by the widespread reports of the miracles which had been done for God's people. And this is why he says: "if perhaps," or that the curses of Balaam

---

[66]Origen had known and been profoundly influenced by a Palestinian Jewish convert to Christianity in Alexandria, a son of a rabbi, who was capable of answering questions about the Hebrew Bible. Cf. Pierre Nautin, *Origène: Sa vie et son œuvre* (Paris: Beauchesne, 1977), p. 417. [67]Lat *Madian*. [68]Lat *synagoga*. [69]Num 22:4. [70]Lit. "that teacher who had believed from the Hebrews." [71]Cf. Ezek 13:20; Rev 21:8; 22:15. [72]Cf. Lk 11:19. [73]Cf. Dan 10:13; Tob 12:15; Lk 1:26. [74]Notice the trinitarian language. [75]Cf. Heb 6:4. [76]Lk 11:15; Mt 9:34; Mk 3:22. [77]Lk 11:19. [78]Num 22:6.

should prevail to such an extent that he can strike *some* of them, but for the others, [they would prevail] to put them to flight in terror and expel them from his land.[79]

6.1. Moreover, he adds: "For I know," he says, "that those whom you bless will be blessed, and those whom you curse will be cursed."[80] I do not believe that the king knew that whomever Balaam had blessed would be blessed; but it seems to me that he said this as flattery. Thus by celebrating and extolling his craft, Balaam might the more readily return with him for the deed. For magic art does not know how to bless, since demons do not know how to do good. Isaac and Jacob know how to bless,[81] as do all the saints; none of the impious know how to bless.

6.2. But finally the ambassadors come to Balaam. For it says: "The elders of Moab and the elders of Midian went and the objects used for divination [were] in their hands."[82] In these arts of divination, which human curiosity has crafted, there are certain things that Scripture has indeed named "objects of divination," but pagan usage speaks of them either as tripods or caldrons or by other terms of this sort. These things have been consecrated for this purpose, as it were, and they are accustomed to be moved and handled by them. The Scripture, plainly divine, names a certain "ephod" in common speech in the prophets, which tradition reports is the garment of those who prophesy. But in the divine Scriptures, prophecy is considered one thing, divination something else; for it says: "There shall not be augury in Jacob, nor divination in Israel. In time it will be told to Jacob and Israel what God will do."[83] So divination is absolutely repudiated; for as we already said above, it is carried out by the action and service of demons.

6.3. So then, Balaam took along the objects used for divination. Since demons were accustomed to come to him, he indeed sees the fugitive demons, but God is present. This is why he claims that God is questioning him,[84] since he no where sees the usual demons obeying him. So God himself "goes to Balaam,"—not that Balaam was worthy for God to come to him, but that they might be put to flight who had been accustomed to be present with him for cursing and doing evil; for from here God was already looking out for his people—therefore God is present and "says to him: Why have these men come to you? And Balaam said to God: Balak son of Zippor,[85] king of Moab, sent them to me, saying: Behold a people has come forth from Egypt and has covered the face of the land, and they settle near me; Go, then, now and curse them for me, if perhaps we shall be able to strike them and cast them out. And God said to Balaam: Do not go with them, do not curse the people; for they are blessed."[86]

7.1. A loftier question arises here, and I do not know whether it is fitting to expose the subject of such a profound mystery and to set it forth to the crowds, and to these crowds that only come to the auditorium of the word of God for a few days and then immediately depart and do not stay longer to meditate on the word of God; nevertheless, for the sake of those who are zealous to learn and who thirst to hear and are able to take in the spiritual meaning, we will say a few things of the many that could be said.[87]

Well then, an objection of the following sort can be raised. Granted that Balaam invokes demons, that he curses the people, that the invoked demons do what they can. Is God unable to defend the people from demons and destroy their power to do evil? Then why was it necessary that he himself go to Balaam and prevent the customary demons from approaching, lest they either tempt his people or try

---

[79]Cf. Num 22:6. [80]Num 22:6. [81]Cf. Gen 27:4; 48:9. [82]Num 22:7. [83]Num 23:23. [84]Cf. Num 22:8. [85]Lat *Balach filius Sephor*.
[86]Num 22:9-12. [87]For Origen's regular criticism of the lack of interest in the preaching that he finds in the members of the church, see *Homilies on Genesis* 10.1; 11.3; *Homilies on Exodus* 12.2; 13.3; *Homilies on Leviticus* 3.7; *Homilies on Joshua* 1.7.

willingly to injure them?

7.2. In response to this, then, although not all that can occur to us should be set forth, yet we will speak "in part"[88] and say that God does not want to condemn the race of demons "before the time."[89] For the demons themselves know that their time is limited to this present age. For this reason, after all, they asked the Lord not to "torment them before the time,"[90] nor to "send them into the abyss."[91] And the reason he has not deprived the devil of his dominion over this world is because there is still need of his works for the battle-training and victories of the blessed. So then, he does not want to violently drag away the remaining demons as well from the intention of his purpose "before the time"; and, therefore, from the start he did not allow them to be invoked by Balaam, lest perhaps those invoked would be destroyed "before the time" and would perish, while God was defending his people.

For it is one thing for a demon to wait on God to provide it with someone whom it can put to the test, such as Job. There are certain limitations when it receives God's authority to do this. God says to it, for instance: "I put under your authority all his things, but you shall not touch the man himself,"[92] or again: "I put him under your authority, but preserve his life."[93] But it is a different matter for demons to wreak havoc without any control, when a magician demands this and compels them by means of certain spells. Assuredly, if freedom of choice were preserved for them in this matter, they would hand the people of God over to destruction; but if freedom of choice is removed [from the demon], this would mean that the rational creature has been condemned and received judgment "before the time."[94] In that case all who could have been crowned in the contest by struggling against them will

have been thwarted. For if freedom of choice is removed from the demons, no athlete of Christ will fight any longer; and with no one fighting, there will be no combat, and when combat has been removed, there will be no reward, no victory.

7.3. For that reason, then, God uses such a way that even the people who are still raw recruits and who had recently begun to be drawn away from the worship of demons are not handed over to demons, and responses are brought to the invoking magician, and the race of demons is not stripped of its capacity of choice. And therefore God anticipates and prevents Balaam from going and the demons from cursing, if he would only cease from the desire. But because he persists in the desire for money, God indulges his freedom of choice and again permits him to go, but he puts his own word into his mouth, preventing the curse from coming into effect by the demons,[95] so as to give opportunity for blessings. And instead of curses he makes Balaam bring forth blessings and prophecies, which can edify not only Israel but also the other nations.

7.4. For if Balaam's prophecies were introduced by Moses into the sacred books, how much more were they copied by those who were living at that time in Mesopotamia, among whom Balaam had a great reputation and who are known to have been disciples of his art? After all, it is reported that from him a race and institution of magicians flourished in parts of the East, which possessed copies among themselves of everything that Balaam had prophesied. They even possessed the following writing: "A star will rise out of Jacob, and a man will spring from Israel."[96] The Magi had these writings among themselves, and that is why, when Jesus was born, they recognized the star and they understood, more than the people of Israel,

---

[88]Cf. 1 Cor 13:12. [89]Cf. Mt 8:29. [90]Cf. Mt 8:29. [91]Cf. Lk 8:31. [92]Job 1:12. [93]Job 2:6. [94]Cf. Mt 8:29. [95]Cf. Num 23:5. [96]Cf. Num 24:17; Mt 2:2. Origen's source for the conjectural link between Balaam and the Magi may be Philo *On the Life of Moses* 1.50.276-277. Philo identifies Balaam as a *magos* and says he was filled with an authentic prophetic spirit. This is close to Matthew's depiction. Moreover Dan 1:20; 2:2; 4:7; 5:7 refers to *magoi* in the Babylonian Empire.

who despised hearing the words of the holy prophets, that the prophecy was being fulfilled. Therefore, based only on these writings that Balaam had left behind, when they knew that the time was near, they came looking for him,[97] and immediately worshiped him.[98] And to declare the greatness of their faith, they venerated the small child as a king.[99]

8.1. But let us return to our theme. Balaam is annoying to God, and he to whom God had already come practically extorts from him permission to go curse the sons of Israel and to invoke demons. "He mounts his donkey,"[100] and the angel who watches over Israel meets him. Of this angel it is written in the Lord's words addressed to Moses: "My angel will go with you."[101] So, to the one pressing on, it is granted for him to go. He is crushed on the way by the donkey. But the magician sees demons; he does not see the angel. Yet "the donkey does see."[102] Not that a donkey was worthy to see an angel, since it was not worthy, but that Balaam might silenced and, as it says somewhere in the Scripture: "a dumb animal responding with a human voice rebuked the madness of the prophet."[103]

8.2. But since many things have already been said about the historical narrative, we should briefly mention in conclusion a few things concerning the allegory. If you should see a contrary power fighting against the people of God, you will understand who it is who sits on the donkey; and if you consider how people are instructed by demons, you will understand who the donkey is. For thus also in the Gospel, you will understand Jesus sending his disciples to "a donkey which was bound and to its colt," as the disciples loose it and lead it away, that he himself "sits on it."[104] And perhaps this donkey, that is, the church, previously carried Balaam, but now Christ, because it has been loosed by

the disciples and it has been released from the chains by which it had been fastened. Thus the Son of God "sits on it" and with it enters into the holy "heavenly city of Jerusalem."[105] And thus the Scripture is fulfilled which says: "Rejoice, daughter of Zion; proclaim, daughter of Jerusalem; behold your king comes to you, meek and sitting on a beast of burden."[106] Doubtless he is calling those who believe from the Jews a "beast of burden," that is, the donkey; and in fact he calls the "new colt" those from the Gentiles "who believe"[107] in Christ Jesus our Lord, "to whom is the glory and power in the ages of ages. Amen."[108]

Homily 14
Numbers 22:15-28

More about Balaam.

1.1. There are more things that remain for us to explain from the reading about Balaam and his donkey. But because the sermon[1] that is being given in the church for the sake of edification is of limited duration, there was not enough time for us to set forth in detail the words of Scripture, so that nothing at all would remain unconsidered, and to present an explanation of each detail. For indeed the latter method would be more in the style of a commentary.[2] Therefore, we return again to the things that seem worthy of investigation. By discoursing on these things by means of whatever interpretation we are capable of giving, we will attempt to set forth this material publicly and discuss it.

1.2. Now in the explanation of the historical narrative itself, it is still difficult to understand how God is said to have "come to Balaam" the first time during the night and to have asked him "who the men were who had come to him,"

---

[97]Cf. Mt 2:8. [98]Cf. Mt 2:2, 11. [99]Cf. Mt 2:2, 11. [100]Num 22:22. [101]Ex 32:34. [102]Num 22:23. [103]2 Pet 2:16. [104]Cf. Mt 21:2-7. [105]Cf. Heb 12:22. [106]Zech 9:9. [107]Acts 21:25. [108]1 Pet 4:11. **Homily 14** [1]Lat *tractatus*. [2]Notice the distinction made by Origen himself between the less detailed "sermon" (*tractatus*) and the more thorough "commentary" (*commentarii*). Rufinus's aim in the present translation is to present Origen's "sermons" more in the form of "commentaries" by drawing on Origen's other exegetical writings. See Rufinus's Preface.

and he replied that "they were sent from Balak," son of Zippor, who had said, "Come, and curse the people for me."[3] And God responded to him: "You will not go with them, nor will you curse the people; for they are blessed."[4] Again a second time it is said: "God came to him at night and said" that he should go with them, but God took care that whatever word he put into his mouth, this is what he should speak.[5] And again a third time, it is said that an angel met him while he was going, to whom his way seemed so ill-chosen and inappropriate that it even wanted to kill him, except that when the "donkey saw the angel," whom Balaam was unable to see, "it turned away."[6] And yet, after [Balaam] is blamed by the angel for why he should have wanted to go, he is again permitted by the same angel to go. Only he is to "take care" of the word that God should put into his mouth, so that this only should proceed and nothing more.[7] Well, all these matters are difficult to explain; yet we will offer you some opportunities of understanding[8] a few of them, as we already said above, in order that you too may do what it written: "Let the wise man become wiser by the things that are heard";[9] and "Give opportunity to the wise man, and he will be wiser."[10]

1.3. But before we come to the point, we should not indeed omit mentioning what those have noticed who look into this passage with more curiosity. In the literature of the Hebrews, the name of God, that is, God, or Lord, is said to be written in different ways. For anything that is called a god is written one way, and the God himself, of whom it is said: "Hear [O] Israel, the Lord your God is one God,"[11] is written another way. Thus that God of Israel, the one God and Creator of all things,[12] is written with a certain determinate symbol comprised of letters, which they call the "tetragrammaton."

So whenever God is written in the Scriptures by this symbol, there is no doubt that the referent is the true God and Creator of the world. But whenever it is written in other letters, that is, common ones, it is considered uncertain whether the referent is the true God or one of those gods of whom the apostle says: "For even if there are those who are called gods, whether in heaven or on earth, just as there are many gods and many lords, yet to us there is one God the Father, from whom are all things, and we through him."[13] Thus, those who read Hebrew literature say that in this passage God is not recorded by the symbol of the tetragrammaton. Let this matter be investigated by one who is able.

1.4. Moreover, with regard to what "God" said to Balaam, as though he were questioning him about the identity of these men, it is asked why he seems to be ignorant.[14] And again, the question is raised about what he says: "Do not curse the people; for they are blessed,"[15] if this can be understood thus, as if he had said: "Do not curse *my* people."

2.1. In the meantime we ourselves say that by a certain dispensation and by the wisdom of God, things in this world are arranged in such a way that absolutely nothing escapes God's purposes, whether it is evil or good. But let us explain what we are saying more clearly. God did not make evil; yet, though he was able to prohibit its being invented by others,[16] he does not prohibit it, but he uses it for necessary causes with those very ones who are its source. For through those in whom there is evil, it makes those who strive for the glory of the virtues manifest and approved. For if evil were to be destroyed, there would assuredly be nothing to oppose the virtues. Virtue, having nothing opposed to it, would not clearly stand out, nor would it become more brilliant and more tested.

---

[3]Num 22:9-11. [4]Num 22:12. [5]Num 22:20, 35. [6]Cf. Num 22:23-30. [7]Num 22:35. [8]Cf. *On First Principles* 2.6.2; 4.2.2; *Commentary on John* 32.22 (14) 291; *Commentary on Matthew* 14.22. [9]Prov 1:5. [10]Prov 9:9. [11]Deut 6:4. [12]Cf. 2 Macc 13:14. [13]1 Cor 8:5-6. [14]Cf. Num 22:9. [15]Num 22:12. [16]Cf. Ezek 28:15.

But an untested and unexamined virtue is no virtue at all. Now if we have said these things without proofs from the divine words, they will seem to have been composed more by a carefully considered human craft than by incontestable truth. So let us investigate whether the divine books contain thoughts of this sort as well.

2.2. Let us consider Joseph. Take away the evil of his brothers, take away their jealousy, take away all the parricidal lying by means of which they vented their rage against their brother, to the point of selling him into slavery;[17] if you remove all this, look at how much of God's plan you would simultaneously eliminate. For you would be simultaneously cutting off everything that happened in Egypt through Joseph for the salvation of all.[18] There would have been no interpretation of the Pharaoh's dream, if Joseph, through his brothers' envy, had not been forcibly separated and had not gone to Egypt.[19] No one would have understood what God had revealed to the king, no one would have stored up grain in Egypt, no one would have cared about the critical situation of the famine by means of prudent foresight.[20] Egypt would have perished and also the neighboring regions would have perished in the famine. Even Israel himself would have died, and his seed would not have gone to Egypt in search of bread.[21] Then the sons of Israel would not have left Egypt accompanied by the wondrous deeds of the Lord.[22] There would have been no plagues on the Egyptians, nor those miraculous powers which God did through Moses and Aaron.[23] No one would have walked through the Red Sea with dry tracks.[24] Mortal life would not have come to know the nourishment of the manna;[25] no flowing water would have gushed forth from the "rock that was following."[26] The law would not have been given to human beings by God; the things that

are reported in Exodus, Leviticus, Numbers and Deuteronomy would not have come to the knowledge of the human race. And, of course, no one would have entered into the inheritance of the fathers and into the Promised Land.

2.3. And that we might come to the matters at hand, take away the evil of this wretched king Balak by means of which he invites Balaam to curse the people,[27] and you will equally remove God's plan for the sons of Israel and the favor of his providence. There will never be those prophecies which are prophesied through the mouth of Balaam to both the sons of Israel and to the nations.

2.4. But if you desire to see this confirmed by means of proofs from the New Testament, if you take away the evil of Judas and eliminate his betrayal, you will at the same time take away the cross of Christ and his suffering; and if there is no cross, there is no "disarming of the principalities and powers," or "triumphing in the wood of the cross."[28] If there had been no death of Christ, assuredly neither would there have been a resurrection, nor would anyone have stood forth as "the firstborn from the dead."[29] But if there had been no "firstborn from the dead," there would be no hope of resurrection for us.[30]

2.5. We should suppose the same thing with regard to the devil himself. If, for instance, he had been prevented from sinning by some sort of compulsion, or if his will for evil had been taken away from him after his sin, this would have simultaneously removed our battle against the trickery of the devil. There would then be no hope of a crown of victory for the one who has fought for it according to the rules.[31] If we did not have opposition, there would be no struggles nor would rewards be doled out to victors, nor would the kingdom of heaven be prepared for those who conquer,[32] nor would

---

[17]Cf. Gen 37:18-36. [18]Cf. Gen 41:25-57. [19]Cf. Gen 37:28. [20]Cf. Gen 41:47-49. [21]Gen 42:1-5. [22]Ex 6:10, 13-27. [23]Cf. Ex 7–11. [24]Ex 14:16, 22 1 Cor 10:1. [25]Cf. Ex 16:13-36; 1 Cor 10:3. [26]Cf. Ex 17:6; 1 Cor 10:4. [27]Cf. Num 22:5-6. [28]Cf. Col 2:15. [29]Cf. Col 1:18. [30]Cf. 1 Cor 15:19-20. [31]Cf. 2 Tim 2:5; 4:7-8. [32]Cf. Mt 25:34; Lk 22:29; Rev 2:7.

"this light and momentary affliction of ours achieve for us a weight of glory beyond measure in the future,"[33] nor would any of us await the immense glory of the future in exchange for our endurance of afflictions.

2.6. From all this one concludes that God not only uses good things for a good work [opus], but also evil things; and that is truly marvelous, that God uses evil vessels for a good work. For in the "great house" of this world, "there are not only vessels of gold and silver, but also of wood and clay; and some are for honor[able], some for shame[ful use],"[34] but both kinds are necessary. But since these vessels of which we are speaking should be understood as endowed with reason and free choice, it is not by accident nor by chance that each becomes either a "vessel of honor" or a "vessel of shame,"[35] but the one who offers himself in such a way that he deserves to be chosen becomes a chosen vessel and a vessel of honor. But the one who lives by unworthy and dishonorable thoughts is formed into a "vessel of shame," not by the Creator, but by himself, by means of the causes given of his shame. Therefore, the Creator did not make them to be this way, but by the justice of his providence and by a certain ineffable method, he dispenses minds of this sort "in accordance with the purpose"[36] of those minds.

2.7. The situation is similar to the way in large cities, for example, those who are the less worthy, the people of low life and despicable conduct, are condemned to perform the lowest and most difficult tasks [opera], works that are nevertheless essential for a city of this kind—they serve, for example, as fire-tenders in the furnaces that heat the baths, so that you can have your comfort and pleasure, or they clean the latrines and perform other services of this kind, so that your life in the city will be pleasant. And while they either do these things on purpose or they suffer them deservedly,

yet their work [opus] brings advancement and advantage to those for whom these good and useful things are prepared. Something similar applies in the things we have set forth: God, to be sure, did not make evil; but he was unwilling to eliminate it absolutely once it had been found in the purpose and intention of those who deviated from the right path.[37] For he foresaw that even if it were of no benefit to those who were making use of the evil, he could still make it useful for those against whom it was being exercised.

2.8. And therefore, on the one hand we should by all means run away, lest evil ever be "found" in us;[38] but in others one should strive to conquer it, not destroy it, since even those in whom evil exists bring some necessary work to the whole. For there is nothing pointless, nothing unprofitable with God, since he either uses a man's good purpose for good things, or he uses an evil [purpose] for things that are necessary. But you will be blessed if, more from the virtues that are in you, the whole of this life is found to attain something good from you, like those of whom the apostle Peter speaks: "May you be as lights in this world, holding fast the word of life."[39] Lights are thus necessary for this world for glory. And what is so delightful, what is so splendid as the effect [opus] of the sun and the moon by which this world receives its illumination?

2.9. Yet in this world there is need of angels as well, who are over the beasts, and of angels who are in charge of earthly practices. There is need, too, of angels who preside at the birth of animals, over the growth of little twigs and plants and over the rest of the fields. And again, there is need of angels who preside over holy deeds, who teach the understanding of eternal light and the recognition of the secrets of God and the knowledge of divine matters. So take heed, lest you cause yourself to be found among

---

[33]2 Cor 4:17. [34]2 Tim 2:20. [35]Cf. Rom 9:20-23. [36]Cf. Rom 8:28. [37]Cf. Ezek 28:15. [38]Cf. Ezek 28:15. [39]Cf. Phil 2:15-16. Origen has mistakenly attributed Paul's words to Peter.

those angels who are in charge of the beasts, if you lead a beastly life,[40] or among those who preside over earthly deeds, if you esteem bodily and earthly things. But instead, make it your goal to be received into the society of the angel Michael, who always offers the prayers of the saints to God.[41] Now you will be received into this number, or into that office, if you persevere always in prayer and remain watchful in it and fulfill what the apostle says: "Pray without ceasing."[42]

2.10. Or at least you may be admitted into the society and office of Raphael, who presides over healing.[43] If you see someone wounded by sins, and pierced by the devil's arrows,[44] you should apply the cure of words and you should bring the medicine of the Word of God, so that you may heal the wounds of sin through penance and point out the medicine of confession. Thus if someone does deeds of this sort in this world, he offers himself to be formed by his Creator in the future age as a "vessel of election and useful to the Lord, prepared for every good work."[45] But if he conducts himself in the opposite way, he will offer himself under God's providential management as a "vessel for shame[ful use]."[46] And I think it is for this reason that both the deeds of the good and of the evil are recorded in the divine books, and the divine Scriptures are composed of both "left" and "right" actions, so that we may understand that with God there are no pointless works, either of the evil or of the good. But now, after this very lengthy but necessary digression, let us return to the subject.

3.1. This Balaam, as we said above, was "divine," that is to say, at times he had foreknowledge of the future by means of the ministration of demons and the magic art.[47] He is asked by Balak the king to curse the people of Israel. Ambassadors come, they carry the instruments of divination in their hands, the nations stand there anxious and astonished, awaiting Balaam's response. They were convinced about him, that he was deemed worthy of divine communication. See now how the wisdom of God causes that "vessel" prepared[48] "for shame[ful use]"[49] to advance for the benefit not only of one nation, but of nearly the whole world. And to this man to whom the demons were accustomed to appear, God appears, forbidding the journey of the evil work.[50] Balaam is stunned and marvels at the authority of the one forbidding this, for evil was not used to displeasing demons. But in the meantime he sends back the ambassadors, saying that he can only do what the word says that God has put into his mouth. The ambassadors return once more, Balaam asks again, again he is annoyed, again he desires to hear.[51] For it is not easy for a greedy man to be without rewards. What then does he hear the second time from God? It says: "If those men have come to summon you, rise and go with them."[52] To be sure God yielded to his greedy will, in order that what is written might be fulfilled: "He let them go in the desire of their heart; they will go in their own wills."[53] But, nevertheless, the counsel of the divine plan is fulfilled. For it is said to him: "Whatever word I put in your mouth, this you shall speak."[54]

3.2. If Balaam had been worthy, God would not have put his word into his "mouth," but into his heart. But now, since the desire for reward was in his heart and he was greedy for money, the word of God is put not in his heart, but in his mouth. For a marvelous and great plan was being carried out. For the words of the prophets that were contained within the Israelite courtyard[55] were not able to reach the Gentiles.[56] But now, through Balaam, who was trusted by all nations, the secret mysteries of Christ would become known to the nations as well, and he

---

[40]Cf. Hermas *Shepherd*, Vision 4.2.4 mentions the angel Thegri, who is the leader of the wild beasts. [41]Cf. Rev 8:3-5; 12:7; Dan 10:21; 12:1; of Raphael in Tob 12:12. [42]1 Thess 5:17. [43]Cf. Tob 3:25; 11:7-14. [44]Cf. Eph 6:16. [45]2 Tim 2:21. [46]2 Tim 2:20. [47]Cf. Num 22:6. [48]Cf. Rom 9:22. [49]Cf. 2 Tim 2:20. [50]Cf. Num 22:12. [51]Cf. Num 22:18, 38. [52]Cf. Num 22:20. [53]Ps 81:12. [54]Num 22:35. [55]Lat *aula*. [56]Or "nations."

would deliver a great treasure to the nations that was carried not so much in the heart and understanding as in his mouth and speech. But lest we be delayed by the details—for there is not time to solve everything—Balaam mounted a donkey and went along the way.[57] An angel met him, doubtless the one who had assisted the sons of Israel. "He opens the mouth of the donkey,"[58] that Balaam might be convicted through the donkey, and he who seemed divine and wise was silenced by the words of a speechless animal.

4.1. But after this, it seems suitable now to touch on a few things concerning the allegory as well. This Balaam, which translates as "vain people," seems to me to represent the character of the scribes and Pharisees of the Jewish people.[59] But Balak, which translates as "exclusion" or "devouring," should be understood to represent the character of one of the spiritual forces of this world of adverse power. These powers long to exclude and devour Israel,[60] not the Israel that is "according to the flesh,"[61] but the one that is according to the spirit. So that power, wanting its enemies to be destroyed and spiritual Israel to be completely annihilated, makes use of no other services than those of the priests, the scribes and the Pharisees. It summons them, it promises them rewards and wages. But they, just as this Balaam does, pretend to refer everything that they do to God and to zeal for God. For they say: "Search the Scriptures and see that a prophet does not arise from Galilee."[62] And again they say: "We have a law, and according to law he ought to die, for he made himself the Son of God."[63] In each of these things, the scribes and Pharisees indeed seem to have a zeal for God, but it is feigned.

4.2. Now as for the donkey on which Balaam was sitting, since the Scripture says: "You will save men and beasts, Lord,"[64] that portion of the faithful can be understood which is likened to animals either for their folly or for their innocence. For thus, too, the apostle says: "But consider your calling, brothers, for not many among you were wise, not many were powerful, not many were well-born; but God chose the foolish things of the world to confound the wise."[65] The Gospel depicts these things in parables when it describes people who have been subjected to those very bad masters, "the scribes and Pharisees," as those who are held fast, as it were, and conquered by them. But they are released by the Lord, not indeed through the Lord himself, but through his disciples. For he says to the disciples: "Go to the village that is opposite you; and you will find a donkey tied up and its colt; loose it and bring it."[66]

4.3. Thus, just as in the Gospel, it is not the Lord himself but the disciples who "loose the donkey," so also here it is not by God himself, but by the angel that "the mouth of the donkey is opened."[67] And just as in the Gospels, those who do not see convict those who see,[68] so also here, those who had been mute convict those with speech. And this is what the Lord said: "Father, I thank you that you have hidden these things from the wise and prudent, and you have revealed them to infants."[69] Therefore, it was the scribes and Pharisees who were sitting on this donkey and were holding it bound. So the angel is angry with them, and were it not for a certain prospective view of the future, it would have destroyed them but saved the donkey, which saw and stood in awe of him who comes to the vineyard and "stands among the vines."[70] However, it pressed "against the wall" the feet of the one sitting on it.[71] Possibly for that reason its old sitter cannot walk, nor can he come to him who says: "Come to me, all you who labor and are burdened down."[72] Nevertheless, the donkey comes, having been brought by the disciples, and on this one on which Balaam once sat, who was greedy for

---

[57]Cf. Num 22:22. [58]Cf. Num 22:28. [59]Cf. Mk 7:6-7. [60]Cf. Rev 12:4. [61]Cf. 1 Cor 10:18. [62]Cf. Jn 7:52. [63]Jn 19:7. [64]Ps 36:6. [65]1 Cor 1:26-27. [66]Mt 21:2. [67]Num 22:28. [68]Cf. Jn 9:35-41. [69]Mt 11:25. [70]Cf. Num 22:24. [71]Cf. Num 22:25. [72]Mt 11:28.

rewards, Jesus now sits.

4.4. Do not be amazed if you see one whom we said contains a figure of the scribes and teachers of the people prophesying about Christ. For we read that Caiaphas also did this, who said: "It is better for you that one man perish for the whole people."[73] But it says: "He prophesied this because he was high priest that year."[74] Thus Balaam too prophesies about Christ, and for that reason no one should be lifted up, even if he prophesies, even if he merits foreknowledge, but let him go back to the apostle's statement, where he considers these matters and says: "Whether prophecies, they will be done away with; whether tongues, they will cease; whether knowledge, it will be destroyed."[75]

And what is it that continues? "Faith," he says, "and hope and love; but the greatest of these is love."[76] And it is love alone, he says, that "never fails."[77] Therefore, love is to be regarded above prophecy, above knowledge, above faith, even above martyrdom itself, as Paul teaches.[78] And love should be cultivated, because even "God is love,"[79] and Christ his Son is love, who deems it fitting to give us the perfection of love. "To him be the glory in the ages of ages. Amen."[80]

Homily 15
Numbers 22:31-41; 23:1-10

On the prophecy of Balaam.

1.1. Although the order of readings that are being read aloud requires that we speak about the things that the lector has expounded, nevertheless since some of the brothers are instead requesting that the things written about the prophecy of Balaam be brought forth into the words of the discussion, I have thought it fair to satisfy the desires of the hearers more than the order of the readings.

So first of all, let us ask with regard to Balaam himself why he is recorded in the Scriptures now as blameworthy, now as praiseworthy? For he is blameworthy when, having been hindered by God from going to the king, he insists on going and, desirous of rewards, he consults a second time, asks of God again, until he is abandoned to his own desires[1] and goes after his own will.[2] He is worthy of blame when he builds altars and offers sacrifices to demons and seeks for divine responses by means of magical equipment. He is worthy of blame when he gives advice that results in the people being seduced by Midianite women and the worship of idols.[3] On the other hand, he is shown to be praiseworthy when the word of God is put in his mouth,[4] when "the Spirit of God comes on him,"[5] when he prophesies about Christ, when he declares in advance to Jews and Gentiles the future mysteries about the advent of Christ, when he bestows blessings on the people instead of curses and extols the name of Israel in mystical terms beyond its visible glory.[6]

1.2. Therefore, since the divine Scripture indicates these things about him, which are so diverse and various, it seems very difficult to me to determine his character definitively, to whom not only this diversity corresponds, but the following can be considered as relevant as well: when he prophesies about himself, as it were, he says: "Let my soul die among the souls of the just, and let my seed become like the seed of the just."[7] Moreover, the Lord testifies something similar about him through Micah the prophet when he says: "My people, what have I done to you? For I called you back from the land of Egypt, and freed you out of the house of slavery, and I sent before your face Moses and Aaron and Miriam.[8] My people, remember what

---

[73]Jn 11:50. [74]Jn 11:51. [75]1 Cor 13:8. [76]1 Cor 13:13. [77]1 Cor 13:8. [78]Cf. 1 Cor 13:2-3. [79]1 Jn 4:16. [80]Rom 11:36.
Homily 15 [1]Cf. Rom 1:24, 26, 28. [2]Lit. "wills." Cf. Ps 81:12. [3]Num 25:1-3; 31:16. [4]Cf. Num 23:5, 16. [5]Cf. Num 24:2. [6]Cf. Num 24:16-19. [7]Num 23:10. [8]Lat *Mariam*.

counsel Balak king of Moab took against you, and what Balaam the son of Beor answered him from the Cords all the way to Gilgal, that the justice of the Lord might be known."[9] Through these things, then, he shows that the reason Balaam son of Beor answered to king Balak all these things that are reported and written down in the books was so that "the justice of the Lord might become known."

1.3. And who do you think will be found so capable that he can show from Balaam's very answers that "God's justice" is manifested[10] in these things? For indeed, if the word of God was put "in his mouth"[11] and "the Spirit of God came on him"[12] and the justice of God is known and manifested from his answers, by all means the things that he says deserve to be believed as nothing but prophetical and divine matters. Although we may have a difficult time finding a Scripture anywhere that says "the Spirit of God came on one of the prophets,"[13] yet we do read of "a vision that he saw,"[14] or a "reception of the word of God," or "the word of God came to so and so,"[15] and certain other things about the prophets. But for the time being, I do not at present recall reading that "the Spirit of God came" on any of the prophets, except that I remember that the following is written about David: "And then from that day on the Spirit of God appeared to" or "shined on David"; yet it does not say "The Spirit of God came on David."[16] Of Saul, in fact, I recall that the following is written: "And the Spirit of the Lord will fall on you and you will prophesy with them, and you will be converted into another man."[17] And again, of the same man it is said: "And the Spirit of the Lord departed from Saul, and an evil spirit from the Lord paralyzed him";[18] and

again: "And it came about when the evil spirit was with Saul, David took up his harp and played it with his hands and plucked it, and it was well with him, and the evil spirit departed from him."[19] I have cited these things because what is written: "And the Spirit of God came on him," can seem ordinary.

1.4. For this reason and in accordance with the things that we had perceived in the discussion above, we also will now attempt to explain how this Balaam represents the character of the scribes, Pharisees and those who are like them. But come now, let us consider the words of his prophecy, which it is written that he spoke when "he took up his parable."[20]

It says: "From Mesopotamia Balak king of Moab summoned me, from the mountains of the east."[21] He calls Mesopotamia the land that lies between the rivers of Babylon, of which it is written: "We sat there by the rivers of Babylon and wept when we remembered Zion."[22] So then, if there is anyone between these rivers of Babylon, if anyone is inundated by the streams of lust and is surrounded by the burning flow of luxury, that one is not said to stand but to sit;[23] and therefore, those who were overtaken there said: "By the rivers of Babylon we sat and wept when we remembered Zion."[24] But they cannot even weep until they have first remembered Zion; for the remembrance of good things makes the causes of evils lamentable. For unless one remembers Zion, unless one gazes at the law of God and the mountains of the Scriptures,[25] he does not begin to weep for his own evils.

1.5. Thus Balaam is called from these rivers, and he is summoned from these mountains of the east. These mountains are those holy moun-

---

[9]Mic 6:3-5. [10]Cf. Rom 1:17. [11]Cf. Num 23:5. [12]Cf. Num 24:2. [13]The instances recorded in Judg 3:10; 6:34; 11:29; 14:19; 15:14 which associate the coming of the Spirit on the judges of Israel with acts of physical strength and strategic military actions do not mention prophecy. However, the instance in 1 Sam 19:20, 23 does link the coming of the Spirit with prophecy among Saul's messengers. Perhaps Origen does not regard the latter as prophets of Israel. [14]Cf. Is 1:1; 13:1; Obad 1:1; Nahum 1:1; Hab 1:1; Zech 9:1; Mal 1:1. [15]Cf. 1 Sam 3:1; 15:10; Jer 1:2; Ezek 1:3 Hos 1:1; Joel 1:1; Jon 1:1; Mic 1:1; Zeph 1:1; Hag 1:1; Zech 1:1. [16]Cf. 1 Sam 16:13. [17]1 Sam 10:6. [18]1 Sam 16:14. [19]1 Sam 16:23. [20]Cf. Num 23:7. [21]Num 23:7. [22]Ps 137:1. [23]Cf. Philo *On the Confusion of Tongues* 66. [24]Ps 137:1. [25]Cf. Ps 121:1.

tains of which it is written: "Her foundations are in the holy mountains,"[26] and again: "Jerusalem, which is built like a city whose sharing of herself is in herself";[27] "mountains surround her, and the Lord surrounds his people."[28] The mountains of Mesopotamia, therefore, are not like that, but they are spoken of as "dark mountains,"[29] and again of the one of which it is said: "Behold, I am against you, O destroying mountain."[30] Those are the mountains in which there is "every height extolling itself against the knowledge of God."[31] Thus it is from those mountains that this Balaam is summoned.

1.6. Now the "East" refers to the condition of these mountains. For the East also has the rising of its light, that light that "transforms itself into an angel of light."[32] It has that light of which it is written: "the light of the impious will be put out."[33] And just as that "light of the impious" and that one which "transforms itself into an angel of light" are opposed to that light which said: "I am the light of the world,"[34] so also this East is opposed to that East of which it is written in Jeremiah: "Behold a man, his name is East."[35] So Balaam came from the regions of the former East, not of the latter. Doubtless he had been enlightened by that morning star[36] of whom it is said: "How did Lucifer, who rose in the morning, fall from heaven?"[37]

2.1. But let us see what Balak king of Moab says to him who summoned him from the midst of the rivers "from the mountains of the east." "Come," he says, "and curse Jacob for me, and come, curse Israel for me."[38] In the Latin language it practically seems to be a superfluous repetition that says: "Curse Jacob for me, and curse Israel for me." But in the Greek text, there is a preposition prefixed to the verb "curse" in connection with the name of Israel.[39] Our translators have omitted it, whether because they believed it had not been spoken properly,

or because they thought that no additional force would be added to the expression by this prefix. But even though it is contrary to our usage, we fashion the words in order that we might gather the sense of the whole. Thus it can be said: "Come, curse Jacob for me, and come, curse even more deeply[40] Israel for me." So the repeated words show by this means that Balak seems to be demanding a curse against Israel with greater violence and intensity than against Jacob. For as long as someone is a mere Jacob, that is, as long as he abides at that level in his actions and deeds, he is attacked with lesser curses. But when he makes progress and already begins to spur on and challenge his "inner man"[41] to "see God" with the eye of his mind unveiled,[42] that person will then be attacked by the enemy, not just with curses, but with "deep curses," that is, with an even more violent hurling of curses.

2.2. But then indeed the mouth of Balaam "was full of cursing and bitterness; and on his tongue were trouble and pain, and he was sitting in ambush with the rich."[43] For he was expecting wages from a rich king, that "he might kill the innocent in secret places."[44] But God, "who alone always does wonders,"[45] works salvation from his enemies; for "he put his word into his mouth,"[46] although Balaam's heart was not yet able to have room for the word of God. For the desire for wages was still in his heart, on account of which, even after the word of God that he had in his mouth, he said to Balak: "Come, and I will give you counsel,"[47] and he taught him how he could cast a stumbling block before the sons of Israel, so that they ate things sacrificed to idols and committed fornication. On that account also, the people fell, and a great plague came against them, until Phinehas killed an Israelite who was fornicating with a Midianite woman and caused the Lord's fury

---

[26]Cf. Ps 87:1. [27]Ps 122:3. [28]Ps 125:2. [29]Jer 13:16. [30]Jer 51:25. [31]2 Cor 10:5. [32]2 Cor 11:14. [33]Job 18:5. [34]Jn 8:12. [35]Zech 6:12. [36]*Lucifer.* [37]Is 14:12. [38]Num 23:7. [39]The LXX has *arasai moi ton Iakōb kai deuro epikatarasai moi ton Israēl.* The second verb has a prefix *epi*, which indicates an intensified form. [40]Lit. "super-curse." [41]Cf. Rom 7:22. [42]Cf. Philo *On the Sacrifices of Cain and Abel* 120; *On Drunkenness* 82; *On the Migration of Abraham* 200-201. [43]Ps 10:7-8. [44]Ps 10:8. [45]Ps 136:4. [46]Num 23:5. [47]Num 24:14.

to cease.[48] And after this, it says, Phinehas led forth an army against the Midianites, and they killed twelve thousand men, including Balaam son of Beor, with the sword.[49]

But we have introduced these things prematurely as a sort of digression, in order to show that Balaam had the word of God not in his heart, but only in his mouth. It remains the case that the things he brings forth, the things he speaks, he speaks from the word of God, and therefore the things he says are God's word.

3.1. Thus he says: "Why should I curse one whom the Lord does not curse?"[50] We use "deep curse" in advance in accordance with the meaning of the Greek term, since we desire to show the force of the word from the prepositional prefix. So what shall we say? The Lord does not *curse* Jacob, or Israel, but do you think he curses anyone else? We read in the Scripture that the Lord speaks to the serpent: "Cursed are you among all the beasts of the earth";[51] and again to Adam: "Cursed is the earth in your works";[52] moreover to Cain: "And now cursed are you from the earth, which opened its mouth to receive the blood of your brother from your hands";[53] and "Cursed are all who make a sculpted or molten image."[54] But lest you think that these things are contained only in the old writings, you will find similar things in the Gospels too. For it is written that the Lord will say to those on his left: "Depart from me, accursed ones, into the eternal fire."[55] Moreover, when he says: "Woe to you, scribes and Pharisees, hypocrites!"[56] and "woe to you rich!"[57] and every expression of this sort, what else does he seem to be insisting on but that they are among the cursed?

3.2. But what shall we say of the command that is given by the apostle, when he says: "Bless and do not curse"[58]? Is it the case, then, that he who sets the example of life for human beings himself does that which he does not will

that people do?[59] This is not so. For with those whom God curses, the person's merit determines who is cursed, and he bears the sentence inasmuch as he does not deceive anyone, neither the nature of the sin nor the affection of the sinner. But because man cannot know this—for one person cannot see or discern the intention and mind of another—therefore, even if the curse is produced by one who judges or who gives a sentence, there cannot be a just motive for cursing when the affections of the sinner are unknown, especially since human perversity knows how to bring forth curses at a time when perhaps it is provoked by insults or injuries. This is the fault the apostle wants to remove when he gives as a necessary command that we should not provoke curses by means of curses and insults by means of insults, that "we bless and do not curse." He wants the vice of insulting speech to be removed; he does not want the truth of judging that is hidden from people to be destroyed, and the right to pronounce judgment.

3.3. And yet, let us listen very carefully to the reason why the Lord does not curse either Jacob or Israel by no less than Balaam himself, or rather, by the word that God put in his mouth.[60] It says: "For from the tops of the mountains I will view him, and from the hills I will understand him."[61] Since, he says, Israel is placed on high mountains and on tall hills, that is, in an exalted and arduous life, for the contemplation and understanding of which one does not become easily suited, unless one ascends to an eminent and exalted knowledge, therefore, he says, God does not curse him. For his[62] life is high and towering, not humble and low. However, it does not seem to me that he has said this about that Israel that is according to the flesh,[63] but about that one whose "citizenship,"[64] while they walk on the earth, "is in heaven."[65] Or, even if these statements are to

---

[48]Cf. Num 25:6-8. [49]Cf. Num 31:6-8. [50]Num 23:8. [51]Gen 3:14. [52]Gen 3:17. [53]Gen 4:11. [54]Deut 27:15. [55]Mt 25:41. [56]Mt 23:29. [57]Lk 6:24. [58]Rom 12:14. [59]Cf. Mt 7:12. [60]Num 23:5. [61]Num 23:9. [62]I.e., Israel's. [63]Cf. Rom 9:4-5. [64]Lat *conversatio*. [65]Cf. Phil 3:20.

be referred to that people, he speaks correctly with a distinction: "I will view" and "I will understand," in order to signify the future time, doubtless that time when "all Israel," by coming to the faith of Christ, "will be saved,"[66] and "he will view from the mountains and the hills."[67] Whom will he view? Doubtless those who have practiced an exalted and heavenly life on earth by their "rising together with Christ."[68] Moreover, what he said about Jacob: "I will see," and then about Israel: "I will understand," even this should be interpreted with a very precise distinction. The former should be related to visible acts, the latter to invisible faith and intelligible knowledge. Or, if we transfer these things to the future age, that is, to the time of resurrection, "I will see Jacob" can be understood as a statement about bodies, but "I will understand Israel" can signify the spirits and souls of those who rise.

3.4. "Behold," it says, "the people will dwell alone and will not be reckoned among the nations."[69] Even according to the letter, this can stand: for only the people of Jacob were not mixed with the rest of humanity nor reckoned among the rest of the nations. For they had certain advantages in their observances and laws. For this reason they were considered to be separated from the other nations. For just as the tribe of Levi was not mixed among the other tribes or numbered among them, in this way as well all Israel is not mixed with the other nations nor is it reckoned among them. In the former people these things would have been in accordance with the form of good things to come,[70] but the true Jacob and the spiritual Israel will truly dwell alone among the nations. For we are truly not reckoned among the other nations if "we have come to Mount Zion and the city of the living God, the heavenly Jerusalem";[71] if we come to spiritual Judea, which is "God's portion";[72] if while on earth, we have

our "citizenship"[73] in heaven; if the borders of the remaining nations are not mixed with our borders; and if Sodom is restored to its ancient state[74] and Egypt returns to its condition; and if some of the other similar things that are written in the prophets [be true of us]. Nevertheless, when they ascend to that Jacob and to the spiritual Israel, to the "church of the firstborn,"[75] no one will be equaled; no one will be mixed, even if those nations are restored in accordance with the statements of the prophets. For unless "the branch of the wild olive tree is grafted and becomes a sharer of the root of the fatness of the olive,"[76] how can it be associated with and joined to Jacob, or Israel, since without that root no one can be called Jacob or Israel? Therefore, if one from Jacob or Israel sins, he cannot be called Jacob or Israel, nor will one who is from the nations who has entered the church of the Lord be reckoned any longer among the nations.

3.5. "Who will track down the seed of Jacob and who will count the families of Israel?"[77] This is similar to what is written, that: "God led Abraham outside and said to him: Look at the sky and count the stars if you can count them. And he said: So shall your seed be. And Abraham believed God and it was reckoned to him for justice."[78] But neither Abraham nor any other human being, nor even any angel, and possibly not even the higher powers, were able to count either the stars or the seed of Abraham, of whom it is written: "So shall your seed be."[79] But God, of whom it is written: "He who counts the multitude of the stars and calls them all by name,"[80] and he who said: "I commanded all the stars,"[81] can "track down the seed of Jacob and count the families of Israel."[82] For he alone knows who Jacob truly is and who Israel truly is. For he looks not to him "who is a Jew in appearance,"[83] nor to that circumcision "which

---

[66]Cf. Rom 11:26. Notice that for Origen Israel's future restoration will take place by their coming to faith in Christ. [67]Cf. Num 23:9. [68]Cf. Col 3:1. [69]Num 23:9. [70]Cf. Heb 10:1. [71]Heb 12:22. [72]Cf. Deut 32:9. [73]Cf. Phil 3:20. [74]Cf. Ezek 16:53, 55. [75]Heb 12:23. [76]Cf. Rom 11:17-18. [77]Num 23:10. [78]Gen 15:5-6. [79]Gen 15:5. [80]Ps 147:4. [81]Is 45:12. [82]Num 23:10. [83]Rom 2:28.

is manifest in the flesh,"[84] but he sees him "who is a Jew in secret and who is circumcised in his heart, not flesh."[85] He is the only one, then, who can count this and track it down. And in accordance with his ineffable and incomprehensible wisdom, he has established these Numbers that we have in hand, which point to that heavenly form, which he alone can know. In this he has commanded that "according to their relatives, according to the houses of their families, let every male be numbered by the heads from twenty-years old and upwards, every one that goes forth in the power of Israel."[86] And a certain consecrated number is gathered from them, as we have already spoken about above, as the Lord granted.[87] But that numbering is only consecrated and pleasing to God at that time when it is counted at God's command. But if someone wanted to count contrary to the Lord's precept, though it may be David himself, though it may be a great prophet, he speaks against the law and is convicted by the prophet and suffers those things that we read are written in the second book of Kingdoms.[88] Therefore, he alone who "counts the multitude of the stars"[89] and who "produced everything by measure, number and weight,"[90] "tracks down the seed of Jacob and counts the families of Israel."[91]

4.1. After this [Balaam] seems to prophesy some things as if concerning himself, when he says: "Let my soul die among the souls of the just, and let my seed be as the seed of the just."[92] But as far as this concerns the person of that Balaam and of that Israel, it did not happen and could not happen; for he did not die among them, but by means of them.[93] So instead, as we have said, it will not correspond to the character of those, who in the present age are considered to be a "vain people," since they are without the grace of the Holy Spirit. At the end of the age, however, when "the fullness of the Gentiles

enters in"[94] and all of these prophecies that are spoken about Israel will be fulfilled in the spiritual Israel, at that time "his soul will die with the souls of the just."[95] For he will receive the faith of Christ in himself, so that they too will say for themselves: "We who have been baptized in Christ, have been baptized into his death. For we were buried together with him through baptism into death";[96] and again: "For if we die together, we shall also reign together."[97] And thus it will truly be fulfilled for the intelligible Balaam, that "his soul will die among the souls of the just."

4.2. Now as for what he says: "And let my seed become as the seed of the just,"[98] this could indeed be understood even about that Balaam, according to the fact that those Magi who came from the east and first worshiped Jesus seem to have been of his "seed," whether by physical descent or by traditional instruction. For plainly it is a fact that they recognized that the star that Balaam had predicted would "rise in Israel."[99] And so they came to worship the king who was born in Israel.[100] Nevertheless, it will correspond with that people according to the things that we have said above; for it is not so much themselves, as their seed that will become like the seed of the just, namely, of those who have been justified in Christ "by believing from the Gentiles."[101] This is why it is clear that, as the apostle says: "Neither circumcision is anything nor uncircumcision, but faith which works through love."[102] And therefore, let no one boast in the antiquity of circumcision or glory in the novelty of uncircumcision, but, as the apostle says: "Let each one test his own work, and only then will he have glory in himself."[103] After all, the prophet also speaks in this way: He says, "Behold a man and his work," and his "recompense" is said to be "in the sight of the Lord,"[104] in Christ Jesus our Lord, to whom is "the glory and the power in the ages of ages. Amen."[105]

---

[84]Rom 2:28. [85]Rom 2:29. [86]Num 1:2-3. [87]Cf. Homily 1. [88]Cf. 2 Sam 24:1-17. [89]Ps 147:4. [90]Wis 11:21. [91]Num 23:10. [92]Num 23:10. [93]Num 31:8. [94]Cf. Rom 11:25. [95]Num 23:10. [96]Rom 6:3-4. [97]2 Tim 2:12. [98]Num 23:10. [99]Num 24:17; cf. Mt 2:2. [100]Cf. Mt 2:11. [101]Cf. Acts 21:25. [102]Cf. Gal 5:6. [103]Gal 6:4. [104]Cf. Is 62:11. [105]1 Pet 4:11.

Homily 16
Numbers 23:11-24

1.1. In the former discussion, we attempted to explain the first part of Balaam's prophecy to the extent that it was possible. Now we are taking up the beginning of the second prophecy, so that, if the Lord deigns to inspire us, we will set forth publicly what occurs to us about it to the best of our ability. I grant that these things are clearly difficult matters, but it seemed inappropriate to me to interrupt the discussion of these things, without explaining the details that we are able to comprehend.

1.2. Therefore, king Balak, as one who was struck and astonished by these things, which he saw Balaam speak contrary to his expectation—for he heard blessings instead of curses—enduring this no longer interrupts his words and says: "What have you done to me? I summoned you to curse my enemies, and behold, you have blessed with a blessing."[1] The embittered king did not bear the sweetness of the blessings, but he seeks curses, he demands curses; for he is related to that one to whom the Lord said: "You are cursed beyond all the beasts of the earth."[2]

But what does the one to whom God had put the word into his mouth answer him in response to these things? "Whatsoever things God has put into my mouth," he says, "shall I not observe to speak these things?"[3] To this Balak, thinking that Balaam had become terrified by the multitude of the Israelite people and that it was for that reason that he did not dare to utter curses, believed that a change of location would be advantageous for him, and he says to him: "Come with me to still another place, from which you will not see them,[4] but you will see a certain part of them, but you will not see all of them, and curse them for me from there."[5] This madman believed that the Israelite grace could be concealed by the obstacle of location. He did not know that "a city set on a mountain cannot be hidden."[6]

1.3. "And he took him," it says, "to the lookout of a field at the top of the hewn mountain, and he built there seven altars, and he offered a calf [and] a ram on an altar. And Balaam said to Balak: 'Stand by your sacrifice, but I will go to inquire of God.' And God met Balaam himself, and he put a word into his mouth and said'"—doubtless God said—"'Return to Balak and you will speak these things.' But he"—that is, Balak—"was standing by his burnt offerings, and all the rulers of Moab with him. And Balak said to him: 'What did the Lord say?'"[7]

1.4. The thing is being carried out, of course, with profane sacrifices, and it is being pursued by means of magic arts and divination; nevertheless, God deems it fitting to be present because he wants "grace to abundantly abound where sin has abounded."[8] He does not flee from these things that were being carried out, not in accordance with Israelite instruction, but in accordance with the error of pagans. Yet [God] is present, not at the sacrifices, but to the one coming to the gathering, and there, especially since the faith and admiration of the pagans is hanging in the balance, he gives his word, and there he announces in advance future mysteries, so that those who are unwilling to believe our prophets may believe their own divines and their own seers.

2.1. It says [Numbers 23:18-24]:

[23:18] "And he took up his parable and said:
    Rise up, Balak, and listen,
    perceive with the ears of a witness,
    son of Zippor.
[23:19] God is not frustrated as man,
    nor as a son of man is he terrified;
    he, when he speaks, will he not act?
    Will he speak, and not continue?

Homily 16 [1]Num 23:11. [2]Gen 3:14. [3]Num 23:12. [4]Lit.: "him," i.e., the people. [5]Num 23:13. [6]Mt 5:14. [7]Num 23:14-17. [8]Rom 5:20.

[23:20] Behold I have been chosen[9] to
bless;
I will bless, and will not turn away
from it.
[23:21] There shall not be trouble in Jacob,
nor shall sorrow be seen in Israel.
The Lord his God is with him,
the splendid things of the rulers
are with him.
[23:22] God, who brought him out of
Egypt,
he is for him as the glory of a
unicorn.
[23:23] For there will not be augury in
Jacob,
nor divination in Israel.
In time it shall be told to Jacob
and Israel,
what God shall perform.
[23:24] Behold the people shall rise up as
a lion's whelp,
and shall exult as a lion;
he will not sleep, until he eats the
prey,
and shall drink the blood of the
wounded.

2.2. Such is the content of the second prophecy in the words of Balaam. So let us examine,
first of all, what he says: "Rise up, Balak, and
listen."[10] For if previously he had not said that
"he was standing near his burnt offering,"
it would not seem to be a great thing to ask
why he says, "Rise, up, Balak." But now, since
[Balaam] exhorts [Balak] to rise up, whom he
had recently said was standing up, the prophetic
words are not to be leisurely passed over. So the
fact that he says earlier that he was standing
at his burnt offering indicates that he was not
standing correctly. For he was standing while
placed in idolatry, and he was standing as an
enemy of God, which was rather not standing,
but falling. Therefore, as one who ought to fall

from that standing position, or rather, as one
who had already fallen, so now by the prophetic
understanding, he commands him to rise up,
inasmuch as he had fallen through the fact that
he seemed to be standing in idolatry. Thus, let
the one who is like this rise up, let him rise up
in spirit, let him rise up in faith and let him
become a witness; if indeed he is converted, he
becomes a witness of faith, but if he remains
in unbelief, he becomes a witness of his own
condemnation.

3.1. But let us hear what he announces to
him: "God is not frustrated as a man, nor as a
son of man is he terrified."[11] You should not
hold this opinion about God, he says, that
you think that he is like a man who could be
frustrated in the things he says. For on many
occasions men are prevented by their vices from
saying what is true. For either they speak while
angry, and when the anger abates, they have
spoken in frustration, or they may speak out
of emotions, greed, boasting and other similar
things. It will turn out that everything they said
while these vices were in control is frustrated
and pointless. But all that God speaks, in whom
there is no passion, no weakness, he speaks for
well-deserving reasons; and therefore, he can
never be frustrated, since whatever is brought
forth by reason cannot lack reason. "Therefore
God is not like man who speaks in frustration,
nor is he terrified like a son of man," or, as we
read in some copies, "nor does he terrify like
a son of man." Among men, terror sometimes
changes one's opinion, but with God, who is
above all things, how can he be terrified into
changing his opinion?

3.2. But if we receive this in accordance
with what we said is read in other copies, that
is, "nor does he terrify as a son of man," this
will seem to be said because men sometimes
make terrors and threats for the sake of boasting, even sometimes to those whom they are
not able to harm. But God does not terrify

<hr />

[9]Lit. "taken." [10]Num 23:18. [11]Num 23:19.

men in this way, as if he could not punish; moreover, if he terrifies, he terrifies with a reason; for he terrifies in order to correct man by the affliction of what he is hearing, so that, when the one who is acting badly has been completely terrified by the threatening word, he may cleanse himself, and the very vengeance due to his own evilly done actions will not reach him. Thus God does not terrify like this, as a man; for man, as we have said, terrifies for the sake of boasting, but God does it for the sake of correction.

4.1. After this it says: "When he himself speaks, will he not do? Will he speak and not continue?"[12] This passage should be read as if one is speaking in the tone of a questioner: What he himself speaks—that is, God—will he not also do it? And what has been spoken, will he not also continue in these things? It is certain that men do not do what they say, and by a blemish of human weakness they do not continue in those things that they speak; for man is mutable, but God is immutable.

But someone can object and say: Did God not fail to carry out the things that he had spoken concerning Nineveh, namely, that after three days it would be overturned?[13] Nor did he accomplish what he said to David, when he promised death and the destruction of the people within three days, and yet it stopped within one day at the hour of dinner?[14]

Now possibly, it will seem that these things are spoken in the form of a question and should not be interpreted absolutely as a pronouncement, but it is a sort of figure of speech, which seems to indicate moderation. Yet he is not expressing the tone of a definitive and irrevocable judgment. Thus a statement seems more moderate when it is written: "When he himself speaks, will he not do it?" than if it was said: "When he himself speaks, he will by all means do it."

4.2. But let us reconsider the passages of Scripture that are recorded both in Jonah and in the books of Kingdoms to see whether there as well they may contain some mystery, as is customary in the divine Scripture. So then, it is written in Jonah: "And the word of the Lord came to Jonah son of Amitai saying: 'Rise and go to Nineveh, the great city, and proclaim in it that the cry of its evil has ascended to me.'"[15] And after he commanded the whale, and it expelled Jonah on the land,[16] it is again written: "And the word of the Lord came to Jonah a second time saying: 'Rise and go to Nineveh, the great city, and proclaim in it according to the proclamation which I have spoken to you.'"[17]

Then, of course, Jonah "preached and said: three more days," or, as the Hebrews claim that the Scripture contains: "Forty more days"— "and Nineveh will be destroyed. But the men of Nineveh believed God, and they proclaimed a fast, and they put on sackcloth, from the least of them to the greatest."[18] And after a few things it says: "And God saw their works and how they had turned from their evil ways, and God repented"—or, as we read in some copies, "pleaded"—"of the evil that he said he would do to them, and he did not do it."[19]

Well, notice in these things that we have taken from the prophet that the statement "Three more days and Nineveh will be destroyed" is not found among the words that God spoke to the prophet; but it says: "When Jonah entered the city, a journey of three days as it were," he himself said: "Three more days and Nineveh will be destroyed." So these words, which were spoken and not done, seem to have been brought forth by Jonah rather than by God.

4.3. Moreover let us cite what is written in the second book of Kingdoms, where it says that when David had numbered the people: "And the word of the Lord came to the prophet Gad, the seer, saying: 'Go, and speak to David:

12Num 23:19. 13Cf. Jon 3:4. 142 Sam 24:13-16. 15Jon 1:1-2. 16Cf. Jon 2:10. 17Jon 3:1-2. 18Jon 3:4-5. 19Jon 3:10.

Thus says the Lord: I will raise three things over you. Choose for yourself one of them that I will do to you.' And Gad went in to David, and denounced him saying: 'Either a famine shall come on your land for three years, or you will flee for three months before your enemies, who pursue you, or death will come against your land for three days. Now then, know and see what answer I shall return to him that sent me.' And David said to Gad: 'Things are very narrow to me on every side. But let me fall into the hands of the Lord instead, for his mercies are many, and let me not fall into the hands of men.' And the Lord gave death to Israel from morning till the hour of dinner, and from the people seventy thousand men died from Dan to Beersheba. And the angel of the Lord stretched out his hand against Jerusalem to destroy it, and the Lord pleaded over the evil and said to the angel who was destroying the people: 'It is enough, withhold your hand.'"[20]

4.4. So observe how in these three threats God is not found to have spoken about "death for three days." For it is recorded among the words of Gad, not in the commands of the Lord, and things spoken through a prophet are not always to be received as statements of God. After all, God also said many things through Moses, yet Moses also commanded some things on his own authority. For in the Gospels the Lord made a very clear distinction when he was asked the question about divorcing a woman. He said that Moses wrote these things to you "in view of the hardness of your heart, but from the beginning it was not so."[21] For "he who made man, made them male and female, and he blessed them and said: for this reason a man will leave his father and mother and will cleave to his wife; and the two shall become one flesh";[22] and he added: "What therefore God has joined together, let man not separate."[23] So you see that even here

God neither commanded nor willed divorce. But Moses wrote that a bill of divorce should be given "on account of the hardness of the heart"[24] of the Jews. Paul, too, makes this clear in his letters, when he says concerning certain ones: "The Lord says, and not I,"[25] and concerning others: "These things I say, and not the Lord,"[26] and again to others: "I do not have a command of the Lord, but I give advice,"[27] and again: "The things I am saying, I am not saying according to the Lord."[28]

4.5. And so, in a similar way, in the other prophets as well, the Lord, and not the prophets, has spoken some things, to be sure, but other things the prophets are speaking and not the Lord. And in this manner the proposed objection will seem to be resolved, since the Lord is revoking and changing for the better not so much his own words as the words of the prophet.

4.6. But I rather think that the earlier solution agrees with the meaning of Scripture as a whole and particularly with those statements where God is said to be "patient and of great mercy and repentant over evils,"[29] and especially with those that are declared by Jeremiah in a general way, in which God is plainly shown, in view of his many mercies and his incomprehensible goodness, to speak and not to do; to speak and not to continue. Thus through Jeremiah God says: "If I should speak until the end"—that is, If I should speak definitively—"against a nation and against a kingdom, to remove them and scatter them, and if that nation converts from its evils, I will repent of all the evils that I had in mind to do to them. And if I should speak until the end about a nation and kingdom to rebuild and replant them, and if they do evils in my sight, so as not to hear my voice, I will repent of all the good things that I had said I would do for them."[30] So how can we prefer the things that

---

[20]2 Sam 24:11-16. [21]Mt 19:8. [22]Mt 19:4-6. [23]Mt 19:6. [24]Cf. Mt 19:8. [25]1 Cor 7:10. [26]1 Cor 7:12. [27]1 Cor 7:25. [28]2 Cor 11:17. [29]Ex 34:6; Ps 86:5; 145:8; Joel 2:13. [30]Jer 18:7-10. Cf. *Homilies on Jeremiah* 18.6.

are said by Balaam in an undecided fashion to these things that were spoken absolutely by Jeremiah, unless it is because the former things [Balaam's words] are to be confirmed as applicable to the negligent and the despisers, but the latter things [Jeremiah's words] are to be heeded in a more hidden fashion by those who are more perfect?

5.1. But after this, Balaam says: "Behold, I have been chosen to bless; I will bless, and I will not turn away from it."[31] Balaam was chosen to bless, not by Balak, but by God, "who put his word into his mouth"[32] in order that he would bless the people, and he does not turn away from this blessing. For even if he wants to, he cannot change the word of God by human language. After this it says: "There shall not be trouble in Jacob, nor shall sorrow be seen in Israel."[33] By these words he openly announces the condition of the future life; for who is there who passes through this life without trouble and sorrow? Not even if one is a Peter or a Paul [could he do that]. For how is Paul not in trouble and sorrow when "three times he is beaten with rods, once he is stoned, three times he is shipwrecked, he is adrift at sea for a night and a day,"[34] and the other countless things he suffers, which he writes concerning his troubles and sorrows? But this will be fulfilled in that place where it is said: "Sorrow and sadness and groaning have fled away."[35]

5.2. However, this does not relate to everyone, but only to those who become Jacob and Israel by their merits. That poor man Lazarus was like this. To be sure he passed the present life in trouble and sorrow, but there it is said to the rich man: "Remember, son, that you received your good things in your life and Lazarus likewise evil things. But now he is at rest, but you are tormented."[36] Thus he is an Israel and a Jacob to whom trouble and sorrow do not come. But that rich man was Israel, to be sure, but he

was Israel "according to the flesh"; for it is said to him that his brothers "have the law and the prophets, let them listen to them."[37] But since he was not Israel "according to the spirit," for that reason trouble and sorrow come on him.

6.1. "The Lord his God is with him, the splendid things of the rulers are with him."[38] For God never abandons his Israel. But let us see of which rulers it is that their splendid things are with Israel. The splendid things of the rulers are their power, their rule and their kingdom. But since there are some rulers who either are to be expelled from their own rule, or perhaps have already been driven out, and in their place and rule those ones are to be introduced who are truly Israelites, all these splendid things, which those rulers had in heaven, who did not keep their own rule, but they abandoned eternal homes,[39] that Israel and Jacob, who has wrestled and conquered[40] will receive, and thus the splendid things of the rulers will be with him.

6.2. "God, who brought him out of Egypt, [is] for him as the glory of a unicorn."[41] To be sure, that Israel was brought out of that earthly Egypt, but this spiritual Israel [is brought] from the Egypt of the world and from the authority of darkness and its glory is as that of a unicorn. Now a unicorn is reported to be an animal that is formed in outward appearance in such a way that it contains a symbol of its own name. We read about this animal frequently in the divine Scriptures, but especially in Job,[42] that the voice of God himself manifests the power and strength of a unicorn. In this, as in very many places, Christ is understood to be indicated. And in the divine Scriptures we have frequently found "horn" recorded for "kingdom." As the prophet also says: "Now the four horns are four kingdoms."[43] And so, under the term unicorn, the following seems to be shown in reference to Christ, that all that he is, is his one horn,

---

[31]Num 23:20. [32]Num 23:16. [33]Num 23:21. [34]Cf. 2 Cor 11:25. [35]Is 35:10. [36]Lk 16:25. [37]Lk 16:29. [38]Num 23:21. [39]Jude 6. [40]Cf. Gen 32:28. [41]Num 23:22. The LXX has *monokerōtos*, which means "with but one horn." [42]Cf. Job 39:9-12. [43]Dan 8:22.

that is, his one kingdom. "For the Father has subjected all things under his feet,"[44] until even the last enemy, death, is destroyed. And Christ possesses one kingdom of everything, "as a unicorn," since, as it is written: "of his kingdom there will be no end."[45] Therefore it says that for him, that is, for that spiritual Israel, there will be glory as is the glory of a unicorn. For this is also what the Lord himself says in the Gospel: "Father, grant to them that just as you and I are one, so also they may be one in us."[46] And therefore, a similar glory will be given to Israel, as is the glory of a unicorn, especially since "he will transform the body of our humiliation to be conformed to the body of his glory."[47]

7.1. "For there will not be augury in Jacob, nor divination in Israel. In time it shall be told to Jacob and Israel, what God shall perform."[48] Since it has already seemed appropriate for us to discuss rather carefully each of the details, it does not seem absurd if we likewise investigate what is augury or divination. For Scripture was pleased to make mention of these things. Otherwise, someone may perhaps fall into these things through ignorance. Now it seems to me that foreknowledge of the future is a neutral matter, in terms of the thing itself, that is, it is neither properly good nor properly evil. For sometimes the foreknowledge of the future can come to the awareness of persons who are even on the devil's side. But of course there is no doubt that when the time and occasion demand it, and when the will of God has been present, foreknowledge is likewise given by God to human beings through the prophets. And that is why we said that it can neither be called properly good, since sometimes it comes from the evil one, nor properly evil, since sometimes it proceeds from God.

7.2. And although examples are at hand in abundant supply from the divine Scriptures, yet we believe that it will suffice if we use the Scrip-

ture that we read in the books of Kingdoms, where it says: "the ark of God was captured by the Philistines[49] and brought to Ashdod,[50] and there they put it in the house of Dagon, and it was found that Dagon had fallen on his face on the ground before the ark of the covenant of the Lord. And the hand of the Lord was heavy on the residents of Ashdod[51] and he scattered them and struck them in their secret parts."[52] "After these things," it says, "the ark entered Akron and the inhabitants of Akron sent and gathered all the satraps of the Philistines and they gathered their own priests and diviners saying: What shall we do with the ark of the Lord? Show us how we shall send it back to its place. The priests and diviners answered: If you send back the ark of the Lord God of Israel, do not send it away empty, but by all means offer it a gift for the transgression, and then you will be healed, and it will be known to you. Otherwise, his hand will not depart from you."[53]

7.3. And after a few things it says: "And now make a new cart and take two cows that have calved on which a yoke has not been set, and yoke the cows to the cart, and lead away their calves behind to their home. And take the ark of the Lord, and put it on the cart, and put likewise on the cart the golden articles which you have offered to it for the transgression, and all the sacred objects. And send it away and let it go and see if it goes by its own way and ascends to its own borders to Beth-shemesh.[54] [If so, the ark] itself caused these great evils for us. But if it does not go that way, we will know that his hand has not touched us, but that these things happened to us by chance."[55] Observe then in these things how the priests and divines contemplate, by means of the indications that have been set forth, the cause of the evils that had come to pass on the Philistines, whether it came from the hand of God and for an injury done to the ark, or whether it happened by chance.

---

[44]1 Cor 15:27. [45]Lk 1:33. [46]Jn 17:21. [47]Phil 3:21. [48]Num 23:23. [49]Lat *Allophylis*. [50]Lat *Azotus*. [51]Lat *Azotians*. [52]1 Sam 5:2-6. [53]Cf. 1 Sam 5:7–6:3. [54]Lat *Bethsamis*. [55]Cf. 1 Sam 6:7-9.

They say: "If it ascends by its own way and to its own borders to Beth-shemesh,[56] it did these evils to us."

7.4. Finally, in what follows it is related: "And when they had placed the ark of the Lord on the cart, the cows led it on the road, opposite to the road which leads to Beth-shemesh,[57] and they did not turn aside to the right or to the left."[58] Well, who would say here, after close examination, that the foreknowledge of the direction taken by the cows was arranged by chance or by some art, and was not the result of some kind of service and operation of demons, who feared the power of the ark of the Lord by which the Philistines were not only being afflicted and punished, but even the very worship of the demons was being destroyed? For each time the ark of the Lord had entered, it cast down their statues and temples. Such, then, is the operation of demons, as it were, in their ministry of foreknowledge. It works by the arts of those who sell themselves out to demons. Sometimes the knowledge is gathered through what they call lots, sometimes it comes through what they call augury, sometimes it even comes from the viewing of scales, which they call the examination of entrails. And in other tricks similar to these, it seems that their foreknowledge is communicated and understood.

7.5. These arts have advanced so far in deceiving the human race that even Manasseh, the son of the most just Hezekiah, was deceived by this error. As the Scripture says, he "built" an altar for the whole army of heaven in the two houses of the Lord.[59] I think that this "army of heaven" is what Paul records as "the spiritual forces of wickedness in the heavenlies."[60] Thus, if there had not been much deception and error in these arts, I do not think that the son of such a great king, who had been trained in the law of

the Lord, could have fallen into these impieties, which are reportedly written about him in the fourth book of Kingdoms. For it says: "And he cast lots and practiced augury, and he made *thyēlēn* (sacrifice),[61] and he made his own sons pass through fire, and he caused wizards to abound. Thus he did evil in the eyes of the Lord and provoked him to anger."[62] Such then were the sins that he committed. It could be said of these things that they were done "with all power, with signs and false prodigies,"[63] so that they could deceive even the elect.[64] For through [Manasseh], the people too were deceived, so that they "did evil in the sight of the Lord, beyond those nations that God had banished from the presence of the sons of Israel."[65]

7.6. Moreover, in the second book of Paralipomenon,[66] similar things are written no less in connection with Manasseh. It says: "And he made groves and worshiped all the army of heaven and served them. And he built altars in the house of the Lord, where the Lord said: In Jerusalem shall be my name for ever. And there he built altars to all the grandeur of heaven in the two houses of the Lord.[67] And he made his own sons pass through the fire in Gehenna; and he practiced lots and did evil deeds and practiced augury and appointed ventriloquists[68] and enchanters, and he multiplied this [wickedness]. Thus he did evil in the sight of the Lord and provoked him to anger."[69]

So I am not in doubt that all these things are done by the operation of demons, that is, augury, the examination of entrails, various kinds of immolation, lots, observance of the movements of birds or animals, and any inspection of scales that would seem to indicate anything about the future. For the demons direct the movements of the birds or animals or scales or lots in accordance with these signs, which

---

[56]Lat *Bethsamis*. [57]Lat *Bethsamis*. [58]1 Sam 5:10-12. [59]2 Kings 21:5. The LXX has "in the two courts of the house of the Lord." [60]Eph 6:12. [61]Rufinus preserves the Greek word here. [62]Cf. 2 Kings 21:6. [63]Cf. 2 Thess 2:9. [64]Cf. Mt 24:24. [65]2 Kings 21:9. [66]*Paralipomenon* is Greek for "matters omitted." This is the name given by the Greek translators to the books of Chronicles, which St. Jerome used as a title in his Latin edition. [67]The LXX and RSV read "in the two courts of the house of the Lord." [68]This is the LXX term for necromancers, i.e., those who communicate with the dead. It does not bear the modern meaning. [69]2 Chron 33:3-6.

likewise showed that the demons are observed by those to whom they handed down the knowledge of this art.

7.7. The one who is a man of God and is numbered in the portion of God[70] must completely repudiate all these things. He should have nothing to do with those things that the demons do by their occult contrivances; otherwise one would once again be associated with demons through these things and would be filled with their spirit and power and would be restored again to the worship of idols. For our divine and heavenly religion renounces all these things. Indeed, in Leviticus it expresses this openly by a law that says: "You shall not practice divination or augury";[71] and after a few things it says: "You will not follow ventriloquists or attach yourselves to enchanters to be polluted by them; I am the Lord your God."[72] And again in Deuteronomy it says: "But if you enter into the land that the Lord your God will give to you, do not learn to act according to the abominations of those nations. There should not be found among you one who purifies his son or his daughter in fire, nor one who divines divination, nor one who allots lots, nor a sorcerer or enchanter or ventriloquist or an observer of portents, nor one who consults the dead. For all who do these things are an abomination to the Lord; for on account of these abominations the Lord your God is destroying these nations from your presence."[73] In all of these things it seems to show that all who are involved in these things are doing nothing else but consulting the dead; for they are dead, since they do not share in life. "But our God is the God of the living and not of the dead."[74]

7.8. To all these laws the following is added as well, that the one who wants to be perfect should learn from no other but from him who

was a prophet chosen through the power of God to minister to the people. Thus it says: "Be perfect in the sight of the Lord your God; for those nations whose inheritance you have taken listen to omens and divinations; but the Lord your God has not granted this to you. For the Lord your God will raise up a prophet from your midst, from your brothers; you will listen to him. By all things whatsoever you have asked of the Lord your God from Horeb on the day of the assembly,[75] when you said: Let us not arrange to hear the voice of the Lord our God, and we will not see that great fire any longer, lest we die."[76]

7.9. God does not want us to become hearers and disciples of demons, that we should learn from demons whatever we want to learn. For it is better not to know something than to learn it from demons, and it is better not to learn from a prophet than to consult those who practice divination. For divination is not divinely given, as some think. On the contrary, it seems to me that it received its name by an anti-phrase,[77] that is, from the opposite, as if it were a thing that comes through men who have been possessed by a demon.[78] But pagan religion believed that everything is divine that is produced through any kind of spirit. In contrast, God commands us to learn nothing from them, lest we become partners of these things and fall into what Isaiah says: "And your words will be brought down to the earth, and your speech will sink down under the earth; and your voice will be as of one speaking from the earth, and your voice will become weak [as it speaks] to the ground."[79]

7.10. For this reason even our Lord Jesus does not deem it fitting to receive testimony from demons, but he says: "Be quiet and come out of him."[80] Likewise his own apostle Paul, imitating him, says: "Grieving he turned and

---

[70]Cf. Deut 32:9. [71]Lev 19:26. [72]Lev 19:31. [73]Deut 18:9-12. [74]Mt 22:32. [75]Lat *ecclesiae*. [76]Cf. Deut 18:14-16. [77]In Greek rhetoric, *antiphrasis* is the use of a word in a sense opposite to its proper meaning. [78]According to the SC editors, it is Rufinus, not Origen, who is speaking in this sentence, since the reproach that "divination is not divinely given" (*divinatio non divinitus datur*) works in Latin, but not in Greek (*manteia*). [79]Cf. Is 29:4. [80]Mk 1:25.

said to the spirit of Python: I command you in the name of Jesus Christ, leave her."[81] Here you may perhaps ask why Paul grieves when he rebukes the spirit of Python. Had it spoken any blasphemy? For it says: "A woman having a spirit of Python" was following Paul and those who were with him, and was shouting, saying: 'These men are servants of the most High God, who are announcing to you the way of salvation.' And she was doing this for many days."[82] From this it is shown that Paul was grieved not because of blasphemy, but because he judged it inappropriate that his words be attested by the spirit of Python. But if Paul does not allow that spirit to give him testimony, but grieves over this, how much more should we grieve if at some time we see that souls are deceived by those who believe in some spirit of Python, as if it were divine, or in a ventriloquist, or in a divine, or in augury, or in any other demons like this?

On this account, then, it says: "There shall not be augury in Jacob, nor divination in Israel."[83]

7.11. But what is added to these things? It says: "In time it shall be told to Jacob and Israel, what God shall perform."[84] What does this mean: "In time it will be told"? When it is opportune, when it is expedient, that is, "In time." Thus if it is expedient that we have foreknowledge of future events, they will be told by God through the prophets of God, through the Holy Spirit. But if they are neither told nor announced, know that it is not expedient for us to have foreknowledge about what is coming. But if they are not told to us for the reason that it is not expedient for us to know these things, those who itch to have foreknowledge about future things by means of various arts and by the invocation of demons are doing nothing else but desiring to learn things that it is not expedi-

ent for them to know. But one should understand that everyone for whom there exists this struggle against the principalities and powers and against the rulers of this world[85] is called a Jacob in respect to these things.[86] And understand as Israel all who see God with the purity of faith and with purity of mind.

7.12. But someone can say, if we should learn about the future from God alone and should not receive a divine or an augur or any other such thing, then we should not even receive Balaam himself. For he is one of those whom the divine verdict prevents us from receiving. But consider this more carefully and remember what we read higher up, where it is said about him that "the Lord put his word into his mouth."[87] Consequently, the things that we are now learning are not from Balaam, but it is the word of God that has been placed in his mouth. For if they were not the words of the Lord, surely the Lord would not have revealed these things to his servant Moses. Since Moses was far off when Balaam spoke these things to king Balak, it is certain that unless God had revealed these things to Moses, he would not have been able to know them.[88]

7.13. But in order to completely destroy divination and augury and other such things, let us fittingly add the following as well. All these things make use of the service of birds and animals, but only kinds that are recorded to be unclean in the law and always found to be lying in ambush against the human race. Surely from this fact, they have indicated things that are favorable and worthy of the service of demons. For dragons and other serpents are presented for service to the Pythons. For augurs and for those who are thought to search for auspices by divining from events, either wolves bear the omens, or foxes or hawks or ravens or eagles or other animals of this sort. I believe it is for

---

[81]Acts 16:18. [82]Acts 16:17-18. [83]Num 23:23. [84]Num 23:23. [85]Cf. Eph 6:12. [86]Cf. Gen 32:24. [87]Num 22:38; 23:5, 12, 16. [88]The meaning apparently is that since Moses was not present when Balaam spoke his oracles to Balak, he must have received revelation about them from God in order to record them in the book of Numbers. See Philo *On the Life of Moses* 2.186; Josephus *Jewish Antiquities* 4.6.

these reasons that in the law Moses marked these out as unclean.[89]

8.1. After this it says: "Behold the people shall rise up as a lion's whelp, and shall exult as a lion."[90] In these things it seems to me that he is describing the confidence of the people who believe in Christ and the freedom that they have in the faith, and the exultation that they bear in hope. For they are compared with a lion's whelp, while they strive for perfection, joyful and swift; in fact they are compared with a lion when they already attain the things that are perfect. For just as a lion and a lion's whelp fear no animal or beast, but all things are subject to them, so also for the perfect Christian, "who takes up his cross and follows Christ,"[91] who can say: "The world has been crucified to me, and I to the world,"[92] all things have been subjected, all things are trampled on.[93] For he despises and condemns all that is in the world, and he imitates him who is called the lion from the tribe of Judah[94] and a lion's whelp, since just as [Christ] himself is the light of the world and has granted to his disciples that they too should be the light of the world,[95] so also, since he himself is a lion and a lion's whelp, likewise he ascribes the name of lion and lion's whelp to those who believe in him.[96]

8.2. But notice that these things are obviously not being said about that people who existed at that time, but about those people who were to come. For it says: "Behold the people *will* arise as a lion's whelp, and *will* exult as a lion."[97] Surely the people he speaks of as about to arise refers to the people who were coming. For if he were speaking about the people who were before his eyes, doubtless he would have said: Behold a people *has arisen* as a lion's whelp. But it is certain

that he is speaking about that people of whom it is also written in the Psalms: "And they will announce his justice to a people who will be born, whom the Lord made."[98] So this people is the lion's whelp, while they still "long for the rational milk without deceit, as new born infants."[99] But they are an exulting lion when, "having become a man, he puts aside the things that belonged to infancy."[100]

9.1. "He will not sleep, until he eats the prey, and drinks the blood of the wounded."[101] In these words, who will be such a contentious defender of the historical narrative, or rather, who will be found so dull, that he would not take refuge by sheer necessity in the sweetness of allegory and shrink back from the sound of the letter? For how will that people, who are so praiseworthy and magnificent, of whom the word lists so many praiseworthy things, come to the point of drinking the blood of the wounded? For God forbids the consumption of blood by so many forceful commands that even we who are called from the Gentiles are necessarily commanded to abstain "both from things sacrificed to idols and from blood."[102]

9.2. So let them tell us who this people are who are accustomed to drink blood. These were the things that those Jews in the Gospel who were following the Lord were scandalized about and said: "Who can eat flesh and drink blood?"[103] But the Christian people, the faithful people, hear these things and embrace them and follow him who says: "Unless you eat my flesh and drink my blood, you will not have life in yourselves; for my flesh is truly food, and my blood is truly drink."[104] And surely, the one who said these things was wounded for men; for "he was wounded for our sins,"[105] as

---

[89]Lev 11:13-19. [90]Num 23:24. [91]Mt 16:24. [92]Gal 6:14. Cf. *Commentary on Romans* 5.9; *Homilies on Judges* 7.2; 8.5. [93]Cf. Lk 10:17-20. [94]Rev 5:5. [95]Mt 5:14. [96]Here Origen gives a rather extensive description of the perfect Christian. F. Ledegang, *Mysterium Ecclesiae: Images of the Church and Its Members in Origen*, BETL 156 (Leuven : Leuven University Press, 2001), p. 36, comments: "What stands out in this is, that he bases these characteristics of the perfect man on the Bible and that he does not only regard the perfect imitation on an ethical level (of among other things asceticism), but in the historical perspective of salvation through the cross and the sovereignty of Christ." [97]Num 23:24. [98]Ps 22:31. [99]Cf. 1 Pet 2:2. [100]1 Cor 13:11. [101]Num 23:24. [102]Acts 15:29. [103]Cf. Jn 6:52-53. [104]Jn 6:53-55. [105]Is 53:5.

Isaiah says. But we are said to drink the blood of Christ not only in the rite of the sacraments, but also when we receive his words, in which are life, as he himself says: "The words that I have spoken are spirit and life."[106] Thus, he himself was wounded, whose blood we drink, that is, we receive the words of his teaching. Moreover, they are no less wounded who have preached his word to us. For when we read their words, that is, the words of his apostles, and when we attain to life from them, we are "drinking the blood of the wounded."

9.3. Therefore it says: "He will not sleep until he eats the prey." For that people who are compared with a lion's whelp or a lion will not rest or sleep until they seize the prey, that is, until they plunder the kingdom of heaven. For "from the days of John, the kingdom of heaven suffers violence, and those who do violence plunder it."[107] Now, that you may recognize very plainly that these things are written about our people, who are covenanted into the sacraments[108] of Christ, listen to how Moses declares similar things on other subjects when he says: "They will drink the cream of cows and the milk of sheep, with the fat of lambs and rams, of the calves of bulls and goats, with the fat of kidneys, of wheat and wine, the blood of the grape."[109] So this is the blood that is called "of the grape," of that grape that is produced from that vine of which the Savior says: "I am the true vine, but the disciples are the branches. But the Father is the vinedresser,"[110] who prunes[111] them so that they may bear more fruit.

Thus you are the true people of Israel, who know how to drink blood and you know how to eat the flesh of the Word of God and drink the blood of the Word of God and to draw the blood of that grape that is from the true vine and from those branches which the Father prunes. The fruit of their branches will de-

servedly be called the "blood of the wounded," which we drink from their words and from their teaching, but only if we are like the lion's whelp, rising up, and like the lion, exulting.

9.4. For the time being, let these things be sufficient commentary on Balaam's second vision. But let us pray to the Lord that with respect to the other things as well that have been prophesied, he may deem us worthy to open up what needs to be understood more clearly, and the meanings that are closest to the truth. And so, by considering these things in the spirit, which have been written down through the Spirit, and by "comparing spiritual things with spiritual things," we may explain what has been written in a way that is worthy of God and of the Holy Spirit who inspired these things, in Christ Jesus our Lord,[112] "to whom is the glory and the power in the ages of ages. Amen."[113]

Homily 17
Numbers 23:25-30; 24:1-9

1.1. We have in hand now the third prophecy from those things which the word of God brought forth through Balaam. Let us discuss some things concerning it as well, as the Lord grants.

Now indeed this wretched Balak was thinking that the divine Balaam lacked the circumstance of location, rather than the will, to speak curses. So he reckoned that it would be advantageous to change location. He said: "Come, and I will lead you to another location, if it pleases God, and you will curse them from there. And Balak took Balaam to the top of Mount Fogor,[1] which extends to the desert."[2]

Now God puts those whom he calls on the top of Mount Sinai;[3] but this Balak, who is opposed to God, "puts Balaam on the top of Mount Fogor." Fogor translates as "delight";

---

[106]Jn 6:63. This is one of the oldest Christian texts that explicitly links Jn 6:53-55 with the sacramental eating of Christ's body and blood in the sacrament of the Eucharist. In the context, Origen does not exclude a metaphorical understanding of the same Scripture as well.
[107]Mt 11:12. [108]Or "mysteries." [109]Deut 32:14. [110]Jn 15:1, 5-8. [111]Or "purges." [112]Notice the trinitarian structure of this conclusion.
[113]1 Pet 4:11. **Homily 17** [1]RSV *Peor*. [2]Num 23:27-28. [3]Cf. Ex 19:2-3.

thus Balak puts people on the top of delight and libidinous desire. For he is a lover of pleasure more than of God, and on that account he puts them on the summit and top of pleasure, in order to exclude them from God. For Balak translates as "excluding" and "devouring." After all this is why Fogor "extends" even "to the desert," that is, to affairs that are void of and deserted by God.

1.2. "And Balaam said to Balak: Construct for me here seven altars, and prepare[4] for me seven calves and seven rams. And Balak did as Balaam told him, and he offered a calf and a ram on [every] altar."[5] The apostle's judgment is clear when he says: "For the things the pagans sacrifice, they sacrifice to demons and not to God."[6] Moreover, the prophet speaks similarly: "They have sacrificed to demons and not to God."[7] Yet, since even the law of God gives commands concerning sacrifices and hands down to the sons of Israel sacrificial rites, perhaps we should ask why these things are commanded to be offered even to God, which apparently have been consecrated to demons. Well, there will indeed be a simple and quick response. We have shown elsewhere[8] that a certificate of divorce was to be given,[9] not by the will of God, who was unwilling that what he had joined together should be separated,[10] but Moses wrote these things on his own "in view of the hardness of heart"[11] of the Jews. Likewise, in this connection, it seems possible that God, as he says through another prophet, "does not eat the flesh of bulls nor does he drink the blood of goats"[12]—and again, as it is written elsewhere: "I did not command you about sacrifices and victims on the day when I led you from the land of Egypt"[13]—but Moses commanded these things to them "in view of the hardness of their heart," as a bad custom to which they had been introduced in Egypt. He did this so that those who were unable to keep themselves from sac-

rificing at the least might sacrifice to God, and not to demons.

1.3. Yet one should consider whether there might be a more hidden and secret reason for sacrificing to God. I mean, consider whether it is possible that sacrifices that are offered to God may result in the destruction of those sacrifices that are immolated to demons. And thus, since through the latter sacrifices, souls are wounded, through the former they are healed. It is just as they affirm who have expertise in medicine. For they maintain that the venom of snakes is driven out by medicine that is made no less from the snakes. So then, the poison of the sacrifices of demons is driven away by sacrifices offered to God, just as also the death of Jesus does not allow the death of sin "to exercise dominion over believers."[14] And indeed, as long as time permitted, sacrifices were confronted with sacrifices; but when the perfect sacrifice came, even the "spotless lamb" who "took away the sin of the whole world,"[15] those sacrifices that were being offered one by one to God already seemed superfluous, since the whole cult of demons has been driven out by this one sacrifice.

But this Balaam, whether in accordance with the intention of his heart, which he had not reformed, or in accordance with that figure by which we said that he represents the character of the teachers and the Pharisees of the unbelieving people, still repeats the offering of victims and still commands sacrifices to be made. For those whose heart does not receive faith in Christ put all their hope in them.

2.1. But what comes next? It says: "And Balaam, seeing that it is good in the sight of the Lord to bless Israel, did not go out according to his custom to meet the auspices, but turned his face toward the desert. And Balaam, lifting up his eyes, observes that Israel had set up their camps by tribes; and the Spirit of God came on

---

[4]Lit. "make." [5]Num 23:29-30. [6]1 Cor 10:20. [7]Deut 32:17. [8]Cf. Homily 16.4.4. [9]Cf. Deut 24:1-4. [10]Cf. Mt 19:5-6. [11]Cf. Mt 19:8. [12]Ps 50:13. [13]Cf. Jer 7:22. [14]Rom 6:9, 14. [15]Jn 1:29.

him. And he took up his parable and spoke."[16]

Perhaps someone is asking how it is that Balaam "sees that it is good in the sight of the Lord to bless Israel." And it will be thought that he came to understand this from the sacrifices that he had offered. For when he sees that none of the demons are present, that no contrary power dares to attend their own victims, that all the servants of wickedness had been shut out, of whom he was accustomed to take advantage in his cursing, on that basis he was able to understand that "it is good in the sight of the Lord to bless Israel."

2.2. However, I prefer to understand the following here, that those people who are now a vain people, and those teachers who detain that people in vanity by not believing in Christ, will one day see, namely, "in the last days,"[17] "when the fullness of the Gentiles enter," and "all Israel" begins to come to the faith of Christ.[18] I mean, at that time those who now "have eyes but do not see,"[19] shall see. For they will lift up their eyes to the higher spiritual meanings, and they will see and understand that "it is good in the sight of the Lord to bless" spiritual "Israel." For they will see Israel arranged by tribes, homes and families, and ready to attain to the glory of the resurrection, "each in his own order."[20] And having "taken up their parable," they will understand what is written in parables. These are things that they neither see nor understand at the present time, because a veil has been placed "over their heart."[21]

Finally, it says, "He did not go out according to his custom to meet the auspices."[22] For by considering the will of God, he will not be carried off by his own usual custom, by foolish and worthless interpretations, to speechless animals and beasts, as those do who infer auspices by means of such things. Instead, he himself will likewise recognize that "God does not care about oxen."[23] In a similar way God does not

care about sheep or birds and other animals, but one should interpret whatever is written about them as having been written for the sake of human beings.[24]

3.1. But let us now see what Balaam utters in the third prophecy. It says: "Balaam son of Beor says, the man who sees truly has spoken, one who hears the words of the Strong One has spoken, one who saw a vision of God in a dream; his eyes have been opened."[25] It is indeed astonishing how Balaam is considered to be worthy of such great praise. The one who "took up his parable" will pronounce these things concerning himself. For how is it that Balaam is "a man truly seeing," who strove after divination and auguries, who was even zealous for magic, as we have shown above? This is very astonishing, unless perhaps such great praises as these should be thought to have been recorded about him in view of what was said above, that "the Spirit of God came on him,"[26] and "the word of God was put in his mouth."[27] For neither Moses nor any other of the prophets will easily be found to have been exalted by such great praises.

3.2. This is why these things seem to me to agree more with that people at the time when they have already been "converted to the Lord, and lay aside the veil that was over their heart. But the Lord is the Spirit."[28] After all, that is why it says: "His eyes have been opened."[29] It is as if those eyes that were closed up to this point will now be opened through the Spirit of God, "who came on him"[30] when the veil was removed.

So now is the time when "he truly sees and he truly hears the words of the Strong One, and he sees the vision of God in a dream,"[31] that is to say, he will see the fulfillment of the times that were indicated in the dreams of the prophet Daniel.[32] He *sees* those visions that were granted to Daniel in dreams, that is, he

---

[16]Num 24:1-3. [17]Acts 2:17. [18]Cf. Rom 11:25. [19]Mk 8:18. [20]1 Cor 15:23. [21]Cf. 2 Cor 3:15. [22]Num 24:1. [23]Cf. 1 Cor 9:9. [24]Cf. 1 Cor 9:10. [25]Lit. "revealed." Num 24:3-4. [26]Num 24:2. [27]Num 23:12. [28]Cf. 2 Cor 3:15-17. [29]Num 24:4. [30]Num 24:2. [31]Cf. Num 24:3-4. [32]Cf. Dan 7:1-2.

will understand and recognize them "with his eyes opened."[33] For he will become like those who said: "But we all with unveiled faces look on the glory of the Lord, having been transformed by the same image from glory to glory, as by the Spirit of the Lord."[34]

3.3. However, I would like to ask which eyes these are that are said to be "opened."[35] Could they perhaps be the ones that in other passages of Scripture are called "the eyes of the earth," as we read in some copies? Could they be what Paul calls "the mind of the flesh," when he says of someone: "Puffed up in vain with the mind of his flesh"?[36] Concerning these eyes, I believe, the serpent as well said to Eve that the Lord knew that "on whatever day you should eat of it, your eyes will be opened";[37] and a little later it says: "and they ate, and the eyes of both of them were opened."[38] For unless there were different kinds of eyes, some being those that are opened by transgression, others being those by which Adam and Eve saw before the former will be opened, Scripture assuredly would never have said to those who had been exposed by transgression, when their eyes were not yet opened: "And the woman saw that the tree was good for eating and pleasing to the eyes for seeing and beautiful to behold, and taking from the tree she ate; and she gave to her husband who was with her, and they ate. And the eyes of both of them were opened."[39] For how is it, if the eyes of both of them had not yet been opened, that the woman "saw that the tree was good for eating and that it was pleasing to the eyes to see? Likewise, with what eyes is it also said to have been "beautiful to behold"?

3.4. But when I hear the voice of my Lord Jesus Christ and understand the power of his goodness, I then turn carefully to what he says: "For judgment I have come into this world, so that those who do not see may see, and those

who see may become blind."[40] For in sinners, the better set of eyes do not see, but those ones do that are called "the mind of the flesh"[41] and which were opened by the counsel of the serpent. Thus the great work[42] of our Lord and Savior is that those ones "become blind" who do not see what the good is with the better eyes, but instead who view what is evil with those eyes that were opened by the counsel of the serpent; and those people who had been blinded in the eyes that the persuasion of the serpent opened may see the good things of the Lord through those eyes which Jesus our Savior came to open. For unless the sight of evil things is first closed off, the viewing of good things will not be opened up. In this sense, then, I interpret that statement of the good God, where he said: "Who made the seeing and the blind?"[43] This refers to those who saw in accordance with Christ, but blind in accordance with the counsel of the serpent.

3.5. We have reminded you of these things in order that it might become clearer what are the eyes that are closed, and what are the eyes that will be opened; at the same time, in order that what is written in the prophet may be understood from these things: "Seeing you will see and you will not see,"[44] that we might know by what eyes they see and by which ones those seeing do not see. So it appears that this Balaam, in view of the fact that "his eyes had been opened,"[45] is speaking about himself when he says, "A man truly seeing," and "the one hearing the words of the Strong One has spoken."[46] For by the same arrangement by which some eyes are closed and others are opened, likewise some ears are understood as needing to be closed, and others as needing to be opened. But if someone wants to take these statements also in accordance with history, he can say that in the fact that "Balaam saw that it is good in the sight of the Lord to bless Israel,"[47] his eyes are shown

---

[33]Num 24:4. [34]2 Cor 3:18. [35]Lit. "revealed." [36]Cf. Col 2:18; Rom 8:5-6. [37]Gen 3:5. [38]Gen 3:6-7. [39]Gen 3:6-7. [40]Jn 9:39. Cf. *Homilies on Ezekiel* 2.3. [41]Cf. Col 2:18; Rom 8:5-6. [42]Lat *opus magnificum*. [43]Ex 4:11. [44]Is 6:9. [45]Num 24:4. [46]Num 24:4. [47]Num 24:1.

to have been opened and that he had become "a man truly seeing." For he saw true things that were coming concerning Israel or concerning Jacob. He will also say that he "heard the words of the Strong One" in that, when God came to him and spoke to him in dreams: "Take care[48] to speak the word that I put into your mouth";[49] and this will be the "vision of God that he saw in his dreams." He will assert that it is by these things that "his eyes were opened," and he was able to see what he saw. These things concern what Balaam has seemed to prophesy about himself in his preamble.

4.1. Well, let us now see what he says in what follows. He says: "How good are your houses, Jacob, your tabernacles, Israel! [They are] as shady groves, as [those] on the rivers of paradise, and as the tabernacles that the Lord set up, as cedars by the waters."[50] With regard to the houses of Jacob that he calls "good," I do not think that he is praising their earthly residences; for no such thing is recorded to have existed among them that was exceptional beyond the other nations. But let us see whether perhaps this may refer to the fact that the people had been divided up by tribes, and each tribe was divided up by clans. And again, the clans were grouped by relatives, and the relatives by the houses of their families. Then again the houses of families were counted by the number of names, individually, that is, "every male twenty years and older who was able to advance to war."[51] Perhaps Balaam beheld these houses in the Spirit and he praises and extols them.

But the meaning that needs to be contemplated does not lie in these considerations of the letter alone, for indeed, what Balaam says, "he speaks, having taken up his parable."[52] So let us also listen to what is said in parables.[53] For if you consider these divisions and arrangements [ordines] of peoples that will be accomplished at the resurrection of the people of the true Israel, when "each rise in his own order [ordine]";[54] if you are able to view those tribes and clans and relatives, in which the relationship is not so much of flesh and blood as of mind and spirit, then you will understand "how good are the houses of Jacob and how good are the tabernacles of Israel."

4.2. Now if you also inquire about the difference between "houses" and "tabernacles" and between "Jacob" and "Israel,"[55] a certain distinction ought to be equally maintained, such as the following. A house is a thing that has foundations, it is stable and fenced off by definite end points. Tabernacles, on the other hand, serve as shelter for those who are always on the way, always moving, and who have not found the end point of their journey. Therefore, Jacob represents those who are perfect in their deeds and work; but Israel stands for those who are zealous in their pursuit of wisdom and knowledge.[56]

Since, therefore, training in works and deeds will one day conclude in a definite end point—for the perfection of works is not without an end—when anyone fulfills all that he was supposed to do and reaches the end of the perfection of works, that very perfection of works will be called his "good house."[57] But there is no end for those who are energetic in their pursuit of wisdom and knowledge—for what limit will there be to God's wisdom? For the more one approaches it, the more he will find greater depths, and the more one has investigated, the more he will discover ineffable and incomprehensible things. Indeed God's wisdom is "incomprehensible and beyond reckoning."[58] On that account, for those who undertake the journey of God's wisdom, he does not praise their houses—for they have not reached the end—but he expresses admiration of the tabernacles in which they are always on the move and making progress. And the more progress they make, the

---

[48]Lit. "observe." [49]Num 22:35. [50]Num 24:5-6. [51]Cf. Num 1:3, 18, 20. [52]Num 24:3. [53]Cf. Mt 13:3. [54]1 Cor 15:23. [55]Cf. Num 24:5. [56]Cf. *Selecta on Numbers* (PG 12.581B); Philo *On the Sacrifices of Cain and Abel* 120. [57]Cf. Num 24:5. [58]Cf. 2 Esd 8:21.

more the road to be traveled is lengthened for them and extends into the measureless. And for this reason, beholding through the Spirit these stages of their progress, he names these things the "tabernacles of Israel."

4.3. And truly, if someone has made some progress in knowledge and has acquired some experience in such matters, he really knows that when he has come to some idea and recognition of spiritual mysteries, his soul tarries there, as it were, in a kind of tabernacle. But when, on the basis of these things it has discovered, it again fathoms other things and advances to other understandings, it picks up its tabernacle from there, so to speak, and heads for the higher things.[59] And there it establishes a seat for its mind, fixed in the stability of the meanings.

And once again from there, on the basis of these things, it finds other spiritual meanings, which doubtless are logical inferences that have come to light by the previously apprehended meanings. And in this way, always "striving for what is ahead,"[60] the soul seems to advance by means of tabernacles, as it were. For there is never a time when the soul that has been set on fire by the spark of knowledge can sink into leisure and take a rest, but it is always summoned from the good to the better, and again from the better to the superior.

4.4. Thus Balaam has very pleasingly and beautifully described this journey to the wisdom of God, when he says: "As shady groves and as [those] on the rivers of paradise, and as the tabernacles that the Lord set up, as cedars by the waters."[61] For those who enter this road, enter through "shady groves"; for the groves are shady for them, the whole assembly of the just and the choir of the holy prophets. For under the shade of the meanings that they find in those writings, their souls are cooled, and by walking in their teachings through the darkness[62] of the groves, so to speak, they are

delighted. They even find "paradises on the rivers," which are similar to and related to that paradise in which is "the tree of life."[63] In fact, we can interpret the rivers as referring either to the Gospels and apostolic Scriptures, or even to the help that angels and heavenly powers give to souls of this sort.[64] For these souls are irrigated and flooded by them and nourished in all knowledge and recognition of heavenly things. Granted that both our Savior is a river "who makes glad the city of God,"[65] and the Holy Spirit is not only himself a river, but he is even given to those in whom "rivers proceed from their belly,"[66] and God the Father says: "They have abandoned me, the spring of living water,"[67] that is to say, it is from that spring that these rivers proceed.[68]

4.5. And so, when they have been flooded by these rivers, the tabernacles of Israel become tabernacles "like those that the Lord set up."[69] But the attentive hearer might be troubled by the present words which mention two kinds of tabernacles. For it says: "How good are your houses, Jacob, your tabernacles, Israel! They are like shady groves, and like [those] on the rivers of paradise."[70] And he again compares the tabernacles with tabernacles and says: "And they are like the tabernacles that the Lord set up."[71] So, in addition to what we just proposed, another explanation can be received. Thus we could say that Jacob's house is the law, and the tabernacles of Israel are the prophets. For he does not praise Jacob himself, but his houses, nor does he praise Israel itself, but its tabernacles. And he praises these things at that time "when his eyes have been opened."[72] For as long as "a veil was placed over the reading"[73] of the law and the prophets, they do not seem to be good tabernacles or praiseworthy houses. But when "the veil is removed," and one begins to understand that the law, as well as the prophets, "is

---

[59]Cf. Col 3:1-2. [60]Cf. Phil 3:13. [61]Num 24:5-6. [62]Lat *opaca*. [63]Cf. Gen 3:22; Rev 2:7. [64]Cf. Heb 1:14. [65]Ps 46:4. [66]Cf. Jn 7:38. [67]Jer 2:13. [68]Notice the trinitarian structure of this thought. [69]Num 24:6. [70]Num 24:5-6. [71]Num 24:6. [72]Num 24:4. [73]Cf. 2 Cor 3:14.

spiritual,"[74] at that time Jacob's houses become good and admirable; and at that time Israel's tabernacles will be worthy of admiration, when you have removed the "letter that kills" and begin to perceive from these things "the life-giving Spirit."[75]

4.6. It can still be understood in another way. He seems to be giving equal praise to the bodies together with the souls of this people who believe and have been perfected, whom Christ has gathered from the nations. The phrase "Jacob's house" would refer to their bodies, just as it is read in a certain little book[76] that Israel is Jacob's house, that is, his body is called Jacob and his soul is called Israel. So likewise also the bodies of the perfect may be called praiseworthy houses. For Jacob is a praiseworthy body, when it is made beautiful by continence and chastity, and sometimes even by martyrdom. In fact the tabernacles can be applied to perfect souls for whom even the name of Israel is befitting, which derives from "seeing God."

4.7. But it says that these tabernacles are "like shady groves, and like [those] on the rivers of paradise, and like the tabernacles which the Lord set up."[77] Thus he is showing that there are other tabernacles that the Lord has set up to which the tabernacles of Israel are similar. It is befitting that I transcend this world to see what are the tabernacles that the Lord has set up. Doubtless they are the ones that he showed to Moses, when he built the tabernacle in the desert, saying to him: "Behold," he says, "you will make everything according to the type that was shown to you on the mountain."[78] So, in imitation of those tabernacles that the Lord set up, Israel should make tabernacles, and each of us should get ready to construct his own tabernacle. This is why it does not seem accidental to me that, on the one hand, Peter, Andrew and the sons of Zebedee were found

to be fishermen by trade,[79] whereas Paul was by trade a "maker of tabernacles."[80] And since they, when called, are converted from the trade of catching fish into becoming fishers of men, when the Lord says: "Come after me, and I will make you fishers of men,"[81] there is no doubt but that Paul too, since he himself was also "called an apostle"[82] through my Lord Jesus Christ, was changed by a similar transformation of his trade. Thus, just as they went from being fishers of fish to fishers of men, so also he was transformed from making earthly tabernacles to constructing heavenly tabernacles.

For he built heavenly tabernacles while teaching everyone the way of salvation, showing them the journey of the blessed mansions in heaven. Paul also makes tabernacles when, by building churches "from Jerusalem in a circuit to Illyricum," he "fulfills the gospel of God."[83] And so he too makes tabernacles in the likeness of the heavenly tabernacles, "which God showed Moses on the mountain."[84]

4.8. Moreover, each of us, if only we have come out of Egypt and dwell in the desert, should dwell in a tabernacle and celebrate a feast day in tabernacles. For just as there was a commemoration of the departure from Egypt by means of the Passover and unleavened bread,[85] so also there was a memory of the commemoration in the desert by means of the tabernacles; for our fathers dwelled in tabernacles in the desert.

But what should these tabernacles be made of except the words of the law and the prophets, the words of the Psalms and all that is contained in the law? For when the soul makes progress from what is written, and always "forgetting the things that are behind, it stretches itself forth to what is ahead,"[86] and moving forward from the lower place,[87] it grows and advances to what is higher, by an increase in the

---

[74]Rom 7:14. [75]Cf. 2 Cor 3:6. [76]Not even Adolf von Harnack, *Der kirchengeschichtliche Ertrag der exegetischen Arbeiten des Origenes*, Texte und Untersuchungen 42.3 (Leipzig: J. C. Hinrichs, 1918–1919), p. 19, was able to identify this book, but suggested a possible referent to the apocryphal book *The Prayer of Joseph*. [77]Num 24:6. [78]Ex 25:40. [79]Cf. Mt 4:18-22. [80]Cf. Acts 18:3. [81]Mt 4:19. [82]Cf. Rom 1:1. [83]Rom 15:19. [84]Cf. Ex 25:40. [85]Cf. Ex 12:11, 17; Num 28:16-17. [86]Cf. Phil 3:13. [87]Cf. Lk 14:10.

virtues. And by that very change of stages, it will deservedly be said to dwell in tabernacles. But consider if these "tabernacles that the Lord has set up"[88] are not also those that the Savior mentions in the Gospel when he says: "Make for yourselves friends from the mammon of unrighteousness, so that when you are in need, they may receive you into eternal tabernacles."[89] But they are said to be "set up"[90] by God insofar as they are not "carried around by every wind of doctrine."[91]

4.9. But these tabernacles are also "like the cedars near the waters."[92] Here he is not speaking of those cedars in which blameworthy pride is rebuked,[93] but the cedars of God which sustain "the branches of that vine that was transferred from Egypt," and in which that fruit rests "whose shade covered the mountains."[94] If you have understood how much rest the journey of wisdom has, how much grace, how much sweetness, do not hesitate, do not be negligent, but undertake this journey, and do not shrink back from the solitude of the desert. For to you who dwell in tabernacles of this sort there will come even heavenly manna, and "you will eat the bread of angels."[95] Only begin, and as we have said, do not let the solitude of the desert frighten you. Even angels will come quickly into your company,[96] which I think are indicated under the form of cedars.

5.1. But now let us see what he prophesies about Christ as well. For it is of him that he says: "A man will come forth from his seed, and he will rule over many nations; and his kingdom will be exalted over Gog, and his kingdom will increase. God led him from Egypt, his glory is as that of a unicorn."[97] Therefore it is Christ who came forth from the seed of Israel according to the flesh.[98] There is no need to explain how he rules over the nations, especially for the one who reads what the Father said to him:

"Ask of me and I will give you the nations for your inheritance, and the ends of the earth for your possession."[99] But what is the meaning of these words: "His kingdom will be exalted over Gog"?[100] Gog translates as "over the roofs," and it is recorded in that passage not, as it is thought, as the name of some nation, but, as in some other passages, the very Hebrew word has been left untranslated, and for this reason it seems to have been spoken as if it referred to some nation. Consequently, the meaning of the statement is this: "and his kingdom will be exalted over the roofs, and his kingdom will increase."

5.2. Now "to be exalted over the roofs" is spoken about the perfection of believers, but "to increase" refers to the multitudes. Thus, in those who are perfect, the kingdom of Christ is exalted "over the roofs," that is, even over those who are in the upper regions and who dwell higher up. For there are perhaps some even in the heavens, beyond whom they advance further, and those who are in the kingdom of Christ are exalted more highly. And therefore, I think, even the Savior himself said: "Let not the one who is on the roof descend to take anything from his house."[101] He was warning that those who have come to the highest perfection should not again descend to the lowly and base things of this world, which are presently called a "house." Moreover, the words: "What you have heard in the ears, proclaim it over the roofs,"[102] no less has this in view. In this way, then, "his kingdom is exalted over Gog, and his kingdom increases."[103] For it increases when the churches are multiplied and the number of believers grows, and the kingdom of Christ increases to such an extent "until the Father places all his enemies under his feet"; and he "destroys the last enemy, death."[104]

6.1. After this it is written, still concerning

---

[88]Lat *fixit*. Cf. Num 24:6. [89]Lk 16:9. [90]Lat *fixa*. [91]Cf. Eph 4:14. [92]Num 24:6. [93]Cf. Ps 37:35. [94]Cf. Ps 80:10. [95]Cf. Ps 78:25; Wis 16:20. [96]Cf. Mk 1:12-13. [97]Num 24:7. RSV *Agag*. [98]Cf. Rom 9:5. [99]Ps 2:8. [100]Num 24:7. [101]Mt 24:17. [102]Mt 10:27. [103]Num 24:7. [104]Cf. 1 Cor 15:25-27.

Christ, that "God led him out of Egypt."[105] This seems to have been fulfilled at that time when, after the death of Herod, he is called back from Egypt. The Gospel indicates this when it says: "Out of Egypt I have called my son."[106] To some these words seem to have been taken from this passage [in Numbers] and were inserted in the Gospels, but to others they seem to come from the prophet Hosea.[107] However, it can also be understood as an allegory, that after he went to the Egypt of this world, the Father led him and took him to himself, so that he could make a way for those who were to ascend to God from the Egypt of this world.[108]

"And his glory is like that of a unicorn."[109] Indeed, by deposing all the kingdoms of the demons, Christ founded his own unique [unum] kingdom, as it were with the glory of a true uni-corn. For we have shown that a horn [cornu] is often the name given to a kingdom. It says, still speaking of the same thing: "He consumes the nations of his enemies, and will suck the marrow of their fat."[110] He himself consumes the nations, it says, which his enemies were possessing. And when the power of the enemy was destroyed, he will suck the marrow of their fat, when he thins out every fatty and carnal meaning from these and converts it into a spiritual understanding. Now the fact that the Scriptures consider "fat" to be a blameworthy condition will be indicated by what it is written: "The heart of this people has become fat,"[111] and elsewhere: "He was sated and grew fat, and the beloved one became recalcitrant."[112]

6.2. Thus he consumes nations and has as food those who believe in him.[113] This is what he himself says in the Gospel: "My food is to do the will of him who sent me."[114] His will, assuredly, was that the nations be converted to the faith. But if, as we have taught above, fat is considered blameworthy, then thin, as the contrary, should be considered praiseworthy. For also "the spirit of wisdom," who is called intelligible, holy, only-begotten and manifold, is likewise declared to be thin [subtilis].[115]

"And with his darts he will pierce the enemy."[116] His darts are his words by which he either conquered the devil, or by which even now he overcomes and transfixes all his enemies and those contradicting him. For all who sin are his enemy, so long as they are sinning. But if one should listen to the words of God, and by recognizing one's sins should be transfixed and pierced by these darts and converted to repentance, the one pierced through by the words of truth will likewise be said to have been transfixed by his darts.

6.3. But after this Balaam also refers to the dispensation of his passion and says: "Lying down, he rested like a lion and like the whelp of a lion; who will rouse him?"[117] He rested like a lion when he was put on the cross and "stripped the principalities and powers, triumphing over them by the wood of the cross,"[118] but as the whelp of a lion, when he rises again from the sleep of death. Now the fact that he is compared simultaneously to a lion and to the whelp of a lion can further be understood as said for the following reason: that in those who are perfect, the name lion is given, but in those who are raw recruits and only starting out, whelp of a lion is named. Now as for these words: "Who will rouse him?" this is said because sometimes he is said to have been raised by the Father, sometimes he even claims that he himself "raises the temple of his own body" after three days.[119] Rightly, therefore, he indicates here the disposition of one who is, so to speak, asking a question.

6.4. "Those who bless you have been blessed, and those who curse you have been cursed."[120] It is certain that those who bless Christ are

---

[105]Num 24:8. [106]Cf. Mt 2:15. [107]Cf. Hos 11:1. [108]Cf. Homily 2.1; *Homilies on Exodus* 3.3; 8.1; Justin *Dialogue with Trypho* 120.3. [109]Num 24:8. [110]Num 24:8. [111]Acts 28:27; cf. Is 6:9-10. [112]Deut 32:15. [113]Cf. Mt 16:8. [114]Jn 4:34. [115]Cf. Wis 7:22. [116]Num 24:8. [117]Num 24:9. [118]Col 2:15. [119]Cf. Jn 2:19, 21; Mt 26:61. [120]Num 24:9.

blessed and have been received into the communion of the Father's blessing; but those who curse him are cursed. For if you consider that people who curse Christ, one even finds it to be a lamentably cursed people. For what else could come to pass for those who curse Wisdom, who curse Truth, who curse Life,[121] except that they lie there banished and exiled from all these good things? For Christ is all these things; and the one who curses Christ, by cursing all these things, as it were, has been condemned by an eternal curse.

6.5. Nevertheless, I think that it is not merely the one who brings forth words of cursing against him who curses Christ, but also the one who, with the name of Christian, acts evilly and behaves basely, and by means of his shameful words and actions causes "his name to be blasphemed among the nations";[122] just as, on the contrary, that one should not be considered to bless who blesses the Lord with words alone, but who causes everyone to bless the name of the Lord by means of his actions, life and character.

And what Balaam indicates by his third prophecy will be fulfilled more in this way, that "those who bless" Christ "will be blessed, and those who curse him will be cursed."[123] For these reasons, let us by all means be on guard against blaspheming the name of Christ through our deeds and actions. Instead let us act in a way that we deserve to be sharers of his blessings. "To him be the blessing and glory in the ages of ages."[124] Amen.

Homily 18
Numbers 24:10-19

1.1. We will now take up the fourth prophecy from the things that Balaam spoke by the Word of God. We want to open up from it what God grants.

Now things similar to this prophecy were previously spoken in the preface, just as above. For it says: "And Balak was enraged against Balaam, and he clapped his hands together; and Balak said to Balaam: I summoned you to curse my enemy, and behold, you have blessed them with a blessing this third time. Now therefore flee to your place; I said: I will honor you, but now the Lord has deprived you of honor."[1] Here it has shown that even Balak understood that Balaam was deceived no longer by the service of demons, but by the power of God he has been transferred to better things, and this is why he says: "The Lord has deprived you of honor."[2] But let us pass over these things which are plain enough and come to what follows.

1.2. "And Balaam said to Balak: Did I not speak to your messengers also whom you sent to me, saying: If Balak should give me his own house full of silver and gold, I shall not be able to go beyond the word of the Lord, to make it good or bad by myself? Whatsoever things God says to me, this I will speak. And now, behold, I am returning to my place."[3] Balaam knows that the responses were not brought to himself by the usual ministers. Instead they came from him who holds authority over all. He seems correct in his declaration that he "cannot go beyond the Word of the Lord and make it small or great by himself."[4] For the one speaking to him was not one who could be changed by sacrifices and gifts, but it was he "with whom there is no change or shadow of change."[5] And therefore, a priest cannot be changed by wages, when God is not moved by gifts.

1.3. And yet, when Balaam is about to depart, he begins to prophesy again and says: "Come, I give you counsel, what this people will do to your people in the last days. And taking up his parable he spoke."[6] But before we come to the explanation of these things that were prophesied, I want to ask what is the meaning and se-

[121]Cf. Jn 14:6. [122]Rom 2:24. [123]Num 24:9. [124]Rev 5:13. **Homily 18** [1]Num 24:10-11. [2]Num 24:11. [3]Num 24:12-14. [4]Cf. Num 24:13. The lemma had "good or bad." [5]Jas 1:17. [6]Num 24:14.

quence of thought in what he says: "Come, and I will give you counsel." Yet no counsel seems to be given, but he says: "What this people will do to your people in the last days."[7] Now surely the statement would have seemed more appropriate if it had said: Come, I prophesy to you what this people will do to your people in the last days. Then there would have been logical coherence; then Balaam would have seemed to prophesy about those things that the people of Israel would do to the people of Balak, or to other nations, and what it would do in power[8] in such a way that they would leave no one from the cities of Moab who would be saved.

2.1. Moreover, the prophecy he adds in what follows, which is about Christ, and in which he says: "A star will arise from Jacob, and a man will arise from Israel, and he will lay waste to the rulers of Moab"[9] would no less have seemed to have been recorded appropriately, if it had been written: Come, and I prophesy to you. But now, what are we to say of what is written: "Come, I give counsel to you, what this people will do to your people"? Let us ask, then, how what is written should be understood: "I give counsel to you."[10]

While continuously searching for the meaning of this myself, I have been unable to discover the complement for this statement, if we are to think that the words: "I give you counsel" have been said by common usage and custom. But instead, I have noticed that the following does fit with what he says: "I give you counsel," that he should be understood to mean: I am now disclosing to you the divine counsel that must be fulfilled in the last days. It has been revealed to me, and I am making it known, so that you may know "what this people will do to your people." In this way, it seemed possible for me to determine the meaning of what he said: "I give you counsel, what this people will do to your people," that is: I am announcing and making known to you the counsel of God.

2.2. Now, of course, in my research in the divine Scriptures, whenever I have been able to encounter some statement similar to these words, it has seemed good likewise to pay attention to it. For example, the apostle says: "For who has known the mind of the Lord, or who has become [his] counselor?"[11] For the "who" here does not mean "no one," but "rare is the one who," or "privileged is the one who." For how could his Only Begotten not have known the mind of God, seeing that he says: "No one knows the Father except the Son and the one to whom the Son wills to reveal"?[12] But what else is it to know the Father if not to know both his counsel and mind? Moreover, the Holy Spirit, who searches even the deep things of God,[13] what does he know if not his mind? Therefore both the Son and the Holy Spirit know the mind of the Lord, and those to whom the Son wills to reveal. But if the Son knows the mind of God, then he is also his counselor. But counselor should not be interpreted in the sense that the Son and the Spirit give counsel to one who does not know what he should do. On the contrary, it means that the Son and the Holy Spirit know and participate in his counsel and will.

2.3. And so in a similar way, Balaam, since God had revealed part of his counsel to him, made Balak share in this and become aware of it. He says: "Come, I give you counsel," as one who truly sees and who truly hears the words of God, just as in the following he says: "Balaam, son of Beor, has spoken, a man who truly sees, hearing the words of God, knowing the knowledge of the Most High, and seeing a vision of God in dreams, his eyes were opened."[14]

We have already spoken above about all these things, since the same things were also written in the preface of the third prophecy. Now the added words, "who knows the knowledge of the Most High" appear only in the present passage. For this is not said above in connection with Balaam. Indeed, it has not been easy for me to find it

---

[7]Num 24:14. [8]Cf. Num 24:18. [9]Num 24:17. [10]Num 24:14. [11]Rom 11:34. [12]Mt 11:27. [13]Cf. 1 Cor 2:10. [14]Num 24:3-4.

recorded about any of the holy prophets at all.

3.1. This is why I am exceedingly astonished over the way this is written about Balaam. To him it was not granted to say what is usual and customary for prophets to say: "Thus says the Lord." Instead, he says: "Balaam has spoken, a man who truly sees has spoken."[15] Furthermore, how will he be so worthy that the following is understood of Balaam, that "he knows the knowledge of the Most High"?[16] For he even taught Balak the king how to cast a stumbling block before the sons of Israel, so that they ate things that had been sacrificed [to idols] and committed fornication.[17] For hardly concerning the holy prophets or apostles will anyone find a statement that they "know the knowledge of the Most High." Granted, Paul said that he had heard unspeakable words, which it is not permitted for men to speak.[18] Yet he did not profess to have "knowledge of the Most High." So let us look more intently, in the hope that perhaps God will deign to reveal something worthy to us concerning these words.

3.2. In the book which among us is usually considered to be among the books of Solomon and is called "Ecclesiasticus," but among the Greeks is called "The Wisdom of Jesus, son of Sirach," it is written: "All wisdom is from God."[19] Possibly we could interpret this to mean that even that wisdom of this world, which is said to be destined for destruction,[20] is from God, and that of the rulers of this world, and if there is any other through which false wisdom is commended. However, in the same little book it is said later on: "For the wisdom of evil is not instruction."[21] By this he surely shows that all instruction that asserts anything false, even if it seems vigorous and truthful and the kind that could scarcely be undermined, nevertheless we should by no means attach the name of wisdom to knowledge of this sort. Well then, what is the

meaning of the statement: "All wisdom is from God"?[22]

To me the following sense seems apparent: we may designate as wisdom given by the Lord either every skill that is considered necessary for human use in a craft, or the knowledge of any matter may be called wisdom given by the Lord. After all, in Job it is written: "Who has given women the wisdom to weave and the knowledge of embroidery?"[23] Moreover, in Exodus it says: "The Lord spoke to Moses, saying: Behold, I have called by name Bezalel,[24] the son of Uri, son of Hur,[25] from the tribe of Judah, and I have filled him with a divine spirit of wisdom and understanding and instruction, so that he may have understanding in every work and be a craftsman in working with silver and gold and bronze, and in chiseling stones, and in all sculpted works, and in wood. Thus he can work according to all the works to which I have appointed him. Moreover, Oholiab[26] the son of Ahisamach,[27] of the tribe of Dan; and I put into his heart understanding with all prudence, that they may do all that I have appointed for you."[28]

3.3. From all these things, then, consider how the craftsman's wisdom is from the Lord, whether in gold or in silver or in any other material, and also the weaver's wisdom. And notice that it can be justly said about all these that the knowledge of these is from the Most High. But if a craftsman's knowledge is declared to be from the Most High, why not the knowledge of geometry, from which, surely, this knowledge is derived, which Scripture names architectonic knowledge? After all, even in Zechariah a geometer's line is spoken of, with which the angel measures Jerusalem.[29] And for this reason I do not think it seems absurd if even this knowledge is said to be from the Most High. But what shall we say of music, in which the most wise David had attained such complete mastery and

---

[15]Num 24:15. [16]Num 24:16. [17]Cf. Num 25:1-3. [18]Cf. 2 Cor 12:4. [19]Sir 1:1. [20]Cf. 1 Cor 2:6. [21]Cf. Sir 19:22. [22]Sir 1:1. [23]Cf. Job 38:36. [24]Lat *Beselehel*. [25]Lat *Or*. [26]Lat *Eliab*. [27]Lat *Achisamach*. [28]Cf. Ex 35:30-35; 36:1; 31:1-6. [29]Cf. Zech 2:1-2.

had acquired instruction in all melodies and rhythms, that from all these things he created sounds on his harp with which he could even soothe a very disturbed king who was harassed by an evil spirit?[30] This is why I do not think that any man of right sense would deny that in the knowledge of all these things, all wisdom is from God. Now indeed, I do not think this can be doubted concerning the knowledge of medicine. For if there is any knowledge from God, which knowledge will more likely be from him than the knowledge of healing, in which both the virtues of plants, the properties of juices and the differences of their effects are discerned?

3.4. Therefore from all these things, it is inferred that even the knowledge of this Balaam, for which he was summoned to curse Jacob from the mountains of Mesopotamia from the east,[31] has its commencement and origin from the Most High. And from that source comes his knowledge by which he had learned about the natures of animals and the movements of birds and the differences in sounds. But these things that he received as knowledge of good things, he had put to evil use. To me this seems similar to the case of one who learned medicine and became acquainted with the virtues of plants and recognized their properties. Doubtless this knowledge is given by God to men for the sake of healing. But suppose this one wishes to convert his purpose and uses all this knowledge, which was granted to bring health to bodies, for evil. And instead of a doctor, he becomes a poisoner; instead of remedies, he brings diseases; instead of healing, he brings death.

3.5. Now that we might understand more fully that the wisdom of all knowledge traces its origin to God, but sinks into evil when men of evil purpose, or even demons, mix in certain corruptions of the wisdom of God, let us reread the things that are written in Daniel about Daniel himself and his three friends. Nebu-

chadnezzar[32] the king handed them over to be educated for three years. He wanted them to become very knowledgeable in his own, that is, his country's, wisdom, namely, that of the Babylonians. And so it is written there that "The Lord gave them knowledge and understanding and prudence in every grammatical art; and to Daniel he gave understanding in all words and in visions and dreams; and they were with the king, and in all speech and prudence and instruction in which the king inquired of them, he found them ten times superior to the sophists and philosophers who were in his entire kingdom."[33]

3.6. Now this indeed is contained in the copies of the seventy translators; but in the codices of the Hebrews I have discovered something even more powerful. Granted that we do not use these codices, but we should mention this for the sake of knowing it. Precisely where we read: "God gave to them understanding and prudence in all grammatical wisdom; and Daniel had understanding in every vision and in dreams,"[34] after a few things, those codices say: "And they stood in the presence of the king, and in every word of wisdom and instruction in which the king inquired of them, he found them ten times superior to all the enchanters and magicians, who were in his whole kingdom."[35]

So from all this it can be understood how Balaam as well said about himself: "He who knows the knowledge of the Most High,"[36] namely, it means that the origin of all knowledge began with him, but through the fault of human malice, with demons inspiring and secretly stealing from it as well, they turned it to destruction. This was allowed to them for the sake of bringing benefit. Let this be our discussion, given to the best of our ability, of his words: "knowing the knowledge of the Most High."

4.1. After this it says: "Who sees the vision of God in dreams, his eyes having been

---

[30]1 Sam 16:23. [31]Cf. Num 23:7. [32]Lat *Nabuchodonosor*. [33]Cf. Dan 1:17-20. [34]Dan 1:17. [35]Dan 1:20. [36]Num 24:16.

opened."[37] We have discussed these things sufficiently in the third vision, and it would be superfluous to repeat the same things.

So let us consider the meaning of what he says in what follows: "I will point to him, and not now; I bless, and he does not draw near."[38] Now in other copies it reads: "I will *see* him, but not now." If this reading is received, it will be thought easier to understand. Thus he is saying that Christ, of whom he says in what follows: "A star will arise from Jacob, and a man will arise from Israel"[39] must be *seen*, but not now. That is to say, not at that time when he was saying these things; for in the last days, when the fullness of times came, God sent his own Son.[40]

But if the text is read in accordance with what we have in our copies, that is: "I will point to him, and not now; I bless, and he does not draw near,"[41] it does not refer to this Balaam through whom these things are being said, but to those whose persona we said[42] is being represented here. For those doctors of the law and the scribes will point to Christ who is prophesied in the law and the prophets, but not now, that is, not at the time when he came, but when "the fullness of the Gentiles enter, and all Israel will begin to be saved."[43] At that time they will point to him and at that time they will bless the one whom they now blaspheme. But the time when these things will be is not drawing near. For it is far off and is to be hoped for at the end of the age. And that is why it says: "I will point to him, and not now," to him, that is, to the people who will be saved at that time.

4.2. After this it says: "A star will arise from Jacob, and a man will arise from Israel."[44] We have already spoken about these things above. It is clearly a prophecy of the star that appeared to the Magi in the east. With it as their guide, they came to Judea seeking him who was born king of Israel, and when they found him they worshiped him when they offered him gifts.[45]

Now what troubles me about this star is that, after it is said in the Gospel that it went ahead of the Magi up to Bethlehem, and "coming, it stood above where the child was,"[46] it says nothing more about whether it departed from there or disappeared or was removed. The Gospel narrative does not indicate anything at all about this. It only says that it came and "stood above where the child was." Thus, perhaps it was similar to what happened at the time of the baptism, when "Jesus was baptized and came up from the Jordan, the heavens were opened for him, and John saw the Spirit of God descending as a dove and abiding above him," and he heard "a voice from heaven saying: This is my beloved Son, in whom I am well pleased."[47] So then, perhaps this star as well, which "came above where the child was and stood there," in a similar way continued to remain on Christ, just as it is said that "the Holy Spirit came in the form of a dove" and "abided on him." And just as we understand that "the Spirit of God came above him and remained on him" in such a way that the Spirit of God never departed from him, so also I think the star which came and stood above him should be understood. It stood above him in such a way that it was never removed from there.

And this is why I am convinced that this star was a symbol of his deity. Indeed, the sequence of the prophecy points to these same things in a coherent fashion, when it says concerning his deity: "A star will arise from Jacob,"[48] but concerning his human nature it says: "and a man will arise from Israel."[49] Thus in both aspects, both according to his deity and according to his humanity, Christ appears to have been clearly prophesied.

4.3. "And he will devastate the rulers of Moab."[50] Now Moab is a nation whose rulers we understand to be none other than the spiritual forces of wickedness and those principalities

---

[37]Num 24:16. [38]Num 24:17. [39]Num 24:17. [40]Cf. Gal 4:4. [41]Num 24:17. [42]Cf. Homily 14.4.1. [43]Rom 11:25. [44]Num 24:17. [45]Mt 2:2-11. [46]Mt 2:9. [47]Mt 3:16-17. [48]Num 24:17. [49]Num 24:17. [50]Num 24:17.

against whom we struggle.[51] Thus, that man from Israel will devastate them when he strips the principalities and powers and fastens them to his cross.[52] For he would not have been able to save the Moabites and lead them to the knowledge of God unless he had devastated those rulers who had held an ungodly dominion over them. "And he will plunder all the sons of Seth."[53] Seth is the son of Adam concerning whom Eve said when he was born: "For the Lord has raised up for me another seed in place of Abel, whom Cain killed."[54] So that is the Seth from whom the whole human race in this world is called;[55] for those who were born from Cain perished in the flood. Thus all men who are in this world are sons of Seth. And when it is said: "He will plunder all the sons of Seth," understand the plunder in the same way as we interpreted it in the section higher up, where it is written: "He will devour the nations of his enemies,"[56] and where he is compared with the whelp of a lion and with a lion.[57]

4.4. So here he takes as plunder all the sons of Seth. Having conquered the adversarial demons, Christ leads them as the plunder of his victory. He carries back as the spoils of salvation the men who were being held under their dominion, just as also in other places it is written of him that: "Ascending on high he led captive a captivity."[58] This means that he led back as a captive and summoned back from death to life that captivity of the human race which the devil had captured unto perdition. Would that Jesus, then, would always hold me captive and lead me as his plunder and that I would be held fast by his chains [vinculis], that I too might merit being called a "prisoner [vinctus] of Christ Jesus,"[59] as Paul boasts concerning himself.

4.5. "And Edom will be an inheritance and Esau his enemy will be an inheritance."[60] Edom is identical with Esau.[61] According to history

he is an enemy of Israel, but at the coming of Christ, it says, he too will be his inheritance, that is, he will be received into the faith and will not be excluded from the inheritance of Christ. But if we consider this spiritually, Edom is understood as the flesh which is in opposition to the Spirit and is its enemy.[62] Thus at the coming of Christ, when the flesh will be subjected to the Spirit through the hope of the resurrection, even the flesh itself will come to the inheritance. For not the soul alone, but the flesh too that was once hostile, will emerge as a sharer of the future inheritance through the obedience of the Spirit.

"And Israel acted in power [virtus]."[63] This means that at that time Edom, or Esau, that is, the nature of the flesh, will be called into the fellowship of the inheritance, when Israel, that is, the soul, will have acted "in power" and will be filled with the virtues [virtus], as is appropriate to each soul. For if the soul does not come to the virtues, but perseveres in indolence, neither will the flesh come to the inheritance, but to the judgment of that one who can destroy both the soul and the body in Gehenna.[64]

4.6. "And he will arise out of Jacob and will destroy the one who has been freed from the city."[65] That one, it says, who will arise like a star out of Jacob will destroy the one who has been freed from the city. Not merely here but in nearly everything that is spoken in the prophetic style of composition, what is said is spoken with extremely confusing and obscure speech. For it did not please the Holy Spirit, who did want something to be written about these things, to lay these things out in the open to be trampled on, so to speak, by the feet of the inexperienced.[66] Instead he so arranged it that, even though things seem to be treated openly, they nevertheless remain protected in secret and mystery, hidden by the obscurity of the words.

---

[51]Cf. Eph 6:12. [52]Cf. Col 2:15. [53]Num 24:17. rsv has *Sheth*. [54]Gen 4:25. [55]Cf. *Commentary on John* 20.4.25-26. [56]Num 24:8. [57]Num 24:9. [58]Cf. Eph 4:8; Ps 68:18; Col 2:15. [59]Cf. Eph 3:1. [60]Num 24:18. rsv has *Seir* rather than *Esau*. [61]Cf. Gen 25:30. [62]Cf. Gal 5:17. [63]Num 24:18. [64]Cf. Mt 10:28. [65]Num 24:19. [66]Cf. Mt 7:6.

And now, therefore, what he says: "He will destroy the one who has been freed from the city," will seem extremely difficult to interpret, unless you take into consideration prophetic usage, of which it is said: "No prophecy can be established by one's own resolution."[67] Nevertheless, let us see if it can possibly be explained in the following manner.

4.7. Let us understand the city here as the world, just as in the Gospels it is said of the luxury-addicted son "who wasted the property of his father," that he went, it says, "to a certain leading personage of a city in that region, who received him and sent him into his field to feed pigs."[68] So here, the city of which that man was a leading personage is understood as this world. Thus Christ "destroys" [perdit] the one who has been freed from this city, that is, the one whom he sets free from this world. For he says to him: "The one who loses [perdet] his soul for my sake, will save it."[69]

Thus, by means of a salvation-bringing destruction, Jesus will destroy the one whom he sets free from the city of this world. And so, we too, if we want to come to salvation and be freed from this world, we ought to lose [perdere] our souls by this beneficial and necessary destruction. For one destroys one's soul in accordance with Christ, who curbs his desires, who cuts off his lusts, who reproves his luxuriousness and lack of discipline, and who never does his own will, but the will of God. This is how the soul is said to be destroyed. For its former life perishes [perit] and it begins to lead a new life, which is in Christ. Now the following statement is likewise similar to this: "If we die together, we will also live together";[70] and this: "Now if you are dead to the elements of the world, how is it, as though living, do you make decrees in this world."[71]

Necessarily, then, it is also being indicated in these things that the one who dies with Christ destroys [perdit] his own soul in this world, and the one who loses [perdiderit] it in this way will find it there, doubtless where the apostle says that "your life is hidden with Christ in God."[72] To him "be the glory in the eternal ages of ages. Amen."[73]

Homily 19
Numbers 24:20-24

1.1. The fifth and final vision of Balaam treats these same matters. As in the other homilies, we will pray to the Lord about this, that he will not in the end abandon us,[1] so that we can hunt for an interpretation of this vision too that is not far from the truth.

So then, it begins with these words: "And when Balaam saw Amalek," it says, "taking up his parable he said: Amalek is the beginning of the nations, and their seed will perish."[2] It seems necessary to me to search in the divine Scriptures to find out in which places or at what time the name of Amalek is written, and to find out from what race that nation descends. For what we are seeking here will be more easily understood if this is set forth from the many passages that have been written about the same subject.

Well, in a reading in Genesis, when five kings came together to fight four kings who were ruling in Sodom,[3] after some things, the following is reported: "And having turned back," it says, "they came to the well of judgment; this is Kadesh,[4] and they killed all the rulers of Amalek and the Amorites who were dwelling in Hazazon-tamar."[5] This is the first passage that I recall seeing Amalek named.

1.2. But someone may perhaps ask whether there are two nations of the same name, since in the list of the sons of Esau and of the chiefs

---

[67]2 Pet 1:20. [68]Cf. Lk 15:13-15. [69]Cf. Lk 9:24. [70]2 Tim 2:11. [71]Col 2:20. [72]Col 3:3. [73]Gal 1:5. **Homily 19** [1]Ps 77:8; Lam 3:31. [2]Num 24:20. [3]Cf. Gen 14:1, 2, 8-9. The original (lxx) text speaks of *four* kings against *five*. [4]Lat *Cades*. [5]Lat *Sasanthem*. Gen 14:7.

who had descended from his tribe, an Amalek is reported. For the following is written: "Now these are the generations of Esau, the father of Edom on Mount Seir. And these are the names of the sons of Esau: Eliphaz, son of Adah, the wife of Esau; and Reuel, the son of Basemath, wife of Esau. And the sons of Eliphaz were Teman, Omar, Zepho, Gatam, and Kenaz. Timna was a concubine of Eliphaz, the son of Esau, and she bore Amalek to this Eliphaz; and these are the sons of Adah, the wife of Esau."[6] And after a few things it says: "And these are the chiefs of the sons of Esau. The sons of Eliphaz, who was the firstborn of Esau: chief Teman, chief Omar, chief Zepho, chief Kenaz, chief Korah, chief Gatam, chief Amalek."[7] This Amalek, then, was a son of Eliphaz, who was the firstborn son of Esau, born from a concubine by the name of Timna.[8]

1.3. But let us go back to the first mention of Amalek, where those who "turned back and came to the well of judgment, which is called Kadesh, killed all the rulers of Amalek."[9] For Kadesh[10] translates as "sanctification" [*sanctificatio*] or "that which is holy" [*sanctum*]; Amalek, on the other hand, translates as "the one devouring the people" or "the one turning aside the people." Therefore, those who turn back to what is holy and who convert themselves to sanctification kill and destroy Amalek, namely, him who devours or turns aside the people. But who else is there who turns aside the people from God if not the contrary power and the spiritual forces of wickedness? Well then, who are the rulers of these? Doubtless it is those principalities against whom the saints do combat. For them there are struggles against the principalities and powers and rulers of this world; yet the saints are unable to overcome them, unless they are converted to sanctity.

1.4. However, in that sanctity, which is Kadesh, there is a "well of judgment."[11] For everyone who converts himself to sanctity always has before his eyes the well of judgment. For he looks forward to the day of judgment and contemplates with a purified heart both the penalties for those who are evil and the blessings for those who are godly. And by doing this, a person wrecks and casts down all the rulers of the Amalekites. But if they do not convert themselves to Kadesh, that is, to sanctity and to the well of judgment, they do not think about the future day of judgment. Such persons are subjected to the rulers of Amalek; for he devours and consumes this people and he turns such a people away from God. Let these things be related as applying to that first Amalek.

1.5. But now let us consider the other Amalek, the "son of Eliphaz the firstborn of Esau, whom Timna his concubine bore to him."[12] His father is Eliphaz, which translates as "God scatters me"; but his mother Timna[13] is translated, first of all, as "that which is itself degenerate," then as "disturbed failure." And surely it is necessary that one born from such parents is Israel's enemy, devouring and turning aside the people. For he was the first to attack the Hebrews in war at Rephidim when they had come out of Egypt. Then, when Moses said to Jesus:[14] "Select men for yourself and go forth and engage Amalek tomorrow; and, behold, I will stand at the top of the hill, and the rod of God will be in my hand. And Jesus did as Moses said to him, and he engaged Amalek; but Moses and Aaron and Ur went up to the top of the hill. And it came to pass when Moses lifted up his hands, Israel prevailed; but when he let down his hands, Amalek prevailed."[15] And after a few things it is again written that "Jesus routed Amalek and drove off his people with

---

[6]Gen 36:9-12. [7]Gen 36:15-16. [8]Lat *Thamna*. [9]Gen 14:7. [10]Lat *Cades*. [11]Cf. Gen 14:7. The RSV leaves *Enmishpat* ("well of judgment") untranslated. [12]Gen 36:12. [13]Lat *Thamnas*. [14]Heb *Joshua*. In the Greek language and in both Origen's and Rufinus's text, the same word, *Jesus*, is used for both names. This identity will be preserved in my translation to clarify the particular emphasis and parallelism Origen draws. [15]Ex 17:8-121

the sword at the time when the Lord said to Moses: Write this for a memorial in a book, and put it into the ears of Jesus, that I will utterly blot out the memory of Amalek from under heaven. And Moses built an altar to the Lord and called the name of it: The Lord my Refuge, and he said that with a hidden hand the Lord combats Amalek from generation to generation."[16] Understand from this very clearly who ought to be understood as Amalek, whom God is said to combat from generation to generation with a hidden, that is, an invisible,[17] hand.

1.6. Moreover, in Deuteronomy it is written as follows: "Remember how many things Amalek did to you on the way, when you had gone forth from Egypt; how he withstood you on the way and cut off your tail, all who were weary behind you; and you hungered and were weary; and you did not fear God."[18] Thus, notice even in these things how Amalek withstood Israel on the way, yet he was unable to cut off his head, but only his tail, that is, he was able to reach those who were behind, who followed last, but not those who "forgetting the things that are behind stretch forth for the things that are ahead."[19] And I think this is why the Lord gave the command in the Gospel and said: "No one who puts his hand to the plow and looks behind is fit for the kingdom of God."[20] And he says this justly; for if someone should be found behind in the tail, Amalek will cut him off.

1.7. Moreover, we will produce still another historical narrative about Amalek, so that what we are seeking may be more clearly observed from more passages of Scripture.

In the first book of Kingdoms, Samuel says to Saul: "The Lord sent me to anoint you king over his people Israel, and now hear the voice of the words of the Lord. Thus says the Lord of powers: I have reconsidered everything that Amalek did against Israel, how he struck him on the way when he was coming up from Egypt.

So now go and strike Amalek and curse and do not spare anything at all that belongs to him, but kill everyone, both man and woman and infants and sucklings and bulls and flocks of sheep and camels and donkeys. And Saul commanded the people, and he looked them over in Galaad,[21] two hundred thousand foot soldiers and three[22] thousand men from Judah."[23]

1.8. "And Saul came to the city of Amalek, and he set an ambush in the valley. And Saul said to Cineus:[24] Go you and depart from the midst of Amalek, lest you be added with him. For you dealt mercifully with all the sons, when they were going up from the land of Egypt. And Cineus[25] departed from the midst of Amalek. And Saul struck Amalek from Evila to Sur,[26] which fronts Egypt. And he took Agag the king of Amalek alive, and he cursed all his people with the edge of the sword. And Saul and the people spared Agag the king, and preserved all that was good from the sheep and cattle, moreover what was fertile from all the good herds, and they were unwilling to destroy them; but everything that was worthless and contemptible they cursed. And the word of the Lord came to Samuel, saying: I repent that I have anointed Saul to be king"[27]

1.9. Here too then, observe how God commands king Saul through the prophet to attack Amalek and not to spare anyone of them, but because he spared Agag, the king of Amalek, he commits an unpardonable offense. He provoked God to such a degree that God said, contrary to what the divine nature receives: "I repent that I have anointed Saul as king."[28] So then, it is not expedient for us to spare that one who turns aside or devours or consumes the people, namely that invisible Amalek, who attacks us and who "withstands on the way" those who want "to go up from Egypt" and to escape "from the darkness of this world" and hasten to the Promised Land. And if he finds us weary and

---

[16]Ex 17:12-16. [17]Cf. Ex 17:16. [18]Deut 25:17-18. [19]Phil 3:13. [20]Lk 9:62. [21]RSV *Telaim.* [22]RSV *ten.* [23]1 Sam 15:1-4. [24]RSV *to the Kenites.* [25]RSV *the Kenites.* [26]RSV *from Havilah as far as Shur.* [27]1 Sam 15:5-11. [28]1 Sam 15:11.

faltering and looking back and placed in the rear and in the tail, he cuts us off and wipes us out. And for this reason, one must always "strive for what is ahead, and hasten to what is before us";[29] or rather, one must ascend to the top of the mountain and our hands must always be raised to heaven in prayer, so that only then will Amalek be conquered and fall.[30]

1.10. Now do you want to know that one does not cross to the holy land or reach the kingdom unless Amalek is first conquered? When David had waged many wars and had had bitter and repeated conflicts against the Philistines,[31] it is nevertheless not written that he obtained the kingdom until he had first completely overcome Amalek. For the Scripture says: "And David returned after Amalek had fallen,"[32] and he received the kingdom of Saul. Yet Amalek himself is described as having first wreaked much havoc among the people of Israel, and he had burned a very large number of their cities.

1.11. For truly before the advent of the true David, the one "who was born from the seed of David according to the flesh,"[33] the spiritual Amalekites, which are the contrary powers, had wreaked much havoc among the people of Israel. Moreover, it says of that David that they had even "captured his two wives."[34] I think this signifies that the first was the Jewish people and the second was the Gentile. "For it is established that all Jews and Gentiles have been shut up under sin."[35] But the outcome of affairs did not remain there; for listen to what David does when he comes. It says: "And David found the Amalekites scattered, eating and drinking, and rejoicing over the plunder they had taken."[36] And it says: "He fell on them from the first night until the evening of the next day."[37] And after this slaughter of the Amalekites, he returned and received the kingdom.[38]

2.1. So then, on seeing this Amalek, "Balaam son of Beor, a man truly seeing and hearing the words of God, who knows the knowledge of the Most High and sees the visions of God, took up a parable," just as it is also written in the former visions.[39] And he said: "Amalek is the beginning of the nations, and their seed will perish."[40] It is certain that the words: "Amalek is the beginning of the nations" can in no way be applied to that Amalek who was in the flesh at that time. For he was not first in terms of the antiquity of his origin. Rather, it is better to refer this to the invisible Amalek, who is called Amalek by virtue of his turning aside people from God and making pagans out of the worshipers of God. And therefore he is rightly called the "beginning of the nations," as it were, as a kind of hostile power that first gave the beginning to men becoming pagans, "by exchanging the glory of the incorruptible God with the likeness of the image of corruptible man and of birds and of four-footed beasts and of serpents,"[41] and "by serving the creation instead of the Creator."[42] For just as Christ has been recorded as the beginning of the people of God,[43] so, on the contrary, Amalek is the beginning of the people who turn away from God and who become pagan.

2.2. "And their seed will perish."[44] Their seed is the conviction and doctrine by which they taught men to turn away from God. So it is that bad seed and evil doctrine will perish, and not those in whom the seed was sown. For they themselves, "when they groan and are converted will be saved."[45] And consider whether this kind of explanation does not provide a suitable rebuttal to those who accuse the God of the law of being cruel and harsh, since he declares not only that the nation of Amalek will perish, but his seed too.[46] Now when the nation is referred to "the spiritual forces of wickedness,"[47] his seed is

---

[29]Phil 3:13-14. [30]Cf. Ex 17:8-13. [31]Lat *Allophylos*. [32]2 Sam 1:1. [33]Rom 1:3. [34]Cf. 1 Sam 30:5. [35]Cf. Rom 3:9; Gal 3:22. [36]1 Sam 30:16. [37]Cf. 1 Sam 30:17. [38]Cf. 2 Sam 5:3. [39]Cf. Num 24:15-16. [40]Num 24:20. [41]Rom 1:23. [42]Rom 1:25. [43]Cf. 1 Cor 11:3; 15:23. [44]Num 24:20. [45]Is 45:22. [46]This was a frequent charge against the God of the Old Testament made by Marcion's followers. [47]Cf. Eph 6:12.

explained as the teaching of pagan superstitions, the worship of idols, and as every sect that would persuade people to turn away from God.

3.1. Now after Amalek, the prophecy recalls Cineus,[48] saying: "And seeing Cineus, he took up his parable and said: Your dwelling place is strong, and if you put your nest in a rock, and if Beor becomes for you a nest of cunning, the Assyrians will lead you captive."[49] It seems to me that he does not name Cineus as very blameworthy; for he is the one to whom Saul said higher up: "Depart from the midst of Amalek, and I will not strike you, since you have dealt mercifully with Israel when they went up from Egypt."[50] So now it is said of this one that "his dwelling place is strong, if he puts his nest in the rock."[51] "The rock is Christ."[52] Thus, if he puts his nest in the rock, his dwelling place is strong, but if not, Beor may become for him "a nest of cunning."[53]

3.2. Beor is the father of Balaam. He can be understood as representing the heretics. Thus the following is apparently intended: Cineus is able to be saved if he puts his nest in the rock, that is, if he locates his hope in Christ and does not surround and circumscribe that nest with the cunning of the heretics. For if that happens, it will not benefit him that it was apparently located in the rock, who is Christ. For he will be captured by the Assyrians, that is to say, by the evil powers, who lead them as captives and receive under their power those whom heretical error has overwhelmed.

Now it seems that the conjunction "and"[54] throws into confusion the interpretation we have given in our explanation concerning Cineus.[55] But one should know that it is common in the Hebrew language to make frequent use of this conjunction, so that sometimes the word "and" abounds and seems to be added where it is not needed, as it appears to our language. Surely this should be accepted with indulgence; for each language has its own peculiarities, which appear to be defects in other languages. Here too, then, the conjunction "and" should be considered as redundant and superfluous.

3.3. So let Cineus beware, let the one who translates as "possessing" beware, I say, even if he possesses and merits that grace to be in the church of Christ, lest the cunning of Beor should encircle him and turn him aside to depraved and perverse doctrines, and on this account he should be handed over to the Assyrians. For those who commit blasphemy while placed in the church are handed over to Satan, as were Phygelus and Hermogenes,[56] of whom Paul says: "Whom I handed over to Satan," he says, "to learn not to blaspheme."[57] So that is the reason that the one who turns aside into heretical blasphemy is handed over to the Assyrians, since Assyrians translate as "those who guide." And the reason they are handed over to those to whom they are handed over is not that they should be lost, or that they should utterly perish, but that they may be guided and corrected and, as Paul himself says: "that they may learn not to blaspheme."[58]

4.1. Now after this, Balaam concludes the words of his prophecy with these words: "And he took up his parable and said: 'Oh, Oh, who will live, when God shall do this? And he will come forth from the hands of the Cithians,[59] and they will afflict Assur,[60] and they will afflict the Hebrews,[61] and they will equally

---

[48]RSV the Kenite. [49]Num 24:21-22. RSV has Kain and Asshur. [50]1 Sam 15:6. [51]Cf. Num 24:21. [52]1 Cor 10:4. [53]Cf. Num 24:22. [54]Or "even." [55]The LXX (Origen's text) of Num 24:21-22 repeats the phrase kai ean ("and if" or "even if"). This would seem to suggest that the threat in the apodosis (the Assyrians will take Cineus captive) will be fulfilled, even if the action of the protasis (Cineus places his nest in the rock) is carried out, which contradicts Origen's interpretation of the passage. Thus Origen explains the "and" as a redundant conjunction. [56]Cf. 2 Tim 1:15, which says that Phygelus and Hermogenes abandoned Paul, but not that they were handed over to the Satan. It is Hymenaeus and Alexander (1 Tim 1:20) who rejected the faith and whom Paul handed over to Satan to learn not to blaspheme. Origen makes the same confused reference in Homilies on Jeremiah 19.14. [57]1 Tim 1:20. [58]1 Tim 1:20. [59]RSV Kittim. [60]RSV Asshur. [61]RSV Eber.

perish.'"[62] The fact that Balaam is said to speak in detail by a parable shames the reader and prevents him from thinking that anything said here is not spoken as though in a parable, but according to the letter.

He says: "Oh, Oh, who will live, when God shall do this?"[63] Here his referent is not this common life, but that one which is according to God, and this is what he says, that when all these things shall happen, when the "star shall arise from Jacob, and a man shall rise out of Israel and shall destroy Amalek and shall cause his seed to perish";[64] that is to say, when Christ comes and destroys the worship of idols and subjugates the power of all demons, who will that one be who is so blessed, so happy, who may see this? That is, who will perceive and understand and believe that God did such things?

4.2. "And they will come forth from the hands of the Cithians,[65] and they will afflict the Assyrians."[66] Cithians translates as "the plague of the end." Thus, those who have been converted to the Lord and who have been instructed by Christ escape the plague that will come at the end of the age on the ungodly; they themselves will afflict the Assyrians, that is, the ones for whom "God will crush Satan under their feet."[67] While engaged in the struggle of piety, they will afflict the Assyrians, namely, the race of demons. For "they will trample on serpents and scorpions and on all the power of the enemy,"[68] and they will afflict them.

4.3. "And they will afflict the Hebrews,[69] and they themselves will equally perish."[70] Hebrews translates as "those passing through."[71] Therefore, this people is likewise called "Hebrew," since they pass through from Egypt to the Promised Land, "from darkness to light,"[72] "from death to life."[73] But since, as we have said, they can only attain this with a struggle

and with intense combat, since they are now placed in a contest, sometimes they afflict, sometimes they are afflicted; sometimes they wound the enemy, but sometimes they are beaten by the enemy. Therefore, even the Assyrians themselves will afflict the Hebrews, that is, the people of God, just as they are afflicted by them; but they, that is, the Assyrians, when they do these things and pour out all their strength to afflict the Hebrews, immediately they themselves will likewise perish. Therefore his words: "And they will afflict the Hebrews, and they themselves will equally perish," must not be interpreted to mean that the Assyrians too will equally perish with the Hebrews; but "equally," that is, "immediately" when they have done these things, when they have afflicted the Hebrews, they themselves will likewise perish. For in Greek the word "equally"[74] can mean "immediately."

4.4. So this will be the end of all things, when even Asshur, to whom those who transgressed from the people of God were "handed over," resulting either in "the destruction of the flesh, so that the spirit can be saved,"[75] or in their "learning not to blaspheme,"[76] will itself likewise perish through "him who has authority to destroy in Gehenna."[77] For the just judge[78] will say to them: "Go into the eternal fire, which God prepared for the devil and his angels."[79] So it is there that Asshur will perish.

4.5. And indeed, once even one sheep out of a hundred sheep was lost, but the good shepherd "left the ninety-nine in the mountains"[80] and went down to this valley of ours, the "valley of tears."[81] He searched for it and found it,[82] and placing it on his shoulders,[83] he carried it back and added it to that group, which had remained safe above. Now with respect to this Asshur, of which it is said that it will perish at the end of all things, I do not know if at some time it could

---

[62]Num 24:23-24. [63]Num 24:23. [64]Num 24:17. [65]RSV *Kittim*. [66]Num 24:24. [67]Rom 16:20. [68]Lk 10:19. [69]RSV *Eber*. [70]Num 24:24. [71]Cf. Philo *On the Migration of Abraham* 20. [72]Cf. Acts 26:18. [73]Cf. Jn 5:24. [74]The Greek term *homothymadon* means "with one accord," "with one mind" and, in a weakened sense, "together." [75]Cf. 1 Cor 5:5. [76]Cf. 1 Tim 1:20. [77]Cf. Lk 12:5. [78]Cf. 2 Tim 4:8. [79]Mt 25:41. [80]Lk 15:4. [81]Ps 84:6. [82]Cf. *Commentary on Genesis* (PG 12.102); *Homilies on Genesis* 13.2. [83]Cf. Lk 15:5.

either be sought for or found. For it perishes[84] not by wandering away, but by its own decision, not by a lapse in its movements, but by a previously hardened persistence. As for what is written: "I will kill and I will make alive, I will lead down below, and I will lead back,"[85] I do not know if this has general application to everyone, or only to those whom the deception of the devil has caused to be led down to death.[86]

4.6. Let these things as well be said by us to the best of our ability concerning the final prophecy of Balaam. Owing to the difficulty in interpreting these passages, I resolved to untangle these things more in the style of a commentary than in the style of one who is giving a homily. But what difference does it make, if only everything is said with edification in view,[87] and if everything leads to the glory of God, "who is blessed into the ages of ages. Amen!"?[88]

Homily 20
Numbers 25:1-10

Concerning the man who committed fornication with the Midianite woman and that the people were consecrated at Beelphegor.[1]

1.1. Today a reading has been given containing, first, a story about the fornication of an Israelite man and a Midianite woman,[2] and second, a story about the visitation of the people,[3] in which, by the Lord's instruction, the people are again commanded to be numbered. For the first numbering had been revoked as null and void owing to the sins that had been committed by those who had been assessed in the previous determination of the numbering. Thus, the number that was written is scrapped and becomes null and void because of sins, and only

transgressions remain in force. Thus it does not help a person to be reckoned by God in the numbering, when that person turns away. But, as the Scripture reports, even their "limbs," which withdrew from God, "fell in the desert."[4] So then, two historical narratives have been recited; but for the time being we will speak about the first one, which describes the fornication of the people. Our hope is that the Lord will deign to bestow some grace, as you pray. And in fact if he grants this, we shall venture to make some remarks on the second narrative as well.

1.2. It says: "And Israel arrived at Sattin,[5] and the people were defiled and committed fornication with the daughters of Moab. And they[6] invited them[7] to the sacrifices of their idols; and the men ate of their sacrifices and worshiped their idols, and were consecrated to Beelphegor;[8] and the Lord was filled with fury against Israel."[9]

Here is shown what we have often mentioned. After Balaam had been checked by the power of God and was not permitted to curse Israel, nevertheless, he wanted to please king Balak and said to him what is written: "Come, I will give you counsel."[10] Now that counsel that he gave was not clarified in that passage, yet it is related and recorded lower down in the same book of Numbers.[11] And it is written in even more detail in the Revelation of John, where the following is contained. It says: "You have there the teaching of Balaam, who taught Balak to cast a stumbling block before the sons of Israel, to eat things sacrificed to idols and to commit fornication."[12]

1.3. So this shows that Balaam gave in to his malice and counseled the king, saying something like the following to him: "This people conquers not by their own strength, but by worshiping God and by guarding their chastity. If

[84]Or "becomes lost." [85]Cf. 1 Sam 2:6. [86]Origen (or Rufinus?) seems quite tentative here about the possibility of universal restoration. [87]Both in the prologue of the present work and in the epilogue (4) of his translation of Origen's *Commentary on Romans*, Rufinus says that edification is the primary goal of his translations. [88]Rom 1:25. **Homily 20** [1]RSV *Baal of Peor.* [2]Cf. Num 25:1-18. [3]Cf. Num 26. [4]Cf. Num 14:29, 32. [5]RSV *Shittim.* [6]I.e., the daughters of Moab. [7]I.e., the men of Israel. [8]RSV *Baal of Peor.* [9]Num 25:1-3. [10]Num 24:14. [11]Cf. Num 31:16. [12]Rev 2:14.

you want to conquer them, first overthrow their chastity and they will be conquered of their own accord. Now you should attack them not by the force of troops, but by the beauty of women, not by the hard strength of weapons, but by the effeminate softness of females. Remove the hand of your armed soldiers to a very great distance from here. Gather together select and beautiful girls and let them go around dancing with their feet and enticing them with their hands. For beauty conquers armed men, good looks captivate the sword, and those who are not conquered in battle will be conquered by beauty. But when the Moabite women perceive that these men have offered their hands to lust and have inclined their necks to sin, do not let the women offer themselves to their lovers before the men have consented to taste of the things sacrificed to idols. Thus, under the compulsion of lust, they will comply with the counsels of the females and first be consecrated to Beelphegor, which is the idol of baseness."

1.4. These were Balaam's counsels. Once they had been received, king Balak at once prepares an army composed not of virile arms but of feminine glamour, an army on fire not with battle fury but with the flames of lust. Shame keeps none of these women in check, modesty curbs not a single one. Love of country and the vice of the nation conspire together with lasciviousness, and a downright depravity appears for the deception. Horror! Lust is scarcely suppressed by the threats of laws, it is scarcely held in check by the terror of the sword! What crime does a woman not perpetrate when she is convinced that she will please the king by the deed and will secure her country's safety? Thus the Israelites are captivated, not by the sword, but by luxury, not by force,[13] but by lust, and they commit fornication with the Midianite women, and the anger of God rises over them.

1.5. Even in these things there are certain mysteries and things that are hidden away in the interior meaning; but first we should let ourselves be edified by the text of the historical narrative. Let us learn from it, since fornication is waging war against us and the javelins of luxury are being hurled at us. But if we do not lack the weapons with which the apostle commands us to be armed, such javelins will be unable to pierce us, if we have at our disposal the "breastplate of justice," the "helmet of salvation, the sword of the Spirit," and above all the "shield of faith"; and if our "feet are shod with the readiness of the Gospel of peace."[14] These are the arms that defend us in such wars. But if we throw such weapons away, at once we are giving the devil an opportunity to wound us and a whole band of demons will "lead us as captives."[15] And on this account the anger of God will rise against us and we will be punished, not only "in the present age," but also "in the future."[16] So then, in these battles that the devil incites against us, it is chastity, justice, prudence, piety and the other virtues that give us the victory. But it is luxury and lust, avarice and impiety and all evil that will cause us to be defeated. So these are the things that the text of the historical narrative has taught us.

1.6. But since John, in his Revelation, includes these things that are written in the law according to history among the divine mysteries [mysteria], and he shows that certain mysteries [sacramenta] are contained in these things, it seems necessary and in accordance with what he has perceived to imitate the method[17] of exposition he has given. First, it is necessary to recall what he says when he writes to the angel of a certain church: "You have there some who hold to the doctrine of Balaam, who taught Balak to cast a stumbling block before the sons of Israel, to eat things sacrificed to idols and to commit fornication."[18] And so, at the time of John the apostle, there were some

---

[13]Lat *virtus*, or "virtue." [14]Cf. Eph 6:14-17. [15]Ignatius *To the Ephesians* 17.1; *To the Philadelphians* 2.2 speaks of being taken captive by the wicked doctrine of the prince of this world and of the heretics. [16]Cf. Mt 12:32. [17]Lat *regula*. [18]Rev 2:14.

in that church to which he was writing who were teaching the doctrine of Balaam. Do you think that this is to be interpreted to mean that in those days there were those who claimed to teach the very things Balaam taught, and those who professed themselves to be teachers of his dogmas and traditions? Or should we instead apply this to mean that if one does the work that Balaam did, he would seem to teach the "doctrine of Balaam"? And just as in the same Revelation, when the "doctrine of Jezebel" is mentioned,[19] this does not mean that someone is teaching from the instructions that Jezebel herself handed down, but that if anyone, for instance, either persecutes God's prophets, as she did, or leads people astray into idolatry,[20] or kills the innocent through false pretexts,[21] that one is said "to hold to the doctrine of Jezebel." So then, if someone produces stumbling blocks for the people of God by means of evil counsels and provokes divine irritation and heavenly wrath against the people, either by sharing in the sacrifices of idols or by serving lust and immorality, this one should be said "to hold to the doctrine of Balaam." So there is an accursed fornication even of the body. For what is so accursed as desecrating the "temple of God"[22] and "taking the members of Christ and making them members of a prostitute"?[23]

2.1. Yet far more accursed is the kind of fornication that is universal in nature in which every kind of sin is equally contained. Now fornication in a general sense is spoken of when the soul, which has been associated with the union of the Word of God and has been joined with it in marriage, so to speak, is corrupted and violated by another, namely, by a foreigner who is hostile to that husband who betroths the soul to himself by faith.[24] Well, the husband

and bridegroom of the pure and chaste soul is the Word of God who is Christ the Lord, just as the apostle also writes: "Now I want to present all of you as a chaste virgin to one husband, Christ; but I fear that just as the serpent seduced Eve by his cunning, perhaps your minds may be corrupted from the simplicity which is in Christ Jesus."[25] So as long as the soul clings to its spouse and listens to his word and embraces him, doubtless it receives from him the seed of the Word; and just as he said: "From your fear, O Lord, we conceived in the womb,"[26] so also it says this: "From your word, O Lord, I have conceived in the womb and I have given birth and I have made the Spirit of your salvation on the lands."[27]

Thus, if the soul conceives from Christ in this way, it generates sons for whose sake it can be said of her that "she will be saved through the generation of sons, if they[28] continue in faith and love and holiness, with sobriety,"[29] even if the soul seems to have first been seduced as Eve had been.[30] And so it is a truly blessed offspring when the soul has had intercourse with the Word of God and when they have embraced one another. From there will be born a noble lineage, from there will arise chastity; from there will issue justice, patience, gentleness and love and the venerable offspring of all the virtues.[31]

2.2. But if the wretched soul abandons the holy nuptials of the divine Word and, deceived by their seductions, hands herself over to the adulterous embraces of the devil and the other demons, doubtless she will generate sons from this, but those about whom it is written: "But the sons of adulterers will be imperfect, and the seed of unlawful intercourse will be banished."[32] Thus all sins are sons of adultery and sons of fornication.

---

[19]Cf. Rev 2:20. [20]Cf. 1 Kings 21:25-26. [21]Cf. 1 Kings 21:1-16. [22]Cf. 1 Cor 3:16. [23]Cf. 1 Cor 6:15. [24]Cf. *Homilies on Song of Songs*; *Homilies on Ezekiel* 8.3; *Homilies on Leviticus* 2.2; *Homilies on Genesis* 2.2. [25]2 Cor 11:2-3. [26]Is 26:18. [27]Is 26:18. [28]I follow the SC editors (who followed Baehrens) in citing the plural *permanserint*, rather than the singular *permanserit*. The reading seems surprising since it appears to make the perseverance of the sons effect the salvation of the mother (soul) retroactively. Migne corrects the reading to the singular without comment. The manuscript tradition of 1 Tim 2:15 is divided between the two readings. [29]1 Tim 2:15. [30]Cf. 1 Tim 2:14. [31]Cf. Gal 5:22-23. [32]Wis 3:16.

And so it is shown that in everything we do, our soul gives birth and generates sons, namely, its thoughts and the works that it does. And if what it does is in accordance with law and in accordance with the Word of God, it gives birth to the Spirit of salvation, and for that reason "it will be saved through the generation of sons."[33] And its sons will be like those of whom the prophet says: "Your sons are like young olive plants around your table."[34] But if what it does is contrary to law and is sin, doubtless it gives birth to evil offspring as a result of a conception from a hostile spirit. For it bears the sons of sin. And these are the accursed generations on account of which some of the saints even curse "the day on which they were born."[35]

2.3. Therefore, there is never a time when the soul is not giving birth; the soul always gives birth, it always generates sons. But that generation is blessed which is generated by a conception from the Word of God, and that is a generation of sons through which "it will be saved." But if, as we said, it conceives from a contrary spirit, it is certain that it gives birth to "sons of wrath prepared for destruction."[36] And perhaps the following passage has in view these two kinds of generations of the soul: "For when they had not yet been born or done anything good or evil, in order that the purpose of God which came according to election might remain, not from works, but from the one who calls, it was said that the greater will serve the lesser, just as it is written: Jacob I loved, but Esau I hated."[37] For these generations of the soul are really like this, they are already loved "before they do anything good," if indeed they are generated from the Holy Spirit; but an accursed conception of an evil will in the soul is deservedly hated, even "before it fulfills any evil," if it is from an evil spirit, by the very fact that the soul gave birth to a will of this sort.

This is perhaps why even the child Canaan is cursed before he was born, as a figure of this mystery. For Ham[38] his father had sinned, and Noah, while prophetically indicating each of the excellent things for each of his sons, when he comes to Ham, says: "Cursed be the child of Canaan."[39] Ham sinned, and Canaan his offspring is cursed and was cursed. And therefore we must pay very keen attention and be on the lookout, that our soul not produce anything that deserves to be cursed. Even if it has not yet fulfilled the deed, yet by the very fact that it is willed and intended, an offspring of this sort will be cursed. But even if this should at some time come to pass—for how easy is it to find someone who is considered to be immune from this sort of generation, that is, from the will to sin?—thus if such a thing should happen, let us inquire from the divine books what remedy is given.

2.4. Well, we have found it written about this in the Psalms: "Wretched is daughter of Babylon, blessed is the one who will repay you the repayment with which you have repaid us. Blessed is the one who will seize and dash your infants against the rock."[40] Even if this "Babylonian" that has been conceived within us has not yet done any work, while it is still an infant, you must not pity it or spare it, but kill it at once—for it is worthy of hatred—destroy it, slay it, "dash it against the rock." "But the rock is Christ."[41] Who then is capable of not waiting at all, until the Babylonian offspring grows within him and increases in him into "works of confusion"? Who will instead, immediately, at the very beginning, when these infants are beginning to be born and are being formed by the movements of the will, and when, so to speak, from the womb of the soul they begin to bring forth their head, that is, the harmful desires that were conceived through the inspiration of an evil spirit, seize them immediately and "dash them against the rock," that is, bring them to

---

[33]Cf. 1 Tim 2:15. [34]Ps 128:3. [35]Cf. Job 3:1; Jer 20:14. [36]Cf. Rom 9:22. [37]Rom 9:11-14. [38]Lat *Cham*. [39]Gen 9:25. [40]Ps 137:8-9. [41]1 Cor 10:4.

Christ? Thus, when they are placed in the presence of his awesome judgment, they will fade away and perish.[42]

2.5. We have said these things about general fornication, which has many forms. Usage identifies one of these forms fornication on account of bodily immorality. But while reading the apostle, when I came to the passage where he says: "He who joins himself to the Lord is one spirit,"[43] and "He who joins himself to a prostitute is one body,"[44] I asked whether there is some other means, in addition to this, whereby one may be joined either to the Lord or to a prostitute. And while investigating this with all my strength, I came to perceive a very profound and hidden meaning in these words of the apostle. For in determining that every soul is joined either to the Lord or to a prostitute, I came to understand that he is calling the virtues[45] "Lord." For Christ is the virtues, that is, the "Word,"[46] "wisdom,"[47] "truth,"[48] "justice,"[49] and others like this. On the other hand, he is calling a "prostitute" all forms of evil that are opposite these. I understand that this was also said by Solomon, insofar as he says of the prostitute: "through her windows she surveys the streets, and if she sees any foolish youth who lacks sense passing near the corners of her house and speaking in the darkness of evening, when the nocturnal stillness and the gloom of night occurs, the woman meets him, having the appearance of a prostitute, which makes the heart of a young man flutter."[50] Thus, she who is called a "prostitute" is evil itself, and the one who joins himself to this prostitute becomes "one body" with evil. So then, just as "the one who joins himself with the Lord," joins himself with wisdom, joins himself with justice, joins himself with piety and truth, and he becomes "one spirit" with all these things, so also "the one who joins himself with this prostitute,"

joins himself with immodesty, impiety, iniquity, lying, and with all the evils of sins together, with which he becomes "one body."

3.1. Nevertheless, "Israel arrived at Sattin."[51] In the translation of Hebrew names, we have found that Sattin in our language means "response" or "rejection." Thus "Israel arrived at" a response or rejection. This was not a good "arrival." After all, look at what happened when they were at this stage.[52] They committed fornication with the Midianite women and were "rejected" by God, not only because they committed fornication, but also because they were consecrated to the idols of the nations and ate what had been sacrificed to idols.[53] Surely this is abhorrent to God. For "what agreement is there between the temple of God and idols?"[54]

But I very much admire as well what the apostle Paul writes about these matters to the Corinthians when he says: "But if anyone sees you who have knowledge reclining in an idol temple, will not his conscience, since it is weak, be built up to eat what has been sacrificed?"[55] For he seems to declare that it is not so much the thing itself that is grave matter, as the stumbling block that comes to the one who sees this and is provoked by the same example, since he is not fortified by the same knowledge. Thus he shows that the one who "while having knowledge reclines in the idol temple" becomes guilty, not so much of damaging himself, as of damaging another.

3.2. But consider whether this was being done solely among the Corinthians, that they were "reclining in an idol temple" and "eating what had been sacrificed to idols." But perhaps, since there were men who were zealous for Greek literature and were lovers of philosophy, they were still being held by the desire for the study of antiquity and were, so to speak, "eating things sacrificed to idols" in the form of the

---

[42]Cf. *Homilies on Joshua* 15.3; *Against Celsus* 7.22. [43]1 Cor 6:17. [44]1 Cor 6:16. [45]Or "powers," "operations." [46]Cf. Jn 1:1, 14. [47]Cf. 1 Cor 1:30. [48]Cf. Jn 14:6. [49]Cf. 1 Cor 1:30. [50]Prov 7:6-10. [51]RSV *Shittim*. Num 25:1. [52]Lat *mansio*, cf. Jn 14:2. [53]Cf. Num 25:2-3. [54]2 Cor 6:16. [55]1 Cor 8:10.

doctrines of the philosophers. Now perhaps these doctrines were incapable of harming those who had received the full knowledge of the truth. But if those who had less instruction in Christ were to emulate those who read such things and those who are still striving hard to study these things, they could be wounded and become overwhelmed by the various errors of the different doctrines. So in this way, it could occur that someone could be harmed by what the one who had full knowledge of the truth was unable to be harmed by. But since love does not seek its own advantage, but that of the many, one should be careful to take in the kind of food of the word that edifies and delights not merely ourselves, but also that does not injure and cause offense to those who look on. Thus, "things sacrificed to idols" consist not merely in foods but also in words. And I think that just as all words that teach piety and justice and truth have been consecrated to God and sacrificed to God, so also all words that have in view unchastity and injustice and impiety are "sacrificed to idols," and the one who receives them, in a manner of speaking, "eats things sacrificed to idols."

3.3. So then, "the people ate from their sacrifices and worshiped their idols."[56] Not only did they "eat" but they "worshiped." Consider the sequence of evil: first lust deceived the Lord's servants, then gluttony of the belly, finally impiety captivated them. But fornication is paid the wages of impiety. If you reread what is written about Solomon, you will find that he, even though he was indeed "the wisest,"[57] "inclined his loins to many women,"[58] though God's law says: "You shall not multiply your wives, lest they make you commit fornication from your God."[59] Thus, although he was the "wisest" and had great merits before God,[60] nevertheless he was deceived because he handed himself over to many wives.[61] I think that the many wives represent the many dogmas and the different

philosophies of the many nations. Though he may have wanted to know and investigate all these things as a very knowledgeable and wise man, he was unable to keep himself within the rule of divine law. Instead, Moabite philosophy deceived him and persuaded him to offer sacrifice in the idol temple of the Moabites, and similarly of the Ammonites; moreover, of the rest of the nations whose wives he is said to have received and to whose idols he built temples and sacrificed.[62] Thus it is a grand thing and truly a work of God to intermingle with many dogmas, as with wives, and yet not to turn aside from the rule of truth, but constantly to say: "There are sixty queens and eighty concubines, and young girls without number; yet one alone for me is my dove, my perfect one; she is the only one of her mother, she is the only one of her that bore her."[63]

3.4. But they "worshiped idols and were consecrated to Beelphegor."[64] Beelphegor is the name of an idol that was worshiped among the Midianites, chiefly by women. So Israel was consecrated into the mysteries of this idol. Yet although we have diligently sought for an interpretation of this name among the Hebrew names, we have found only that it is written that Beelphegor is a "form of baseness."[65] Yet he was not willing to declare which or what sort or whose form of baseness it was. I believe the translator deliberated about this with integrity and was unwilling to pollute the ears of his hearers. Therefore, since there are many forms of baseness, every single form of baseness out of the many that exist are called Beelphegor. This is why one must know that everyone who does anything base and turns aside into any form of baseness is consecrated to the demon of the Midianites, Beelphegor. Moreover, through every sin that we commit, especially if we sin no longer surreptitiously, but with enthusiasm and feeling, doubtless we are consecrated to that

---

[56]Num 25:2. [57]Cf. 1 Kings 4:31. [58]Sir 47:19. [59]Deut 17:17; 1 Kings 11:2. [60]Cf. 1 Kings 4:29; 10:24. [61]Cf. 1 Kings 11:1. [62]Cf. 1 Kings 11:7-8. [63]Song 6:8-9. [64]RSV *Baal of Peor*. Num 25:2-3. [65]Cf. Philo *On the Change of Names* 107.

demon whose concern it is to bring about that sin we are committing. And perhaps it will happen to us to be consecrated to as many demons as sins we commit;[66] and for each transgression, we receive the mysteries, as it were, which they say belong to this or that idol.

3.5. And possibly it was for this reason that the apostle said: "For already the mystery of iniquity is at work."[67] Thus, the evil spirits "go around" and "seek" how they can deceive each one,[68] and consecrate everyone to their mysteries by luring them into sin. Without one's perceiving or understanding what is going on, the demons introduce each one, for instance, through the sin of fornication to the demon of the Midianites, and they consecrate one person to Beelphegor, they consecrate someone else to baseness. In a similar way, through the other sins, as we have said, human beings are consecrated to other demons.

But you should observe very carefully what is written, and "stand in the ways and ask what are the eternal ways of the Lord, and what is the good way, and enter on it."[69] Do not approach the gates of a house of evil. But if you sense an evil spirit is speaking in your heart, to lead you to carry out some sin, understand that it wants to lead you into it in order to consecrate you to a demon. It wants to lead you to receive the devil's mysteries, the mysteries of iniquity.[70] And this, I think, is what the apostle writes: "Now when you were Gentiles, going after the form of idols, as you were led."[71] By which one or ones were you "led"? By evil spirits, of course, you were led into the works of sins.

3.6. Every vigilant hearer who listens to this will possibly say: "So what shall we do? If evil spirits go around each of us and lead and drag off into sin, but there is no one else who would draw toward justice, who would summon and lead to chastity, to piety: how will the way not appear as wide open to destruction?[72] Indeed,

no access to salvation will ever be granted." On the contrary, pay more careful attention, if you can consider with me interior mysteries by opening the eye of our heart,[73] and you will see the extent to which greater care is exercised in secret for our salvation than the faculties for deceiving are granted. There is present to each one of us, even to the "least"[74] who are in the church of God, a good angel, an angel of the Lord, who guides, warns and governs, who for the sake of correcting our actions and imploring mercy, daily "sees the face of the Father who is in heaven,"[75] as the Lord indicates in the Gospels. And again, according to what John writes in the Apocalypse, an angel presides generally over each church,[76] who is either praised for the deeds done well by the people, or is even blamed for their transgressions.

3.7. In this connection I am deeply moved with admiration of this tremendous mystery, that God cares about us so much that he even allows his angels to be blamed and rebuked for us. For just as when a child is handed over to a pedagogue, if perchance he appears less instructed in the worthy disciplines in a way that does not accord with his father's nobility, immediately the blame is transferred to the pedagogue. It is not the child who is rebuked by the father so much as the pedagogue, unless the boy has become stubborn and has shown contempt for the pedagogue's warnings and, prone to lewdness and brashness, has despised his salutary words and complied instead with those that encourage excess and which provoke lewdness.

As to what becomes of that soul, learn from the words of the prophet: He says: "The daughter of Zion will be abandoned as a tent in a vineyard, and as a storehouse for cucumbers, as a city that has been attacked";[77] and again: "Its wall will be removed, and it will be for trampling, and all who pass along that way will

---

[66]Cf. *Homilies on Joshua* 15:5. [67]2 Thess 2:7. [68]Cf. 1 Pet 5:8. [69]Jer 6:16. [70]Cf. 2 Thess 2:7. [71]1 Cor 12:2. [72]Cf. Mt 7:13. [73]Cf. Eph 1:18. [74]Cf. Mt 18:10. [75]Mt 18:10. Matthew's text has "always" for Rufinus's "daily." [76]Cf. Rev 1:20; 2:1, 8, 12, 18; 3:1, 7, 14. [77]Is 1:8.

plunder it,"[78] and "every fierce beast will feed on it."[79] It will suffer these things, if it does not acquiesce to the warnings of its angel, who is placed over it for salvation. For the soul has its own choice, and it is free to turn in whatever direction it wants; and this is why God's judgment is just, for the soul obeys either good or evil advisors of its own accord.

3.8. Do you want me to show you something still more from the divine Scriptures, namely, how much more care God has for the salvation of human beings than the devil has for their destruction? Would not the diligence of the angels have been enough help against the snares of the demons and against those who draw men into sin? The Only Begotten[80] himself, the very Son of God, I say, is present; he himself defends, he himself stands guard, he himself draws us to himself. Listen to the way he says: "And behold, I am with you all the days until the consummation of the age."[81] Nor is it enough for him to be with us, but he even uses a kind of force in order to draw us to salvation; for he says elsewhere: "But when I am lifted up, I will draw all things to myself."[82] You see how he not only invites the willing but also "draws" all. Do you want to hear how he "draws" even all? He did not give permission to the one who wanted "to go and bury his father,"[83] nor give him any time, but he says to him: "Leave the dead to bury their own dead; but you, follow me."[84] And elsewhere he says: "No one who puts his hand to the plow and looks back is fit for the kingdom of God."[85]

3.9. But if you want to know still more about this mystery,[86] I will show you from the Scriptures that even God the Father himself does not neglect the management of our salvation; but he himself not only calls us to salvation, but he also "draws" us. For this is what the Lord says in the Gospel: "No one comes to me unless my heavenly Father draws him."[87] Moreover, the "householder" who "sends his servants to invite friends to the wedding of his son," after those who had first been invited made excuses, says to his servants: "Go out to the roads and street corners, and whoever you find, compel them to enter."[88] So then, we are not only invited by God, but we are also drawn and compelled to salvation.

But neither is the Holy Spirit absent from providential concerns of this sort.[89] For he himself says: "Separate for me Paul and Barnabas for the ministry for which I have appointed them."[90] And again, he hinders Paul from going into Asia and again compels him to go to Jerusalem, predicting to him that chains and imprisonment await him there.[91] But if "the angels of the Lord surround those who fear him, to rescue them,"[92] if God the Father, the Son and the Holy Spirit not only encourage and challenge, but also "draw," how is it not the case that greater care by far is carried out on our behalf leading to salvation than is achieved by the adversaries leading to death?

Let these things be said concerning the words: "the people were consecrated to Beelphegor."[93]

4.1. "And the Lord was filled,"[94] it says, "with fury against Israel. And the Lord said to Moses: Take the rulers of the people and show them to the Lord facing[95] the sun, and the anger of the fury of the Lord will be turned away from Israel."[96]

In discussing these things, I do not know if we will offend certain people; but even if we do offend them, "it is more necessary to obey and serve the word of the Lord than the favor of men."[97] Israel sinned, "the Lord told Moses to take all the rulers and show them to the Lord facing the sun." The people sin, and the rulers are shown "facing the sun," that is to say, they

---

[78]Is 5:5. [79]Ps 80:13. [80]Cf. Jn 1:18. [81]Mt 28:20. [82]Jn 12:32. [83]Cf. Mt 8:21. [84]Mt 8:22. [85]Lk 9:62. [86]Lat *sacramentum*. [87]Jn 6:44. [88]Cf. Lk 14:21-23; Mt 22:3, 9. [89]Notice again the trinitarian arrangement of Origen's theological thought. [90]Acts 13:2. [91]Cf. Acts 16:6; 21:11-12. [92]Ps 34:7. [93]Num 25:3. [94]Lit. "angry." [95]Lat *contra*. [96]Num 25:4. [97]Acts 5:29.

are brought forth to be tested, to be exposed by the light.

You see what the situation is for the "rulers of the people": not only are they convicted for their own transgressions, but they are even forced to given an account for the sins of the people, lest it be their fault that the people transgressed. Perhaps they failed to teach; perhaps they failed to warn them and were not careful to rebuke those who were the first to do wrong, so as to prevent the spread of the malady to more people. For it impends on the rulers and teachers to do all these things. For if, through their inaction, through their lack of protective concern for the multitude, the people sin, it is they who are "shown" and they who are "brought forth" to judgment. For Moses, that is, the law of God, convicts them of negligence and sloth; and the wrath of God will be turned against them, and it "will cease from the people."[98] If men would think about this, they would never desire or intrigue for leadership of the people. For it is enough for me to be convicted for my own offenses; it is enough for me to give account for myself and for my sins. What need is there for me to be shown up for the sins of the people as well, and to be "shown before the sun," before which nothing can be hidden, nothing kept dark?

4.2. But perhaps even here there may be some hidden and secret meaning, which teaches us something more than this general exposition seems to contain. For possibly this passage can also be applied to those "rulers of the people" of whom we spoke a little earlier. For the angels shall come to the judgment with us and they will stand for us "before the sun of justice,"[99] lest perhaps some cause of our transgressing lies with them; lest perhaps they failed to expend sufficient work and effort on our behalf, so as to call us back from the fatal defilement of sins. For unless there were something even in them, which seemed to be blameworthy in our cause,

the words of Scripture would never have said to the angel of this or that church: "You have some," for instance "who hold the teaching of Balaam";[100] or "You have abandoned your first love"[101] or "your patience,"[102] or the other things of this sort that we have already mentioned above, on account of which in the Apocalypse the angels of each church are blamed.

For if, for instance, the angel who has received me as his assignment from God expects a reward for the things I have done well, it is certain that he will also expect to be blamed for those deeds of mine that were not done well. And that is why they are said to be "shown facing the sun," doubtless to make it clear whether it was through my disobedience or through the angel's negligence that the sins were committed which led to my being consecrated to Beelphegor, or to some other idol, according to the character of my sinning. But if my ruler—I mean the angel assigned to me—did not fail, but counseled me to right action, and spoke in my heart, at least insofar as conscience called me back from sin, but I despised his warnings, scorned the restraint of conscience, and rushed headlong into sin, for me there will be a double punishment, one for despising my adviser and another for offending in the deed I committed.

4.3. Of course, you should not be surprised if we say that angels come to judgment together with men, since Scripture says: "The Lord himself will come to judgment with the elders of the people and with its rulers."[103] Thus the rulers are "shown," and if the fault is in them, God's anger "ceases from the people." Therefore we should exercise keener vigilance over our actions, knowing that it is not we alone who shall stand "before God's tribunal"[104] for our deeds, but also the angels, as our rulers and guides, who shall be brought into judgment on our account. For this is why Scripture says: "Obey those placed over you, and comply with them in all things; for they watch as those who shall give

---

[98]Num 25:4. [99]Mal 4:2. [100]Rev 2:14. [101]Rev 2:4. [102]Cf. Rev 3:5. [103]Is 3:14. [104]Rom 14:10.

account for your souls."[105]

5.1. After this it is reported: "When Phinehas son of Eleazar son of Aaron the priest" saw that an Israelite man entered to a Midianite woman, "he took a lance[106] in his hand, entered the place of prostitution and pierced both of them through their shameful places."[107] And because of this, it says, "the Lord said to Moses: Phinehas son of Eleazar, son of Aaron, has quelled my wrath."[108]

These things may have edified the first people; but for you who are redeemed by Christ, a physical sword has been removed from your hands.[109] In its place the "sword of the Spirit"[110] has been given, and you must seize the latter sword. And if you see an Israelite thought prostituting itself with Midianite whores, that is, rolling about with devilish thinking, I do not want you to spare it, I do not want you to hesitate, but strike at once, destroy it immediately. Cut through the very womb too, by investigating the secrets of its nature and penetrating to that very seat of sin, lest it should conceive any longer, lest it generate any longer and the accursed offspring of sins should contaminate the encampments of the Israelites. For if you do this, immediately you will quell the Lord's wrath; for you have anticipated the day of judgment, which is called a "day of wrath and fury."[111] And by exterminating the seat of sin from yourself, which here is called the womb of the Midianite woman, you will come through secure to the day of judgment.

And therefore let us rise up and pray[112] that we may always find that "sword of the Spirit"[113] prepared,[114] through which the very seeds and receptacles of sins may be destroyed, and God will become propitious to us through the true Phinehas, our own Lord Jesus Christ, to whom be "the glory and power in the ages of ages. Amen."[115]

Homily 21
Numbers 26

Concerning the fact that the people were numbered a second time.

1.1. We are reading "Numbers," and in an earlier reading, time prevented us from saying anything about the second numbering; but now it is convenient to return to what was omitted and excluded.

So, by the Lord's command, the people were numbered the first time, but since those who had been admitted at first "fell"[1] owing to their continuing in transgressions, a second people, who succeeded in place of the lapsed, are called to the number in a renewed generation, and what had not been said of those earlier ones is said about them. For after the number had been compiled by tribes, groups, houses and families, the Lord says to Moses: "For them the land will be distributed by lot from the number of names. To those who are more, more will be given by lot, and to those who are fewer, you will give a smaller inheritance."[2] If concerning the former ones it had been said that "to them the land will be distributed by lot," surely it would have been false that they "fell in the desert"[3] on account of their transgressions. Therefore, what was not said about the first ones is said about those who came later, to whom everything that is promised has been fulfilled.

1.2. Now I do not want you to think that these things are deduced from the text of the historical narrative alone; they are mysteries that are recorded through the image of the law. For the first people, who are "of the circumcision," are rejected, and a second people, who are gathered "from the nations" are introduced, and that is the one who obtains the fathers' inheri-

---

[105]Heb 13:17. [106]Rufinus uses a rare word, *siromastes* (Gk *seiromastēs*), lit. a pit-searcher, or instrument used by tax-gatherers in probing corn-pits, etc. Cf. C. T. Lewis and C. Short, *A Latin Dictionary* (Oxford: Clarendon, 1975), ad loc. Jerome uses the same word of Phinehas's spear in *Epistles* 109.3; 147.9. [107]Cf. Num 25:6-8. [108]Num 25:11. [109]Cf. Mt 26:52. [110]Eph 6:17. [111]Rom 2:5. [112]Cf. Lk 22:46. [113]Cf. Eph 6:17. [114]Cf. Lk 22:36. [115]Cf. 1 Pet 4:11. **Homily 21** [1]Cf. 1 Cor 10:5. [2]Num 26:53-54. [3]Cf. 1 Cor 10:5.

tance. And from whom is it obtained? Not from Moses, but from Jesus.[4] For even Moses, if he gives an inheritance to anyone, does not give it inside the Jordan, nor does he cross the Jordan at all, but he gives land beyond the Jordan, not land "flowing with milk and honey,"[5] but land that is suitable for cattle and that can nourish dumb animals and irrational beasts more than rational human beings. But the land that my Jesus gives to the second people is a land "flowing with milk and honey,"[6] or rather, it is a honeycomb of honey that is beyond the entire earth. And Moses does not give an inheritance by lot,[7] nor does he distribute by allotment, nor can he repay the merits of each by a divine allotment, "by groups and houses and families and names."[8] Jesus alone does this, to whom "the Father has handed over all judgment."[9] He knows how to pay out his people with a worthy and befitting mansion,[10] not merely "by tribes and families and houses," but even each one "by name."[11]

1.3. Yet there are some among these who rise above the condition of an allotment and are not led to an allotment at all. All the Levites, that is, all who abide in the service of God intently and unceasingly, and who carry out a continuous and vigilant watch in his service, do not receive an allotment among the others.[12] But their allotment is not on earth at all, but it is mentioned that the Lord himself is their inheritance.[13] In the Levites it appears to me that they are being indicated who are not hobbled by any hindrances of bodily nature, but having transcended the glory of all visible things, have set their mode and practice of life in the wisdom of God alone and in his Word. They seek nothing bodily, nothing that is foreign to reason. For they have desired wisdom, they have desired the knowledge of God's secrets, and "where their heart is, there is also their trea-

sure."[14] Therefore they do not have an inheritance on earth, but they transcend the highest heights of heaven and they will always be delighted there in the Lord, always in his word, always in his wisdom and in the pleasure of his knowledge. For them, this will be their food, their drink, their riches; this will be their kingdom. They will be like this, then, and they will be in these things, for whom the Lord himself will be their inheritance.

1.4. But those who are inferior and have not reached the summit of the stages of advancement will receive an inheritance of land, though of a rather lofty and robust land. For "the land of the living"[15] is promised, which is assuredly called the "land of the living" because it does not know death. And they are the "lambs" and those "blessed ones," but more blessed are those who will no longer see "through a mirror and in a riddle," nor in physical essences, but "face to face."[16] They will see God, irradiated by the illumination of wisdom and having become capable of pure divinity through the purity of their heart.[17] They have their portion not in creation but in the Creator, "who is over all things God blessed unto the ages."[18]

2.1. Thus it says: "From the number of names to those who are more, more will be given in the allotment, and to those who are fewer in number, you will give a small inheritance; to each his inheritance will be given as he was assessed."[19] This is what the historical narrative teaches, that, if a tribe is considered to be more numerous among the people, a greater extent of land should be allotted; but if it is assessed to be of a lesser number of men, it should be contented with a smaller possession.

But since we are saying that the division and inheritance of this land contains the earthly form and "image of the good things to come,"[20] and points to the form of that heavenly in-

---

[4]Heb *Joshua*. [5]Cf. Josh 5:6. [6]Josh 5:6. [7]Or "to clergy." [8]Cf. Num 1:20. [9]Cf. Jn 5:22. [10]Or "stage," Lat *mansio*. Cf. Jn 14:2. [11]Cf. Jn 10:3. [12]Cf. Homilies 3.2; 10.1; *Homilies on Leviticus* 15.3. [13]Cf. Num 18:20. [14]Mt 6:21. [15]Cf. Ps 27:13. [16]Cf. 1 Cor 13:12. [17]Cf. Mt 5:8. [18]Rom 9:5. [19]Num 26:53-54; 33:54. [20]Cf. Heb 10:1.

heritance that is awaited by the faithful and the saints, I ask, in respect to this inheritance that one must hope for, who are "those who are more" and who are the "few"? I find that the "few" are considered more blessed than "those who are more." For they are called "many" who have taken the journey down the "broad and spacious way that leads to destruction";[21] but they are called "few" who have gone down the "narrow and constricted way which leads to life."[22] And again, it is said of some: "How few they are who are saved!"[23] and again of others: "when iniquity is multiplied, the love of many"—not of few—"will grow cold."[24] Moreover, in the ark that Noah constructed, when the measurements are given from heaven, for the lower sections the length is recorded as "three hundred cubits and the width fifty;[25] but when his structure rises up to the higher parts, it is forced to become narrow and is compressed within the limits of a "few" cubits, so that its summit is finished to within the space of a single cubit.[26] For this reason in the lower parts where the rooms were considered "broad and spacious," both beasts and cattle were located; but in the higher sections there were birds, and in the highest parts which were more narrow and constricted, there rational man is located. But the very summit is pressed into a single cubit; for all things are gathered into a monad, which, however, in the number three hundred cubits indicates the mystery of the Trinity, and man is placed near this mystery, inasmuch as he is rational and has a capacity for God.[27]

2.2. Moreover, from this we may gather indications as to what is the difference between few and many. Take the whole number of the human race and pick out those who are faithful from all the nations: doubtless they will be fewer than the whole. Then select the bet-

ter ones from the number of the faithful: it is certain that the number will be far lower. And again, from those whom you have chosen, select the more perfect ones: you will find even fewer. And the more you continue to make choices, the more you will find them to be scanty and very few, until you finally come to someone who confidently says: "I labored more than all of them."[28]

Thus, "those who are more" will receive more land and more of a physical inheritance; but the "few" will attain to a small amount of land, since they have more in the Lord; but some will receive absolutely no earthly inheritance, if they become worthy to be priests and ministers of God; for "of these" the Lord will be their whole inheritance.[29] And who is so blessed that among the few he receives either a small amount of land, or that among the chosen priests and ministers he merits in the allotment of his inheritance to have room for the Lord alone? For granted they receive some land on account of their beasts of burden,[30] yet it is from that land that borders on cities and is attached to cities.

2.3. Yet these words which say that the inheritance is multiplied to those who are more can be understood in still another way as well. For one just man is considered as "more" in accordance with the fact that "he is accepted by God."[31] After all, it is even written: "Through one wise man a city will be considered, but the tribes of the unjust will be desolated."[32] And one just man is reckoned for the whole world, but the unjust, even if they are many, are considered by God as scanty and as nothing.

So there is a praiseworthy multitude, as we see was said to Abraham as well, when "he led him outside and said to him: look at the sky if you are able to number the stars; thus will be your seed."[33] Consider here how the just man

---

[21]Cf. Mt 7:13. [22]Cf. Mt 7:14. [23]Lk 13:23. [24]Mt 24:12. [25]Cf. Gen 6:15. [26]Cf. *Homilies on Genesis* 2.1. Origen envisioned Noah's ark to be in the shape of a pyramid. For an artistic depiction, see the reproductions of the art works of Lorenzo Ghiberti and Paolo Uccello in E. Wind, "The Revival of Origen," in *Studies in Art and Literature for Belle Da Costa Greene*, ed. D. Miner (Princeton: Princeton University Press, 1954), between pp. 414 and 415. [27]Cf. Clement *Miscellanies* 6.11.87.2. [28]1 Cor 15:10. [29]Cf. Num 18:20. [30]Cf. Josh 14:4. [31]Acts 10:35. [32]Sir 16:4. [33]Gen 15:5.

is interior and always abides in what is interior, since it is "inside" that "he prays to the Father in secret,"[34] and "all the glory of the king's daughter," that is, of the royal soul, "is within."[35] Nevertheless, God "leads him outside," when circumstances demand it and the rational order of visible things demands it. Therefore, even in this way, to the many who are "as the stars of heaven in multitude,"[36] an inheritance is multiplied; and to the scanty few, namely those who, even if they are many in number, nevertheless are considered scanty due to the unworthiness and commonness of their life, a scanty inheritance is appointed.

3.1. It says: "The distribution of the inheritance will be by lot."[37] This is indeed commanded, but when I come to the Scriptures, I see that Moses himself, to whom these things are commanded, does not make use of an allotment in the division of the inheritance of "Reuben, Gad and the half-tribe of Manasseh."[38] Moreover, Jesus son of Nun gives to the tribe of Judah and Caleb an inheritance outside the allotment;[39] he also grants to the tribe of Ephraim and the half-tribe of Manasseh an allotment that is outside. For others a lot is cast, and "the lot fell first on Benjamin,"[40] and from there it fell on the rest of the tribes as well. This is why I think that in that blessed inheritance of the kingdom of heavens,[41] there will be some who do not attain an allotment. They will not be numbered with the others, even though they are holy. Instead, theirs will be a certain choice and exceptional inheritance, as it was for Caleb, from the tribe of Judah, and for Jesus himself, the son of Nun.

For instance, when provinces and spoils are divided out to victors after a battle, in the division of the spoils the outstanding and exceptional warriors are not conducted to an allotment with the rest of the soldiers. Instead, the best and most distinguished of the spoils are appointed for them, owing to the merit of their virtues. But the others rightfully enjoy an allotment, but it is solely by right of victory. It seems to me that my Lord Jesus will act like this. Indeed, for certain people whom he knows labored more abundantly than the others[42] and whose splendid deeds and lofty virtues he himself recognizes, he appoints for them glories and honors that are exceptional and, if I may speak boldly, similar to his own.

Or does he not seem to you to confer something resembling his own blessedness to his most beloved disciples, when he says: "Father, I want that where I am, they also may be with me,"[43] and again when he says: "You will also sit on twelve thrones judging the twelve tribes of Israel,"[44] and again: "Just as you are in me, Father, and I am in you, that they too may be one in us"[45]? None of these things occur by lot, but they are given by the privilege and choice of him who alone sees into human hearts and minds, who deigns to lead us too into an allotment of the saints, even if it is not among the exceptional and chosen allotments and those that are above an allotment. "To him be the glory and the power in the ages of ages. Amen."[46]

Homily 22
Numbers 27:1-23

Concerning the daughters of Salphaat[1] and concerning Moses' successor.

1.1. There were five daughters whose names are even preserved in the Scripture.[2] They were born of Salphaat, a certain Israelite, who "died in the desert"[3] without having left behind a male descendant. So these daughters of Salphaat plead to Moses and demand an allotment of a paternal inheritance, saying: "Lest the name

---

[34]Cf. Mt 6:6. [35]Ps 45:13. [36]Heb 11:12. [37]Num 26:55. [38]Cf. Num 32:33; 34:14; Josh 18:7. [39]Cf. Josh 14:13. [40]Josh 18:11. [41]Cf. *On First Principles* 2.3.7; *Homilies on Joshua* 12.1; Clement *Salvation of the Rich* 3.1. [42]Cf. 1 Cor 15:10. [43]Jn 17:24. [44]Mt 19:28. [45]Jn 17:21. [46]Cf. 1 Pet 4:11. **Homily 22** [1]RSV Zelophehad. [2]Cf. Num 27:1. [3]Num 27:3.

of their father be blotted out from the midst of his people, because no male-son was born to him."[4] Moses consults with God about this matter.[5] And the clemency of Almighty God does not spurn or despise the question that is being brought by his children, and not only does he deem it fitting to give an answer, but he goes so far as to approve and embrace their words, in order to establish eternal rights for humanity from these things, rights that are to be observed in all ages. For "the Lord, speaking to Moses, says: The daughters of Salphaat have spoken rightly; you will give them a possession in the midst of their father's brothers, and you will give their father's allotment to them. And you will speak to the sons of Israel, saying: If a man dies and has no son, you will give his inheritance to his daughter. But if he has no daughter, you will give his inheritance to his brother. But if he has no brothers, you will give his inheritance to his father's brother. But if his father has no brothers, you will give the inheritance to the member of the household who is his nearest relation from his tribe, and he will receive his inheritance. And this shall be to the sons of Israel an ordinance[6] of judgment, as the Lord has established it to Moses."[7]

1.2. What relevance this has according to the historical narrative is plain to everyone who knows that these laws are kept not only by the sons of Israel, but also by all men, at least those who live by laws. This is why it appears that the boldness[8] of the daughters of Salphaat not only conferred the inheritance to them, but even gave to the world perpetual rights for living. You see what great usefulness there is even in the historical narrative in the law of God. Who can ever dissolve these laws that the whole world uses?[9]

But let us nevertheless look for a means by which we can also be edified spiritually. For it can happen that I may have no daughters according to the flesh, nor any land the inheritance of which can be received. What then? Will this law not be operative with one in this situation? Will it be superfluous to anyone that it was sanctioned by the voice of God? Therefore, in the spiritual law as well, let us seek the identity of these five daughters whose father, even though he died for some sin,[10] nevertheless they themselves receive an inheritance because of the word of God.

1.3. Above,[11] when we were discussing spiritual sons, we showed that the virtues of the soul and the senses[12] of the mind are called sons. Doubtless it seems consistent and befitting to understand likewise as daughters the works that are fulfilled in the service of the body. After all, that is why the number *five* is attributed to them; for there are five bodily senses with which every work is fulfilled in the body.[13] So these are the five daughters, that is, the perfection of works, even if they are orphaned from their father and remain orphans. Yet they are not cast away from the inheritance, nor are they excluded from the kingdom, but they receive a portion of the inheritance in the midst of the people of God.

But indeed let us see who their father is, who is said by them to have died.[14] "Salphaat,"[15] it says. Now Salphaat translates as "shadow in his mouth." Understanding is the father of works. Well it often happens, and there are not a few among our brothers whose understanding is not very profound or deep, but their senses[16] have died out, as it is written about someone: "And his heart died within him."[17] That one, then, even though he is not sensitive to spiritual interpretation, but is dead, yet if he bears daughters, that is, works of service, works of obedience, works of God's commands, he will obtain an inheritance of earth with the Lord's

---

[4]Num 27:4. [5]Cf. Num 27:5. [6]Lat *iustificatio.* [7]Num 27:6-11. [8]Lat *libertas,* lit. "freedom." Cf. Homily 24.3.5. [9]Cf. Philo *On the Life of Moses* 2.234-245. [10]Cf. Num 27:3. [11]Cf. Homily 20.2. [12]Here and below there is a play on the term *sensus,* which means both "bodily senses" and "meanings." [13]Cf. Homily 5.2.2; Philo *On Planting* 133. [14]Num 27:3. [15]RSV *Zelophehad.* [16]Or "meanings," Lat *sensus.* [17]1 Sam 25:37.

people. To be sure he will be unable to be numbered among those whose "portion is the Lord, whose inheritance is God";[18] he will not be able to be received into the number of ministers and priests; yet he will receive an inheritance in the Promised Land in the ordering of the people. "For many are called, but few are chosen."[19]

1.4. Yet the reason why this Salphaat could not produce sons, but only daughters, is shown from the interpretation of his name. For, as we said, the name translates as "shadow in his mouth." So you see that if the one who has the *shadow* of the law in his mouth, and not "the very image of things,"[20] this one, since he is unable to perceive anything spiritual or of deep understanding, but only the *shadow* of the law is in his mouth, he cannot generate living spiritual meanings.[21] Yet he can generate works and deeds, which are the services of a more simple life. And for this reason the clemency of God shows in this that those who are more innocent, even though they lack sense, nevertheless if they have good works, they are not excluded from the inheritance of the saints. Thus it is right that they are spoken of as daughters of Salphaat.

2.1. After this, a law of God concerning succession is established, so that, in the first place a son succeeds, secondly, a daughter, thirdly a brother, fourthly the father's brother;[22] but the fifth rank does not designate any fixed person, but whoever was "nearest[23] out of the whole family"[24] is to succeed. Here the meaning of the historical narrative is so complete and perfect that it does not seem necessary to ask anything further.

However, if someone is well instructed in the spiritual laws and radiates with a fuller light of knowledge, he can understand these different ranks of succession and how it is that the one who is a male son is first in line to obtain the heavenly inheritance by the merit of his learning and knowledge; the daughter is the one who

is second in line by the privilege of works; the third ranking is called the brother, due to some sort of sympathy and imitation. For there are some who do nothing of their own accord and by their own understanding; yet they are placed among the brothers by the imitation of others, because they seem to do the same things that those ones do who are provoked by their own understanding. Therefore, to them as well the third rank of inheritance is granted under the designation of the name of brother.

2.2. Now the fourth rank, which he names "father's brother," can possibly be understood of that order of men who try to fulfill what has been heard from the fathers and what has been received from the narratives about the ancients and, not so much moved by their own thoughts or stirred up by the admonitions found in the present instruction, as instructed by tradition and custom alone, nevertheless, they do something good. Thus in the final recorded ranking, comes that one who in some manner was "nearest" to these. It is as if he were saying: If someone has done anything good, either occasionally, or by the truth of instruction, he will not lose the wages for his good work, but he will receive a place of inheritance from the Lord who bestows this. Now these things may perhaps seem to have been set forth publicly by us boldly and presumptuously, yet it will not be absurd if, by proposing "spiritual things by means of spiritual things,"[25] we encourage them with the desire to strive after a more hidden interpretation.

3.1. After this a story is reported that is both remarkable as a narrative and magnificent in its signification. For it is recorded how "God told Moses to go up on the mountain."[26] He was to survey and contemplate the whole Promised Land from there, and then he was to die there.[27] But that man, who had more concern for the people than for himself, prays to the Lord "to provide a man" who will rule the people, "lest it

---

[18]Deut 32:9. [19]Mt 22:14. [20]Cf. Heb 10:1. [21]Or "senses," Lat *sensus*. [22]Cf. Num 27:8-10. [23]Lit. "nearer." [24]Num 27:11. [25]Cf. 1 Cor 2:13. [26]Num 27:12. [27]Cf. Num 27:13.

happen," it says, "that this congregation be like sheep without a shepherd."[28]

3.2. Well, first of all, notice how one who is perfect and blessed dies not in a valley, nor on some level place on earth, or on some hill, but on a mountain, that is, in a steep and arduous place. For the consummation and perfection of his life was passed "on high." Moreover, he is commanded to contemplate with his eyes the whole Promised Land and to carefully perceive everything from his eminent position. For it was not right that anything remain unknown to one who is about to obtain the summit of perfection, but it is fitting for him to have knowledge of everything that is seen and heard. I believe that the reason for this is that for all these objects that he had known under their physical appearance while he was in the flesh, having [now] become in the spirit and having become pure mind, he comprehends their rational causes and reasons, as one who is hastening quickly to the auditorium and school of wisdom. For what benefit will seem to come to one who is about to depart from this world and who will receive the end of his life immediately from showing him lands and places for which he would not need to endure toil, nor would he receive any benefit?[29]

3.3. Frankly, the words that follow terrify me and make me fearful and hesitant to speak. For they relate to that great Moses, the servant and friend of God, with whom God spoke face to face,[30] through whom such awesome and menacing signs and wonderful miracles were accomplished.[31] What indeed does God say to him? "And you yourself will be added," it says, "to your people, just as Aaron your brother was added on Mount Or."[32] And as if explaining the cause of his death, he says: "Because you transgressed my word in the desert of Sin, when the congregation refused to sanctify me. You

did not sanctify me at the water before them."[33] So is Moses likewise at fault? He himself likewise fell into a sin of transgression, he himself likewise came to be under sin. I believe that this is why the apostle said with confidence: "Death reigned from Adam up to Moses";[34] for it approached "up to Moses" and did not spare him. And therefore, I think, he said that "Sin entered into this world, and through sin death, in that all sinned";[35] and again: "God enclosed all under sin, in order to have mercy on all."[36] But "thanks [be] to our Lord Jesus Christ," who "freed us from the body of this death,"[37] so that "where sin abounded, grace would super-abound."[38] For how could Moses free anyone from sins, when even to himself it is said: "You transgressed my word in the desert of Sin, and you did not sanctify me at the water before the sons of Israel"?[39] Thus it is clear to everyone that the former one alone should be sought as the only one: "who committed no sin, nor was deceit found in his mouth."[40]

4.1. But for now let us consider the grandeur of Moses. When he was about to depart from the world, he prays to God to provide a leader for the people. What are you doing, O Moses? Are not Gershom and Eleazer your sons? Or, if you have some hesitations about them, does not your brother, a great and famous man, have sons?[41] Why not pray to God for them, to have them appointed leaders of the people? But let the rulers of the churches learn not to ordain as their successors those who are linked to them by blood relation, nor those who are associated by proximity of the flesh. They should not transmit a hereditary rule in the church, but should defer to God's judgment and not select one whom human affection recommends. Instead let them allow the matter of the election of a successor be completely determined by God's judgment.

---

[28]Num 27:17. [29]Lat *gratia*. [30]Cf. Josh 1:7; Ex 33:11. [31]Cf. Num 14:11. [32]Num 27:13 LXX. The RSV does not have "on Mount Or." [33]Num 27:14. [34]Rom 5:14. [35]Rom 5:12. [36]Rom 11:32. [37]Rom 7:24-25. [38]Rom 5:20. [39]Num 27:14. [40]1 Pet 2:22. [41]Or possibly "Are not your brother's sons great and famous men?"

Was Moses unable to choose a leader for the people, and to choose by a true judgment and by a fair and just decision, to whom God had said: "Choose elders for the people whom you yourself know that they are elders"?[42] And he chose the sort of men on whom "the Spirit of God immediately rested and they all prophesied."[43] Who then was as capable of choosing a leader for the people as Moses? But he does not do it, he does not choose, he does not dare. Why does he not dare? So that he will not leave to posterity a presumptuous precedent. But listen to what he says: "May the Lord God of spirits and of all flesh provide a man over this congregation, who will go out before their face and who will go in, and who will lead them forth and lead them back."[44] Thus, if a man of the stature and quality of Moses does not allow to his own judgment the selection of a leader of the people, the appointment of a successor, who will there be who would dare to do this, whether from the people, who often are accustomed to be stirred up by shouts for favors, or who perhaps are provoked by financial gain; or even from the priests themselves? Who will there be who would judge himself capable of doing this, unless it be revealed to someone who prays and asks the Lord?

4.2. Just as God also says to Moses: "Take to yourself Jesus the son of Nun, a man who has the Spirit of God in himself, and you will lay your hands on him; and you will set him before Eleazar the priest, and you will give him a charge before all the congregation, and you will give a charge concerning him before them; and you will put your glory[45] on him, that the sons of Israel may listen to him."[46] You hear plainly the ordination of a leader of the people so clearly described that it scarcely requires an explanation. Here there is no shout of acclamation of the people, there is no question of blood relationship, there is no consideration of near relations. To near relations let the inheritance

of fields and estates be left; let the governance of the people be transmitted to one whom God has chosen, namely, to the kind of man who "has the Spirit of God within him,"[47] as you have heard is written, and "the commands of God are before him,"[48] and who is very well known to and familiar with Moses, that is, who possesses the glory[49] and knowledge of the law, so that the sons of Israel can hear him.

4.3. But since all these things are crammed full of mysteries, we cannot omit mentioning the more precious ones, even though these things which are commanded according to the letter seem useful and necessary. So let us consider what Moses' death means: doubtless it means the end of the law,[50] but of that law which is said to be "according to the letter." Now what is this end? It is namely the cessation of the sacrifices and of the other things which are commanded in the law by a similar observance. So then, when these things receive their end, Jesus takes up his rule. "For Christ is the end of the law for justice to all who believe."[51] And just as it is said about the former things, that "All were baptized into Moses in the cloud and in the sea,"[52] so also it may be said about Jesus that "all were baptized in the Holy Spirit" and in water.[53] For it is Jesus who passes through the waters of the Jordan, and in a certain manner even then baptizes the people in them.[54] And he is the one who divides out to all the land of inheritance, the holy land, not to the first people, but to the second; for the first people, on account of their transgression, "fell in the desert."[55] Of the time of Jesus, it is said that "the land rested from wars."[56] It was impossible to say this of the time of Moses. But this is said of Jesus my Lord, not of that son of Nun.

4.4. And would that my land would cease from wars! Indeed it can cease, if I fight faithfully for Jesus my leader. For if I obey my Lord Jesus, my flesh will never rise up in insurrec-

---

[42]Num 11:16. [43]Num 11:25. [44]Num 27:16-17. [45]Lat *claritas*. [46]Num 27:18-20. [47]Num 27:18. [48]Ps 18:22. [49]Lat *claritas*. [50]Cf. Rom 10:4. [51]Rom 10:4. [52]1 Cor 10:2. [53]Cf. Jn 1:33. [54]Cf. Josh 3:15-16; 4:10-11. [55]1 Cor 10:5. [56]Josh 11:23.

tion against my spirit,[57] nor will my land be attacked by pagan adversaries, that is, it will not be goaded on by various lusts. So let us pray that Jesus may reign over us and that our land will cease from wars, cease from the attacks of carnal desires. And when these have ceased, then each one will rest "under his own vine and under his own fig tree,"[58] and under his own olive tree. For under the covering of the Father and of the Son and of the Holy Spirit,[59] the soul will rest that has recovered peace between the flesh and the spirit within itself. To the eternal God be the "glory in the ages of ages. Amen."[60]

Homily 23
Numbers 28:1–29:39

Concerning what is written: "My gifts, my presents," and concerning the various feasts.

1.1. If the observance of sacrifices and the legal institutions which were given to the people of Israel as a type had been able to exist until the present time, doubtless these things would have excluded the faith of the gospel, through which, since the advent of our Lord Jesus Christ, the nations are being converted to God. For in those things that were being observed then, there was a splendid religion that was filled with all reverence. Even from the very first sight of it, it amazed the one who looked on. For who, on seeing what was called the sanctuary or the sacred place, and on gazing at the altar, on seeing the priests, too, standing in attendance and carrying out the sacrifices and surveying the entire order whereby all those things were being done, would not have thought that this was the most complete rite by which God the Creator of all things ought to be worshiped by the human race?

1.2. But thanks to the advent of Christ,

our souls have been torn away from gazing on such things. He has guided them to the consideration and contemplation of heavenly and spiritual things; and indeed he destroyed what seemed great on earth, and transferred the worship of God from the visible to the invisible, and from the temporal to the eternal.[1] But indeed, the Lord Jesus Christ requires ears that can hear and eyes that can see.[2] This is also why, since we now have the law that was given through Moses[3] in our hands and want to show that it is a "spiritual law,"[4] we require that your ears and eyes be the kind that do not look back to those things that have been destroyed, but which seek these things where "Christ is sitting at the right hand of God," and that you be mindful of "what is above, not what is on the earth."[5]

So let this be sufficient as what has been said first, in place of a preface, as that which we had to say.

2.1. But now let us come to the things that are written.

It says: "And the Lord spoke to Moses, saying: Charge the sons of Israel and you will say to them: Observe to offer to me on my feast days my gifts, my presents, my victims for a sweet-smelling savor. And you will say to them: These are my victims, which you offer to the Lord."[6] No one offers anything of his own to God, but what he offers is the Lord's, and one does not so much offer one's own things as return to him what are his own things. So this is why the Lord, when he wanted to write laws of sacrifices and gifts that are to be offered to him by men, first of all clarifies the rationale for all these things that were to be offered, and he says: "Observe to offer to me on my feast days my gifts, my presents, my victims for a sweet-smelling savor." These gifts, he says, concerning which I will charge you to offer to me on

---

[57]Cf. Gal 5:17. [58]Cf. 1 Kings 4:25. [59]Cf. Mt 28:19. [60]Cf. 1 Pet 4:11. **Homily 23** [1]Cf. *Commentary on Romans* 9.1.1; Theresia Heither, *Translatio Religionis: Die Paulusdeutung des Origenes in seinem Kommentar zum Römerbrief* (Cologne, Germany: Böhlau, 1990), pp. 57-83. [2]Cf. Mt 13:13, 16. [3]Cf. Jn 1:17. [4]Rom 7:14. [5]Col 3:1-2. [6]Num 28:1-3.

my feast days are my presents, that is, they are given to you from me. For all that the human race possesses, it has from me. So he says this to prevent anyone from believing that in his offering of gifts to God he is conferring some benefit on God. For by thinking that, an impious man would arise in the very gift by which he seemed to be worshiping God. For what is so impious as the man who thinks that he is conferring something on a needy God? Necessarily then, as we have said, he first teaches man to know that whatever man offers to God, he is returning it to God rather than offering it to him.[7]

Let us moreover look at the sense of the words: "What you offer to me on my feast days."[8]

2.2. So, does God have his own feast days? He does. For to him, human salvation is a great feast. I think that a feast takes place with God through every single believer, through all who are converted to God and make progress in the faith. How do you think it causes him joy, when the one who had been unchaste becomes chaste, and the one who has been unjust cultivates justice, and the one who had been impious becomes pious? All such conversions of every one of these people give rise to festivities with God. Now there is no doubting the fact that our Lord Jesus Christ too, who even poured out his own blood for our salvation, celebrates a very great feast, when he sees that it was worth the effort that he "humbled himself and taking on the form of a slave, became obedient to death."[9] And the Holy Spirit equally offers a feast, when he sees more temples prepared for himself in those who are being converted to God.[10]

2.3. Now what should I say about the angels, to whose festival of rejoicing all are said to come who are converted to the Lord? Or is there not great feasting among them when they "rejoice in heaven over one sinner who repents than over ninety-nine just men who do not need repentance"?[11] So the angels as well celebrate a feast day. They rejoice over those who flee the fellowship of demons and hasten to join themselves to the angelic fellowship by the practice of the virtues.

2.4. Perhaps what I am trying to say may be surprising: that we seem to provide grounds for feasting and rejoicing with God and the angels; we, while placed on earth, supply the occasion of rejoicing and exultation in heaven, while walking on the earth, "we have our citizenship[12] in heaven,"[13] and through this means, doubtless, we bring about a feast day in heaven. But just as our good actions and progress in the virtues give rise to rejoicing and festivity with God and angels, so I fear that our evil manner of living[14] brings about lamentation and sorrow, not only on earth but also in heaven. And perhaps likewise human sins strike God himself with grief. Or is this not the voice of one who is grieving, when he says: "It grieves me that I made man on the earth"?[15] Moreover, there are these words of our Lord and Savior in the Gospel, when he says: "Jerusalem, Jerusalem, you who stone prophets and kill those sent to you, how often have I wanted to gather your sons, as a hen gathers her chicks under her wings, and you were unwilling!"[16] And lest you think that it is said only about the ancients, that they "stoned the prophets," I too, today, stone the prophet, if I do not listen to the words of the prophet, if I spurn his admonitions; and as far as is in me, I kill the one whose words I do not listen to, namely by treating his words as if they were spoken by a dead man.

2.5. Moreover, the following are the words of God who is lamenting for the human race, in which it is said through the prophet: "Alas for me! For I have become as one who gathers straw in the harvest and as grape clusters in the

---

[7]This whole paragraph reveals how alien Origen's doctrine of grace was from the spirit of Pelagius. [8]Num 28:2. [9]Phil 2:7-8. [10]Cf. 1 Cor 3:16. Notice the trinitarian structure of this paragraph. [11]Lk 15:7. [12]Lat *conversatio*. [13]Phil 3:20. [14]Lat *conversatio*. [15]Gen 6:6. [16]Mt 23:37.

vintage, since there is no ear or grape to eat for the first fruits! Alas my soul, for the reverent has perished from the earth, and there is no one who corrects among men!"[17] These are the words of a Lord grieving for the human race. For he came to gather the harvest, and instead of a harvest he found straw; and he came to gather the vintage, but instead of the vintage he found a few grape clusters, namely the apostles. Unless the Lord Sabaoth had left them for us as seed,[18] and "unless a grain of wheat had fallen into the earth to bear more fruit,"[19] "we would have become like Sodom, and we would have been like Gomorrah."[20]

With the angels of God too, as we said above, "there is joy in heaven over one sinner who repents."[21] It is certain that where joys are celebrated on behalf of the good, there will be lamenting for those in the opposite condition. Thus, if they rejoice over the convert, necessarily they would grieve for the sinner.

2.6. So this is why "Jerusalem sinned a great sin,"[22] according to what is written in the Lamentation.[23] She came into confusion and all her feasts perished and her solemn days, since they killed my Lord Jesus Christ in the holy place and on a feast day. And this is why he says to them: "Your new moons and sabbaths and your feast days my soul hates."[24] Now here [in Numbers], when he gives commands about gifts, when there are as yet no sins, he says: "my feast days";[25] but when there is sin, the Lord does not say "my" but "your feast days."[26]

But all these terms in which God is said to grieve or rejoice or hate or be made glad should be interpreted as being said by Scripture as figures of speech and in a human manner of speaking. The divine nature is completely estranged from all passion and affective change. It always abides in the peak of beatitude, immutable and undisturbed.

3.1. Since therefore we have the laws for feasts in hand and the present words concern this subject, let us diligently investigate the order of the feasts in order to be able to conclude from these orders and from the rite of sacrifices how each one can prepare a feast for God by his own actions and by his holy manner of life.[27]

Well, the first feast of God is the one called "perpetual."[28] For a command is given concerning these morning and evening sacrifices, which are offered perpetually and without any interruption whatsoever. Thus, when he commands the rites of the feasts, he does not come first of all and immediately to the Passover feast, nor to the feast of Unleavened Bread, nor to that of Tabernacles, nor to the others about which commands are given; but he has recorded this one first, in which he commands a perpetual sacrifice to be offered. The reason for this is so that each one who wants to be perfect and holy may know that it is not merely now and then that one must celebrate a feast for God, but at other times, there is no need to celebrate a feast. On the contrary, always and perpetually the just person should celebrate the feast day. For the sacrifice that is commanded to be offered perpetually, both in the morning and in the evening, indicates this, that in the law and the prophets, which point to the morning time, and in the teaching of the gospel, which points to the evening time, that is, to the evening of the world, it points to the coming of the Savior, it persists with a perpetual intention. So it is of these kinds of feasts that the Lord says: "And you will observe my feast days." Thus it is a feast day of the Lord, if we offer him a sacrifice perpetually, if "we pray without intermission,"[29] so that "our prayer may ascend like incense in his sight in the morning, and the lifting up of our hands may become an evening sacrifice to him."[30] So then, this is the first celebration of a perpetual sacrifice, which must be fulfilled by worshipers of the gospel in this manner that we

---

[17]Mic 7:1-2. [18]Cf. Is 1:9; Rom 9:29. [19]Cf. Jn 12:24. [20]Cf. Is 1:9; Rom 9:29. [21]Lk 15:7. [22]Lam 1:8. [23]Rufinus uses the singular for the title of this book. [24]Is 1:14. [25]Num 28:2. [26]Is 1:14. [27]Lat *conversationibus sanctis*. [28]Cf. Num 28:6. [29]1 Thess 5:17. [30]Ps 141:2.

have explained above.

3.2. But since, as the prophetic words have clearly shown, the feast days of sinners "are converted into mourning" and "their singing into lamentation,"[31] it is certain that the one who sins and celebrates days of sin cannot be celebrating a feast day; and therefore on those days on which he sins, he cannot be offering a perpetual sacrifice to God. But the one who preserves justice[32] and keeps himself from sin can make such an offering. But it is certain that on the day on which he interrupts this and commits sin, on that day he is not offering a perpetual sacrifice to God.

I fear to say something that is given to be understood based on the apostolic sayings, lest I seem to cause grief in some people. For if "the prayer of the just is offered like incense in the sight of God, and the lifting up of hands is his evening sacrifice,"[33] but the apostle says to those who are married: "Do not deprive one another, except by consent for a time, that you may be free for prayer, and again be unto this very thing,"[34] it is certain that the perpetual sacrifice is impeded in those who serve conjugal needs.[35] This is why it seems to me that the offering of a perpetual sacrifice belongs to that one alone who has pledged himself to perpetual and continual chastity. But there are other feast days for those who perhaps are not able to offer the sacrifices of chastity perpetually.

4.1. Now the second feast, after the feast of the perpetual sacrifice, is recorded to be the sacrifice of the sabbath, and it is necessary that every saint and just person celebrate the feast of the Sabbath as well. Well, what is the feast of the Sabbath, if not that feast of which the apostle says: "So a sabbath,"[36] that is, the observance of the sabbath,[37] "will be left for the people of God"?[38] Therefore, leaving behind the Judaic observances of the sabbath, let us see what sort of observation of the sab-

bath there ought to be for the Christian. On the day of the sabbath, no worldly activity is supposed to be carried out. Thus if you cease doing secular works and carry out nothing worldly, but make room for spiritual works, if you come together at church, give ear to the divine readings and discussions, think about heavenly things, show concern for the future hope, keep the coming judgment before your eyes, do not look to present and visible things, but to the invisible and future things, this is how the Christian observes the sabbath.

4.2. But even the Jews should have observed these things. After all, even among them, if there was a craftsman, a builder or any other such worker, he takes it easy on the sabbath day. But the reader of the divine law, on the other hand, and the teacher, does not leave off from his work, and yet they are not defiling the sabbath; for this is what the Lord says to them: "Or have you not read that the priests in the temple violate the sabbath and are without an offense?"[39] Therefore, the one who has ceased from the works of the world and makes room for spiritual actions is the one who carries out the sacrifice of the sabbath and celebrates the feast day of the sabbaths. He "carries no burdens on the road";[40] for every sin is a burden, as the prophet says: "They have weighed down on me like a heavy burden."[41] He "kindles no fire,"[42] namely, that fire of which it is said: "Go in the light of your fire and in the flame which you have kindled."[43] On the sabbath each one stays in his own place and does not go forth from it. Well, what is the "place" of the spiritual soul? Its place is justice, truth, wisdom, sanctification, and everything that Christ is; this is the "place" of the soul. It is not proper for the soul to go forth from this place, so that it may keep the true sabbaths and accomplish the feast day with the sacrifices of the Sabbath, as the Lord

---

[31]Amos 8:10. [32]Cf. Mic 6:8. [33]Cf. Ps 141:1-2. [34]1 Cor 7:5. [35]On the way marriage can impede the prayer life, see *On Prayer* 31.4; *Homilies on Genesis* 5.4. [36]Lat *sabbatismus*. [37]Lat *sabbatum*. [38]Heb 4:9. [39]Mt 12:5. [40]Neh 13:19. [41]Ps 38:4. [42]Ex 35:3. [43]Is 50:11.

also said: "He who *stays* in me, I too [will *stay*] in him."[44]

4.3. Now as for what we have called true sabbaths, if we ask anew and more deeply what are the true sabbaths, [we find that] the observance of the true sabbath is beyond this world. For what is written in Genesis, that "The Lord rested on the sabbath day from his works,"[45] we do not see either that this was done then, on the seventh day, or that it is even being done now. For we see God always working, and there is no sabbath on which God does not work, on which he does not "bring forth his sun on the evil and on the good and send rain on the just and on the unjust";[46] on which he does not "bring forth hay on the hills, and grass for the benefit of men";[47] on which he does not "strike and heal,"[48] "go down into the nether world and come back up again";[49] on which he does not "kill and make alive."[50] This is why the Lord too in the Gospels, when the Jews accused him of working and healing on the sabbath, responded to them: "My Father is working still, and I am working."[51] There he shows that God does not rest from his management of the world and from his providence over the human race on any sabbath day of this world. For he made creatures in the beginning, and he brought forth their substances,[52] as far as could suffice for the perfection of the world, which he knew himself, being the Creator of things. But he does not cease his oversight and management of these substances "till the consummation of the age."[53]

4.4. So the true sabbath on which God will "rest from all his works"[54] will be the future age. At that time "grief and sadness and groaning will flee,"[55] and God will be "all in all."[56]

On this sabbath may God grant to us as well the celebration of a feast day with him and rejoicing in these festivities with his holy angels, by offering "a sacrifice of praise and pay-ing back our vows to the Most High,"[57] which "our lips have here specified."[58] Perhaps at that time as well, the perpetual sacrifice, which we have expounded above, will be offered in a better fashion. For then the soul will be better able to attend to God perpetually and to offer a sacrifice of praise "through the great High Priest,"[59] who is a "priest forever in the order of Melchizedek."[60]

5.1. The third feast is recorded to be the day of the new moon [*neomenia*] on which a sacrifice is also offered.[61] Now the new moon is called *neomenia*. So this is the feast when the moon is renewed. But it is called "new" when it comes nearest to the sun and is closely conjoined with it, so that it is concealed under its brightness. But perhaps it may seem remarkable, or rather, superfluous, that the divine law gives a precept about this. For what does the observance of a new moon feast have to do with religion, that is, when it is it is conjoined with the sun and is closely united with it? Should these things be considered according to the letter, they will seem not so much religious as superstitious. But the apostle Paul knew that the law is not speaking about these things, nor was the Holy Spirit prescribing that rite which the Jews seem to observe. And this is why, to those who received the faith of God, he said: "Let no one then judge you in respect to food or drink, or in the part of a feast day or new moon or sabbath; which are a shadow of things to come."[62] So, if the sabbath, which we explained above to the best of our abilities, is a shadow of things to come, and the new moon [*neomenia*] is a shadow of things to come, it is certain that the other feasts likewise are shadows of things to come.

5.2. But now let us consider the new moon [*neomenia*]. We have said that it is called a feast of the new moon when the moon begins to be renewed and comes nearest the sun and is

---

[44]Jn 15:5. [45]Gen 2:2. [46]Mt 5:45. [47]Ps 147:8. [48]Job 5:18; Deut 32:39. [49]1 Sam 2:6. [50]1 Sam 2:6; cf. Deut 32:39. [51]Jn 5:17. [52]Cf. Homilies 6.2.1; 7.4.4. [53]Mt 28:20. [54]Gen 2:3. [55]Is 35:10. [56]1 Cor 15:28; cf. Col 3:11. [57]Ps 50:14. [58]Ps 66:14. [59]Heb 4:14. [60]Heb 5:6, 10; 6:20. [61]Num 28:11. [62]Col 2:16-17.

absolutely conjoined with it. Christ is the "sun of righteousness";[63] if the moon, that is, his church, which is filled with his light, is joined and completely united with him, so that, as the apostle says: "whoever joins himself with the Lord, let him become one spirit with him,"[64] then it celebrates the feast of the new moon; for then it becomes new, "when it casts off the old man, and puts on the new, who is created according to God,"[65] and thus it will deservedly carry on the solemnity of renewal, which is the feast of the new moon.

Ultimately, that is when it can neither be seen nor understood by human viewers. For when the soul has completely united itself to the Lord and has totally yielded itself to the splendor of his light, and thinks absolutely no earthly thought, seeks nothing worldly and does not strive to please men, but devotes itself completely to the light of wisdom and to the warmth of the Holy Spirit, having become "thin and spiritual,"[66] how can it be seen by human beings or apprehended by human eyes? For "animal man" cannot understand or perceive the spiritual.[67] And therefore it will most fittingly celebrate the feast day and will slaughter the sacrifice of the new moon to the Lord, since it has been renewed by him.

6. The solemnity of the Passover is placed fourth among the feasts of God, during which feast a lamb is killed. But you should look to the true lamb, "the lamb of God who takes away the sin of the world,"[68] and say that "Christ our Passover has been sacrificed."[69] Let the Jews eat lamb's flesh[70] in a carnal sense, but let us eat the flesh of the Word of God; for he himself said: "Unless you eat my flesh, you will not have life in yourselves."[71]

What we are now saying is the flesh of the Word of God, but only if we set it forth not as "vegetables" for the weak[72] or as the nourish-

ment of "milk" for children.[73] If we speak what is perfect, robust[74] and strong, we are setting out the flesh of the Word of God for you to eat. For where there are mystical words, where there are doctrinal and solid words that are brought forth in a way that is filled with faith in the Trinity, when the mysteries[75] of the spiritual law of the age to come are expanded on, once the "veil of the letter has been removed";[76] when the soul's hope is torn away from the earth and cast toward heaven and is located in those things that "eye has not seen nor ear heard nor have they ascended into the heart of man."[77] All these things are the flesh of the Word of God. The one who is able to consume these things with a perfect understanding and with a purified heart[78] truly offers the sacrifice of the Passover feast and celebrates the feast day with God and his angels.

7. After this feast, or rather, continuous with it, follows the feast of Unleavened Bread,[79] which you will celebrate worthily if you banish all the "leaven of evil" from your soul and you keep the "unleavened bread of sincerity and truth."[80] For one should not think that the Almighty God writes laws for men on account of yeast, and that this is why he commands the "the soul is banished from the people,"[81] if perchance it comes to light that he spilled in his house a little of this yeast that comes from flour. This does not seem to me to be an interpretation that is worthy of the divine laws: that the divine majesty was so greatly concerned that he claims to be equally offended on account of this yeast, that because of it he would command the soul, which he himself made "in his own image and likeness,"[82] to be banished and destroyed. Instead, it is a question of God's shrinking back and deservedly shrinking back, if the soul is "leavened" with a spirit of evil, wrath and wicked-

---

[63]Mal 4:2. [64]1 Cor 6:17. [65]Eph 4:24. [66]Wis 7:22-23. [67]Cf. 1 Cor 2:14. [68]Jn 1:29. [69]1 Cor 5:7. [70]Or "meat," here and below. [71]Jn 6:53. [72]Cf. Rom 14:2. [73]Cf. 1 Cor 3:2; Heb 5:12. [74]Cf. Heb 5:14. [75]Lat *sacramenta*. [76]2 Cor 3:16. [77]1 Cor 2:9. [78]Cf. Mt 5:8. [79]Cf. Num 28:17. [80]1 Cor 5:8. [81]Num 9:13. [82]Cf. Gen 5:3.

ness, and if it "rises" in its disgraceful conduct.

God does not want these things to be in the soul, and if we do not get rid of yeast like this from the house of our soul, we will be deservedly banished. But you should not take this lightly, even if you seem to be fermenting only a little evil within yourself, for "a little leaven corrupts the whole lump."[83] And therefore, do not be negligent concerning the small sin, since from one sin another is born. For just as justice is generated from justice, and chastity from chastity—for if someone begins to be chaste at first in a modest degree, once the leaven of chastity has been received, he becomes more chaste on a daily basis—so also the one who has once implanted the leaven of evil within himself, however small an amount, daily he becomes more wicked and worse off in himself. And this is why, if you want to celebrate the feast of Unleavened Bread with God, do not allow even a little bit of the leaven of evil[84] to reside within yourself.

8. After this follows a sixth feast, which is called the feast "of the New Produce,"[85] that is, when the first fruits are offered from the new harvest. For when the field is sown and carefully cultivated and the crop reaches maturity, then, at the perfection of the harvest, the feast of the Lord is carried out. So if you too want to celebrate the feast day of the New Produce with God, look to where and how you sow your seed, that you may be able to reap the kind of harvest from which you may cause him to rejoice and to celebrate the feast day. You will not otherwise be able to fulfill this unless you listen to the apostle when he says: "He who sows in the Spirit, from the Spirit will reap eternal life."[86] If you sow and reap in this way, you will truly celebrate the feast day of the New Produce. Ultimately, this is the reason the prophet admonishes and says: "Renew the new ground

for yourselves, and do not sow among thorns."[87] Thus the one who from day to day renovates his heart and inner man renews new ground for himself and does not sow among thorns, but on the good earth, which returns to him a harvest thirtyfold, or sixtyfold, or one hundredfold.[88] So he is the one who "sows in the Spirit,"[89] and gathers the "fruit of the Spirit."[90] Now the fruit of the Spirit is, first of all, joy.[91] And the one who reaps joy deservedly celebrates the feast day of the New Harvest, especially if at the same time he reaps also "peace and patience and goodness and gentleness."[92] If he gathers other fruits like these, he will celebrate the feast of the New Harvest to the Lord in a most worthy fashion.

9. Then follows the feast of Weeks. For just as among the days, every seventh day is observed as the sabbath, and it is a feast, so also among the months, every seventh month is the sabbath of months.[93] So then, a feast is celebrated on it, which is called "Sabbath of Sabbaths," and a memory of Trumpets occurs on the first day of the month. But who is it who carries out the feast of the memory of Trumpets, if not the one who can commit to memory and store up inside the "treasure of his heart"[94] the prophetic Scriptures, the Gospels and the apostolic writings, which resound, as it were, with a certain heavenly trumpet? The one who does this, then, and who "meditates on the law of God day and night,"[95] carries out the feast of the memory of Trumpets. Moreover, if someone can earn those graces of the Holy Spirit by which the prophets were inspired, and can say in the melody of the Psalm: "Sing at the beginning of the month with the trumpet, on the day of its eminent solemnity,"[96] and who knows how to "rejoice unto him with Psalms,"[97] he celebrates the solemnity of Trumpets worthily unto God.

---

[83]1 Cor 5:6; Gal 5:9. [84]Cf. 1 Cor 5:8. [85]Lit. "new things," Lat *novorum*; cf. Num 28:26. Later, Origen calls it "New Harvest." [86]Gal 6:8. [87]Jer 4:3. [88]Cf. Mt 13:8. [89]Gal 6:8. [90]Gal 5:22. [91]Cf. Gal 5:22. [92]Gal 5:22. [93]Num 29:1. [94]Lk 6:45. [95]Ps 1:2. [96]Ps 81:3. [97]Ps 105:2.

10. There is still another feast, when "they afflict their souls" and humble themselves to God, while celebrating the feast.[98] What a marvelous feast! The affliction of the soul is called a feast day! For this is a day of propitiation,[99] it says, on the tenth day of the seventh month. Consider then if you want to celebrate the feast day, if you want to afflict your soul and humble it in order to make God rejoice over you. Do not allow it to carry out its own desires; do not permit it to stray into sensuality; but to the extent that it can be done, afflict it and humble it. After all, both the feast of the Passover and of Unleavened Bread are said to have "bread of affliction,"[100] nor can anyone celebrate a feast day unless he eats bread of affliction and eats the Passover with bitterness. For it says: "You will eat unleavened bread with bitterness," or with bitter herbs.[101] So you see the nature of the feasts of God; they do not welcome things that delight the body physically, they do not will anything that is lax, hedonistic or luxurious, but they demand the affliction, bitterness and humility of the soul, because "he who humbles himself will be exalted with God."[102] Thus the day of propitiation also demands this; for when "the soul becomes afflicted and humbled in the sight of the Lord,"[103] then God is propitiated to it, and then that one comes to it whom "God set forth as a propitiator through faith in his blood,"[104] Christ Jesus, its Lord and Redeemer.

11.1. Now indeed let us consider the final feast day of God, which is when God is made glad over man. It says: "Tabernacles."[105] He is made glad over you, then, when he sees you dwelling in this world in tabernacles, when he sees that you have a heart and purpose that are not fixed and established on earth, nor one that longs for what is earthly,[106] nor one that regards the "shadow of this life" as if it were your own eternal possession, but [if he sees you] placed

here as if you were passing through and hastening to the true country from whence you came forth, to paradise, and saying: "I am a sojourner and a foreigner, like all my fathers."[107] For the fathers also dwelled in tents, and "Abraham, with Isaac and Jacob, co-heirs of the same promise, dwelled in huts,"[108] that is, in tents. So then, when you become a foreigner and a sojourner on earth, and your mind is not fixed and rooted in earthly desires, but you are prepared to move on quickly and you are prepared "always to stretch forth for what is ahead,"[109] until you reach the "land flowing with milk and honey"[110] and take possession of the inheritance of the future things, if, I say, God finds you in this condition, he rejoices over you and will celebrate a feast day for you.

11.2. These things concern the present; but in the future, if you want to consider how the feast days are celebrated, raise your senses a little from the earth, if you can, and forget for the time being the things that are held before your face. Indeed, imagine to yourself how "heaven and earth are passing away,"[111] and "this whole form of the world is passing away,"[112] but a "new heaven and a new earth"[113] will be established. Remove from your sight even the light of this sun and ascribe to that world which is coming a light that is sevenfold beyond this sun; or rather, to speak in accordance with the authority of Scripture, ascribe that the "Lord himself is its light."[114] Consider the angels attending in glory, consider the powers, authorities, thrones, dominions and every very brilliant name of the heavenly powers, not only that is named in the present age, but that is named even in the future. Among all these consider and determine how the Lord's feast days can be celebrated, what feasts are there, what joys, what extent of gladness. For from these spiritual feasts of which we have spoken above, even

---

[98]Cf. Num 29:7. [99]Num 29:11. [100]Deut 16:3. [101]Ex 12:8. [102]Lk 14:11. [103]Cf. Jas 4:10. [104]Rom 3:25. [105]Lat *scenopegia* (Gk *skēnopēgia*), lit. "setting up of tents." [106]Cf. Col 3:1-2. [107]Ps 39:12. [108]Heb 11:9. [109]Phil 3:13. [110]Ex 33:3. [111]1 Cor 7:31. [112]1 Cor 7:31. [113]2 Pet 3:13. [114]Cf. Is 60:1-2, 19; Jn 8:12; Rev 21:23-25.

if they are great and true, especially when they are carried out spiritually in the soul, nevertheless they are "in part" *[ex parte]*, not complete. For as the apostle said: "We know in part *[ex parte]* and we prophesy in part *[ex parte]*."[115] So it is consistent that we carry out the feast day "in part" *[ex parte]*.

11.3. Now, in order that you may know that these things are so, let us go back to the words of Paul himself, which he recorded about feast days and new moons, and notice how he has carefully said: "Let no one," he says, "judge you in respect to food or drink or in respect to a part of *[in parte]* a feast day."[116] Consider very carefully, therefore, how he did not say: in respect to a feast day, but: "in respect to a part of *[in parte]* a feast day." For while we are in the world, we celebrate the feast day in part *[ex parte]*, not completely *[ex integro]*. For we are interrupted by the burden of the flesh, even if don't want to be; we are pummeled by its lusts, we are pierced by cares and disturbances. "For the corruptible body"—as a very wise man says—"weighs down the soul and oppresses the much-thinking mind."[117] Therefore, in this world the saints celebrate the feast day *in part*, "because they know in part and they prophesy in part. But when the perfect comes, the things that are in part will be destroyed."[118] For just as what is in part yields to perfect knowledge, and what is in part yields to perfect prophecy, so also the feast that is in part gives way to the perfect feast. For the world cannot contain what is perfect, where, as we have said, the body's need suggests now food, now drink, now sleep, now it even arouses anxiety of whatever extent is necessary for the present life. Doubtless all these things are interruptions to the continuous celebration of the feast of God.

But when the moment comes that was spoken about those who will be restored in the sanctuary—but only if we are worthy to belong to those who are to be restored, who

will neither hunger nor thirst,[119] nor will they sleep, nor will they labor, but they will be ever-watchful, as the ever-watchful life of angels is said to be[120]—then there will be the true and uncorrupted feast, of which feast the ruler and bridegroom and Lord will be Jesus Christ himself, our Savior, "to whom is the glory and power in the ages of ages. Amen!"[121]

Homily 24
Numbers 28–30

Concerning the sacrifices that are commanded to be offered at each feast, and concerning vows that are made to God.

1.1. For a long time, all who have to be instructed in the higher disciplines consider as annoying the effort involved in learning the rudiments, as long as they ignore the goal and the benefit of the instruction to which they are being introduced. But when the perfection of the discipline has been attained in order, then it will delight the initiates to have endured the trouble of the elementary instruction. Well, in holy and divine matters, there are also certain primary elements to which those who are striving for the perfection of blessedness are introduced. In the song of Exodus, the servant of God plainly indicates this when he says: "Introduce them and plant them on the mountain of your inheritance, in your prepared habitation, which you prepared, Lord."[1] The apostle Paul too knew that there are certain primary elements of instruction and that one arrives at perfection only at a later time. For when writing to certain people he said: "For although you should now be teachers on account of the time, you again need to be taught the initial elements of the words of God; and you have become those for whom milk is needed, not strong food. For all who feed on milk are inexperienced in the words of justice; for he is an infant. But

---

[115]1 Cor 13:9.   [116]Col 2:16.   [117]Wis 9:15.   [118]1 Cor 13:9-10.   [119]Rev 7:16.   [120]Cf. Sir 16:27.   [121]1 Pet 4:11.   **Homily 24**   [1]Ex 15:17.

solid food is for the perfect, who have their senses trained for the capacity of taking things in, for the distinction between good and evil."[2] And again elsewhere he mentions that the letter of the law and every Scripture of this sort are "elements of the world."[3]

1.2. And so, for the time being the things that pertained to those who were being instructed in the first elements seem annoying to us when we first hear them; for when things are read about the sacrifices of rams and goats and calves to any hearer who wants to learn about things that pertain to salvation, they judge that writings of this sort bring no benefit to them, as far as pertains to what has been heard. But if someone is found who can remove the "veil that is placed over the reading of the Old Testament,"[4] and can then investigate the true sacrifices that cleanse the people on feast days, then he will see how marvelous and splendid are the things that are here indicated, which are considered superfluous and superstitious to the ignorant.

But Paul, and any who are like him, recognized these things more fully from Wisdom itself, and more perfectly from the Word of God. But we will attempt to discuss some things in summary fashion that pertain to the rite of sacrifices, which lead to general edification, to the extent that we can determine these things from their writings, in which they have given certain indications to us, as though through a shadow and image.[5]

1.3. As you have learned from the things that were read aloud, at the feast of the Passover, it is recorded that a lamb purifies the people. On other feasts it is a calf, and on others a goat or a ram or a she-goat or calves.[6] So, a lamb is one of the animals that are taken for the purification of the people. Our Lord and Savior himself is said to be this lamb. For John who is greater than all the prophets understood him thus.[7]

And he attested to this when he said: "Behold the lamb of God, behold who takes away the sin of the world."[8] But if the lamb which is given to purify the people refers to the person of our Lord and Savior, it seems consistent that the other animals as well, which are assigned to these same uses of purification, ought to refer similarly to certain persons who confer some purification on the human race.

1.4. So consider whether it is possible that, just as our Lord and Savior was led "like a lamb to the slaughter,"[9] and was offered on the altar as a sacrifice, and gave remission of sins to the whole world, so perhaps also the blood of other saints and just men, "which was poured out from the blood of the just Abel to the blood of the prophet Zechariah, who was killed between the temple and the altar,"[10] is poured out for expiation for some part of the people, the blood of one man [having been poured out] like [the blood] of a calf, of another, like that of a goat, or of a she-goat, or of some other of these [animals]. Who, then, would dare to be facile about asserting whether these things apparently need to be referred to the characters of the prophets who were slain in this world, or of those who say: "for we are afflicted with death all day long for your sake, we are reckoned as sheep for the slaughter";[11] or even to the higher powers, to whom governance of the human race has been given? For these animals must not be considered according to their outward form, but figuratively they are to be referred to this or that person.

1.5. For not even the Lord Jesus Christ himself is called a "lamb" because he is, as it were, changed and converted into the form of a lamb. On the contrary, he is called "lamb" who has the will and goodness to propitiate God to human beings and to grant pardon for sins. Such a one rose up for the human race as an immaculate and innocent sacrifice of a lamb, by means

---

[2]Heb 5:12-14. [3]Cf. Gal 4:3, 9; Col 2:8, 20. [4]Cf. 2 Cor 3:14. [5]Cf. Heb 10:1. [6]Ex 12:3; cf. Num 28:19-20; 29:2-4. [7]Cf. Lk 7:26. [8]Jn 1:29. [9]Cf. Acts 8:32. [10]Mt 23:35. [11]Ps 44:22; Rom 8:36.

of which the divine is believed to be reconciled with humans.

In this way, then, perhaps even if there is one who belongs to the angels and heavenly powers, or one of the just men, or even one of the holy prophets and apostles, who rather earnestly intercedes for the sins of men, this one who has been offered for the divine propitiation like a ram or a calf or a goat can be understood to be a sacrifice for the sake of procuring the purification of the people. Or does it not seem that Paul offered himself as a burnt offering, like a ram or a goat, for the people of Israel, when he said: "But I was desiring that I myself be accursed from Christ for my brothers, who are my kinsmen according to the flesh"[12]? Now do you want proof that Paul offers himself as a sacrifice to be slain? Listen to his words elsewhere: "For I am now being sacrificed, and the time of my dissolution"—or, as we read in the Greek copies, "return"—"is near."[13]

1.6. So in this way, in a figurative manner, in order to reconcile God to humans, it can seem that one person is offered as a goat or calf or ram for the feast of the New Produce, another for the feast of the Sabbath, another for the feast of Tabernacles. For as long as sins exist, sacrifices for sins are necessarily required. For suppose, for instance, that sin did not exist. If sin did not exist, it would not have been necessary for the Son of God to become a lamb, nor would there have been need that he be slain when he was in the flesh, but he would have remained what he was in the beginning, "God the Word.[14]

But since "sin entered into this world,"[15] but the necessity of sin demands propitiation, and propitiation does not happen apart from sacrifice, it was necessary that a sacrifice for sin be provided. And since the kinds of sin were diverse and various, the sacrifices of different animals are commanded, doubtless which

corresponded with the varieties of sins. So in this way, as we have said, one of the saints or angels or men becomes a calf, who intercedes on that feast for the transgressions of the people, but another becomes a ram on another feast, through whose intercession the purification for sins takes place.

1.7. But if men can be purified from sins and be more pure, the sacrifices are also diminished. For if there are sacrifices for sins, and for a multitude of sins they are multiplied, doubtless for a reduction of sins they are diminished. Now we have indications of this fact in the present passages of Scripture, that is, in the last feast of Tabernacles, when sacrifices are commanded to be offered over a period of eight days. And "on the first day," as if there is still an abundance of sins, "fourteen calves" are commanded to be offered.[16] But on the second day, as sins are reduced, the sacrifices too are diminished and thirteen calves are offered. "On the third day, twelve," and after this, eleven, and so on, as if by the purifications, as the multitude of sins decreases over the days, consequently the number of sacrifices also is reduced.

1.8. In this way, then, understand the method of purification likewise for the management of the whole world. For not only do things on earth need purification, but also things in heaven. For destruction threatens heaven as well; for thus the prophet says: "The heavens will perish, and all will grow old like a garment, and you will wrap them up like a cloak and they will be changed."[17] Contemplate, therefore, the purification of the whole world, that is, "of the heavenly things and the earthly things and of things below."[18] Consider how many sacrifices all these things need, how many calves they require, how many rams, how many goats. But in all these, there is one "lamb" who was able to take away the sin of the entire world.[19] And the reason the other sacrifices ceased is because this

---

[12]Rom 9:3. [13]2 Tim 4:6. See Homily 10.2 above. [14]Cf. Jn 1:1. [15]Rom 5:12. [16]Cf. Num 29:12-38. [17]Ps 102:26. [18]Phil 2:10. [19]Cf. Jn 1:29.

was the kind of sacrifice that a single sacrifice was sufficient for the salvation of the whole world.

1.9. For others forgave sins by means of prayers; he alone forgave them by his authority. For he said: "Son, your sins are forgiven you."[20] So then, the world is instructed to seek remission of sins, in the first place, through different sacrifices, until it comes to the perfect sacrifice, to the completed sacrifice, "a year-old lamb," that is perfect, who takes away the sin of the whole world,[21] through which it celebrates spiritual feasts, not for the satisfaction of the flesh, but for the progress of the spirit, when the mind's spiritual sacrifices are offered for purification. For it befits God that the victim of the heart be offered up in sacrifice, and that the "sacrifice of a broken spirit,"[22] not of flesh and blood, be slain. For even if "we knew Christ once according to the flesh, but now we no longer know him,"[23] and therefore let us celebrate the feast day in spirit and let us slay spiritual sacrifices.

To the best of our ability, we have discussed these things about the diversity of sacrifices. As for their clear interpretation, that one knows it to whom "all things are bare and revealed, nor is any creature invisible to his sight."[24]

2.1. After this the law of vows is recorded and Moses makes use of a new beginning in this legislation; for he says: "Any man-man who has vowed a vow to the Lord."[25] Why the repetition of the term? It is as if it were not sufficient to have said: Any man who vows a vow to the Lord. So why does he say: "Man-man," and what is the significance of the double mention of the term man? It seems to me that this should not be passed over in silence.[26] The apostle teaches that there is an "inner man" and an "outer man,"[27] and

the former is being "renewed from day to day according to the image of him who created him";[28] but the latter is visible and is being corrupted. Thus, when one already reaches that stage of progress that the law of God is received and vows are offered to the Lord—but no one can offer vows to the Lord unless he has something within himself and in his essence[29] that he can offer to God—that outer man is not adequate to receive the law of God, nor to offer vows on its own—for it cannot have anything worthy of God—but rather it is that inner man who has something within itself to offer to God; for in that one is the dwelling place of the virtues, in that one is all understanding of knowledge, in that one is the renovation of the divine image. When it has recovered its form in which God made it in the beginning, and when it has received the beauty of its previous form by the restoration of the virtues, then it can offer vows to God and then it will no longer be called merely a "man," but a "man-man."

2.2. For the one who does not cultivate the inner man, who does not take care of it, who does not build it up in the virtues, adorn it with good character, train it in divine principles of education, does not seek after God's wisdom, expends no effort to attain knowledge of the Scriptures, this one cannot be called a "man-man," but only a "man" and an "animal man."[30] For that inner man, to which the name "man" more truly and nobly belongs, has been lulled to sleep within him and has fallen into fleshly vices and into the cares and concerns of this world. Thus the designation of the name [of inner man] cannot be considered to apply. This is why each one of us has more than enough to do so that, if perhaps one sees the inner man laid out prostrate within himself, overwhelmed by

---

[20]Mt 9:2. [21]Cf. Ex 12:5; Jn 1:29. [22]Ps 51:17. [23]2 Cor 5:16. [24]Heb 4:13. [25]Num 30:2. [26]Cf. *Homilies on Ezekiel* 3.8. "Homo, homo" (LXX *anthrōpos, anthrōpos*) corresponds to the Hebrew idiom *'îš 'îš*, according to which the repetition of single words is used to express a distributive sense ("every man"). See *Gesenius's Hebrew Grammar*, ed. E. Kautzsch, 2nd ed. by A. E. Cowley (Oxford: Clarendon, 1988), §123c. Origen follows the Jewish interpretative tradition in seeing a mystical meaning in the unusual construction. Similarly, Philo *On Giants* 33, said that the repeated word was a sign that God means not the man who is compounded of soul and body, but the man whose life is one of virtue. [27]Cf. 2 Cor 4:16. [28]Col 3:10. [29]Lat *substantia*. [30]Cf. 1 Cor 15:44-45.

the filth of sins and by the rubble of the vices, he may quickly remove all sources of uncleanness from him, he may quickly extricate him from all defilement of flesh and blood, he may finally be converted to repentance, recall the memory of God to himself, revive the hope of salvation. For these things must not be sought from anywhere outside, but the opportunity for salvation is within us, as the Lord said: "For behold the kingdom of God is within you."[31] For the capacity for conversion is within us; for when "you groan and are converted, you will be saved."[32] It is at that time that you will be able "to repay your vows to the Most High"[33] worthily, and be called a "man-man."

2.3. Now a vow is when we offer something of ourselves to God. So, God first wants to receive something from us and in this way he wills to bestow his generosity on us, so that he seems to be bestowing his gifts and presents on those who deserve them and not on the undeserving. But what is it that God wants to receive from us? Listen to the thought of Scripture: "And now, Israel, what does the Lord your God require of you, but to fear the Lord your God, and to walk in all his ways, and to love him with all your heart and all your soul and all your strength?"[34] So this is what God requires of us. If we do not first offer these things, we will receive nothing from him. And in another passage we read: "Give glory to God"[35] and "Give greatness to God."[36] If you have given glory, you will receive glory; for this is what God himself says: "I will glorify those who glorify me."[37]

2.4. Indeed, I say that if we offer him our justice, we will receive from him God's justice; and if we offer him our chastity, that is, our body's, we will receive from him the chastity of the Spirit;[38] and if we offer him our mind, we will

receive from him his mind, as the apostle has said: "But we have the mind of Christ."[39] Now when we have offered what is in us to God, and he has granted what is his to us, then we will truly no longer be called merely a "man," but a "man-man." For both men have been becomingly adorned with the perfection of their title.

2.5. So these are the vows that one should pay out who is called a "man-man." I know that different vows are referred to in the Scriptures. Hannah vowed the fruit of her womb to God and consecrated Samuel in the temple.[40] Another vowed to God whatsoever should meet him on his return after the victory, and when his daughter met him, he paid in full the vows with tears.[41] Others offer as vows to God calves or rams or houses or other things of this sort that are without reason.

2.6. In fact, the one who is called a Nazarene has made a vow of his own self to God.[42] For this is the vow of the Nazarene, which is beyond every vow. For to offer up a son or daughter or cattle or land, all this is outside ourselves. But to offer oneself to God, and to please him not with someone else's effort, but with one's own, this is more perfect and more excellent than all vows. For whoever does this is an "imitator of Christ."[43] For he gave to man "the earth, the sea and all that is in them."[44] He also gave the sky for man's obedient service; he granted the sun too, and the moon and the stars for the service of men; he bestowed on humanity the rain, the winds and everything that is in the world. But after all this he gave himself: "For God so loved the world that he gave his only-begotten Son"[45] for the life of this world. So what great thing will a man be doing, if he offers himself to God, for whom God first offered his own self?[46]

---

[31]Lk 17:21. [32]Is 45:22. [33]Ps 50:14. [34]Deut 10:12. [35]Ps 68:34. [36]Deut 32:3. [37]1 Sam 2:30. [38]See Homily 20:2 above for his definition of "chastity of the Spirit." [39]1 Cor 2:16. [40]1 Sam 1:11. [41]Cf. Judg 11:31. [42]Cf. Num 6. [43]Cf. 1 Cor 11:1. [44]Acts 14:15. [45]Jn 3:16. [46]Hans Urs von Balthasar cites this impressive passage in *Theo-Drama: Theological Dramatic Theory*, vol. 5: *The Last Act*, trans. G. Harrison (San Francisco: Ignatius, 1998), p. 383, where he states: "For Origen this gift of oneself is at the center of Christian truth: it is a straightforward, natural response to God's gift of himself to me in and through 'whatever is in the world.'" My colleague Jay Martin informed me of this reference.

2.7. So if you "take up your cross and follow Christ,"[47] if you say: "It is no longer I who live, but Christ lives in me,"[48] if "our soul thirsts and longs"[49] "to return and be with Christ,"[50] as the apostle said, and takes no delight in the enticements of the present world, and if it fulfills spiritually the whole law that is given concerning the Nazarenes, then it has offered to God its very self, that is, its own soul. The one who lives in chastity, vows his body to God in accordance with him who said: "Now the virgin thinks about how she may be holy in body and spirit."[51] For even the word "holy" [sancta] has this in view; for they are called saints [sancti] who have vowed themselves to God. Whence also if a ram, for instance, is vowed to God, it is called holy [sanctus]. It is not permissible to fleece it for common usage. Moreover, if a calf is devoted to God, it no less is called holy [sanctus], and it is not permissible to yoke it up for common work. From this, therefore, we may gather what it means that a man vows himself to God. If you are vowed to God, you must imitate the calf, which is not permitted to serve human works, or to do anything that pertains to men and to the present life. But whatever pertains to the soul and to the observance of divine worship, this is what you must both do and think about.

3.1. But meanwhile, the present reading contains different kinds of vows. For if the one who vows is a man, he is said to be free in his vows and subject to no one.[52] But if a woman takes a vow, if indeed she is in the home of her father,[53] her vow depends on the choice of her father; and if he refuses it, she is freed; but if he does not refuse it, both he and the daughter are held liable to it.[54] But if, after the father does not refuse it, she does not repay the vow, sin remains on the daughter herself. But it is decreed likewise with respect to the husband, that if, in the home of the husband, the wife makes some

vow, and the husband hears but does not refuse it, he will be held liable for the vow equally with his wife; but if he refuses it, both the woman and the husband are free; but if both are silent, as we said, both are held liable.[55] This is what is written.

3.2. But we must pray to God that he deign to give an understanding that is worthy of himself, whereby we can heed these things in a way that is proper in the interpretation of the words of God. Of all of us who live under God's law and who are reckoned to belong to his church, some live under fathers, some live under husbands. Now if the soul is in infancy and has the beginning stages of divine learning, it should be believed to be living under a father. But if it has already become more mature, so that it is capable of having a husband and conceiving the seed of the Word of God, and if it is capable of the secrets of spiritual instruction, this soul is said to be placed under a husband. For this is what Paul said of the Corinthians: "Now I want to present all of you as a chaste virgin to one husband, Christ."[56] But respecting those who are more perfect and eminent than these, it is not said of them that they are under a husband, but listen to the way Paul speaks about himself and those like him: He says: "Until we all reach perfect manhood, the measure of age of the fullness of Christ."[57] Thus, no one domineers over this soul, which is reaching perfect manhood, with respect to vows, but it has authority and freedom of its own vows.

3.3. Now if the soul is still of the feminine sort, over which either the husband or the father domineer in respect to vows, the blame is not always in itself, but sometimes it traces back to the husbands or the parents. Though it may be difficult to make an application concerning this, yet we will introduce what can occur to us, as the Lord grants it. We have said on repeated occasions that the care and oversight

---

[47]Cf. Mt 10:38. [48]Gal 2:20. [49]Cf. Ps 42:1-2. [50]Phil 1:23. [51]1 Cor 7:34. [52]Cf. Num 30:2; 1 Cor 9:19. [53]Cf. Num 30:3. [54]Cf. Num 30:3-5. [55]Cf. Num 30:7. [56]2 Cor 11:2. [57]Eph 4:13.

of souls that are in the church of God is carried out by angels, and we have shown that they too come to the judgment along with men, so that it may be established in that divine examination whether men sinned by their own sloth, or through the negligence of their advisers and guardians. So it seems to me that in this passage as well the same things are being indicated under a mystery, and it is shown that some souls carry on under them as daughters, others live as wives, in accordance with what we made clear above. Thus, if one of these souls desires to offer and vow something to God, if indeed what it vows is overhasty and less fitting, it is the duty of that angel, as its guardian and adviser, to reprimand the one making the vow and blunt his audacity. But if, on hearing the vow, the angel does not check it and issue a warning, the soul is set free from blame, but the angel itself will remain liable for the vow.

3.4. Now this is how one should interpret what happens with those who are inferior. But in those who are perfect, God himself is present, as it is written of the people of Israel: "But the Lord himself led them."[58] Now after they transgressed and made themselves inferior to the others, they are handed over to the angel. This is why Moses said: "Unless you yourself come with us, do not lead me forth from here."[59] Moreover, God says of someone else: "I am with him in tribulation";[60] and elsewhere he says: "Do not be afraid to go down to Egypt, for I will be with you."[61] Therefore, God himself is present with the just and the chosen, but angels are present with the inferior, in accordance with the things we have said above. They govern and oversee them, and sometimes transfer their vows to themselves, sometimes they leave to them the responsibility for their vows.

3.5. But we should strive to become a "perfect man in the measure of age of the fullness of Christ."[62] Let us use our liberty in respect to

vows, and thus hasten to "cleave to the Lord," so that we may be "one spirit"[63] with him, rather than with the angel, that he himself may remain with us and we in him.[64] Let there be nothing feminine in us, nothing that belongs to the age of infancy. Let there be no need in us for our being abandoned by the Father to "tutors and overseers,"[65] but let us hasten to hear those words from our Lord and Savior in which he says: "The Father himself loves you."[66] "To him be the glory in the ages of ages. Amen!"[67]

Homily 25
Numbers 31:1-54

Concerning the vengeance carried out against the Midianites.

1.1. Higher up the sons of Israel committed fornication with the Midianite women, and this was a stumbling block by which they offended the Lord and "provoked to wrath the Holy One of Israel."[1] So now, after Israel endured what it endured, it says: "The Lord spoke to Moses, saying: Execute the vengeance[2] of the sons of Israel from the Midianites, and in the end you will be added to your people."[3]

So then, since the stumbling blocks which had happened to the Israelites had taken place through a subterfuge of the Midianites—for they had secretly introduced the women who seduced them into sinning before the Lord—the Israelites endured vengeance for their sin, yet a rather mild and sparing one, but those who were the cause of their sinning are subject to a much more powerful vengeance.

1.2. We are taught from this that to offer an occasion of sin is far more serious than for someone to sin. The Lord also indicates this when he says: "It would have been better for a man not to be born, or for a millstone to be tied around his neck and to be cast into the depths

---

[58]Ex 12:51. [59]Ex 33:15. [60]Ps 91:15. [61]Gen 46:3-4. [62]Eph 4:13. [63]1 Cor 6:17. [64]Cf. Jn 15:4. [65]Cf. Gal 4:2. [66]Jn 16:27. [67]Rom 11:36. **Homily 25** [1]Cf. Is 1:4. [2]Lit. "avenge the vengeance." [3]Num 31:2.

of the sea, than to cause one of these little ones to sin."[4]

At the same time it is necessary to observe that some indeed presume to use the term "stumbling block" improperly. One speaks of a stumbling block [scandalon] when some deception is constructed that leads to sin in one who is walking on the right road, and a cause for sinning is exposed, just as also the Midianites secretly introduced women to the Israelites, who had been "walking in the law of the Lord,"[5] and guarding their chastity. These women seduced them into sinning. Thus to offer an occasion of sin is to "make a stumbling block" [scandalizare]. Nevertheless, vengeance is given, but it is much more serious against those who made the stumbling block, who supplied the cause of the sin, than against those who sinned.

1.3. At the same time, observe what he added to these things. It says: "At last you too will be added to your people."[6] Whenever we converse with the Samaritans, who deny the resurrection of the dead and do not have faith in the future world, we should press them with these words that the Lord speaks to Moses, that he "will be added to his people." For no one is added to those who do not exist. Thus it is established that there exists a people to which it is said that Moses will be united after his departure from this life. Since therefore the Samaritans do not believe in the prophets, from whom faith in the resurrection of the dead could be more clearly proven, at least they should be convinced and healed on the basis of these books of Moses, which they do receive and whose authority they do confess; but only if it is proper for Babylon too to be healed.[7] So this is a passage that clearly points to the resurrection of the dead. For it indicates that there is a people to which Moses must be added after his death and to whom he must be transferred in view of his merits.

2.1. After this it says: "Moses spoke to the people saying: Arm [men] among you and wage war against Midian,[8] pay back vengeance from the Lord against Midian; a thousand from a tribe and a thousand from a tribe; send [men] from all the tribes of Israel to make war."[9]

Pay attention to the reading. For the mind needs to concentrate not only on hearing the words, but on considering the realities. Remember the past, listen to the present, pay attention to the things that follow. Compare the former things with what comes later, and contemplate the greatness of the divine forces.[10] Once the sons of Israel were six hundred thousand armed men who went forth against Midian, and they were all conquered, for there was sin among them. But now, the Midianite victors, who had put to flight six hundred thousand, are defeated by twelve thousand men, that you may know that Israel does not conquer by the multitude or by the number of soldiers, but it is justice and piety among them that conquers. Ultimately that is the reason it is said in their Benedictions that if they will keep the law of the Lord, one of them would pursue a thousand and two would turn ten thousand.[11]

2.2. So you see that one saint who prays is much more powerful than countless sinners who wage war. "The prayer of the saint reaches heaven."[12] How will it not also defeat an enemy on earth? And therefore, in every way one should strive "to seek first" and "to keep" the "justice of God."[13] If you obtain it and preserve it, justice itself will subject all your enemies to you, if, as the apostle says, you "put on the breastplate of justice and are girded with the truth," if you "take up the helmet of salvation and the sword of the Spirit," and before everything else, the "shield of faith by which you can extinguish all the flaming arrows of the evil

---

[4]Cf. Mt 26:24; Mk 9:42; 14:21. This is a composite citation that resembles Clement of Rome's blending of the two ideas in *1 Clement* 46.8. [5]Ps 119:1. [6]Num 31:2. [7]Cf. Jer 51:8. [8]Lat *Madian*. [9]Num 31:3-4. [10]Or "powers," "virtues." [11]Cf. Lev 26:8. [12]Cf. Sir 35:17. [13]Cf. Mt 6:33.

one."[14] For, equipped with such weapons, you will put to flight all the encampments of the devil and his whole army, and you will sing confidently: "If an army encamps against me, my heart will not fear; if a battle is engaged against me, I will hope in this."[15]

2.3. Thus twelve thousand assemble against the Midianites, and it says: "they killed every male among them; and they killed with the sword their kings, and Balaam, son of Beor, along with the rest of their slain."[16] This present passage of Scripture plainly shows what we had asked above,[17] namely, how it could be proven from the Scriptures that it was by the counsel of Balaam that Midianite women were secretly introduced to seduce the sons of Israel into committing fornication. For it says that he was "killed with the sword," as the author of the stumbling block that was sent in to the sons of Israel. Now the Scripture speaks of him in what follows still more clearly in this fashion: "And Moses said to them: Why have you let all the females live? For they are the ones who made apostates of the sons of Israel in accordance with the word of Balaam."[18]

2.4. But the kings of the Midianites are killed, and those who were first conquered by the women now, having atoned and done penance, even conquer kings. From this we should understand how much a conversion to God can do, how useful the correction of sins is. Every male and all the kings of the Midianites are conquered and destroyed by those who were corrected and reformed through the Lord's correction and through repentance of their deeds.

3.1. Well then, reference is made to five kings of the Midianites who were overcome by Israelite soldiers. Moreover, the divine Scripture even took care to record their names. It says: "Evi, Rekem, Zur, Hur and Reba."[19] These are the ones who reign among the Midianites,

whom everyone who wages war for God should overcome and completely annihilate. For "Evi" translates as "beastly" or "savage." And how can you "please him who has commended you"[20] if you do not cut off from yourself and completely destroy beastly and savage morals? How can you arrive at the blessedness of the meek[21] unless you first kill "Evi" and hand over to death the savageness of all anger? I think that divine Scripture did not report these names for the sake of the history, but it is adapting them to rational grounds and to realities. For do you think there could be anyone so foolish as to give the name "Beastly" to his own son? On the contrary, I think that the divine word was looking ahead to the condition of souls. It wanted to show us that we must wage war against vices of this sort, we must dislodge these vices from their habitations in our flesh, we must put these kings to flight from the kingdom of our body. This is clearly what the apostle indicates when he says: "Therefore do not let sin reign in your mortal body."[22]

3.2. Now do you want to see that names are adapted to realities, not only among the saints, but also among pagans and barbarians? Of saints it is of course known that Abram was called Abraham,[23] and Sarai Sarah,[24] and Jacob Israel.[25] But let us show that this custom is practiced also among the barbarians. Had not one of the sons of Israel received from his parents the name Joseph?[26] But when he moved to Egypt and stood before Pharaoh, his name was changed, and Joseph was named Zaphenath-paneah,[27] which Pharaoh composed in his own language and which derived from the revelation of secrets and dreams. And it is not to this Joseph alone that Pharaoh applies a name on the basis of a reality, but Daniel too in Babylon is named "Balthasar,"[28] and Hananiah, Azariah and Mishael[29] are called Shadrach, Mishach,[30]

---

[14]Cf. Eph 6:14-17. [15]Ps 27:3. [16]Num 31:7-8. [17]Cf. Homily 20:1. [18]Num 31:15-16. [19]Cf. Num 31:8. Lat *Evin, Rocon, Sur, Ur, Roboc.* [20]2 Tim 2:4. [21]Cf. Mt 5:5. [22]Rom 6:12. [23]Cf. Gen 17:5. [24]Cf. Gen 17:15. [25]Cf. Gen 35:10. [26]Cf. Gen 30:24. [27]Lat *Psonthomphanec.* Cf. Gen 41:45. [28]RSV *Belteshazzar.* [29]Lat *Ananias, Azarias, Misael.* [30]RSV *Meshach.*

and Abednego.[31] Thus you see that both the names of Israelites as well as those of barbarian men are applied in the law not fortuitously, but to realities and rational grounds. Therefore Moses named the king of the Midianites as he himself had assessed that he deserved to be called. It is beastly savageness, he says, who reigns in the Midianites, and not only that, but there is another king among them by the name of Rekem,[32] which in our language means "worthlessness." Thus, worthlessness reigns in the nation of the Midianites.

3.3. For in truth there is much worthlessness and vanity in this world, or rather, there is "vanity of vanities," and "all is vanity,"[33] which the soldier of God has to overcome and conquer. Now, he conquers worthlessness who carries out nothing in a worthless way or superfluously or what is not relevant and to the point, who is mindful of that precept of the Lord where he says that "men will give an account on the day of judgment even for an idle word."[34] But in this life, nearly all that men speak and do is idle and worthless. For every act and every word is called worthless that is not done solely for God's sake or for the sake of God's command.

3.4. There is also another king of Midian, Hur,[35] and this translates as "irritation." You see what sort they are who reign among the Midianites. It is necessary to be opposed to them all, or rather, it is befitting that those who follow God destroy and kill them. For they are referred to in the law not so much as the names of kings, as of vices that reign in men, and it is not so much the wars of nations that are being described, as of fleshly lusts that wage war against the soul.[36]

3.5. After all, those who are reigning in the vices are said to be "*five* kings." Thus we are most plainly taught that every vice that reigns

in the body is dependent on the *five* senses. So these five senses must be destroyed from the kingdom of the Midianites, so that vices may no longer reign through them, but justice; nor should what they see look to a stumbling block, but to edification. For among the Midianites these senses that were inclined toward stumbling were reigning in order to cause stumbling blocks and to seduce. And this is why the Lord commanded that "if your eye causes you to stumble, pluck it out";[37] if your hand or foot [causes you to stumble], cut if off.[38] So you see that he commands the kings of those who cause stumbling blocks to be cut off and destroyed. He says: "It is better for you to enter into the kingdom of God one-eyed and crippled and lame than to be cast into Gehenna with these."[39] Assuredly in these statements he is not commanding the eye of our body to be gouged out, nor our hand and foot to be cut off, but he orders us to cut off the mind that thinks carnal thoughts and that is on fire with fleshly lusts, so that "our eyes may see right things,"[40] and our ears may hear right things, and our taste may "taste the Word of God,"[41] and "our hands may feel and touch the Word of life."[42] And this is how, once the kings of the Midianites have been destroyed, and the affections that lead to stumbling blocks are cut off, justice reigns in us, our very Lord Jesus Christ, "who became for us justice from God and peace and redemption."[43]

3.6. Therefore, by the Lord's command to the sons of Israel, wars were carried out against the Midianites, abundant spoils from them are reported, an immense quantity of gold and silver and of other objects, a very great number of beasts and prisoners.[44] But since all these things are considered unclean among the Israelites, a suitable purification is applied to each of these things; and fire purifies the things that are

---

[31]Lat *Sidrac, Misac, Abdenago*. Cf. Dan 1:7. [32]Lat *Rocon*. [33]Eccles 1:2. [34]Mt 12:36. [35]Lat *Ur*. Cf. Num 31:8. [36]Henri de Lubac, *History and Spirit: The Understanding of Scripture According to Origen*, trans. A. Nash (San Francisco: Ignatius, 2007), p. 133 writes: "[Origen] would have been astonished to learn that the day would come when it would be seriously believed that he had intended to deny the literal existence of the kings of Midian and the reality of the wars remembered in the Bible." [37]Cf. Mt 5:29-30. [38]Cf. Mk 9:43-44. [39]Cf. Mk 9:42-47. [40]Cf. Prov 4:25. [41]Cf. Heb 6:5. [42]Cf. 1 Jn 1:1. [43]1 Cor 1:30. [44]Cf. Num 31:11-12.

made from metals, but the things that are more fragile and cannot endure fire are commanded to be purified by water.[45] Thus they make two equal divisions of all the spoils, so that one part is "for those who had gone out to war," and the other part is for those who stayed back in the camps.[46] They are also commanded to offer some of these things as gifts of God; on the one hand, those who had gone out to war [offer] "one head out of five hundred"; but those who had remained in the camps, "one out of fifty."[47] And the number of everything gathered together is reported.[48] This is what the historical narrative contains.

4.1. But let us see what spiritual meaning is indicated in these things. Among the people of God are some, as the apostle says, who "fight for God." Doubtless they are those who do not get involved in worldly affairs.[49] And they are the ones who "go out to war"[50] and fight against hostile nations and "against the spiritual forces of wickedness"[51] on behalf of the rest of the people and of those who are weaker, whether due to their age, sex or resolve. But they fight by means of prayers and fasts, justice and piety, gentleness, chastity and all the virtues of self-control, as if they were armed with the weapons of war. And when they return to the camp victorious, both the weak and those not called to fight, and those who cannot go out, enjoy the fruits of their labors. Yet one must know that everything that is taken from these nations is unclean; and possibly all that is taken from this world or is captured in battle is unclean and requires purification; and some of these things "will pass through fire," but for others a purification by water will be sufficient.[52]

4.2. Now both men and beasts are taken in battle when "all understanding is taken captive to obedience to Christ."[53] For unless we have fought under the Word of God, we will not be able "to take captive" the understanding of those who think differently from Christ, and lead them to the obedience of Christ. But they are few who can fight and conduct these battles; of the six hundred thousand and more armed men, who seem to fight for God, only twelve thousand are selected; the rest are left in the camps. Now consider with me the people of God who are in the church, how many are they, of those who are able to fight for the truth, who can resist those who contradict, who know how to conduct wars of the Word. Blessed are they who can fight for all the people and defend the people of God and bring back spoils in abundance from the enemies. Nevertheless, even the remaining portion of the people who seem unwarlike, if they quietly stay behind in the camps, if they carry on in silence and do not withdraw from Moses, but abide in the law of God, they too will receive a part of the spoils. For an equal portion will come, not numerically, to be sure, but as much as is given to the remaining people as is given to those twelve thousand who took the spoils in their victorious conquest.

4.3. Who, on hearing these things, will not be summoned to the army of God? Who will not be inspired to fight for the church and resist the enemies of truth, namely, those who teach men either to attack the church's doctrines or to strive after pleasure and luxury? Thus, the one who fights against these and destroys the vices, either in themselves or in their neighbors, will receive much of the spoils, multiplied fifty times beyond the others; for in such a great number, the quantity seems to be increased, when twelve thousand are compared with six hundred thousand.

4.4. However, both portions are commanded to make an offering to God. Those who conquered [are to offer] "one out of five hundred,"[54] but those who stayed home, "one out of fifty."[55] Now Scripture testifies that both five hundred

---

[45]Cf. Num 31:22-23. [46]Cf. Num 31:27. [47]Cf. Num 31:28-30. [48]Cf. Num 31:32-40. [49]2 Tim 2:3-4. [50]Cf. Num 31:27. [51]Eph 6:12. [52]Cf. Num 31:23. [53]2 Cor 10:5. [54]Cf. Num 31:28. [55]Cf. Num 31:30.

and fifty are holy numbers; and this is why the Savior said in the Gospels: "To a certain man who was a money-lender, there were two debtors; one of them owed five hundred denarii and the other fifty. Since they did not have the means to repay, he forgave both."[56] Moreover, when a monad, that is, one, is added to seven weeks, it makes the fiftieth day, which is called the feast of Pentecost. Similarly, when the perfection of one decade is added to seventy weeks, it comes to the number five hundred. But seventy weeks are more than seven, as much as the number five hundred is more excellent and perfect than fifty. After all, this is why, in the parable of the Gospel that we set forth above, our Savior declares that the one to whom the five hundred denarii that he owed were forgiven "loves more" than the one to whom fifty [were forgiven].

5.1. Finally, in the present reading, it is written that Eleazar the priest spoke, not to all the people, but only "to those who are returning from battle." For it says: "And Eleazar the priest spoke to the men of virtue[57] who were returning from the battle."[58] So you see that the word of God addresses "men of virtue." For those who go forth to war are men of virtue. In fact, if anyone does not want to fight and engage in war, if anyone does not want to strive after divine studies and abstinence, he does not want to fulfill what the apostle said: "But whoever strives in a contest, is self-controlled in all things."[59] Thus the one who does not "strive in the contest," and is not self-controlled in all things, and does not want to be trained in the word of God and to "meditate on the law of the Lord day and night,"[60] this one, even if he may be called a man, nevertheless cannot be called a "man of virtue." But in fact, this one of whom the words of divine Scripture are now concerned, who brings back spoils from the enemies, is called a

man of virtue; for this is a sign of his remarkable praise, that Scripture says that "Eleazar the priest spoke to the men of virtue, who were returning from battle."

Which of us is well prepared to go forth to war and struggle against the adversaries, so that he can be called a "man of virtue"? But just as the self-controlled life and the effort for abstinence and the struggles of contests cause each one to be called a "man of virtue," so, on the contrary, a life that is remiss, negligent and lazy causes one to be called a man of laziness. So if you want to be called a "man of virtue," "put on Christ the Lord,"[61] who is the "power[62] of God and the wisdom of God,"[63] and unite yourself to the Lord in all things, so that you may become "one spirit with him,"[64] and then you will become a "man of virtue."

5.2. Therefore, in this world we live in a time of war; [we have] a battle against the Midianites,[65] either against the vices of our flesh, or against the contrary powers. The choir of angels watches us, the pious expectation of the heavenly powers is in suspense over us, as to when or how we may return from the battle, as to what amount of booty each of us will carry back. And they watch very carefully and examine very anxiously, which of us brings back more gold from here, which one even displays a quantity of silver from there, which one carries out precious stones. They even seek to find out if anyone carries out copper or iron or lead, moreover, whether anyone perchance carries back a vessel of wood, of clay, or anything else like this that has necessary uses in a large house. For "in a large house, there are not only vessels of gold and silver, but also of wood and clay."[66] So they carefully inquire about when we have gone forth from there, what each of us is carrying out; and each one is tested according to the things that he has carried out, according to his effort exhib-

---

[56]Lk 7:41-42. [57]The LXX has *andras tēs dynameōs*, lit. "men of power," which means "army" in this context (cf. "armed *forces*"). Rufinus translates the Greek term by *virtus*, which means "virtue" or "power." [58]Num 31:21. [59]1 Cor 9:25. [60]Cf. Ps 1:2. [61]Cf. Rom 13:14. [62]Lat *virtus*. [63]Cf. 1 Cor 1:24. [64]1 Cor 6:17; cf. Eph 4:4. [65]Lat *Madianitas*. [66]2 Tim 2:20.

ited in the consideration of the spoils. Likewise the merit of one's dwelling place[67] will be calculated. However, all these things are tested, the things that came through fire [are tested] through fire, and the things that came through water [are tested] through water; for "fire will test the quality of each one's work."[68]

6.1. So this is why it says: "This is the ordinance[69] of the law, which the Lord appointed for Moses. Beside the gold and silver and brass and iron and lead and tin, every thing that passes through fire, have it pass through fire and it will be cleansed; moreover they will be purified with the water of purification; everything, whatsoever does not pass through fire shall pass through water. And on the seventh day you shall wash your garments, and you will be clean; and after this you will enter into the camp."[70] You see how everyone who has gone forth from the combat of this life requires purification. But if this is so, allow me to be bold in saying something in accordance with the authority of Scripture: no one who goes forth from this life can be clean.

For consider carefully what the text of the historical narrative indicates. They went forth to fight on behalf of the sons of Israel, they killed the Midianites; but in killing them, as far as concerns the order of history and the letter of the law, they pleased God—for they fulfilled the will of God; however, in this act of killing their adversaries, they are said to have become unclean, and therefore it is said to them: "And you will wash your garments on the seventh day, and you will be clean; and after this you will enter into the camp."[71] Thus, those who fight have become polluted, in view of the fact that they have touched unclean enemies, and because they assembled against them and had combat with them.

6.2. And so, I myself, even if I am able to conquer the devil, even if I am able to reject the unclean thoughts and the evils that he suggests to my heart when these things come, or, if I can kill them after they have entered into me and prevent them from becoming effective, and if I am able and capable of trampling on the head of the dragon;[72] nevertheless, I am necessarily polluted and defiled in the process, in that I have striven to trample on him who is polluted and defiled. And, to be sure, I will be blessed for having been able to overcome him; however, I am unclean and polluted, since I have touched one who is polluted, and for this reason I am in need of a purification. Doubtless this is why Scripture says that "no one is clean from filth."[73] Thus we all need purification, or rather, purifications. For many different kinds of purifications await us. But these things are mysterious and inexpressible.

6.3. For who can explain to us what are the purifications that are prepared for Paul or Peter or others who are like them, who have fought so much, who have blotted out so many barbaric nations, who have laid low so many enemies, who have taken so much spoil, so many triumphs, who return from the slaughter of the enemies with blood-stained hands, whose "foot is stained with blood,"[74] and who have "washed their hands in the blood of sinners"? Indeed, "in the morning they killed all the sinners of the land,"[75] and they "banished their image from the city of the Lord."[76] They indeed conquered and destroyed the different nations of demons. For if they had not conquered them, they would not have been able to take captives from them, this whole number of believers, and "bring them to the obedience of Christ,"[77] and subjugate them to his "gentle yoke," and place on them his "light burden."[78] So who is blessed enough to succeed them in these battles and to kill all the Midianites and to be justified[79] by their blood?

---

[67]Lat *mansio*; cf. Jn 14:2. [68]1 Cor 3:13. [69]Lat *iustificatio*. [70]Num 31:21-24. [71]Num 31:24. [72]Cf. Gen 3:15. [73]Job 14:4. [74]Ps 68:23. [75]Ps 101:8. [76]Cf. Ps 72:20 LXX. [77]2 Cor 10:5. [78]Cf. Mt 11:30. [79]The choice of this verb seems to depend on Num 31:21, which uses Gk *dikaiōma* (Lat *iustitia*).

For one is said to pour out the blood of demons, who rescues those who are under their dominion. But he will be washed of this blood and he will be purified in the kingdom of God, so that, having become purified and clean, he can enter the holy city of God, as Christ Jesus our Lord opens the door for him,[80] or rather, who is the "door"[81] of that city of God, "to whom is the glory in the ages of ages. Amen."[82]

Homily 26
Numbers 31–32

On the sum of the number of the sons of Israel.

1.1. If anyone looks rather carefully at the reading, he will detect in many passages in the divine volumes that there are different levels of progress and merits among the people who comprise the faithful. We gather this no less from the present reading, from what is written: "And all who had been appointed rulers throughout the tribes in the army, the tribunes and the centurions,[1] came to Moses, and they said to Moses: We your servants[2] have gathered the sum of our male warriors, and none of us dissents. And we have brought a gift to the Lord, each man whatsoever he found, [having offered] a vessel of gold, a necklace or armlet or ring or bracelet or little chain, to make propitiation for us before the Lord."[3]

So the chosen rulers who were appointed over the army speak to Moses, and they offer gifts to God for the things that have been done well, saying: "We are your servants, who have taken the sum of the warriors of the sons of Israel." Now the "sum of warriors" refers to those twelve thousand men who were chosen from all the tribes of Israel to engage the Midianites. Thus, there are many warriors among the people of God, and there are very many who are unwarlike; and again, among the

warriors there are some who are called the "sum of the warriors," doubtless those who rise above those who are called warriors, just as the warriors rise above those who are unwarlike. And again, there are some who are more lofty than those who are called the "sum of the warriors," namely, those who were appointed over those rulers and were preferred to each of the thousands of the chosen ones. Thus, there is much diversity in that rank[4] that is called "warriors."

1.2. Moreover, among the unwarlike ones themselves there is no less a diversity. For they are not all equally and in one rank[5] called "unwarlike." For some are so unwarlike that they could never become warriors, as is the case, for example, with the elders and with all females; also, with those who have the status of slaves. But the age of boyhood[6] is unwarlike in a way that holds out the hope of one day becoming warlike, namely, when "it reaches perfect manhood, in the measure of age."[7] At that time, not only are warriors made from boys, but they even hope to come into the "sum of warriors" and be chosen and numbered among the twelve thousand, or even put ahead of these and to be rulers of the chosen ones.

2.1. Consider, now, the state of the present age and notice how everything is full of wars and all human life is beset by invisible battles and attacks of demons. In fact, among God's people there are some who are so robust in faith and so armed with virtues that they wage wars against enemies of this sort on a daily basis. They are always battle-ready, and they not only guard themselves against the plots of the enemies, but others as well, who are not able to fight because of their sex, age or status as slaves. They protect these people by the word of teaching, by the example of life and by the earnestness of their admonitions. But this is only valid if these people do not lack faith; for whether people are warriors or unwarlike, it is impos-

---

[80]Cf. Jn 10:9; Rev 3:20. [81]Cf. Jn 10:9. [82]Cf. Gal 1:5. **Homily 26** [1]Rufinus uses anachronistic terms here. [2]Lit. "boys," Lat *pueri*.
[3]Num 31:48-50. [4]Lat *ordo*. [5]Lat *ordo*. [6]Lat *puerilis aetas*, picking up on *puer* from the lemma. [7]Cf. Eph 4:13.

sible to be saved without faith.

2.2. However, among the warriors themselves, at any rate those who fight for God, consider that some are so prepared and ready that "they entangle themselves in absolutely no secular affairs, in order to be able to please the one who has commended them."[8] Moreover, they "meditate on the law of God day and night."[9] So those who are like this are called the "sum of the warriors."

After all, it is not said of the common number of warriors that no one among them dissents,[10] but it is said of those who are called the "sum of the warriors." For in those who are like this, there is no dissent, no discord. For they are the ones of whom it is said: "But the heart and soul of the believers was one, nor did any of them say anything was his own, but they shared everything in common."[11] So these are the "sum of the warriors," among whom no one dissents. They are the ones who by fighting took the most gold and all the silver and every ornament, whether for the head, arms or even fingers, that is to say, they offer to God whatever they have in thoughts and deeds. For they know that his gifts are his presents,[12] and this is why no one dissents among them. For they could not offer gifts to God while in dissension.

I think that they are the ones who, according to the Gospel, carefully observe that precept that the Lord and Savior commands: "But if, when offering your gift at the altar, you remember that your brother has something against you, leave your gift there at the altar, and go first to be reconciled with your brother, and then come and offer your gift,"[13] namely, in order that they may "lift their hands to God without anger and dissension."[14] So these are the ones who say: "We have gathered the sum of our male warriors, and none of them dissents; and we have offered the gift to the Lord."[15]

2.3. Therefore, it is extremely urgent for

us to learn the discipline of harmoniousness. For just as in music, if a harmony of the notes is made consonantly, it produces the agreeable sound of a song with rhythm. But if some dissonance occurs on the lyre, a very displeasing sound is produced and the pleasantness of the song is ruined. The same applies to those who fight for God. If they have discords and dissensions among themselves, everything will be displeasing and nothing will seem acceptable to God, even if they wage many wars, even if they carry back many spoils and offer many gifts to God. For it will be said to them: "Put down your gift at the altar, and first go to be reconciled with your brother."[16] Then you too can be numbered among those who are the "sum of the male warriors" and say that "None of us dissents."[17]

2.4. I will say something even more. Unless you become the kind of person who in no way dissents from God's commands, and who is not out of harmony with any of the Gospel precepts, you will not be able to conquer the enemy, you will not be able to overcome the opponent. For in the very fact that you dissent, you have already been conquered. And through the very thing in which you are discordant with God, you are overcome by the devil. But if you want to conquer the enemy and be the "sum of the warriors," "cleave to God"[18] and be in concord with him, just as that one who said: "Who will separate us from the love of God? Tribulation or anguish or hunger or nakedness or danger or sword?"[19] And again: "Neither life nor death nor the present nor the future nor height nor depth nor another creature can separate us from the love of God, which is in Christ Jesus."[20] One who is like that dissents in nothing whatsoever; one who is like that can conquer Midianites and "kill all the sinners of the land,"[21] and "destroy their image from the city of the Lord."[22] So then, I too ought to destroy

---

[8] 2 Tim 2:4. [9] Ps 1:2. [10] Cf. Num 31:49. [11] Acts 4:32. [12] Cf. Num 28:2. [13] Mt 5:23-24. [14] Cf. 1 Tim 2:8. [15] Num 31:49-50. [16] Mt 5:24.
[17] Num 31:49. [18] Ps 73:28. [19] Rom 8:34. [20] Rom 8:38-39. [21] Ps 101:8. [22] Ps 72:20 LXX.

sinners from within myself and from the land of my flesh and kill fornication, uncleanness, passion, evil desire and greed. For these are the sinners of my land, which I will only be able to banish and kill if I do not dissent from God's commands. And then I will truly be worthy to offer gifts to God.

2.5. It says: "Every golden vessel, necklace or armlet or ring or bracelet or little chain."[23] A "necklace" is an ornament of wisdom. For in Proverbs it is said of wisdom that the one who has acquired it "places a golden necklace around his neck."[24] An "armlet" and a "ring" are ornaments of the hands in which the indications of works are symbolized; likewise also the "bracelet." Now the "little chains," on the other hand, indicate the link between the word and doctrine.

It says: "To propitiate God for us."[25] If we say that God becomes propitious to men for the sake of gold, consider how absurd, or rather, how impious it would be judged. For this is considered to be notorious even in a good man, if his inferiors placate him by giving him gold. Well then, how much more inappropriate is it to think this of God? This is why I think the method of this ecclesiastical exposition is established, which teaches that through the outward form of gold, the virtues of the soul are indicated and doing of good works, which alone are worthy to be offered to God by humans, and for the sake of these alone, it befits God to become propitious to men.

2.6. It says: "And Moses and Eleazar the priest took the gold from all the tribunes and centurions, and brought it to the tabernacle of testimony, a memorial to the sons of Israel before the Lord."[26] You see that the things that are said do not relate to what is viewed visibly, but to what the mind remembers. For blessed is the one who remembers that he has done a good work "before the Lord" and has offered to God well-pleasing gifts, the virtues of the soul and the ornaments of piety.

3.1. After this, a story follows about the inheritance of "Reuben[27] and Gad and the half-tribe of Manasseh."[28] Since it is our intention to discuss a few things from this narrative, we first want to awaken the attention of the hearers and raise their minds to the contemplation of the spiritual meaning. Everything that is said has to be carefully examined. This applies not merely to the words that are spoken, but also particular attention needs to be paid to the persona of the one who is speaking. For instance, if it is a child who is speaking, we adapt our minds to listen to the speech of a child. We do not look for anything more in what is said except to the extent that a child was capable of understanding. But if the one who speaks is a man, at once we reflect on whether the things that are said are worthy of the man. And again, if that man who speaks is educated, we examine his statements likewise in view of his learning. But if the man is ignorant and uneducated, we receive what is said in another way. So likewise, if the one who speaks is older and is a man of much proven experience, insofar as he has grown old in his learning, the corresponding expectation of his statements will be far greater.

3.2. Listen, now, to why we have said these things as a preface to the historical narrative about the inheritance of Reuben, Gad and the half-tribe of Manasseh, which we intend to explain. The one who is narrating these events that we are reading is neither a child, as we have described above, nor is he some sort of man or older man or any human being at all. And that I might say something more, he is not an angel or one of the heavenly powers, but, just as the tradition of the elders holds, it is the Holy Spirit who is the narrator of these things. For how could Moses have narrated things that happened from the origin of the world, or that would be done at the end of it, apart from the inspiration of the Spirit of God? How could he

---

[23]Num 31:50. [24]Prov 1:9. [25]Num 31:50. [26]Num 31:54. [27]Lat *Ruben*. [28]Num 32:33.

have prophesied about Christ, unless it were by the Holy Spirit speaking to him? For thus Christ himself testifies to him and says: "If you believed Moses, you would surely also believe me; for he wrote about me; but if you do not believe his writings, how will you believe my words?"[29] And so it is established that these things were spoken through the Holy Spirit, and for that reason it seems fitting that these things be understood in accordance with the dignity, or rather, in accordance with the majesty of the one who is speaking.

Moreover, I consider it to be very appropriate to recall in this place what Abraham said in response, when he heard the rich man who was in torments ask him to allow him to go and warn his brothers to live piously, lest they too should descend to that place of torments. Abraham said: "They have Moses and the prophets; let them listen to them."[30] Clearly he was not speaking of embodied men as "Moses and the prophets," but he was identifying as "Moses" the things that were written down by Moses through the dictation of the Spirit of God.

3.3. So then, one should say: Since these things have been written in this manner, if Abraham sends me to the statements of Moses, that by reading them, I can escape that place of torments, how will it help me escape Gehenna if I read:

– how the sons of Reuben and the sons of Gad and the half-tribe of Manasseh receive an inheritance from Moses "on the other side of the Jordan," since they had more herds than the other tribes?[31]

– and that Moses says to them: See to it that you do not provoke God, as those ten did who were sent with Jesus and Caleb to explore the land, and who said: "the land is such and such, and we cannot take it"?[32]

– and that the sons of Reuben and the others

with him responded to these things: Give us this land and its inheritance and "we will no longer seek a land of inheritance inside the Jordan"[33] with our brothers, but we will leave here our beasts and our gear and our women and our children,[34] but our men will go together with you and will cross the Jordan?[35]

– and that after this Moses commends them to Jesus son of Nun[36] and to Eleazar the priest, the son of Aaron,[37] but on the condition that they cross with the sons of Israel and fight with them against the enemies who were on the other side of the Jordan, until the land is freed from them,[38] and then they may receive the land that they had demanded of king Sihon and of king Og?[39]

– and to them alone an inheritance outside the Jordan is given through Moses, but to all the others it is given through Jesus[40] inside the Jordan?[41]

Consequently, someone will say: What benefit do these things have in relation to what Abraham said: "They have Moses and the prophets; let them listen to them"?[42] That is, how will those who read and hear these things avoid going down into that place of torments?

3.4. Now we have said these things in order to stir up the souls of the hearers, so that they may look more carefully at the things that are read or spoken, and so that in the writings of Moses, once the veil of the letter has been removed, they may understand what is written in such a way that they find that things are said in every detail, things which, if they are understood and observed, can keep the hearers from being brought to that place of torment, where that rich man was taken, who despised hearing these things that are written in a hidden fashion. Instead, may [the souls of the hearers] go to the bosom of Abraham, where Lazarus rested. So let us pray to the Lord that "the veil may be

---

[29]Jn 5:46-47. [30]Lk 16:23-31. [31]Cf. Num 32:1, 22, 29, 33. [32]Cf. Num 32:8-10, 12. [33]Cf. Num 32:19. [34]Cf. Num 32:26. [35]Cf. Num 32:27, 32. [36]Lat *Nave*. [37]Cf. Num 32:28. [38]Cf. Num 32:20-22. [39]Cf. Num 32:33. [40]Recall here as elsewhere that *Jesus* is the Greek form of the Hebrew *Joshua*. [41]Cf. Josh 1:6; 23:4. [42]Lk 16:29.

removed from our hearts during the reading of the Old Testament,"[43] so that we may be able to see the things that are hidden and concealed in the writings of Moses, in accordance with the warning of the prophet who says: "And unless you have heard in secret, your soul will weep."[44]

3.5. And indeed, in view of the things that have been asserted higher up, I think no one can be in doubt about the fact that these things are mysteries and contain a divine meaning. Not even one who is insatiably attached to "Jewish fables" can doubt this.[45] Nevertheless, just as I think that no one denies this, so I think that to know these things clearly, that is, the things that are present and the things that are being indicated in these narratives, things in which the "figure of realities" is covered under this veil, belongs to the same Holy Spirit who inspired these things to be written,[46] and to our Lord Jesus Christ, who said of Moses: "For he wrote about me,"[47] and to the almighty God, whose ancient plan for the human race is not openly indicated, but veiled in the letters.[48]

But let us pray from the heart to the Word of God, who is his only-begotten[49] and who "reveals the Father to whom he wills,"[50] that he may deign to reveal these things even to us. For in these things are the mysteries of his promises, "which he promised to those who love him, that we too may know what things have been given to us by God."[51] Moreover, you should help us by your prayers and consider carefully not so much we who are speaking as the Lord who enlightens those whom he has found worthy of enlightenment. By the contemplation of these things, may he deign to grant to us as well "the word in the opening of our mouth."[52]

But come now, if you have raised your hearts to the Lord and have asked for the illumination of his holy Word, let us come to a thorough investigation of the meaning of these things that seem to be hidden.

4.1. It has already been repeatedly said, both by our predecessors[53] and by ourselves, that the figure of the exodus from Egypt is understood in two ways. For both when someone is led from the darkness of errors to the light of knowledge, and when one is converted from an earthly way of life[54] to a spiritual manner of life,[55] he seems to have made an exodus from Egypt and to have come to a solitude, that is, to that state of life in which, by means of silence and quiet, one becomes practiced in the divine laws and is imbued with heavenly speech. Educated and guided by these things, when he has crossed the Jordan, he hastens to the Promised Land, that is, through the grace of baptism, he arrives at a life according to the gospel.[56]

Moreover, we said that there is a figure of the exodus from Egypt when the soul abandons the darkness of this world and the blindness of bodily nature and is transferred to another world, which is described as the "bosom of Abraham" in the story of Lazarus,[57] or as "paradise" in the story of the thief who believed from the cross,[58] or as whatever other places or stages there might be which are known to God.[59] Passing through these and coming to that "river" which "makes glad the city of God,"[60] the soul that believes in God receives within itself the allotment of the inheritance promised to the fathers.

4.2. So then, since the departure out of Egypt and the transition to the desert and from there the entrance into the inheritance of the holy land is described in a twofold manner, let us now see what Reuben, Gad and the half-tribe of Manasseh mean.

The inheritance which is given through Moses and is decreed "beyond the Jordan" comprises, for certain secret and mysterious reasons, a figure of the entire human race in the

---

[43]Cf. 2 Cor 3:14-16. [44]Jer 13:17. In my judgment the SC editors have misplaced the comma in their text. The context makes clear that it belongs after *occulte*. [45]Cf. Tit 1:14. [46]Cf. 2 Tim 3:16. [47]Jn 5:46. [48]Notice the trinitarian structure of this statement. [49]Cf. Jn 1:18. [50]Cf. Mt 11:27. [51]Cf. 1 Cor 2:9, 12. [52]Cf. Eph 6:19. [53]Cf. Philo *On the Migration of Abraham*. [54]Lat *conversatio*. [55]Lat *spiritalia instituta*. [56]Lat *ad evangelica instituta perveniat*. [57]Cf. Lk 16:22. [58]Cf. Lk 23:43. [59]Cf. Jn 14:2. [60]Cf. Ps 46:4.

twelve tribes of the sons of Israel; or at least [it is a figure] of all human beings who have come to the knowledge of God. Thus, some portion of them, through Moses, attain an inheritance "beyond the Jordan," but a portion also through Jesus receives an inheritance "across the Jordan" in the Promised Land.

And indeed, the ones for whom an inheritance is decreed "beyond the Jordan" are the "firstborn." Although they are less noble, although they are not without faults, nevertheless they are firstborn. For Reuben is the firstborn of Jacob.[61] Although he defiled his father's bed, nevertheless he is firstborn.[62] Moreover, Gad, although he was from a maidservant, nevertheless he too is a firstborn.[63] Manasseh too, whose half-tribe inherits "beyond the Jordan," though he was born of an Egyptian woman is nevertheless a firstborn.[64] Thus, all these are firstborn and for that reason they represent the first people who receive the allotment of their inheritance "beyond the Jordan," not through our Lord Jesus, but through Moses.

4.3. Now consider very carefully as well the reason why the first [trustees] obtain an inheritance "beyond the Jordan" and away from the others. It says: "Our beasts and flocks are many."[65] So this is the reason why the first people was not able to obtain an inheritance of that land, "which flows with milk, which abounds with honey, which is honey-sweet beyond the whole earth."[66] Nor were they able to recognize the "Word made flesh,"[67] because they had many beasts and many herds. For the "animal man cannot understand the things of the Spirit of God, nor make spiritual judgments,"[68] since "when man was in honor, he did not understand, but he was likened to the foolish beasts and he became like them."[69] For these reasons, they obtained an inheritance beyond the waters of the Jordan and made themselves strangers to the holy land. So that people received an inheri-

tance through Moses. They received only the land of two kings. For Moses was not able to kill more than two kings, whose land he divided for the peoples who have "many animals and many flocks."

4.4. But to those who cross the Jordan, Jesus[70] divides the land. Although they too have animals and flocks, nevertheless they are not so extensive as to prevent them from crossing the Jordan, but they strive to cross the Jordan with their animals, women and children, and to obtain the things promised to their fathers. The former, however, because of their flocks, beasts, women and children, were unable to cross the Jordan and enter into faith of Christ, which is the Promised Land.

5.1. Moses rebukes them, however, and "says to the sons of Reuben and to the sons of Gad: Shall your brothers go into combat and you sit here? Why do you pervert the hearts of the sons of Israel that they do not cross over into the land that the Lord is giving them?"[71] Even though he had rebuked them with words like this, it says: "The sons of Reuben and the sons of Gad approached him and said: We will build here folds for our sheep and flocks, and cities for our possessions, and we will arm ourselves and go before the sons of Israel as an advance squadron until we bring them into their own place."[72] And by making these promises, they appeased Moses, so that he commended them to Jesus and Eleazar. For thus it is written: "And Moses presented them to Eleazar the priest and to Jesus son of Nun and to the rulers of the families of the tribes of Israel. And Moses said to them: If the sons of Reuben and the sons of Gad cross the Jordan with you, each man armed for battle before the Lord, and you obtain the land in your sight, you shall give to them the land of Gilead[73] for a possession."[74]

5.2. We have found that the term "earth"[75] is recorded in the divine Scriptures with different

---

[61]Cf. Gen 35:23. [62]Cf. Gen 49:4. [63]Cf. Gen 35:26. [64]Cf. Gen 41:51. [65]Num 32:1. [66]Cf. Ezek 20:6; Jer 3:19; Num 14:7. [67]Cf. Jn 1:14. [68]1 Cor 2:14. [69]Ps 49:12. [70]Heb *Joshua*. [71]Num 32:6-7. [72]Num 32:16-17. [73]Lat *Galaad*. [74]Num 32:28-29. [75]Or "land."

significations. First indeed, this earth in which we dwell was not called earth from the beginning, but "dry [land]," and after this, what had formerly been called "dry [land]" received the name "earth."[76] In the same way, that visible heaven was not called "heaven" from the beginning, but was first named "firmament," and afterward it was designated by the term "heaven" as well. Yet "in the beginning" of creation, God is said to have made "heaven and earth," and later "dry [land]" and then "firmament."[77] Now do you want proof that "dry [land]" is one thing in the Scriptures, and "earth" is something else? Listen to the words of Haggai the prophet: "Once more I will shake the heaven and the earth and the sea and the dry [land]."[78] You see how the prophet records "earth" as one thing, and "dry [land]" as something else.

5.3. Moreover, in many passages of Scripture, we have found that "earth" is named in a praiseworthy sense, but we do not easily read that "dry [land]" is recorded in a praiseworthy sense. For even Adam, after his sin, is driven out into this place, as a blameworthy place, which is named "dry [land]." For previously he was not on the "dry [land]," but on the "earth"; for the paradise is not in the "dry [land]" but on the earth. Moreover, what the Lord promises to the meek in the Gospel is not "dry [land]" but the "earth." For he says: "Blessed are the meek, for they will inherit the earth."[79] And likewise in the Gospel, the seed that gives fruit, a hundredfold, sixtyfold and thirtyfold, is said to be "earth," not "dry [land]."[80] And I think that there is a certain progression of going from dry land to earth, just as there was a progression for this "dry [land]" to be called "earth." For all of us, while we are unfruitful and bear no fruit of justice, chastity and piety, are "dry [land]." But if we begin to cultivate ourselves and till our idle souls for a harvest of virtues, we go from being "dry [land]" to "earth," which multiplies

the seed when a pleasing crop has been received.

5.4. Thus even in the kingdom of God, there is a certain earth which is promised to the meek,[81] and an earth which is said to be "of the living,"[82] and an earth that is located on high, of which the prophet speaks to the just: "And he will exalt you so that you inherit the earth."[83] Therefore, the soul that believes in God obtains the inheritance of that earth, after it makes an exodus from the Egypt of this world; and in one place are those who have lived under the law, but in another place those who have been governed by the faith and grace of Jesus Christ. Nevertheless, those who seem first and who were governed by Moses will not be the first to obtain the inheritance decreed for them, unless they themselves cross with those whom Jesus governs, and fight with them against the enemies, and establish them in their homes; and thus they themselves will obtain the inheritance, which they earned under their commander Moses.

6.1. But unless these things are proven from the divine Scriptures, they will seem to be fables. So then, let Paul be produced as a suitable witness for these things, who in his epistle to the Hebrews, when he describes all those fathers and patriarchs and prophets who pleased God through faith,[84] after the enumeration of them all, in the final conclusion, says the following about them: "And all these, having received the testimony of faith, did not receive the promises, since God was providing something better for us, so that they would not be perfected without us."[85] It is as if these nine and a half tribes were saying of those two and a half tribes that the reason they did not receive the promise of that land beyond the Jordan, which was decreed to them through Moses, was because "God was providing something better for us, so that they would not be perfected without us." So, for that reason, they cross with

---

[76]Cf. Gen 1:9-10. [77]Cf. Gen 1:1. [78]Hag 2:6. [79]Mt 5:5. [80]Cf. Mt 13:8. [81]Cf. Mt 5:5. [82]Cf. Ps 142:5. [83]Ps 37:34. [84]Cf. Heb 11:1-38. [85]Heb 11:39-40.

us armed for battle, and they help us wage war and fight the enemies. But those who cross are armed, they are brave and powerful men; but all the others, who are a lazy and unwarlike band, remain "beyond the Jordan."

But if there are any brave men among them, they abandon their animals, flocks and all their possessions, and fight with us against the enemy, until our enemies are conquered, until we take the inheritance of the good land, the land of milk and honey.[86]

6.2. For who doubts that each of the holy fathers helps us by means of prayers and strengthens us by their deeds and encourages us by their examples?[87] Moreover, they help us by their books, through the things that they left behind for us in writing for remembrance. They teach and instruct us how to conduct the struggle against the hostile forces and how to endure the battles of the contests. Thus they fight on our behalf, and they enter in arms first, ahead of us. For since we have them as examples and see the things they have done bravely through the Spirit, we arm ourselves for spiritual combat, and we struggle against the "spiritual forces of wickedness in the heavenlies."[88] Ultimately, it is in this way that those who campaign under the commander Jesus destroy thirty kings and more and receive their lands by the allotment of the inheritance.[89] For once the spiritual forces of wickedness have been expelled from the heavenlies, they receive the inheritance of the heavenly kingdom, which Jesus our Lord apportions.

7.1. It seems that there can be yet a third way of explaining this, namely, that in the sons of Israel, that is, in the people of the church, some are understood to be spiritual and to receive inside the Jordan an inheritance of land "flowing with milk and honey," that is to say, by receiving the sweetness of wisdom and knowledge. Their land is surrounded and irrigated by the river of

God, which is filled with the waters of divine understanding. But others are carnal, who have too many beasts and flocks, that is, fattened and dull senses. They were like this, of whom the apostle said: "You are so senseless that though you began with the Spirit, now you are finishing with the flesh?"[90] and: "O senseless Galatians, who bewitched you from obeying the truth?"[91] Moreover, each of us, if we do not arm ourselves and get rid of crude and brutal senses, and hasten to the spiritual understanding, we will remain "beyond the Jordan." Nor will it be possible to pass through the river of wisdom which "gladdens the city of God,"[92] that is, [it gladdens] the soul that has room for God. [If we do not arm ourselves,] we will not penetrate to the inner aspects of the Lord's words, which are "sweeter than honey and the drippings of the honey-comb."[93] Instead, we will attain only to that land in which two kings were killed, when it is said to him: "I decided to know nothing else among you than Christ Jesus and him crucified."[94]

7.2. But the one who is able to cross the Jordan and to penetrate to the inner regions, by following our Lord Jesus there, he will kill more than thirty kings,[95] possibly those of whom it is said that "The kings of the earth took their stand, and the rulers were gathered together against the Lord and against his Christ."[96] Once these kings have been expelled and laid out prostrate, one will recognize the more hidden mysteries, until one comes even to that place where the throne of God is, and Jerusalem, the city of the living God,[97] not that Jerusalem which is "enslaved with her sons" on the earth, but that heavenly one, "which is free and is the mother of us all."[98] May our commander and Lord Jesus Christ deign to bring us to this inheritance. "To him be the glory in the ages of ages. Amen."[99]

---

[86]Cf. Ex 33:3-4. [87]Cf. 2 Macc 15:12-16. [88]Cf. Eph 6:12. [89]Cf. Josh 12:24. [90]Gal 3:3. [91]Gal 3:1. [92]Ps 46:4. [93]Ps 19:10. [94]1 Cor 2:2. Origen seems to interpret Paul's words here disjunctively, as if "Christ Jesus" and "him crucified" have different mystical referents, when in fact they have the same referent. Cf. Homily 26.4.3. [95]Cf. Josh 12:24. [96]Ps 2:2. [97]Cf. Heb 12:22. [98]Gal 4:25-26. [99]1 Pet 4:11.

Homily 27
Numbers 33:1-49

Concerning the stages of the sons of Israel.

1.1. When God founded the world, he created innumerable different kinds of foods. This was owing to the diversities that exist, either of human desire or in the nature of animals. Not only is this the reason why, when a man sees the food of animals, he knows that it was created not for him but for the animals; but the animals themselves know their own food, and, for example, the lion uses certain foods, the deer, others, the ox, others, and birds, others. Moreover, among human beings there are certain differences in the foods that are sought, and one person, who is quite healthy and strong in his physical constitution, requires strong food and he "believes and has confidence to eat all things."[1] He is like a very strong athlete. But if someone feels that he is rather weak and without strength, he enjoys vegetables and does not receive strong food owing to his own weakness. Now if someone is an infant, even though he cannot indicate this with his voice, still in reality he seeks no other nourishment than that of milk. And so, each individual, whether owing to age or strength or the health of his body, longs for food suitable to himself and corresponding to his strength.

1.2. If you have considered this illustration from physical realities sufficiently, let us now move on from these things to the understanding of spiritual things. Every rational nature needs to be nourished by foods that are proper to it and that correspond to it. Now the true food of a rational nature is the Word[2] of God. But just as in the nourishment of the body, we have just granted many differences, this also applies to the rational nature, which feeds, as we have said, on reason and the Word[3] of God. Not every nature is nourished by one and the same

Word. That is why, as in the physical illustration, the food some have in the Word of God is milk,[4] that is, the clearer and simpler doctrine. This normally consists in moral instruction, which is customarily given to those who are starting out in divine studies and who are receiving the first elements of a rational education.

1.3. And so, when some such reading from the divine books is recited, in which there seems to be nothing obscure, they gladly receive it, for example, the brief books of Esther, Judith or even Tobit, or the precepts of the book of Wisdom. But if the book of Leviticus is read to him, his mind immediately stumbles and he flees from it as from something that is not his own food. For the one who had come to learn how to worship God and how to receive his commandments concerning justice and piety, hears precepts given about sacrifices and the rites taught that concern immolation. Why should one not immediately turn away from what is heard and, so to speak, refuse the food as not suitable for him?

1.4. Moreover, when the Gospels or the apostle or the Psalms are read, another person joyfully receives them, gladly embraces them, and rejoices in gathering from them, as it were, certain remedies for his weakness. But if the book of Numbers is read to him, and especially those passages which we now have in hand, he will judge that there is nothing advantageous, nothing as a remedy for his weakness or that will benefit the salvation of his soul. Instead, he will immediately reject it and spit it out, as heavy and burdensome foods and as those that are not suitable to a sick and weak soul. But if I may return to the illustration from the physical world, if understanding were given to a lion, for example, he will not immediately blame the abundance of grasses that has been created, because he himself feeds on raw meat, nor will he say that they were made by the Creator need-

---

Homily 27 [1]Rom 14:2. [2]Lat *sermo.* [3]Lat *verbum.* [4]Cf. 1 Cor 3:2.

lessly, because he does not use them as food; neither should a human being, because he uses bread and other nourishment suitable to him, blame God for making snakes, which apparently supply food for deer. Nor should the sheep or the ox, for example, find fault with the fact that it has been given to other animals to feed on meat, though for them grasses alone suffice for them to eat.

1.5. Now it is just the same way in the case of rational food, I mean that of the divine books. One should not immediately blame or reject a Scripture which appears rather difficult or obscure to understand, or which appears to contain things that cannot be used by the beginner and infant,[5] by the one who is weaker,[6] by those who are less strong in understanding all things, and who thinks that nothing applies to him that is useful or health-bringing. Rather, one should consider that, just as God's creation consists in snakes, sheep, human beings and straw, and the very diversity of these things points to the praise and glory of the Creator, because they either supply food or take in food in a suitable and timely fashion for each of those for whom they were created; so also each individual, insofar as he perceives himself healthy and strong, takes in all these things, which are the words of God, and in which there is different food according to the capacity of the souls.

1.6. Now if we inquire quite carefully, for example, into the reading of the Gospel or into the apostolic instruction in which things you seem to take delight and in which you reckon is found the food most suitable and agreeable to you, how many are the things that have escaped your notice, if you investigate and thoroughly scrutinize the Lord's commands? But if what seems obscure and difficult must be immediately shunned and avoided, you will find so many obscure and difficult things even in the passages about which you are very confident,

such that, if you hold to this judgment, you will be forced likewise to give them up. Yet there are very many things in these [writings] that are spoken openly and simply enough to edify the hearer of limited intelligence.

1.7. Now we have said these things first in the preface to stir up your minds, since we have in hand a reading of this sort, one that is hard to understand and seems superfluous to read. But we cannot say of the Holy Spirit's writings that there is anything useless or superfluous in them, even if they seem obscure to some. But what we need to do instead is to turn the eyes of our mind toward him who ordered this to be written and to ask him for an understanding of these things, so that if there is weakness in our soul, he who "heals all its illnesses"[7] may heal us; or if we are of limited intelligence, the Lord may be with us, guarding his children, and may nourish us and lead us to the "measure of age."[8] For both are within us: to attain health from our weakness and to the age of maturity[9] from our childhood. But it is up to us to ask this of God. Yet it belongs to God to "give to those who ask and to open to those who knock."[10] Let this be enough for the preface.

2.1. Now let us come to the beginning of the reading that has been recited, so that with the Lord's help we may be able to summarize the main points and explain their meaning, even though we may not expect total clarity. Well then, it says: "These are the stages[11] of the sons of Israel, from when they went forth out of the land of Egypt with their power[12] by the hand of Moses and Aaron. And Moses wrote down their starting places[13] and stages by the Word of the Lord,"[14] and so on. You have heard that Moses wrote these things down "by the Word of the Lord." Why did the Lord want these things to be written down? Was it so that this passage in Scripture about the stages the sons of Israel made might benefit us in some way, or

---

[5]Cf. Heb 5:13. [6]Cf. Rom 14:2. [7]Ps 103:3. [8]Cf. Eph 4:13. [9]Lit. "manhood." [10]Cf. Mt 7:7. [11]Lat *mansiones*. [12]Lat *virtus*. [13]Lat *profectiones*. [14]Num 33:1-2.

that it would bring us no benefit? Who would dare to say that what is written "by the Word of God" is of no use and makes no contribution to our salvation, but merely narrates an event that happened, and which, to be sure, passed on by back then, but now pertains in no way to us when it is related? This opinion is impious and foreign to the catholic faith. It belongs only to those who deny that the one and only wise God of the Law and the Gospels is the Father of our Lord Jesus Christ.[15] So let us attempt, in a summary fashion, so far as time allows, to investigate what a faithful interpretation should understand from these stages.

2.2. Now when the discussion above gave us the opportunity of speaking about the departure[16] of the sons of Israel from Egypt,[17] we said that in a spiritual sense there can be seen a double exodus from Egypt, either when we leave our pagan life and come to the knowledge of the divine law, or when the soul leaves its dwelling place in the body. Therefore, these stages, which Moses now describes "by the Word of the Lord," have both in view.

2.3. For to be sure it is concerning those stages in which the soul, divested of the body, or rather, clothed again with its own body, will dwell, that the Lord declared in the Gospel by saying: "With my Father are many stages;[18] otherwise I would have told you: I am going to prepare a stage for you."[19] So then, these are the many stages that lead to the Father. And for each of them, what the reason is, what advantage comes to the soul by its sojourn there, or what instruction or enlightenment one receives, is something only the Father of the future world knows,[20] who says of himself: "I am the door."[21] "No one comes to the Father except through me."[22] Perhaps he will become the door for each soul in each of the different stages, so that it may enter through him and go out through him

and find pasture,[23] and then again enter another stage and from there another, until it reaches the Father himself.

But suddenly we have nearly forgotten our preface and have raised your hearing to lofty heights. Let us then, by all means, return to what happens among us and in us.

2.4. The sons of Israel were in Egypt; they were being afflicted with mortar and brick for the works of Pharaoh the king,[24] until they groaned and cried out to the Lord.[25] And he heard their groaning and sent his Word to them by Moses and led them out of Egypt. And we, then, when we were in Egypt, I mean in the errors of this world and in the darkness of ignorance, by doing the works of the devil in lusts and pleasures of the flesh, the Lord had pity on our affliction[26] and sent the Word, his only-begotten Son,[27] who brought us forth, snatched from the ignorance of error to the light of the divine law.

3.1. But first of all consider the reason of the mystery. If one observes it carefully, he will find in the Scriptures that there were forty-two stages in the departure of the sons of Israel from Egypt; and, further, the coming of our Lord and Savior into this world is traced through forty-two generations. For this is what the Evangelist Matthew records when he says: "From Abraham to David the king, fourteen generations, and from David to the deportation of Babylon, fourteen generations, and from the deportation of Babylon to Christ, fourteen generations."[28] Therefore, those who ascend from Egypt make forty-two stages, the same number as these forty-two stages of generations that Christ made when he descended to the Egypt of this world.

And Moses has recorded this quite carefully when he says: "The sons of Israel ascended with their power."[29] What is their "power" unless it is Christ himself, who is the "power of God"?[30]

---

[15]Cf. Rom 15:4, 6. This statement is directed against Marcion. [16]Lat *profectio*. [17]Cf. Homily 26.4.1-2. [18]Lat *mansiones*. [19]Jn 14:2. [20]Cf. Is 9:6. [21]Jn 10:9. [22]Jn 14:6. [23]Cf. Jn 10:9. [24]Cf. Ex 1:14. [25]Cf. Ex 2:23. [26]Cf. Ex 3:7. [27]Cf. 1 Jn 4:9. [28]Mt 1:17. [29]Lat *virtus*. Num 33:1. [30]1 Cor 1:24.

Thus the one who ascends, ascends with him who descended from there to us, so that he can reach the place from which that one descended, not by compulsion, but by dignity, so that what was spoken might be true, that: "He who descended is the one who also ascended."[31]

Therefore, the sons of Israel by forty-two stages reach the beginning of the taking their inheritance. In fact the beginning of the taking the inheritance was when Reuben, Gad and the half-tribe of Manasseh receive the land of Gilead.[32] And so the number of Christ's descent is established through forty-two fathers according to the flesh, as through forty-two stages of one who is descending to us. And the ascent of the sons of Israel up to the beginning of the promised inheritance is established through the same number of stages.

3.2. If you have understood how great a mystery that number of the descent and ascent contains, come now and let us begin to ascend through the things by which Christ descended and make that first stage, which he made last of all, namely, when he was born of the Virgin. And let this be the first stage for us who wish to go out of Egypt. In it we abandoned the cult of idols and the worship of demons—not gods—and believed that Christ was born of the Virgin and the Holy Spirit, and that the Word made flesh came into this world.[33] After this, let us now strive to go forward and to ascend one by one each of the steps[34] of faith and the virtues. If we dwell in them for such a long time until we come to perfection, we will be said to have made a stage at each of the steps of the virtues until, when we reach the height of our instruction and the summit of our progress, the promised inheritance is fulfilled.

4.1. Moreover, when the soul sets out from the Egypt of this life to head for the Promised Land, it necessarily goes by certain ways and, as we have said, carries out certain fixed stages. I think the prophet was mindful of this when he said: "I remembered these things, and I poured out my soul on me, since I would depart for the place of the admirable tabernacle, up to the house of God."[35] Those stages and those tabernacles are what he speaks of in another place: "How lovely are your tabernacles, O Lord of the virtues![36] My soul longs and faints for the courts of the Lord."[37] For that reason the same prophet says in another passage: "My soul has sojourned much."[38] So understand, if you can, what these sojourns of the soul are, in which it laments with a certain groaning and grief that it has been sojourning for too long. But the understanding of these things is faint and obscured, so long as it is still sojourning. But when the soul has returned to its rest, that is, to its homeland in paradise, it will be taught more truly and will understand more truly what the meaning of its sojourn was. The prophet viewed this under a mystery and said: "Return, my soul, to your rest; for the Lord has done good to you."[39]

But for the time being the soul sojourns and makes a journey and makes stages, doubtless being governed by means of these stages through the providential oversight of God for the sake of some advantage, as is said in one passage: "I have afflicted you, and fed you with manna in the desert, which your fathers did not know, so that what is in your heart might be made known."[40] So these are the stages by which the journey from earth to heaven is made.

4.2. Who will be found so capable and aware of the divine secrets, who can describe the stages of that journey and the ascent of the soul and explain the toils and resting places of each location? For how will one explain that after the first, second and third stage, Pharaoh is still in pursuit? That the Egyptians are in pursuit? And that, granting they do not catch them, nevertheless they keep on pursuing? And, granting

---

[31]Cf. Eph 4:8-10. [32]Cf. Josh 17:5-6. [33]Cf. Jn 1:1, 9, 14. [34]Lat *gradus*. [35]Ps 42:4. [36]Lat *virtutes*. Or "powers." [37]Ps 84:1-2. [38]Ps 119:6 LXX (120:6 RSV). [39]Ps 116:7. [40]Deut 8:2-3.

they were drowned, yet they did conduct a pursuit? How will one express the significance of the fact that the people of God, who had been saved only after a few stages, first sang the song, saying: "Let us sing to the Lord, for he has been honored gloriously; he has thrown the horse and rider into the sea"?[41] But, as I have said, I do not know who would dare to explain the stages one by one and also to make conjectures about the characteristics of the stages by considering their names. Nor do I know if the understanding of the one who is speaking is equal to the weight of the mysteries, or if the hearing of the listeners is capable of understanding.

4.3. For how will one explain the encounter of war with the Amalekites, or the different temptations, and how will one tell about those whose "limbs fell in the desert,"[42] and that not all the sons of Israel absolutely, but the sons of the sons of Israel were able to reach the holy land? And [how will one explain] that that entire ancient people, whose life and dwelling had been with the Egyptians, fell; but only a new people that did not know the Egyptians reached the kingdom, with the exception of the priests and the Levites? For if anyone could find a place in the order of priests and Levites, if anyone could have no portion in the lands but the Lord himself, that one does not "fall in the desert," but reaches the Promised Land. This is why, if you do not wish to fall in the desert, but to reach the promises of the fathers, you should not have your allotment on the earth, nor should you have anything in common with earth. Let your portion be the Lord alone, and you will never fall. Therefore, the ascent from Egypt to the Promised Land is carried out, through which, as I have said, we are taught in mysterious descriptions the ascent of the soul to heaven and the mystery[43] of the resurrection from the dead.

5.1. Now names are recorded for the stages.

For it did not seem befitting that every other place under heaven, that is, mountains, valleys and fields, should make use of names, but that the ascent by which the soul ascends to the kingdom of God should not have names for its stages. The stages of the ascent bear names that have been adapted to the mysterious themes; and it has as its guide not Moses—for he did not know where he was going[44]—but the pillar of fire and the cloud,[45] that is, the Son of God and the Holy Spirit, just as the prophet says in another place: "The Lord himself was leading them."[46] Such, then, will be the ascent of the blessed soul, when all the Egyptians have been drowned, and the Amalekites and all who had attacked it [perish]. And by passing through each of the different stages, that is, those "many [stages]"[47] that are said to be with the Father, it will be more fully enlightened, and going from one to another, it constantly gains greater increases in its enlightenment, until it grows accustomed to endure looking on the "true light" itself, "which enlightens every man,"[48] and bears the splendor of its true majesty.

5.2. But if we go back to the second explanation that we mentioned above, we shall understand that the stages point to the progress of the soul when placed in this life, which, after its conversion from a pagan life, it follows not so much Moses as the law of God, and not so much Aaron as that priest who remains forever.[49] Before it comes to perfection, it dwells in the wilderness, where, of course, it is trained in the commandments of the Lord and where its faith is tested by temptations. And when it conquers one temptation and its faith has been proved by it, from there it goes to another one; and it passes as it were from one stage to another; and then, when it prevails over the things that have happened and endures them faithfully, it moves on to another stage. And thus, the progress through each of the tempta-

---

[41]Ex 15:1. [42]Num 14:32; 1 Cor 10:5. [43]Lat *sacramentum*. [44]Cf. Heb 11:8, where the words refer to Abraham. [45]Cf. Ex 13:21. [46]Ps 78:14; cf. Deut 1:32-33. [47]Cf. Jn 14:2. [48]Cf. Jn 1:9. [49]Cf. Heb 6:20.

tions of life and faith will be said to have stages, in which increases in virtues are acquired one by one, and what is written is fulfilled: "They will go from virtue to virtue,"[50] until the soul reaches its final end, or rather, the highest degree of the virtues, and it crosses the river of God and receives the promised inheritance.

6.1. And so, by using a twofold manner of explanation, we should consider this entire sequence of stages which has been read aloud, so that progress may come to our soul from both, when we learn from them both how this life that has turned from error and follows the law of God ought to be led, and how great an expectation we have of the future hope that is promised on the basis of the resurrection.[51] For in this way I think that an interpretation worthy of the laws of the Holy Spirit may be taught in regard to what is read. For what benefit is there in my knowing the location in the desert which is said to be, for example, where the sons of Israel camped as they were passing through? Or what progress is conferred on those who read and who "meditate on the law of God day and night,"[52] especially since we see what great care the Lord took in describing these stages in detail, so that their description was inserted this second time in the divine laws? For those names were already mentioned, granted with some differences, at that time when the sons of Israel are said to have lifted up through each different place from that place, and to have camped at that place. And now, again through the Word of the Lord, they are commanded to be recorded by Moses. And for the very reason that this description is repeated a second time, it seems to me to correspond well with the mystery of this explanation that we have proposed. For they are repeated twice in order to show two ways for the soul: one by which the soul placed in flesh trains itself in the virtues through the law of God, and by ascending through certain steps

of progression it goes, as we have said, "from virtue to virtue," and uses these progressions as stages as it were. But the other way is the way by which the soul, when it is about to ascend to heaven after the resurrection, neither suddenly nor unseasonably, ascends to the heights, but it is led through "many stages,"[53] through which it is enlightened stage by stage, and it always receives an increase of splendor, illumined at each stage by the light of wisdom, until it reaches the Father of lights himself.[54]

6.2. So it says: "The sons of Israel went forth with their power."[55] That power was with them that had said: "I will go down with you to Egypt."[56] And it is because that power was with them that the prophet says: "And there was no one weak among their tribes."[57]

Now they went forth "by the hand of Moses and Aaron."[58] The one hand of Moses does not suffice for going forth from Egypt; the hand of Aaron is also sought. Moses represents the knowledge of the law; Aaron, the skill in making sacrifices and immolations to God. Thus it is necessary for us, when we come forth from Egypt, to have not only the knowledge of the law and of faith, but also a harvest of works by which one pleases God. For the reason the hand of both Moses and Aaron is mentioned is so that you may understand "hand" to mean works. For if when I make my exodus from Egypt and convert to God, I cast away pride, then I have sacrificed a bull to the Lord by the hand of Aaron. If I have destroyed aggressive passions and licentiousness, I should believe that I have killed a goat for the Lord by the hands of Aaron. If I conquer lust, [I have sacrificed] a calf; if folly, I will seem to have sacrificed a sheep. In this way, then, when the vices of the soul are purged, the "hand of Aaron" is at work within us; and the hand of Moses is in us when we are enlightened from the law to understand these very things. And

---

[50]Ps 84:7. The Latin *virtus* means both "virtue" and "power." [51]Cf. 1 Pet 1:3. [52]Ps 1:2. [53]Cf. Jn 14:2. [54]Cf. Jas 1:17. [55]Lat *virtus*, which also means "virtue." Num 33:1. [56]Cf. Gen 46:4. [57]Ps 105:37. [58]Num 33:1.

the reason both hands are necessary for those making an exodus from Egypt is so that there may be found in them not only the perfection of faith and knowledge, but also that of deeds and works. And yet, these are not two hands, but one. For [it says]: "by the *hand* of Moses and Aaron" the Lord led them forth, and not by the *hands* of Moses and Aaron. For there is a single work for each hand and a single fulfillment of perfection.

7. It says: "And Moses wrote down their starting places[59] and their stages[60] by the Word of the Lord."[61] He wrote them down, then, "by the Word of the Lord" so that when we read them and see how many starting places and stages lie ahead of us on the journey that leads to the kingdom, we may prepare ourselves for this way and, by considering the journey that lies ahead of us, we may not allow the time of our life to be wasted by laziness and negligence. Otherwise, while we linger in the vanities of this world and take delight in each of the sensations that come to our sight or hearing or even to touch, smell and taste, the days may slip by, the time may pass, and we shall not find any opportunity for completing the journey that lies ahead, and we may faint while only halfway there. And it will come to pass to us what is reported of certain ones who were unable to reach the destination, but their "limbs fell in the desert."[62] Thus, we are making a journey, and the reason we have come into this world is so that we may pass "from virtue to virtue,"[63] not to remain on the earth for earthly things, like the man who said: "I will pull down my barns, and build larger ones, and I will say to my soul: Soul, you have many good things laid up for many years, eat, drink, be merry."[64] Otherwise, the Lord may say to us, as he said to him: "Fool! This night your soul will be taken from you."[65] He did not say "this day," but "this night." For

he is destroyed at night, like the firstborn of the Egyptians,[66] as one who "loved the world"[67] and its darkness and who belonged to "the rulers of the darkness of this world."[68] Now this world is called darkness and night, because of those who live in ignorance and do not accept the light of truth. But those who are like this do not set out "from Rameses," nor do they pass on "to Succoth."[69]

8.1. But let us see when the sons of Israel first set out "from Rameses." It says: "In the first month, on the fifteenth day of the month."[70] By the Lord's command, on the fourteenth day of the month[71] they celebrated the Passover in Egypt, killing a lamb the day before they set out; and they who were still in Egypt performed a kind of beginning of the feast. Therefore, on the following day, which is the first day of Unleavened Bread, on the fifteenth day of the first month, they set out from Rameses and come to Succoth to make the day of the feast of unleavened bread there. "Who is wise and will understand these things? Or discerning and he will know them?"[72] Or rather, who is there who even understands them "in part," as the apostle says: "For we know in part, and we prophesy in part"?[73] Who understands how we celebrate the feast days even "in part," so that "no one will pass judgment on us in part for a feast or a new moon or a sabbath"?[74] For every feast day that is carried out on earth by human beings is carried out "in part," not completely, or with the perfect title of a feast. But when you come forth from that Egypt, then you will have a perfect feast; then you will keep the "unleavened bread of sincerity and truth"[75] to perfection; then you will celebrate the day of Pentecost in the wilderness; and then perhaps for the first time you will receive the heavenly food of manna and will carry out each of the different feasts about which we spoke earlier so far as we were able.[76]

---

[59]Lat *profectiones*. [60]Lat *mansiones*. [61]Num 33:2. [62]Heb 3:17; cf. 1 Cor 10:5. [63]Ps 84:7. [64]Lk 12:18-19. [65]Lk 18:20. [66]Cf. Ex 12:29. [67]Cf. 1 Jn 2:15. [68]Cf. Eph 6:14. [69]Cf. Num 33:3, 5. [70]Num 33:3. [71]Cf. Ex 12:6, 18. [72]Hos 14:9. [73]1 Cor 13:9. [74]Col 2:16. [75]1 Cor 5:8. [76]Cf. Homilies 23, 24.

8.2. But know that after that Passover that happened in Egypt, we found that a Passover was kept once in the desert, when the law was given,[77] and another, as we have observed, in Numbers;[78] and after this, it was never again carried out except in the Promised Land. Therefore, "on the fifteenth day of the first month," on the following day after the Passover, which is the first day of Unleavened Bread, "the sons of Israel set out from Rameses with a high hand," it says, "in the sight of all the Egyptians."[79] What is the "high hand"? For it says in another place: "Let your hand be lifted up."[80] Where there is no human or earthly work but a divine one, there the term "high hand" is found. For "hands" are quite often spoken of where works are to be understood. So it says: "with a high hand in the sight of all the Egyptians, they set out."

8.3. It says: "And the Egyptians were burying their dead."[81] The dead were burying their own dead,[82] but the living were following the Lord their God. After this it is said that "and on their gods the Lord made vengeance."[83] Moreover, in Exodus it says the following: "And on all the gods of the Egyptians the Lord will make vengeance."[84] Now here it says that "the Lord *made* vengeance on them." "There are some who are called gods, whether in heaven or on earth,"[85] the apostle says. Moreover, in the Psalms it is said: "All the gods of the nations are demons."[86] Thus, it calls, not the images, but the demons who dwell in the images "gods" on whom "the Lord made vengeance." But I would like to ask how God makes vengeance on the demons, when assuredly the day of vengeance and of judgment has not yet come.

8.4. Now I think that this vengeance is carried out on the demons when a person who had been deceived by them to worship idols is converted by the Word of the Lord and worships the Lord. And from the work of conversion itself, vengeance is inflicted on him who had deceived. And similarly, if someone who had been deceived by demons to commit fornication is converted to purity, esteems chastity and weeps for his error, the demon is scorched by that man's tears of repentance and is set on fire, and thus vengeance is meted out to the author of the deception. And likewise, if someone turns away from arrogance to humility, from luxury to thrift, by these acts each one whips and tortures the different demons who had deceived them in these matters.

8.5. Into what great torments do you think they are driven if they see someone who according to the Lord's word, "sells everything he possesses and gives to the poor"[87] and "takes up his cross and follows" Christ?[88] But beyond everything and beyond all punishments are the kinds of torments that arise for them when they see someone engaged in the study of the Word of God and seeking out the knowledge of the divine law and the mysteries of the Scriptures with attentive exertions. This sets them all ablaze; and in that fire they are completely burned up, since they had darkened human minds with the darkness of ignorance, and by this means they had succeeded in making God unknown, in causing the zealous pursuit of divine worship to be transferred to themselves. What vengeance do you think is meted out to them, what fire of punishments is inflicted on them, when they see these things opened by the light of truth, and the clouds of their deceit dispersed by knowledge of the divine law?

8.6. For they possess all who live in ignorance; and not merely those who are still in ignorance, but they frequently go to those who have known God, and attempt once again to bring about works of ignorance in them. No sin is accomplished without them. For when someone commits adultery, surely this is not without a demon; or when a man is seized by excessive

---

[77]Cf. Ex 13:3. [78]Cf. Num 9:1-2. [79]Num 33:3. [80]Ps 10:12. [81]Num 33:4. [82]Cf. Mt 8:22. [83]Num 33:4. [84]Ex 12:12. [85]1 Cor 8:5. [86]Ps 96:5. [87]Cf. Mt 19:21. [88]Cf. Mt 16:24.

anger, or when one plunders someone else's goods; and "the one who sits against his neighbor and slanders him,"[89] and the one who "puts a stumbling block in the way of his mother's son"[90]—it is not without a demon. And therefore, we must be active in every way, lest we stir up against us once more the firstborn of the Egyptians, or their gods, whom the Lord struck down and destroyed, if we give them an opportunity to work in us what God hates. But if we keep ourselves away from all of them, in the way we have already spoken of above, then "the Lord has inflicted vengeance on all the gods of the Egyptians," and they receive punishments from our amendment and conversion.

9.1. So then, the sons of Israel come forth from Egypt, and "setting out from Rameses, they come to Succuth."[91] This sequence[92] of setting out and the distinction of the stages are quite necessary and must be observed by those who follow God and set their minds on progress in the virtues. With respect to this order I remember that already in other places, when we said a few things for the sake of edification, which the Lord deigned to grant, we pursued this subject, but we shall now once again call to mind a few things.

So the first starting place is "from Rameses";[93] and, whether the soul starting out from this world goes to the future age, or is converted from the errors of life to the way of virtue and to the knowledge of God, it "sets out from Rameses." For in our language, Rameses means "confused agitation" or "agitation of the worm."[94] Clearly by this is shown that everything in this world is set in agitations and disorders, and also in corruption—for this is what the worm indicates. It is not fitting for the soul to remain in these things, but it should set out and come to Succuth.[95] Now Succuth translates as "tabernacles." Therefore, the first progression

of the soul is that it be taken away from earthly agitation and realize that it must dwell in tabernacles, like a sojourner, and like one making a journey, so that it can be, as it were, ready for battle and encounter those who lie in wait for it unhindered and free.

9.2. From there, when the soul feels that it is now ready, it "sets out from Succuth and camps at Buthan."[96] Buthan means "valley." We have said that the stages refer to progress in the virtues. Now a virtue is not acquired except by training and effort, nor is it tested as much in prosperity as in adversity. Thus one comes to a valley. Now in valleys and in lower places, the struggle against the devil and the contrary powers takes place. So then, a contest must be carried out in the valley, and in the valley one must fight. After all, even Abraham fought against the barbarian kings in the Valley of Salt,[97] and there he gained a victory. So then, this wayfarer of ours descends to those who are in deep and low places, not to linger there, but to gain a victory there.

9.3. "But they set out from Buthan and camped at the mouth of Iroth."[98] Iroth translates as "village." For one does not yet come to the city; nor is what is perfect already held, but first and for the moment some small things are captured. For progress consists in coming to great things from small ones. So they come to the "mouth," that is, to the first entrance of a village, which is an indication of a manner of life[99] and of moderate abstinence. For an excessive and immoderate degree of abstinence is dangerous at the beginning stages.

Now Iroth is situated opposite "Beelsephon and opposite Magdalum."[100] Beelsephon translates as "the ascent of the watchtower or citadel." So then, the soul ascends from small things to great things, and it is not yet placed in the watchtower itself, but "opposite" the watch-

---

[89]Cf. Ps 101:5. [90]Cf. Ps 50:20; Rom 14:13. [91]Num 33:5. RSV *Succoth.* [92]Lat *ordo.* [93]Lat *Ramesse.* [94]Cf. Philo *On Dreams* 77; *On the Posterity of Cain* 56; Jerome *Epistle* 78.3. [95]Lat *Sochoth.* [96]Num 33:6; RSV *Etham.* [97]Cf. Gen 14:10. [98]Num 33:7; RSV *Pi-hahiroth.* [99]Lat *conversatio.* [100]Num 33:7; RSV *Baal-zephon, Migdol.*

tower, that is, in sight of the watchtower. For it begins to watch and to look for the future hope and to contemplate the height of the progressions and little by little one grows, while it is more nourished by hope than fatigued by toils. This camp or stage is "opposite Magdalum," but not yet in Magdalum itself. For Magdalum means "magnificence." So then, since it has in view both the ascent of the watchtower and the magnificence of the things to come, [the soul,] as we have said, is fed and nourished by great hopes. For it is now situated in starting places, not in perfection.

10.1. After this, "they set out from Iroth and pass through the midst of the Red Sea, and they camped at the bitterness."[101] We have said that the time of the progressions is a time of dangers. How hard a temptation it is to pass through the midst of the sea, to see the waves rising in mass, to hear the noise and crashing of the raging waters! But if you follow Moses, that is, the law of God, the waters will become for you a "wall on the right and left," and you will make a journey on "dry ground in the midst of the sea."[102] Moreover, it can happen that the heavenly journey that we have said the soul is making has some waters; it is possible that waves too may be found there. For one part of the waters is "above the heaven" and another part is "below the heaven,"[103] and for the time being we endure the waves and billows of these waters which are "below the heaven." May God grant that they always be quieted and calmed and not stirred up by any blowing winds.

10.2. But meanwhile, when we come to the crossing of the sea, although we see Pharaoh and the Egyptians in pursuit, we will not be afraid. Let there be no fear of them, no terror. Let us only believe in the "one true God and his Son Jesus Christ, whom he sent."[104] But if it is said that "the people believed in God and in his servant Moses,"[105] we also believe accordingly in Moses, that is, in the law of God and the prophets. So be firm, and in a little while you will see "the Egyptians lying on the seashore."[106] Now when you see them lying there, rise up and sing out in songs to the Lord, and praise him who "sank the horse and rider in the Red Sea."[107]

10.3. So "they camped at bitterness."[108] Do not be terrified or afraid when you hear of "bitterness." For as the apostle teaches: "no discipline seems sweet at the moment, but bitter; but later it yields the very sweet and peaceful fruit of justice to those who have been trained by it."[109] After all, even the unleavened bread is commanded to be eaten with bitter [herbs];[110] nor is it possible to reach the Promised Land unless we pass through bitterness. For just as physicians put bitter [substances] in medicines with a view to the health and healing of those who are sick, so also the physician of our souls, with a view to our salvation, has willed that we suffer the bitterness of this life in various temptations, knowing that the end of this bitterness gains the sweetness of salvation for our soul; just as, on the contrary, the end of the sweetness found in physical pleasure yields a bitter end in the inferno of punishments, as the example of that rich man shows.[111] You, then, who are entering on the journey of virtue, should not turn back from camping at "bitterness." For you will set out even from there, just as the sons of Israel did.

11.1. It says: "They set out from bitterness and came to Elim."[112] Elim is where there are twelve springs of water and seventy [-two] palm trees.[113] You see, after bitterness, after the hardships of temptations, what pleasant places receive you! You would not have come to the palm trees unless you had endured the bitterness of temptations, nor would you have come to the sweetness of the springs unless you

---

[101]Num 33:8; rsv *Marah*. The Latin text consistently uses the plural, "bitternesses." [102]Cf. Ex 14:22. [103]Cf. Gen 1:7. [104]Jn 17:3; cf. Ex 14:31. [105]Ex 14:31. [106]Ex 14:30. [107]Cf. Ex 15:1. [108]Num 33:8. Lit. "bitternesses." [109]Heb 12:11. [110]Cf. Ex 12:8. [111]Cf. Lk 16:19-25. [112]Num 33:9. Lat *Aelim*. [113]Cf. Num 33:9.

had first overcome what was sad and harsh; not indeed that the end of the journey and the perfection of all things is here; but God, who governs souls, has on this journey placed some places of refreshment into the midst of our toils, so that the soul may be refreshed and restored by them and may more readily return to the toils that remain.

Now Elim translates as "rams." Rams are the leaders of flocks. Who then are the leaders of Christ's flock if not the apostles, who are also the twelve springs? But since our Lord and Savior chose not only those twelve[114] but also seventy others,[115] for that reason there are not only twelve springs recorded, but also there are seventy palm trees. For they too are called apostles, as Paul himself says when he is explaining the resurrection of the Savior. He says: "he appeared to those Twelve,[116] then to all the apostles."[117] There he is showing that there are other apostles besides those twelve. Therefore, this pleasantness awaits you after bitterness, this rest after the toil, this grace after temptation.

11.2. "They set out from Elim and camped by the Red Sea."[118] Notice that they do not enter the Red Sea—it is enough to have entered it only once. Now they "camp by the sea," that they may see the sea and view its waves, but in no way fear its motions and assaults.

"And they set out from the Red Sea and camped in the desert of Sin."[119] Sin translates as "bramble bush" or "temptation." Thus, the hope of good things now begins to smile on you. But what is the hope of good things? "The Lord appeared from the bramble bush" and gave responses to Moses;[120] and this was the beginning of the Lord's visitation to the sons of Israel. But it is not in vain that Sin also translates as temptation. For visions usually involve

temptation as well. For sometimes an angel of wickedness "transforms himself as an angel of light."[121] And for that reason one must be on guard and exercise great care in order that you may knowingly discern the kind of visions. This is what Jesus the son of Nun did, when he saw a vision and knew that there was a temptation in it. He immediately questioned the one who appeared to him and said: "Are you of us, or of the adversaries?"[122] So then, when the soul sets out and comes to the place where it begins to distinguish between visions, it will then be proven to be spiritual if "it knows how to discern all things."[123] Ultimately, that is why one of the spiritual gifts given by the Holy Spirit is recorded to be "the distinguishing of spirits."[124]

12.1. "And they set out from the desert of Sin and came to Raphaca."[125] Raphaca translates as "health." You see the order of the progressions, how when the soul is once made spiritual and begins to see heavenly visions, it arrives at health, so that it deservedly says: "Bless the Lord, my soul, and all that is within me, [bless] his holy name!"[126] Which Lord? The one, it says, "who heals all your infirmities, who redeems your life from destruction."[127] For there are many infirmities of the soul: avarice is an infirmity of it, indeed the worst one; pride, anger, boasting, fear, inconstancy, timidity and the like. When, Lord Jesus, will you cure me of all these infirmities? When will you heal me so that I may say: "Bless the Lord, my soul, who heals all your infirmities," so that I may be able to make a stage at Raphaca, which is healing?

12.2. It would take too long if we wanted to go through each of the stages and explain one by one what is suggested by contemplating their names. Nevertheless, let us run through them in a brief and summary fashion, not to offer you a full exposition, since time certainly does not

---

[114]Cf. Mk 3:14; Jn 6:70. [115]Cf. Lk 10:1. [116]Cf. 1 Cor 15:5. It is noteworthy that Origen reads "twelve" here. Several Western (Greek) manuscripts read "eleven." Bruce M. Metzger, *A Textual Commentary on the Greek New Testament*, 3rd ed. (London and New York: United Bible Societies, 1971), p. 567, calls the latter reading a "pedantic correction," since "Twelve" may have been an official designation. [117]1 Cor 15:5, 7. [118]Num 33:10. [119]Num 33:11. [120]Cf. Ex 3:2. [121]2 Cor 11:14. [122]Josh 5:13. [123]Cf. 1 Cor 2:15. [124]1 Cor 12:10. [125]Num 33:12; rsv *Dophkah*. [126]Ps 103:1. [127]Ps 103:3-4.

allow that, but to offer you opportunities for understanding.

Well then, "they set out from Raphaca and come to Halus."[128] Halus translates as "toils." Do not be surprised that toils follow health. For the soul acquires health from God in order to accept toils with delight and not unwillingly. For it will be said to it: "You will eat the toils of your harvest; you are blessed, and it will be well with you."[129]

After this they come to "Raphidin."[130] Now Raphidin translates as "praise of judgment." Praise most justly follows after toils. Yet of what reality is the praise for? Judgment, it says. So the soul that judges and discerns correctly becomes worthy of praise, that is to say, the soul that "judges all things spiritually and is itself judged by no one."[131]

12.3. After this it "arrives at the desert of Sina."[132] Sina itself is a place in the desert that was earlier mentioned as "Sin."[133] But this place is, rather, the name of the mountain that is in that desert; it is called Sina after the name of the desert. Thus, after the soul has been made praiseworthy in judgment and begins to have a right judgment, then God gives it the law, since it has begun to be capable of receiving divine secrets and heavenly visions.

From there one arrives at the "tombs[134] of lust."[135] What are the tombs of lust? Doubtless it is where lusts are buried and covered over, where all desire is quenched and the flesh no longer "lusts against the spirit"[136] by its having been put to death by the death of Christ.[137]

After this they come to "Aseroth,"[138] which translates as "perfect halls," or "blessedness." Consider quite carefully, O my wayfarer, what the order of the progressions is. After you have been buried and have handed over to death the lusts of the flesh, you will come to the breadth of the halls, you will come to blessedness. For

blessed is the soul that is no longer beset by any vices of the flesh.

12.4. From there one arrives at "Rathma,"[139] or "Faran." Rathma translates as "complete vision," and Faran means "visible face." Why should the soul not grow in such a way, that when it has ceased being beset by the harassments of the flesh, it has complete visions and receives a perfect understanding of things, namely by recognizing more fully and more deeply the causes of the incarnation of the Word of God[140] and the reasons of his dispensations?

From there one arrives at "Remmon Phares,"[141] which in our language means "a lofty cutting away," that is, when the separation and distinction of great and heavenly realities from earthly and lowly things takes place. For as the understanding of the soul grows, the knowledge of lofty things is supplied to it and it is given judgment, by means of which it knows how to cut away what is eternal from what is temporal, and to separate what is perishable from what is everlasting.

12.5. After here one arrives at "Lebna,[142] which translates as "whitening." I know that in some passages whitening is recorded in a blameworthy fashion, as for example when it is said: "whitened wall"[143] and "whitened tombs."[144] But here, the whitening is that concerning which the prophet says: "You will wash me and I shall be whiter than snow";[145] and again Isaiah: "If your sins are like scarlet, I will whiten them like snow, and I will make them gleam like wool."[146] And again in the Psalm: "They will be whitened with snow in Zalmon."[147] And the hair of the Ancient of Days is said to be gleaming, that is, white like wool.[148] So then, this whitening must be understood to come from the splendor of the true light and to descend from the brightness of heavenly visions.

---

[128]Num 33:13; RSV *Alush.* [129]Ps 128:2. [130]Num 33:14; RSV *Rephidim.* [131]Cf. 1 Cor 2:15. [132]Num 33:15; RSV *Sinai.* [133]Cf. Num 33:12. [134]Lat *monumenta.* [135]Num 33:16; RSV *Kibroth-hattaavah.* [136]Gal 5:17. [137]Cf. Rom 6:2-4; 7:4. [138]Num 33:17; RSV *Hazeroth.* [139]Num 33:18; RSV *Rithmah.* [140]Cf. Jn 1:14. [141]Num 33:19; RSV *Rimmon-perez.* [142]Num 33:20; RSV *Libnah.* [143]Acts 23:3. [144]Mt 23:27. [145]Ps 51:7. [146]Is 1:18. [147]Ps 68:14. [148]Cf. Dan 7:9.

After this a stage takes place in "Ressa,"[149] which among us could be called "visible" or "praiseworthy temptation." Why is it that no matter what great progress the soul makes, temptations are still not taken away from it? This is why it is clear that temptations are exercised on it as a kind of protection and defense. For just as meat becomes rotten if it is not sprinkled with salt, no matter of what quality it consists, so also the soul. If it is not somehow salted with constant temptations, it immediately becomes negligent and dissolute. This is confirmed by the saying "every sacrifice will be salted with salt."[150] Ultimately, this is why even Paul said: "And to keep me from being too elated by the loftiness of revelations, a thorn was given me in the flesh, an angel of Satan, to harass me."[151] So this is the visible or praiseworthy kind of temptation.

12.6. From here one arrives at "Macelath,"[152] which is "principality" or "staff." By these two terms is indicated both power and that the soul has progressed to the point that it rules over the body and obtains this by that the staff of power; or it has power not only over the body but over the whole world, when it says: "But the world has been crucified to me, and I to the world."[153]

From there one comes to "Mount Sephar,"[154] which is called "sound of trumpets." The trumpet is a sign of war. Therefore, when the soul senses that it has been armed with so many outstanding virtues, it necessarily goes forth to the war it has "against the principalities and powers, and against the rulers of this world."[155] Or, at least, the trumpet sounds in the Word of God, that is, in the word of preaching and teaching, to give "a meaningful sound by the trumpet," so that the one who hears it "can prepare himself for war."[156]

After this one comes to "Charadath,"[157] which in our language signifies "made compe-

tent"; just as indeed he himself says, that: "He has made us competent to be ministers of a new covenant."[158]

12.7. From there a stage is made at "Maceloth,"[159] which translates as "from the beginning." For the one who strives for perfection contemplates the beginning of things, or rather, he refers everything to him who was "in the beginning,"[160] and he never separates from that beginning.

After this one makes a stage at "Cataath,"[161] which is "encouragement" or "endurance." For it is necessary for someone who wants to be of use to others to endure many things and to bear them all patiently, as it is said of Paul: "For I will show him how much he must endure for the sake of my name."[162]

From there one comes to "Thara,"[163] which is understood among us as "contemplation of amazement." We cannot express the Greek word, which they call *ekstasis*, with a single word in the Latin language, that is, when the mind is struck with admiration over some great reality. Thus, the contemplation of amazement means a time when the astounded mind is amazed by the knowledge of great and marvelous things.

12.8. After this one comes to "Matheca,"[164] which translates as "new death." What is the new death? When "we die together with Christ and are buried together with Christ, that we may also live together with him."[165]

From there one comes to "Asemna,"[166] which is said to mean "mouth" or "bones." Doubtless through these things the virtue and strength of endurance is being revealed.

Now from here a stage is made at "Mesoroth,"[167] which is thought to mean "one who excludes." What do they exclude? Doubtless the wicked suggestions of the opposing spirit from their thoughts. For this is what the wisdom

---

[149]Num 33:21; RSV *Rissah.* [150]Lev 2:13. [151]2 Cor 12:7. [152]Num 33:22; RSV *Kehelathah.* [153]Gal 6:14. [154]Num 33:23; RSV *Shepher.* [155]Eph 6:12. [156]1 Cor 14:8. [157]Num 33:24; RSV *Haradah.* [158]2 Cor 3:6. [159]Num 33:25; RSV *Makheloth.* [160]Jn 1:1. [161]Num 33:26; RSV *Tahath.* [162]Acts 9:16. [163]Num 33:27; RSV *Terah.* [164]Num 33:28; RSV *Mithkah.* [165]2 Tim 2:11; cf. Rom 6:4. [166]Num 33:29; RSV *Hashmonah.* [167]Num 33:30; RSV *Moseroth.*

of God says: "If the spirit of one having power rises up against you, do not leave your place."[168] Thus, the place must be held and the adversary must be excluded, lest he find a place in our heart, as the apostle says: "Give no place to the devil."[169]

After this one arrives at "Baneain,"[170] which means "springs" or "filters," that is, where one draws from the springs of the divine words until one filters them by drinking. Now the word "filter" [excolat] comes from colare [to strain], and not from colere [to cultivate]. Thus, a person filters the word of God when he does not pass over even the "least commandment," or rather when not even "one iota or one dot" from the word of God are considered superfluous to his understanding.[171]

After this one comes to "Galgad,"[172] which translates as "temptation" or "something packed together." Temptation, as I see it, is a kind of strength and defense for the soul. For it is so interconnected with virtues that no virtue appears to be seemly or complete without them. And for that reason for those making progress toward virtue, there are various and frequent stages involving temptations.

When you pass through them, you will camp at "Tabatha."[173] Tabatha translates as "good things." Thus, one will not come to good things except after the experience of temptations.

From there, it says, they "camped at Ebrona,"[174] which is "passage." For everything must be passed through, since, even if you come to good things, it is necessary that you pass through to better things, until you come to that good in which you should always remain.

After this one reaches "Gasiongaber,"[175] which translates as "the counsels of a man." If someone ceases to be a child in understanding, he arrives at the counsels of a man, just as that one did who said: "But when I became a man,

I laid aside the things that belonged to childhood."[176] Thus, the counsels of a man are great, as that one also says: "the counsel in a man's heart is deep water."[177]

12.10. From there one comes again to "Sin."[178] Sin is once again "temptation." For we said that there is no other way of clearing the way to enter on this journey. It is just as if, for instance, some goldsmith wanted to make a necessary vessel. He brings it often to the fire; he strikes it repeatedly with his hammers; he smoothes it often with razors, so that it becomes more purified and is brought to that form and beauty that the craftsman is looking for.

After this one camps at "Pharancades,"[179] which is "holy fruitfulness." You see where the person has come from; you see that holy fruitfulness follows the furrows of temptations.

Then one camps at "Mount Or,"[180] which translates as "a mountaineer." For one comes to the mountain of God in order to become a "rich mountain and a swelled[181] mountain";[182] or it derives from the fact that one who always dwells on the mountain of God is called a mountaineer.

12.11. The stage at "Selmona"[183] follows after this one. This translates as "shadow of the portion." I think the shadow mentioned is the one about which the prophet said: "The Spirit[184] of our face is Christ the Lord, to whom we said: In his shadow we will live among the Gentiles."[185] Moreover, similar to this one is the shadow about which it is said: "The Spirit of the Lord will overshadow you."[186] Thus, the shadow of our portion, which offers us shade from all the heat of temptations, is Christ the Lord and the Holy Spirit.

Now from here we come to "Phinon,"[187] which we think translates as "brevity of the mouth." For the person who can view the mys-

---

[168]Eccles 10:4. [169]Eph 4:27. [170]Num 33:31; rsv Bene-jaakon. [171]Cf. Mt 5:18-19. [172]Num 33:32; rsv Hor-haggidgad. [173]Num 33:33; rsv Jotbathah. [174]Num 33:34; rsv Abronah. [175]Num 33:35; rsv Ezion-geber. [176]1 Cor 13:11. [177]Prov 20:5. [178]Num 33:36; rsv Zin. [179]Num 33:36; rsv Kadesh. [180]Num 33:37; rsv Mount Hor. [181]The Greek word means "curdled like cheese." [182]Cf. Ps 68:15. [183]Num 33:41; rsv Zalmonah. [184]Or "breath" or "wind." [185]Lam 4:20. [186]Lk 1:35. [187]Num 33:42; rsv Punon.

tery of Christ and of the Holy Spirit, even if he sees or hears things "which it is not permissible for men to speak,"[188] will necessarily have brevity of the mouth, since he knows to whom, when and how he ought to speak about the divine mysteries.

After this one comes to "Oboth."[189] Although we have not found a translation of this name, nonetheless we do not doubt that in this name as well, as in all the others, the rational meaning of the progressions is preserved.

There follows after this the stage that is called "Gai,"[190] which translates as "chasm."[191] For through these progressions one approaches the "bosom of Abraham," who says to those who are in torments: "Between you and us a great chasm has been fixed."[192] Thus he rests also in his bosom, just as the blessed Lazarus did.

12.12. From there one comes in turn to "Dibon-gad,"[193] which bears the meaning "beehive of temptations." Observe the marvelous caution of divine providence! Behold now this wayfarer on his heavenly journey is very close to the highest perfection by a succession of virtues, and yet temptations do not leave him. But I hear of temptations of a new kind: it says: a "beehive of temptations." Scripture describes the bee a praiseworthy creature. Kings and commoners make use of its labors for their health.[194] This is rightly understood of the words of the prophets and the apostles and of all who wrote the sacred books. And I think this can be understood most worthily as the beehive, that is, the entire canon[195] of the divine Scriptures. So then, for those who strive for perfection, there is some temptation even in this beehive, that is, in the prophetic and apostolic words. Do you wish to see that the temptation in them is not the least one? I find written in this beehive: "See to it," it says, "that when you see the sun and the moon, you do not worship these things, which

the Lord your God has reserved for the Gentiles."[196] Do you see what a temptation proceeds from that beehive? And again when it says: "You shall not revile the gods."[197] And again [there is temptation] in the beehive of the New Testament, where we read: "Why do you wish to kill me, a man who has told you the truth?"[198] And again the Lord himself says in another place: "This is why I speak to them in parables, so that seeing they may not see, and hearing they may not understand, lest they should be converted and I would heal them."[199] Moreover, when the apostle says: "In their case the god[200] of this world has blinded the minds of the unbelievers."[201] And you will discover many temptations of this kind in this divine beehive to which it is necessary that each of the saints come, so that even by means of these things it may be known how perfectly and religiously he is thinking about God.

12.13. After this one comes now to "Gelmon Deblathaim,"[202] which translates as "contempt of figs," that is, where earthly things are completely scorned and despised. For unless we spurn and treat with contempt what seems to delight us on earth, we cannot pass on to the heavenly things.

For there follows after this the stage at "Abarim opposite Nabau."[203] The former word means "passage," but Nabau translates as "separation." For when the soul has made its journey through all these virtues and has ascended to the height of perfection, it then "passes" from the world and "separates." This is what is written of Enoch: "And he was not found, because God had translated him."[204] Someone like this, even if he seems to be still in the world and to dwell in flesh, nonetheless is not "found." Where is he not found? He is not found in any worldly activity, in any fleshly affair, in any worthless conversation. For God has "translated

---

[188]2 Cor 12:4. [189]Num 33:43. [190]Num 33:44, 45; RSV *Iye-abarim* or *Iyim*. [191]Lat *chaos*. [192]Lk 16:26. [193]Num 33:45. [194]Cf. Prov 16:24. [195]Or "enumeration." [196]Deut 4:19. [197]Ex 22:28. [198]Jn 8:40. [199]Mt 13:13-15. [200]Or "God." [201]2 Cor 4:4. [202]Num 33:46; RSV *Almon-diblathaim*. [203]Num 33:47; RSV *Abarim, Nebo*. [204]Gen 5:24.

him" from these things and has established him in the realm of the virtues.

The last stage is "east of Moab by the Jordan."[205] Now the reason this race takes place at all and is run is so that one may reach the river of God, that we may dwell near the flowing wisdom and be watered by the waves of divine knowledge; so that having thus been purified by them all we may merit to enter the Promised Land.

For the time being, these are the things we have been able to touch on in passing and to bring forth before the public concerning the Israelites' stages according to one method of exposition.

13.1. Now possibly this kind of exposition, which relies on the meaning of Hebrew terms, may seem contrived and violently forced to those who do not know the conventions of that language. Therefore, we shall give a comparison in our language as well, by which the logical method we have used may be clarified. There is a literary game in which boys receive the first elements [of education]. Some of the boys are called the "abcd's" others, "syllabarians"; others, "namers"; and others, "counters." Now when we hear these terms, we know from them which of the boys has made progress. Likewise in the liberal arts, when we hear a passage recited or a consolation or an encomium or any other topics in order, we notice a youth's progress by the name of the topic. So why should we not believe that by these names of places, as in the names of topics, there can be indicated stages of progress for those who are learning by divine instructions? And just as the students appear to linger in each different topic and to make, as it were, stages in them, and they set out from one to another, and again from it to another, so also, why should not the name of the stages and the progression from one to another, and from it again to another, be believed to indicate the

mind's progress and to signify the increase of the virtues?

13.2. But I leave the other aspect of the exposition to be inferred and contemplated from this one by any who are prudent. For it is enough to have given opportunities to the wise,[206] since it is not expedient that the minds of the hearers remain completely idle and lazy. Therefore, by making a comparison with this exposition, let that other exposition be measured, or rather, let something more penetrating and more divine be contemplated. "For God gives the Spirit not by measure,"[207] but because "the Lord is Spirit,"[208] he "blows [spirat] where he wills."[209] And we desire that he may inspire [adspiret] you as well, so that you may perceive things that are better and loftier than these in the words of the Lord, as you make your journey through the places we have described in accordance with our mediocrity. Thus we ourselves may also be able to walk with you on that higher and loftier way, as our Lord Jesus Christ leads us, who is "the way and the truth and the life,"[210] until we reach the Father, "when he hands over the kingdom to God the Father"[211] and subjects every principality and power to him. "To him be glory and power in the ages of ages. Amen."[212]

Homily 28
Numbers 34–35

1.1. The last story that is recorded in the book of Numbers is the one in which the Lord commands Moses "to give orders to the sons of Israel,"[1] that when "they have entered the holy land," they may know how to take possession of its inheritance and that they should observe the boundaries of their limits in these things. And after this, with the Lord himself now describing this, it is said: "toward Africa," that is, toward the west, the boundary of that place should be observed, and of that place toward the east,

---

[205]Num 33:48. [206]Cf. Prov 9:9. [207]Jn 3:34. [208]2 Cor 3:17. [209]Jn 3:8. [210]Jn 14:6. [211]Cf. 1 Cor 15:24. [212]1 Pet 4:11. **Homily 28**
[1]Num 34:2.

and thus the Lord himself indicates through the four regions of the sky certain names which the people of God ought to keep in that earthly Judea.

Now one of the more simple hearers will say that here too there are things that are necessary and useful even according to the letter. For no one should go beyond the borders that have been appointed through the Lord's command, and one tribe should not dare to violate the boundaries of another. But what will we do when no possibility remains for the Jews, not merely to invade the borders of another [nation] in these lands, but even of possessing them at all? For they have been banished from that land, they are exiles and refugees, and those who now possess and guard the boundaries are not those whom the divine law appointed, but those whom they have entrusted the rights of victors. What, I ask, will we do, who read these things in the church? If we read them according to the sense of the Jews, they will really seem superfluous to us and pointless.

1.2. But I am one who reads what is written about Wisdom: "I went out after her as a tracker."[2] I want to go out after her, and since I do not find her in the physical realities, I desire to pursue her tracks and investigate where she is going and to see into which rooms she leads my understanding. For I think that if I am able to follow her with care and to investigate her ways, she will give me some opportunities from the Scriptures to understand how it is, even in these passages we need to explain, if we believe what Paul says in a mystery, that those who serve through the law are serving "the shadow and image of heavenly things."[3] And if, no less in accordance with the judgment of that man, the law, of which this reading that we have in hand is a portion, "contains a shadow of the good things to come,"[4] it seems logical and necessary that everything that is described in the law

that seems to concern earthly things is really a shadow of the good things of heaven; and the whole inheritance of that land, which is called the "holy land"[5] and the "good land,"[6] is an image of the good things of heaven. As we have already said, these things, which are mentioned as good things on earth, contain a shadow and an image of the heavenly things.

2.1. But to elevate my words and your understanding a little bit, and to gain an access, as it were, into the things that we are saying need to be attended to, let us make use of a certain comparison. No one doubts that every place in the land of Judea, every mountain, every city and village, is designated by certain names. Nor is there a single place that lacks a name, but each one is referred to by its own designations; for instance, the Canaanites have given their name to their own locales, or the Perezites no less to their places, and the Amorites or Hittites[7] or even the Hebrews.

So then, according to the judgment of Paul where he says that earthly things are a "shadow and pattern of the heavenly things,"[8] there will perhaps be no negligible distinctions of localities in the heavenly regions as well. You will see the names and designations by which they are distinguished, and whence these are derived, and that names are assigned not only to the districts of heaven but also to all the stars and heavenly bodies. For "he that made the multitude of the stars," as the prophet says, "gives names to them all."[9] Concerning these names very many secret and cryptic statements are contained in the books which bear the name of Enoch.[10] But since these books do not appear to have any recognized authority with the Hebrews, we will for the present postpone citing examples from the things that are identified in them. Instead let us pursue our investigation of realities from the things that we have in hand, concerning which no doubts can arise.

---

[2]Sir 4:22. [3]Heb 8:5. [4]Heb 10:1. [5]Cf. Ex 3:8. [6]Cf. Deut 8:7. [7]Lat *Euaei*. [8]Heb 8:5. [9]Ps 147:4. [10]Cf. Enoch 69-82. This work is cited in Jude 14-16.

2.2. In the divine law, then, the land of Judea is described in the words of God, and it is said that this must be referred to an "image of heavenly things." Now in heaven, it is expressly declared by the apostle that there is a city of Jerusalem and a Mount Zion.[11] So it is logical that, just as round about the earthly Jerusalem there are situated also other cities and villages and various districts, so too that heavenly Jerusalem, in accordance with the image of earthly things, has also round about it other cities and villages and various districts. The people of God and the true Israel must one day be settled in these through the true Jesus—of whom that Jesus, the son of Nun, bore an image—and they will receive an inheritance by a distribution of an allotment, that is, in consideration of their merits.

So if the Lord now says that in the distribution of the land, the boundaries of this tribe, say, are such and so, but the boundaries of another are different, this owes perhaps to the fact that the merits of those who are to obtain the inheritance of the kingdom of heaven are diverse. This is why this distinction of boundaries is commanded to be carefully marked out with respect to these tribes as well. Thus we should know that these diversities of merits must be taken into account in every case.

For example, consider the person who has lived so negligently that, to be sure, for his faith he deserves to be reckoned among the sons of Israel, but for his negligent life and for the laxity of his conduct, he ought to be assigned to the tribe of Reuben or Gad or the half-tribe of Manasseh. He does not receive an allotment of his inheritance inside the Jordan but outside of it. But someone else, who by the improvement of his life and by the way of life he has purposed for himself, has rendered himself to be such a person that, for reasons known only to God, he deserves to be assigned to the tribe of Judah, or even to the very tribe of Benjamin, in which

Jerusalem itself and the temple of God and the altar stand. And one will be in this tribe, another in that.

And in this manner these things which are reported as written in the book of Numbers are a sort of shadow of the future allotment in heaven, at any rate for those who, through Jesus our Lord and Savior, as we have said, will receive the inheritance of the kingdom of heaven.

2.3. There, I believe, there will also be carefully maintained those privileges of the priests that are foreshadowed here. They are ordered to be separated off from the sons of Israel, in localities that are near the cities and adjoining the very walls.[12] There too, I believe, there will be those cities the pattern of which is here described, which the writer calls "cities of refuge."[13] Not every murderer may flee to these, but those who have committed manslaughter. For perhaps there are some sins which make us murderers, if we commit them willingly and on purpose. But there are others for which a certain place is decreed for us and prepared by God's command, if we commit them unawares. There, I believe, for a certain period, those of us who have committed involuntary sins must dwell; provided, that is, we are found clean and free from sins which have been committed deliberately. And this is why certain "cites of refuge" are separated off.

There are some who think that even the situation and grouping of particular stars can be termed and accounted a city in heaven. This is something on which I do not dare to speak definitively. For I see that all creation "has been made subject in hope because of him who subjected it."[14] And yet "it awaits freedom in the redemption of the sons of God."[15] Doubtless [it is waiting for] something more splendid and more lofty.

3.1. So if, as we said, "the law contains the shadow of the good things to come," and they who serve under the law serve the "copy and

---

[11]Cf. Heb 12:22. [12]Num 35:2. [13]Num 35:11. [14]Rom 8:20. [15]Rom 8:21.

shadow of heavenly things,"[16] and the contemplation of the realities will be considered "now through a mirror and in a riddle, but then face to face,"[17] I believe also that with respect to the manner of life[18] that we are now said to have "in heaven through outward form and in a riddle, but then face to face,"[19] those who will be deserving will have citizenship[20] in heaven. So if, by the logic of the realities and by fidelity to the promises, it is necessary that we be translated from earth to heaven, I think that it will not be apart from an allotment based on merits that our Lord Jesus will establish each one in these heavenly places, in this or that part and habitation of heaven.

3.2. But there are likewise great differences among the lands. For instance, [it is one thing] to dwell in fertile and abundant locales that overflow with goods, where there is a pleasant climate, humane education, and where liberal institutions are not lacking. But it is a far different matter to dwell in unfertile locales and in squalid regions where there is a lack of things, or in locales that are scorched by heat, or are frozen because of cold and frost; or, indeed, in locales where there are no laws, but a monstrous and savage barbarism, where wars never cease and there is never calm.

Now these things are decreed to each one not without a certain hidden dispensation of God and justice of his judgment: so also in these locales there will be something similar, so that in no one would the "shadow of the heavenly things" on earth be considered absolutely pointless. So then, there as well, as we said, there will be a "city of refuge," and there will be another in the desert, just as Bosor is said to be a city in the desert in the inheritance of Reuben.[21]

4.1. Moreover, the following inference must no less be maintained, that God, at the beginning of the world, "when he dispersed the sons of Adam, appointed the boundaries of the nations according to the number of the angels of God," or, as we read in other copies, "according to the number of the sons of Israel."[22] And thus the sons of that Adam were dispersed, just as their merits or a consideration of Adam himself demanded. What will we say of the future, when the divine dignity begins not to disperse, but to dispense the sons of the last Adam, who was made not into "living soul,"[23] but into a "life-giving spirit,"[24] not at the beginning, but at the end of the world? And not as those "who all died in Adam," but as those "who are all made alive in Christ"?[25] Doubtless there will be a dividing up and distribution, which must be requited not merely in view of the merits of those who are being managed, but also in consideration of the last Adam, in whom all are said to be made alive.

4.2. But who among us is of the quality that he merits coming to this kind of distribution and to that allotment of the heavenly inheritance? Who will be so blessed that his allotment will come in Jerusalem, that he would be where the temple of God is, or rather, that he would himself be the temple of God?[26] Who is so blessed that he would celebrate feast days where the divine altar smells of perpetual fires? Who is so blessed that he places his own sacrifice and the sweet-smelling incense on that fire of which the Savior said: "I have come to cast fire on the earth"?[27] Who is so blessed that he always celebrates the Passover there, "in the place that the Lord his God has chosen,"[28] and there carries out the day of Pentecost and the feast of propitiation and the solemnity of tabernacles, not only through a shadow, but through the very form and truth of the realities?

4.3. Which of us will be considered worthy of selection for such a blessed allotment, when God begins to divide the sons of the last Adam, not as to the one to whom he says: "You will have authority over five cities,"[29] or to whom he

---

[16]Heb 8:5. [17]1 Cor 13:12. [18]Lat *conversatio*. [19]Cf. Phil 3:20. [20]Lat *conversatio*. [21]Cf. Josh 20:8; RSV *Bezer*. [22]Deut 32:8. [23]Cf. Gen 2:7. [24]1 Cor 15:45. [25]Cf. 1 Cor 15:22. [26]Cf. 1 Cor 3:16. [27]Lk 12:49. [28]Cf. Deut 12:25. [29]Lk 19:19.

says: "You will have authority over ten cities";[30] nor to whom he says: "Enter into the joy of your Lord";[31] but to whom he says: "You also sit with me on twelve thrones, you yourselves even judging the twelve tribes of Israel"?[32] Of them he says: "Father, I want that where I am, they too may be with me";[33] I want them likewise to be kings, so that I may be "King of kings";[34] I also want them to have lordship, so that I may be "Lord of lords."[35]

Blessed are those who will reach this summit of blessedness; blessed are those who have climbed to these heights of merits, and blessed is our God, who has promised these things "to those who love him."[36] These are the ones who are truly numbered by God in the sacred Numbers, or rather, they themselves are those whose "hairs of their head have been numbered,"[37] by Jesus Christ our Lord, "to whom is the glory and the power in the ages of ages. Amen."[38]

---

[30]Lk 19:17. [31]Mt 25:23. [32]Mt 19:28. [33]Jn 17:24. [34]Cf. Rev 19:16. [35]Cf. Rev 19:16. [36]Cf. 1 Cor 2:9. [37]Mt 10:30. [38]1 Pet 4:11.

Subject Index

Aaron, 4, 6, 11, 14-18, 23-27, 32, 35-45, 58, 59, 81, 85, 117, 131, 137, 163, 169, 172-74

Adamantius, xxv, xxvi, 1, 63

Alaric, xxvii, 1

almond(s), 42-43

alphabet, 7, 13

altar, 12, 15, 17, 19, 29, 35-40, 47, 48, 52, 53, 68, 85, 91, 97, 102, 118, 139, 148, 161, 185, 186

Anderson, Gary, 47

angel(s), 11, 19, 20, 31, 39, 40, 45, 54-58, 62, 76, 79, 80, 82-84, 87, 89, 94, 106, 108, 112, 121, 123, 128-30, 140, 141, 143, 144, 146, 147, 149, 153, 158, 162, 178, 180, 186

antiphrasis, 98

archangel(s), 56

ark, 133

Assyrian, 3, 55, 120, 121

Augustine, St., 1, 2, 13, 49

Babylon(ians), 55, 56, 78, 86, 113, 125, 154, 155, 179

Baehrens, xxxi, 124

Balaam, 71-95, 99-116, 119-24, 130, 155

Balak, 74, 75, 77, 80-87, 91, 92, 95, 99, 101, 102, 110-12, 122, 123

Balthasar, Hans Urs von, xxi, xxxii, 151, 155

baptism, xix, xxv, xxix, 9, 17, 22, 26, 47, 54, 66, 68, 70, 90, 114, 138, 164

baptismal liturgy, 17, 70

Barnabas, Epistle of, 25

Basilides, 36, 65

Benedict XVI, Pope, xxiv

Beyer Moser, M., xxvi

blood, 24, 26, 30, 31, 47, 48, 64, 74, 75, 88, 92,

100-102, 105, 137, 138, 140, 146, 148, 150, 151, 159, 160

Borret, M., xxxii

Brenton, Sir Lancelot, xxxii

bronze/brass, 35-37, 112, 159

Brown, Raymond E., xxxi

Buchheit, V., xxvi

Bultmann, Rudolf, xxix

Caleb, 30, 37, 134, 163

Cassiodorus, xxv, 2

catechumen, xix, 9

Catholic, 36, 170

censer, 35-40

census, 4, 13

centurion, 160, 162

cherubim, 17, 19, 48, 49

church, 6, 8, 11, 15, 21, 24-26, 35, 36, 45, 46, 51-57, 59, 66, 71-73, 79, 89, 107, 108, 120, 123, 124, 128, 130, 137, 142, 144, 152, 153, 157, 167, 184

Cicero, 49

Clark, E., xxiv

Clement of Alexandria, 3, 18, 36, 49, 133, 134

Clement of Rome, xxv, 154

circumcision, 17, 24, 42, 50, 51, 53, 60, 90, 131

consubstantiality, xxvi, 63

continence, 2, 7, 54, 107

cross, 12, 42, 48, 81, 100, 109, 115, 152, 164, 175

Crouzel, H., xx, xxiv, xxix

Cyprian, 1

Daly, Robert, 47

D'Ambrosio, M., xxxi

Daniélou, Jean, xxiv, xxxi, 46, 55, 56

darkness, 20, 27, 30, 31, 37, 95, 106, 118, 121, 126, 164, 170, 174, 175

Decius, emperor, xxi

Demetrius, bishop, xix, xx

demon(s), xxiii, 12, 20, 23,

30, 31, 34, 46, 58, 71, 75-79, 83, 85, 97-99, 102, 103, 109, 110, 113, 115, 121, 123, 124-29, 140, 159, 160, 171, 175, 176

Denzinger, H., xxiii

devil, xxi, 9, 20, 37, 40, 42, 47, 68-72, 78, 81, 83, 96, 109, 115, 121-24, 128, 129, 131, 155, 159, 161, 170, 176, 181. *See also* Satan

Dialogue of Adamantius, xxii, xxv, xxvi, 63

dictation, 2, 163

Dolan, J., xxiv

Donatus, 1

donkey, 71, 74, 79, 80, 84, 118

Doutreleau, L., xxxii, 49, 60

Dunkle, B., 49

East, 75, 78, 86, 87, 90, 113, 114, 183

eleven, 149, 178

Enoch, book of, xxviii, 182, 184

Erasmus, xxi, xxiv, 9

Eucharist, 17, 101

Eusebius, xix, xx, xxiii, xxv, 1

faith, 3, 9, 11, 24, 25, 29-32, 34, 36-38, 44, 46, 47, 50, 54, 56, 59, 63, 65-71, 79, 84, 85, 89-92, 99-103, 109, 115, 120, 123, 124, 133, 138-40, 143, 144, 146, 154, 160, 161, 165, 166, 170-74, 185

fast, 19, 93, 157

Fifth Ecumenical Council, xxi, xxiii

fifty/fiftieth, 14, 18, 19, 133, 157, 158

fire, 1, 11, 35, 36, 39, 40, 65, 72, 73, 82, 88, 97, 98, 106, 121, 123, 142,

156, 157, 159, 172, 175, 181, 186

first fruits, 49, 52-62, 141, 145

foreknowledge/foreknow, 38, 47, 83, 85, 96, 97, 99

forgiveness/pardon, 18, 19, 35, 47, 118, 148

free will/choice, 67, 78, 82, 129, 133, 134, 152

Gabriel, angel, 76

Gehenna, 65, 97, 115, 121, 156, 163

Gesenius, 150

Godin, A., xxiv

gold, 15, 36, 40, 41, 49, 50, 82, 96, 110, 112, 156, 158-62, 181

goths, 1

grace, 2, 9, 12, 16, 19, 27, 37, 41, 44, 54, 57, 74, 90, 91, 108, 120, 122, 137, 140, 145, 164, 166, 178

Gregory of Nazianzus, xxv

Gregory Thaumaturgus, xx

Hammond, C., xxi, xxvi, xxvii, 2

Hanson, R., xxix, xxxi

Harnack, Adolf von, 107

hearer, 4, 9, 11, 19, 20, 26, 27, 54, 58, 85, 98, 106, 127, 128, 148, 162, 163, 169, 183, 184

hēgemonikos, 3

Heither, Theresia, 139

heretic(s), xxiii, xxv, xxvi, xxxi, 1, 25, 36, 39, 65, 120, 123

Hexapla, xxi, 60

Hilary, 13

Hippocrates, 13

Hippolytus, xx, 70

Holy Spirit, 2-5, 9, 21-27, 41, 49, 53, 60, 63, 65, 66, 68, 76, 90, 99, 101, 106, 111, 114, 115, 125,

129, 138-40, 143-45,
162-64, 169, 171-73,
178, 181, 182
homothymadon, 121
honey, 5, 37, 50, 132, 146,
165, 167
idol/idolatry, 45, 85,
87, 92, 98, 100, 112,
120-30, 171, 175
Ignatius of Antioch, xix,
123
incense, 17, 19, 35, 36, 39,
40, 48, 141, 142, 186
inspiration, 56, 101, 113,
125, 145, 157, 162,
164, 183
Irenaeus, 24, 25, 36, 65
iron, 67, 158, 159
Jerome, xx, xxi, xxii, xxiv,
xxv, 1, 2, 71, 97, 131,
176
Jerusalem, 11, 31, 51, 54,
79, 87, 89, 94, 97, 107,
112, 129, 140, 141, 167,
185, 186
Jezebel, 124
Josephus, 22, 99
Julia Mammaea, xxi
Justin Martyr, 109
Justinian, emperor, xxiii,
xxiv
Kalvesmaki, Joel, 13
Kannengieser, C., 63
Korah, 35, 36, 117
law of nature, 49
Ledegang, F., xxxii, 4, 44,
70, 100
Leonides, xix
leprosy, 23-29
Lienhard, J., xxx
light, 17, 19-21, 37, 43, 62,
65, 82, 87, 100, 106,
121, 130, 136, 142,
144, 146, 164, 170,
172-75, 178, 179
Lubac, Henri de, xxii-
xxxii, 5, 22, 156
Lucifer, 56, 87
magi/magic/magician, 70,
74-79, 83, 85, 90, 91,
103, 113, 114, 126
manna, 3, 9, 17, 26, 49, 81,
108, 171, 174

Marcion, xxx, 25, 26, 36,
39, 65, 67, 119, 170
Martens, Peter, xxxi
Martin, Jay, 151
martyrs/martyrdom,
xix-xxiii, 1, 47, 48, 54,
85, 107
McGuckin, John, xx, xxviii
McKenzie, J., xxix
Melania, xxv, 2
merit (deserve), 3, 14, 26,
28, 30, 33, 47, 53, 54,
55, 57, 58, 60, 61, 66,
67, 68, 70, 72, 73, 82,
85, 86, 88, 92, 95, 101,
108, 110, 115, 120,
125, 127, 132, 133,
134, 136, 144, 145,
151, 154, 156, 159,
160, 178, 183, 185,
186, 187
Messina, xxvi, 1
Methodius, xxiii
Metzger, Bruce, 178
Michael, angel, 76, 83
Miriam, 23-29, 86
Moab, 67, 68, 72,74-77, 86,
87, 91, 111, 114, 115,
122, 123, 127, 183
Murphy, F., xxiv
Nautin, Pierre, 76
Nazarene, 3, 151, 152
New Testament, 39, 49,
51, 81, 178, 182
Nicaea, xix, xxv, xxvi,
63
Noah's ark, shape of, 133
Og, 73, 163
Old Testament, transla-
tor's introduction, 14,
36, 39, 50, 119, 148,
164
Origen's works
Against Celsus, xxi;
xxii; xxix; 7.22
(126)
*Commentary
on John*, xxii;
1.35(40).260 (55);
2.31(25).189 (55);
20.4.25-26 (115);
32.22(14).291 (80)
Commentary on Mat-

thew, xxii; 14.21
(33); 14.22 (80)
*Commentary on
Romans*, xxii;
2.13.21 (25); 3.8
(49); 5.7.8 (68);
5.9 (100); 7.14.2
(55); 7.16.1-4 (41);
8.12.6 (55); 9.1.1
(139); 10.31 (33)
*Commentary on Song
of Songs*, xxii; xxii;
1.4 (68); 2 (49);
2.1 (24)
*Commentary Series
on Matthew*, xxii;
53 (33); 101 (33)
*Dialogue with Hera-
clides*, xxi; xxiii; 3
Homilies on Exodus,
xxii; 1.5 (55); 3.3
(109); 7.1 (41); 8.1
(109); 9.3 (18); 9.6
(36); 12.2 (77);
13.3 (77)
Homilies on Ezekiel,
xxii; 1.2 (34); 1.5.2
(33); 1.15 (49); 2.3
(104); 3.8 (150);
4.8 (xix); 8.3 (124)
Homilies on Genesis,
xxii; 1.7 (68); 2.1
(xxiii, 133); 2.2
(124); 2.5 (18);
5.4 (142); 8 (xxix);
10.1 (77); 11.3
(77); 13.2 (121);
15.3 (55); 16.6
(18, 55)
Homilies on Jeremiah,
1.15-16 (73); 18.6
(94); 19.14 (120)
Homilies on Joshua,
xxii; 1.7 (77); 1.9.3
(4); 12.1 (134);
15.1 (31); 15.3
(126); 15.5 (128)
Homilies on Judges,
xxii; 5.2 (xxix); 7.2
(100); 7.12 (xix);
8.5 (100)
*Homilies on Leviti-
cus*, xxii; 2.2 (124);

2.4 (47); 3.7 (77);
4.6 (21); 7.5 (73);
8.4 (25); 9.1 (48);
13.4 (18); 15.3
(132)
Homilies on Luke,
xxii; 35 (55); 35.3
(33); 4.2 (59)
*Homilies on Song of
Songs*, xxii; 1.6
(24); (124)
On First Principles,
xxi; xxii; xxiii; xxv;
3; 33; 34; 55; 60;
80; 134
On Prayer, xxii; xxiii;
48; 142
Palladius, xxv, 2
Pamphilus, xx-xxiii, xxiv
Passover, 17, 18, 50, 60,
107, 141, 144, 146, 148,
174, 175, 186
pedagogue, 5, 128
Pelagius, 140
persecution, 37-39, 47,
71, 124
Pharaoh, 3, 28, 55, 75, 81,
155, 170, 171, 177
Philo, xxviii, 18, 21, 22,
40, 42, 49, 64, 69, 78,
86, 87, 99, 105, 121,
127, 135, 150, 164, 176
philosophy, xix, 3, 46, 49,
59, 70, 113, 126, 127
Phinehas, 87, 88, 131
Pinianus, 2
prayer/pray, 2, 6, 9, 17, 19,
23, 29, 32, 35, 38, 39,
47, 48, 54, 61, 62, 71,
75, 76, 83, 101, 107,
116, 119, 122, 131,
134, 136-39, 141, 142,
150, 152, 154, 157, 163,
164, 167
Prayer of Joseph, 107
Procopius, 24
progress, 2, 4, 11, 29, 44,
54, 56, 58, 68, 69, 87,
105-7, 140, 150, 160,
166, 171-83
propitiation/propitiatory,
17, 19, 38, 40, 48, 131,
146, 148, 149, 160,

162, 186

punishment, 9, 26, 33, 34, 37, 42, 43, 45, 93, 97, 123, 130, 175-77

Raphael, angel, 76, 83

renunciation of the devil, 70

rest, 5, 19, 21-24, 44, 62, 95, 101, 106, 108, 109, 138, 139, 143, 163, 171, 178, 182

Reuben, 4, 10, 11, 134, 162-65, 171, 185, 186

Rhegium, 1

rod, 35, 41-44, 117

Rombs, R. xxiii

Runia, D., xxviii

sacrament, 15, 101, 123, 129, 144, 172

Satan, 32, 70, 71, 120, 121, 180. *See also* devil

renunciation of, 70

Scheck, Thomas, xxiii, 67

serpent/snake, 31, 71, 74, 75, 88, 99, 102, 104, 119, 121, 124, 169

Severus, emperor, xix, xxi

Shepherd of Hermas, 33, 83

Sihon, 69-74, 163

silver, 36, 41, 82, 110, 112, 156, 158, 159, 161

spies/explore, 30, 32, 163

sprout, 35, 41-44

stage(s)/mansion(s), 4, 68, 106, 107, 108, 126, 132, 150, 152, 159, 164, 168-83

star, 3, 8, 63, 69, 78, 87, 89, 90, 111, 114, 115, 121, 133, 134, 151, 184, 185

Stoics, 3, 49

teacher/doctor, 6, 11, 17, 21, 31, 46, 54, 55, 59, 76, 85, 102, 103, 114, 124, 130, 142, 147

temple(s), 13, 19, 23, 29, 47, 70, 97, 109, 124, 126, 127, 140, 142, 148, 151, 185, 186

temptation, 10, 172, 177, 178, 180-82

Tertullian, 67

tetragrammaton, 80

Thegri, 83

Thomas Aquinas, St., 49

Tollinton, R., xxxii

tribunes, 160, 162

Trinity, xxiii, xxvi, 5, 13, 49, 60, 63, 76, 101, 106, 129, 133, 140, 144, 164

truth, 5, 17, 24, 26, 30, 36, 40, 42, 48-51, 55, 56, 60, 63, 67, 70, 73, 81, 88, 101, 109, 110, 112, 116, 126, 127, 136, 142, 144, 151, 154, 156, 157, 167, 174, 175, 182, 183, 186

Twelve, 10, 13, 32, 41, 88, 134, 149, 154, 155, 157, 160, 165, 177, 178, 187

Ursacius, xxvi, 1

Valentinus/Valentinians, 65, 67

Villegas, G., xxix

virgins, 7, 54, 124, 152, 171

widowhood, 54

Williams, R., xxvi

Wind, E., 133

wisdom, 3, 8, 15, 17, 21, 22, 24, 41, 42, 43, 50, 55, 61, 63, 64, 66, 69, 80, 83, 90, 105, 106, 108, 109, 110, 112, 113, 126, 132, 137, 142, 144, 148, 150, 158, 162, 167, 168, 173, 180, 183, 184

works, 6, 8, 14, 16-19, 33, 34, 40, 41, 44, 48, 59, 70, 74, 75, 78, 82, 83, 87, 88, 90, 93, 97, 98, 105, 112, 125, 128, 135, 136, 142, 143, 152, 162, 170, 173-75

Zelophehad (Salphaat), 134-36

Zippor, 74, 77, 80, 91

Zipporah, 64

Scripture Index

Genesis
1:1, *166*
1:1–2:3, *29*
1:7, *177*
1:9-10, *166*
2:7, *186*
3:15, *71, 159*
3:22, *106*
5:3, *144*
6:15, *133*
9:6, *64*
13:13, *37*
14:1, *116*
14:2, *116*
14:7, *116, 117*
14:8-9, *116*
14:10, *176*
16:13-14, *62*
16:15, *51*
17:5, *155*
17:9-14, *50*
17:15, *155*
18:32, *38*
21:3, *51*
21:25, *62*
24:13-15, *62*
24:42-46, *62*
25:30, *115*
26:15, *42, 64*
26:17-22, *62*
26:18, *42*
26:22, *42*
27:1-29, *10*
27:4, *77*
29:3-12, *64*
29:34, *10*
30:22, *12*
30:24, *155*
32:24, *72, 99*
32:28, *72, 95*
32:30, *55*
35:10, *55, 155*
35:23, *165*
35:26, *165*
37:18-36, *81*
37:28, *81*
41:25-57, *81*
41:45, *155*
41:47-49, *81*

41:51, *165*
46:4, *173*
48:9, *77*
49:4, *165*

Exodus
1:14, *170*
2:12, *25*
2:23, *170*
3:2, *178*
3:7, *170*
3:8, *184*
7–11, *81*
7:10, *74*
7:12, *75*
7:20, *74*
7:21, *75*
7:22, *75*
8:18, *75*
12:3, *17*
12:5, *50, 150*
12:6, *174*
12:8, *17, 177*
12:11, *107*
12:17, *107*
12:18, *174*
12:23, *39, 40*
12:29, *12, 174*
13:3, *175*
13:21, *172*
14:6-28, *3*
14:22, *177*
14:31, *177*
15:1, *177*
16:13-36, *81*
16:19-20, *9*
17:6, *4, 81*
17:8-13, *3, 119*
17:11, *75*
17:16, *118*
19:2-3, *101*
20:5, *44*
20:6, *44*
20:24, *48*
23:17, *59*
25:10-30, *17*
25:17, *19*
25:17-18, *48*
25:18, *19*

25:22, *19*
25:40, *107*
26:33-34, *16*
27:1, *48*
31:1-6, *112*
31:18, *49*
32:4-5, *10*
32:27-29, *10*
33:3-4, *167*
33:11, *137*
35:30-35, *112*
36:1, *112*

Leviticus
1:1, *4*
19:18, *39*
20:7, *60*
23:15, *18*
25:10, *18*
26:8, *154*

Numbers
1:1-4, *2*
1:1-54, *2*
1:3, *105*
1:18, *105*
1:20, *105, 132*
2:1-2, *10*
2:1-34, *6*
2:2, *39*
2:3, *5*
2:3-9, *11*
2:18-24, *11*
2:32, *4, 6*
3:3, *14*
3:4, *14*
3:5-39, *9*
3:6-9, *14*
3:33-34, *14*
3:39, *13*
3:39–4:49, *13*
3:43, *13*
4:1-49, *16*
4:2, *14*
4:4, *14, 15*
4:5, *15, 19*
4:5-6, *16*
4:5-15, *19*
4:7, *14, 15, 19*

4:9, *14, 15, 19*
4:11, *15*
4:12, *15*
4:13, *15*
4:14, *15*
4:15, *15*
4:18, *15*
4:20, *16*
4:24-28, *14*
4:29-33, *14*
4:31-32, *20*
4:47, *18*
7:3, *15*
7:7-8, *15*
7:7-9, *16*
7:9, *15, 17*
8:24-25, *18*
9:1-2, *175*
11:16-17, *20*
11:16-25, *20*
11:24, *21*
11:25, *21*
12:1, *20, 24, 25*
12:1-15, *20*
12:4-15, *23*
12:9, *27*
12:10, *24, 27*
12:12, *28*
12:14, *24, 25*
12:15, *25*
13:3-4, *32*
13:18-33, *24*
13:26, *32*
13:31-33, *37*
14:1-4, *32*
14:1-8, *24*
14:1-38, *32*
14:6-7, *32*
14:6-9, *30, 37*
14:7, *30, 165*
14:10, *32, 37*
14:11, *137*
14:22, *33*
14:23, *33*
14:29, *33, 122*
14:31-33, *33*
14:32, *122*
14:34, *43*
16:36, *35*

16:36-40, *36*
16:38, *35, 36*
17:1, *35*
18:1, *47*
18:1-7, *44*
18:3-32, *49*
18:8-19, *49*
18:8-32, *49*
18:10, *56*
18:20, *132, 133*
18:24, *56*
20:17, *10*
21:2, *21*
21:7, *35*
21:16-23, *62*
21:17, *64*
21:18, *64*
21:21, *69*
21:21-22, *73*
21:24-35, *71*
21:28, *72*
21:33, *73*
22:1-14, *71*
22:5, *74*
22:5-6, *81*
22:6, *77, 83*
22:8, *74, 77*
22:9, *80*
22:12, *74, 83*
22:15, *74*
22:15-28, *79*
22:18, *83*
22:20, *83*
22:22, *84*
22:23-30, *80*
22:24, *84*
22:25, *84*
22:28, *84*
22:31-41, *85*
22:38, *83*
23:1-10, *85*
23:1-24, *91*
23:5, *78, 85, 86*
23:7, *86, 113*
23:9, *89*
23:11-24, *91*
23:16, *85*
23:18-24, *91*
23:25-30, *101*

24:1-9, *101*
24:2, *85, 86*
24:3-4, *103*
24:5, *105*
24:6, *108*
24:10-19, *110*
24:13, *110*
24:15-16, *119*
24:16-19, *85*
24:17, *78*
24:18, *111*
24:20-24, *116*
24:21, *120*
24:21-22, *120*
24:22, *120*
25:1, *126*
25:1-3, *112*
25:1-10, *122*
25:1-18, *122*
25:2-3, *126, 127*
25:6-8, *88, 131*
26:51, *74*
26:59, *14*
26:61, *36*
27:1, *134*
27:1-23, *134*
27:3, *135*
27:5, *135*
27:8-10, *136*
27:13, *136*
28–30, *147*
28:1–29:39, *139*
28:2, *161*
28:6, *141*
28:16-17, *107*
28:17, *144*
28:19-20, *148*
28:26, *145*
29:2-4, *148*
29:7, *146*
29:12-38, *149*
30:2, *152*
30:3, *152*
30:3-5, *152*
30:7, *152*
31–32, *160*
31:1-54, *153*
31:6-8, *88*
31:8, *155, 156*
31:11-12, *156*
31:16, *122*
31:21, *159*
31:22-23, *157*

31:23, *157*
31:27, *157*
31:28, *157*
31:28-30, *19, 157*
31:30, *157*
31:32-40, *157*
31:49, *161*
32:1, *163*
32:8-10, *163*
32:12, *163*
32:19, *163*
32:20-22, *163*
32:22, *163*
32:26, *163*
32:27, *163*
32:28, *163*
32:29, *163*
32:32, *163*
32:33, *134, 163*
33:1, *170, 173*
33:1-49, *168*
33:3, *174*
33:5, *174*
33:9, *177*
33:12, *179*
34–35, *183*
34:14, *134*

Deuteronomy
1:32-33, *172*
1:39, *33*
7:9, *44*
8:7, *184*
12:25, *186*
18:14-16, *98*
24:1-4, *102*
25:5-10, *29*
30:15, *42*
32:9, *56, 89, 98*
32:39, *143*

Joshua
1:6, *163*
1:7, *137*
3:15-16, *138*
4:10-11, *138*
5:6, *132*
9:1-2, *31*
10:23-24, *31*
12:24, *167*
14:4, *133*
14:13, *134*

15:5, *128*
17:5-6, *171*
18:7, *134*
18:28, *31*
20:8, *186*
23:4, *163*

Judges
3:10, *86*
6:34, *86*
7, *100*
11:29, *86*
11:31, *151*
14:19, *86*
15:14, *86*
16:15-17, *3*

1 Samuel
2:6, *122*
2:25, *45*
3:1, *86*
5:7–6:3, *96*
6:7-9, *96*
15:10, *86*
16:13, *86*
19:20, *86*
19:23, *86*
30:5, *119*
30:17, *119*

2 Samuel
5:3, *119*
5:6-7, *31*
24:1-17, *90*

1 Kings
3:16-28, *23*
4:25, *139*
4:29, *127*
4:31, *127*
6:15, *23*
10:24, *127*
11:1, *23, 127*
11:2, *127*
11:7, *23*
11:7-8, *127*
13:1-6, *23*
13:17-24, *23*
21:1-16, *124*
21:25-26, *124*

2 Kings
21:6, *97*

Job
3:1, *125*
38:36, *112*
39:9-12, *95*

Psalms
1–15, *1*
1:2, *158*
12:6, *36*
27:13, *132*
37, *33*
37:35, *108*
42:1-2, *152*
46:4, *164*
50:20, *176*
68:15, *181*
68:18, *115*
72:20, *159*
78:25, *108*
80:10, *108*
81:12, *85*
86:5, *94*
87:1, *87*
91:5, *20*
91:6, *20*
91:12, *20*
101:5, *176*
121:1, *86*
141:1-2, *142*
142:5, *166*
145:8, *94*

Proverbs
4:25, *156*
9:9, *183*
16:24, *182*
22:20, *4*
22:20-21, *42*

Ecclesiastes
1:2, *61*

Song of Solomon
6:11, *42*

Isaiah
1:1, *86*
1:4, *153*
1:9, *141*
6:9-10, *109*
9:6, *170*
10:12, *55*

10:12-13, *55*
13:1, *86*
14:12, *32*
29:4, *98*
45:22, *35*
60:1-2, *146*
60:19, *146*
62:11, *90*

Jeremiah
1:1, *42*
1:2, *86*
1:11, *42*
1:13, *42*
3:19, *165*
7:22, *102*
17:10, *5*
18, *94*
19, *120*
20:14, *125*
51:8, *154*

Lamentations
3:31, *116*
4:2, *41*

Ezekiel
1:3, *86*
13:20, *76*
16:53, *89*
16:55, *89*
20:6, *165*
28:15, *80, 82*
36:21, *7*

Daniel
1:1, *55*
1:7, *156*
1:17-20, *113*
1:20, *78*
2:2, *78*
4:7, *78*
5:7, *78*
7:1-2, *103*
7:9, *179*
10:13, *76*
10:21, *83*
12:1, *83*

Hosea
1:1, *86*
11:1, *109*

Joel
1:1, *86*
2:13, *94*

Obadiah
1:1, *86*

Jonah
1:1, *86*
2:10, *93*
3:4, *93*

Micah
1:1, *86*
6:8, *142*

Nahum
1:1, *86*

Habakkuk
1:1, *86*

Zephaniah
1:1, 86

Haggai
1:1, 86

Zechariah
1:1, *86*
2:1-2, *112*
9:1, *86*

Malachi
1:1, *86*

Matthew
2:2, *78, 79, 90*
2:8, *79*
2:11, *79, 90*
2:15, *109*
3:1-7, *38*
4:18-22, *107*
5:5, *155, 166*
5:6, *19*
5:8, *132, 144*
5:9-10, *37*
5:12, *61*
5:17, *51*
5:18-19, *181*
5:20, *53*
5:28, *52*
5:29-30, *156*

5:44, *38, 39*
5:45, *52*
6:6, *134*
6:22, *17*
6:31, *6*
6:33, *154*
6:34, *6*
7:6, *115*
7:7, *169*
7:12, *72, 88*
7:13, *128, 133*
7:14, *133*
7:23, *40*
8:21, *129*
8:22, *175*
8:29, *78*
9:34, *76*
10:17, *47*
10:28, *115*
10:37, *10*
10:38, *152*
11:12, *30*
11:27, *164*
11:30, *159*
12:32, *123*
12:36-37, *57*
12:46, *21*
13:3, *105*
13:8, *145, 166*
13:13, *139*
13:16, *139*
13:35, *72*
13:36, *21*
13:38, *53*
14, *33, 80*
15:17, *58*
16:8, *109*
16:24, *175*
17:1-3, *26*
17:3, *29*
17:5, *27*
18:10, *128*
19:5-6, *51, 102*
19:8, *94, 102*
19:21, *175*
21:2-7, *79*
22:3, *129*
22:9, *129*
24:24, *97*
25:34, *67, 81*
25:41, *40*
26:24, *154*
26:52, *131*

26:61, *109*
28:19, *63, 139*

Mark
1:12-13, *108*
3:14, *178*
3:22, *76*
5:9, *31*
7:6-7, *84*
9:42, *154*
9:42-47, *156*
9:43-44, *156*
14:21, *154*

Luke
1:26, *76*
1:67, *53*
2:37, *19*
7:26, *148*
7:41, *18*
8:31, *78*
9:3-6, *52*
9:24, *116*
10:1, *178*
10:17-20, *100*
11:19, *76*
12:5, *121*
13:23, *3*
13:27, *40*
14:10, *107*
14:21-23, *129*
14:32, *74*
15:5, *121*
15:13-15, *116*
16:19-25, *177*
16:22, *164*
16:25, *33*
18:8, *38*
19:16-18, *68*
20:35, *47*
21:12, *47*
22:29, *81*
22:36, *131*
22:46, *131*
23:43, *164*
35, *33, 55*

John
1:1, *126, 149,
171*
1:9, *171, 172*
1:14, *126, 165, 171,
179*

1:17, *4, 139*
1:18, *129, 164*
1:29, *149, 150*
1:33, *138*
2:19, *109*
2:20, *13*
2:21, *109*
3:5, *26*
4:6, *62*
4:6-26, *63*
4:10, *64*
4:10-11, *67*
4:13-14, *63*
5:22, *33, 132*
5:24, *121*
6:51, *58*
6:52-53, *100*
6:53-55, *101*
6:58, *58*
6:70, *178*
7:23, *50*
7:38, *106*
7:52, *84*
8:11, *34*
8:12, *146*
9:35-41, *84*
10:3, *132*
10:9, *160, 170*
10:16, *24*
12:24, *141*
14:2, *4, 68, 126,
132, 159, 164,
172, 173*
14:6, *110, 126*
14:12, *31*
14:30, *71*
15:4, *153*

Acts
2:40, *11*
8:13, *9*
8:18-19, *9*
8:32, *148*
10:1-48, *53*
10:44, *53*
10:47, *9*
12:13, *55*
12:15, *55*
16:6, *129*
18:3, *107*
21:11-12, *129*
21:25, *53, 90*
26:18, *121*

Romans
1:1, *107*
1:3-4, *60*
1:5, *66*
1:17, *86*
1:20-21, *67*
1:24, *85*
1:26, *85*
1:28, *85*
2:17-28, *50*
2:26-27, *17*
2:28, *53*
2:28-29, *51, 60*
2:29, *24, 60*
3:9, *22, 119*
3:12, *38*
3:25, *48*
5:1, *37*
6:2-4, *179*
6:4, *180*
6:12, *67*
6:13, *67*
6:16, *67*
6:19, *67*
7:4, *179*
7:14, *17*
7:22, *60, 87*
8:2, *4, 58*
8:4-5, *28*
8:5-6, *104*
8:17, *26*
8:28, *82*
8:34, *35*
8:36, *148*
9:4-5, *88*
9:5, *108*
9:19, *41*
9:20-23, *82*
9:22, *83, 125*
9:24, *33*
9:29, *141*
10:4, *138*
11:4, *10*
11:17-18, *89*
11:25, *24, 90,
103*
11:26, *89*
11:32, *24*
13:14, *158*
14:2, *144, 169*
14:13, *176*
15:4, *8, 170*
15:6, *170*

15:13, *61*
15:16, *31*

1 Corinthians
1:24, *158*
1:30, *126*
2:6, *112*
2:6-7, *21*
2:9, *164, 187*
2:10, *111*
2:12, *164*
2:13, *136*
2:14, *16, 144*
2:15, *178, 179*
3:2, *144, 168*
3:16, *124, 140, 186*
4:1, *16*
5:5, *121*
5:7, *17*
5:8, *17, 145*
5:10, *74*
6:15, *124*
7:28, *23*
8:7, *45*
9:5-14, *52*
9:9, *103*
9:10, *103*
9:13, *52*
9:14, *52*
9:19, *152*
9:22, *44*
10:1, *81*
10:3, *58, 81*
10:4, *4, 81*
10:5, *33, 131, 172, 174*
10:18, *84*
11:1, *151*
11:3, *119*
13:2-3, *85*
13:11, *3, 5*
13:12, *5, 16, 78, 132*
15:5, *178*
15:10, *134*
15:19-20, *81*
15:20, *53, 58*
15:22, *186*
15:23, *4, 119*

15:24, *183*
15:25-27, *108*
15:44-45, *150*

2 Corinthians
3:6, *107*
3:14, *106, 148*
3:14-16, *164*
3:15, *103*
3:15-17, *103*
3:16, *13, 14, 27, 38*
3:18, *16*
4:6, *24*
4:16, *150*
10:5, *73*
11:23-26, *38*
11:25, *95*
12:4, *112*

Galatians
1:5, *160*
3:22, *119*
3:24, *5*
4:2, *54, 153*
4:3, *148*
4:4, *114*
4:9, *148*
5:6, *90*
5:9, *145*
5:17, *115, 139*
5:22, *145*
5:22-23, *124*

Ephesians
1:18, *17, 128*
3:1, *115*
4:4, *158*
4:8, *115*
4:8-10, *171*
4:13, *160, 169*
4:14, *108*
4:22, *39*
4:24, *39*
5:2, *57*
6:12, *31, 99, 115, 119, 167*
6:14, *31, 174*
6:14-17, *123, 155*

6:16, *31, 83*
6:16-17, *73*
6:17, *31, 131*
6:19, *164*

Philippians
2:15-16, *82*
3:13, *106, 107*
3:19, *6*
3:20, *32, 89, 186*
4:4, *61*

Colossians
1:16, *31*
1:18, *53, 81*
1:24, *47*
2:3, *41*
2:8, *148*
2:15, *81, 115*
2:16, *24, 53*
2:16-17, *17*
2:18, *104*
2:20, *148*
3:1, *89*
3:1-2, *32, 106, 146*
3:5, *68*
3:11, *143*

1 Thessalonians
5:10, *68*

2 Thessalonians
2:7, *128*
2:9, *97*

1 Timothy
1:20, *120, 121*
2:1, *62*
2:8, *161*
2:14, *124*
2:15, *124, 125*
3:13, *4*
5:17-18, *52*

2 Timothy
1:11, *31*
1:15, *120*
2:4, *6*
2:5, *81*

2:11, *68*
2:20, *83*
3:16, *164*
4:7-8, *81*
4:8, *121*

Titus
1:14, *74, 164*
2:3, *6*
3:5, *26*

Hebrews
1:14, *106*
3:3, *35*
4:12, *9, 25*
4:15, *57*
5:1-2, *47*
5:12, *144*
5:13, *169*
5:14, *144*
6:4, *76*
6:5, *156*
6:20, *172*
8:5, *14, 56*
9:2, *19*
9:3-4, *48*
9:4, *19*
9:4-5, *17*
9:5, *19*
10:1, *6, 8, 50, 51, 89, 132, 136, 148*
10:34, *61*
11:1-38, *166*
11:8, *172*
11:17, *68*
11:29, *29*
12:4, *34*
12:22, *14, 31, 79, 167, 185*

James
1:17, *173*
4:10, *38, 146*

1 Peter
1:3, *173*
1:23, *9*

2:2, *100*
2:9, *16*
2:22, *22*
4:1-5, *8*
4:11, *16, 24, 62, 131, 134, 139*
5:4, *57*
5:8, *128*
5:11, *32, 35*

1 John
1:1, *156*
2:1, *35*
2:1-2, *35*
2:8, *39*
2:13, *3*
2:15, *174*
2:16, *34*
3:23, *39*
4:9, *170*

Jude
14-16, *184*

Revelation
1:4, *11*
1:11, *11*
1:16, *25*
1:20, *128*
2:1, *56, 128*
2:7, *81, 106*
2:8, *56, 128*
2:12, *128*
2:18, *128*
2:20, *124*
3:1, *128*
3:5, *130*
3:7, *128*
3:14, *56, 128*
3:20, *160*
8:3-5, *83*
12:4, *84*
12:7, *83*
19:16, *56, 57, 187*
21:8, *76*
21:23-25, *146*
22:15, *76*